Strategies for Sustainable Development

Strategies for Sustainable Development
Experiences from the Pacific

EDITED BY
JOHN OVERTON & REGINA SCHEYVENS

ZED BOOKS
LONDON & NEW YORK

Strategies for Sustainable Development was first published
in the UK and the USA by
Zed Books Ltd, 7 Cynthia Street, London N1 9JF, UK,
and Room 400, 175 Fifth Avenue, New York, NY 10010, USA

Published in Australasia by
University of New South Wales Press
University of New South Wales
Sydney 2052 Australia
in 1999

Distributed in the USA exclusively by
St Martin's Press,
Room 400, 175 Fifth Avenue, New York, NY 10010, USA

First published in 1999

A catalogue record for this book
is available from the British Library.

ISBN 1 85649 641 4 Cased (Zed Books)
ISBN 1 85649 642 2 Limp (Zed Books)

Cover design by Andrew Corbett
Typeset in 9/11pt Palatino by Long House, Cumbria, UK
Printed in Malaysia

Contents

List of Figures

List of Tables

List of Text Boxes

A note on currencies used

Throughout this book, a variety of local and international currencies is referred to. There has been considerable variation in exchange rates in recent years and a general, and sometimes major, decline in the value of regional currencies against the major American and European currencies. Where local currencies are used with reference to former periods of time, a note is included on the value of the currency at that time. In other cases the following table may be used as a guide to relative values:

PACIFIC ISLAND REGION EXCHANGE RATES (JUNE 1998)

Country	*Symbol*	*Value to $US*
Australia (dollar)	$A	1.67
Fiji (dollar)	$F	2.01
French Polynesia (franc)	CFP	110.30
New Zealand (dollar)	$NZ	1.96
Papua New Guinea (kina)	K	2.12
Solomon Islands (dollar)	$SI	4.80
Tonga (pa'anga)	$T	1.60
Vanuatu (vatu)	$V	131.74
Samoa (tala)	$S	2.98

Abbreviations

APEC	Asia Pacific Economic Cooperation
AusAID	Australian Agency for International Development
CMT	customary marine tenure
CSR	Colonial Sugar Refining Company
DEC	Division of Environment and Conservation (Samoa)
EEZ	Exclusive Economic Zone
FFA	Forum Fisheries Agency
FIA	Forest Industries' Association
FMP	Forest management plan
FSC	Forest Stewardship Council
FSM	Federated States of Micronesia
GDP	Gross domestic product
GEF	Global Environment Facility
GNP	Gross national product
ICDs	Integrated conservation and development areas
IFOAM	International Federation of Organic Agricultural Movements
IHDP	Integrated Human Development Programme
IUCN	International Union for the Conservation of Nature and Natural Resources
KFPL	Kolombangara Forest Products Limited
LMC	Lihir Management Company
MIRAB	Migration, remittances, aid and bureaucracy
NGO	Non-governmental organisation
NTFP	Non-timber forest products
NZODA	New Zealand Official Development Assistance Bureau
ODA	Official Development Assistance
PRA	Participatory rural appraisal
SIDT	Solomon Islands Development Trust
SNF	Swedish Society for Nature Conservation
SPARTECA	South Pacific Regional Trade and Economic Cooperation Agreement
SPEC	South Pacific Bureau for Economic Cooperation
SPREP	South Pacific Regional Environmental Programme
SWIFT	Solomon Western Islands Fair Trade
TFF	Tax Free Factory
TTPI	Trust Territory of the Pacific Islands
UK	United Kingdom
UNCLOS	(III and IV) UN Convention on the International Law of the Sea
UNDP	United Nations Development Programme
UNEP	United Nations Environment Programme
USAID	United States Agency for International Development
WCED	World Commission on Environment and Development
WTO	World Trade Organization

Acknowledgements

This book represents a collection of chapters by researchers working in the Pacific Islands region. We have been assisted by our various universities, the University of the South Pacific, Massey University and the University of Canterbury, and we acknowledge the financial assistance of those institutions and the support of colleagues therein. The New Zealand Ministry of Foreign Affairs and Trade has also been instrumental in supporting much of the research undertaken, either through scholarship support for Pacific Island students studying in New Zealand or by research grants for New Zealand researchers working in the Pacific Islands. We are particularly grateful for their continuing support in these areas. In addition, the editors wish to thank Massey University and the International Social Sciences Institute, University of Edinburgh for their support in providing facilities to assist with the editing of this book, and Karen Puklowski for her cartographic skills in producing the diagrams and maps. We would also like to thank the Pacific Island people who participated in the fieldwork and research of the various authors and who generously shared their experiences and knowledge with us.

All the views expressed in this book are those of the respective chapter authors and not necessarily those of the institutions or individuals mentioned above.

About the Contributors

Imam Ali is a Lecturer in Geography at the University of the South Pacific in Fiji. He is a specialist in rural development and has conducted research on a major resettlement scheme in the state of Sabah in Malaysia and on the sugar industry in Fiji.

Kalaveti Batibasaqa lives in Fiji, where his family holds land both on the coast and in the interior. He has been active in opposing logging of tropical rainforests in Fiji, and is currently studying at Massey University in New Zealand to gain the technical skills to work with communities to undertake village-based sustainable development programmes.

Ross Cassells is a Senior Lecturer in the Faculty of International Studies, International Pacific College, New Zealand. A forester by profession, he developed a method for valuing the subsistence use of tropical rainforest in the Solomon Islands. This was used to compare subsistence values with logging royalties as well as to calculate compensation for the illegal logging of customary land. He has a particular interest in social forestry as applied in developing nations, having worked extensively in this field in the Solomon Islands and Cambodia.

Ned Hardie-Boys is a Senior Policy Analyst at the Ministry of Maori Development (Te Puni Kõkiri) in Wellington, New Zealand. He has conducted research on how the concept of sustainable development has been incorporated into the development of conservation areas in Western Samoa. Ned is particularly interested in how sustainable development practices relate to local level socio-economic and cultural contexts.

Kirsti Hooker is a graduate in Geography from the University of Canterbury. Her master's thesis research was on return migrants in the Cook Islands in 1994 and since graduating she has been a teacher of geography at Rangitoto College in Auckland.

Peter Horsley is a Senior Lecturer in the School of Resource and Environmental Planning at Massey University, where he teaches environmental law and resource management. He is currently involved in a major research project developing collaborative management models that will enable Maori and European communities and government agencies to share the responsibility for protecting and restoring their local environment. He is also working with customary landowners in the Fiji Islands to establish village-based protection and development projects that are guided by *vanua* principles.

Peter King is a researcher at the Family Centre Social Policy Research Unit in Lower Hutt, New Zealand. He has conducted research into land tenure and relationships between social and physical space in northern Kiribati, using a framework which combines practice theory and ecological theory. He is presently engaged in poverty and migration research.

Leonard Lagisa is currently employed as a senior research officer by Lihir Management Company , a wholly owned subsidiary of Rio Tinto Zinc involved in managing the gold mining project on Lihir Island, Papua New Guinea. He completed a master's degree in Geography at Massey University in 1996, at that time studying the Lihir mine and its impacts upon women. His subsequent employment has involved monitoring social impacts of the Lihir mining development and preparing recommendations for the company.

Warwick Murray is lecturer in Human Geography at the University of the South Pacific, Fiji. He gained his PhD from the University of Birmingham in 1996, after spending a year in Chile carrying out research on the globalisation of fruit, neoliberalism and small-scale farming. His general areas of interest are economic geography, development, the global agro-food complex, rural change and Latin America. Since taking up his position at USP, he has been involved in research on global/local change and rural development in the South Pacific. To date he has undertaken research in Tonga, Fiji, Niue and the Cook Islands.

John Overton is Professor of Development Studies at Massey University. He has had a long-standing interest in rural transformations and has worked in Fiji, Malaysia and Kenya. He is the author of *Land and Differentiation in Rural Fiji* (1989) and *Colonial Green Revolution* (1994) and has a particular interest in colonial land and agricultural policies, changing land tenure systems and the sustainability of agriculture.

Nick Purdie is currently a doctoral candidate in Human Geography at the Australian National University. His specific interests include the human-environment interface in the context of human livelihoods, and he has undertaken research on the relationship between local livelihoods and a sustainable development project in the Solomon Islands. His doctoral research is into the development of socio-environmental imaginaries and livelihood in Eastern Indonesia.

Salome Samou is a Solomon Islander who did her BA degree in Anthropology at the University of Auckland, graduating in 1988. She was a curator at the Solomon Islands Museum and has recently completed her Postgraduate Diploma in Development Studies at the University of the South Pacific.

Regina Scheyvens received her doctorate in Development Studies after conducting research on women's organizations in the Solomon Islands. She is currently a lecturer in Geography at Massey University and her present research interests include gender issues, tourism and sustainable development. As well as working in the Solomon Islands and Papua New Guinea, she has recently undertaken research in Southern Africa.

Donovan Storey is a lecturer at the Centre of Development Studies at the University of the South Pacific, Fiji. His research interests include urban issues, including sustainability, poverty and governance, the politics of development, non-government organizations and development studies. His regional interests lie in South East Asia and the Pacific Islands.

Randolph Thaman is Professor of Biogeography at the University of the South Pacific. He has had very extensive research and teaching experience in the Pacific Island region and his research interests have spanned agriculture, nutrition, pollution, home gardening and agroforestry. He has also been active in promoting issues of concern for health and the environment within the region. His published work includes two books edited with W.C. Clarke – *Food and National Development in the South Pacific* (1983) and *Agroforestry in the Pacific Islands* (1993) – and a host of articles and conference papers.

Judith Varcoe is a Project Manager for the Social Research Unit at CM Research, Wellington. She has spent time in the Cook Islands studying economic and social development, and she now works on a wide range of social research topics in New Zealand including welfare, broadcasting, education and families.

Richard M. Wartho is a Law Librarian at Victoria University of Wellington. He has an MA in Geography from the University of Canterbury and a particular interest in the geopolitics of the Pacific Islands.

CHAPTER 1

Sustainable Development and the Pacific Islands

JOHN OVERTON

Sustainable development is a concept fraught with imprecision and inconsistencies yet cogent in its broad appeal. The literature spawned on the subject in recent years has been extensive and wide-ranging. It has led to the exploration of diverse theoretical avenues, it has encompassed a wide range of disciplinary approaches and it has fostered changes in development practice world-wide. Yet its very success in attracting wide support is also its failing – it seems to offer little to inform practice beyond principles and platitudes.

There is a need to examine sustainable development from new perspectives and seek new insights. Hitherto, sustainable development has been framed largely in terms of global environmental concerns. The wide acknowledgement of the potential dangers of climate change, sea-level rise, loss of biodiversity, air and water pollution and land degradation, and the acceptance that these malign impacts are inextricably linked to contemporary processes of human economic development, have enabled the emergence of a single, broad concept – sustainable development – to encompass the supposed guiding principle for their amelioration. That sustainable development has also been able to encompass concerns for poverty eradication, social justice and the meeting of basic human needs is more a sign of the vagueness of the term, and the political necessity to acknowledge these issues as being of equal importance, than any strong conceptual or operational linking of the environmental and social objectives. The social perspective still seems a junior partner in the sustainable development coalition.

Similarly, the local perspective is frequently seen as subordinate to the global. True, the importance of local action to achieve sustainable development is well recognised in the literature and by environmentalist movements, yet it is global concerns (whether environmental impacts, inequalities of development or new theories) that dominate the sustainable development literature. General issues, after all, seem to attract more interest and sell more books than studies of small communities and what they do and think. We are more swayed by evidence of commonalities than we are by difference. Furthermore, sustainable development seems mostly concerned with ideas which focus on global issues ('think global ...'), and translating these into a myriad of small-scale activities ('... act local'), than those which arise from the multiplicity of local needs, aspirations, resources and ideologies and challenge existing global discourses of developmentalism and environmentalism.

In such a context, an examination of sustainable development in a Pacific Island context, and one which lays stress on sustainable livelihoods, is timely. The islands of the Pacific Ocean have not, to date, figured prominently in publications on sustainable development. More concerned with the seemingly wider impacts of deforestation in the Amazon Basin or desertification in the Sahel, and mindful perhaps of the relatively small populations and land areas of the island states of the Pacific Ocean region, sustainable development literature has mostly by-passed the Pacific or, as we suggest below, seen it simply as a 'victim' of external environmental degradation. Yet it should be seen as a critical region. The Pacific Ocean spans a third of the planet's surface area, it contains both some of the most marginal, and some of the most productive, environments for human habitation, it contains great cultural and environmental diversity, and its human history reveals many examples of both sustainable and highly destructive use of fragile environments. In addition, as this book will demonstrate, there are many examples in the region of activities which may signal the ways in which environmental and social concerns can be translated into viable and sustainable economic activities.

Sustainable Development

The topic of sustainable development has spawned a very large and expanding literature. Such work has done much to examine some of the philosophical underpinnings of sustainability and expose many of the different layers of meanings of the term. To a large extent, however, 'sustainable development' remains an elusive concept. It has wide popular appeal, it has been adopted by a wide range of development agencies and it does constitute a long-term desirable goal for development processes (World Bank 1992). Yet it lacks conceptual rigour, offers little by way of direct policy implications and there are widely differing views on what sustainable development means (Tisdell 1988).

Sustainable development is a concept that represents a compromise. Environmentalism and a concern for the global environment have created the impetus for a mode of change that addresses the need to preserve the integrity of ecological systems and minimise environmental damage. Such concerns, in many ways, are 'anti-development', for they see that conventional models of economic development, based on industrialisation, resource extraction and sustained growth in material consumption, inevitably impose severe pressures on the environment through resource depletion, waste disposal or disturbance of natural ecosystems (Redclift 1984:56). The search for sustainability, from this perspective, seeks to minimise growth, preserve the natural environment and seek stability (Adams 1995:94). On the other hand, writers with a concern for poverty and social inequalities have rightly highlighted that much environmental damage is as much a consequence as a cause of poverty (WCED 1987). They suggest that development is essential as a precondition to achieving environmental sustainability for as long as people live in poverty or in unjust and inequitable societies, they will have little alternative but to put increasing pressure on the environment. 'Sustainable development', then, represents a compromise in that it suggests that the twin goals of environmental sustainability and human economic development are compatible, attainable and mutually inseparable (Simon 1989, Redclift 1991). What it does not do adequately is suggest how the apparent gap between the two sides can be bridged in practice.

Sustainable development also presents a long-term strategic goal rather than a short-term policy agenda. To be 'sustainable' our environmental, economic and social systems have to be able to exhibit a high degree of stability and integrity over a very long period of time. This repositions the horizon for development far into the future and across succeeding generations, rather than into what can be foreseen easily in planning or project cycles. It is open-ended and requires a commitment to the future. The best-known definition of sustainable development – 'development which meets the needs of the present without compromising the ability of future generations to meet their own needs' (WCED 1987:43) – encompasses this future-oriented view whilst avoiding having to explain some key and contentious underlying concepts (such as 'development', 'needs', 'compromising') or suggesting how the goal can be achieved.

Fundamental to understanding what sustainable development means is an appreciation of three general perspectives on it: ecological, economic and social. Each – despite considerable variation within the perspective – involves differing conceptions of sustainable development and vastly different policy implications.

Ecological sustainability

'Sustainability' usually means 'environmental sustainability' and the environmental/ecological bases of sustainable development are very strong. This perspective puts emphasis on the natural environment and ecosystems, and sees their preservation as fundamental to the future of human existence. It rests upon a number of ecological principles and frameworks for analysis, including ecosystems, the biosphere, natural production systems, carrying capacity, the laws of physics and natural cycles (Rees 1990).

Bearing these biological and physical principles in mind, a quite strict view of sustainability is presented, one that puts much value on the maintenance in perpetuity of natural environmental systems but is inherently suspicious of the human role in the environment. This ecological perspective sees current patterns of human activity and resource use as inherently unsustainable and points to the ways humans are destroying key ecosystems and species at an alarming rate. It places the environment at the centre of the sustainability debate, not just in a position where it has to be 'accounted for' like other factors (Shiva 1992).

The perspective has led to different views on how sustainability might be achieved. In its mild form it calls for a minimisation of resource use. Put another way, humans should stop 'cashing in' ecological capital (non-renewable resources) and live only off the sustainable 'interest'. Yet this need not put a stop to development. Economic growth is necessary and possible, it is believed, though such growth should not harm the environment irrevocably. It might be termed 'ecodevelopment' – development which is based upon responsible and sustainable use of environmental resources (Adams 1990: 51–6). It involves, in particular, the idea of environmental 'management', carefully managing the earth's resources in such a way that natural productivity is increased and basic human needs are met. It is therefore an 'accommodating' view (allowing development to occur) (O'Riordan 1981:376).

It is this mild and reformist view of environmental sustainability that has gained widespread acceptance because it seems to be a 'win-win' situation: you can have development *and* environmental protection. Big development agencies, such as the World Bank, and Third World governments are more inclined to accept this view than the more radical interpretations. Yet others remain sceptical that a win-win scenario is ever possible and argue that this perspective is too bland and vague to be of any practical use (*The Ecologist* 1993).

A second, more radical strategy places much more emphasis on ecological principles. It can be thought of as 'ecocentric' (putting nature first). It has perhaps two strands: one is known as 'communalist' (a strong preservationist view within a steady state economy with zero growth) while the more radical view stresses 'deep ecology' (preservation of nature above all else – the 'earth first' notion) (Naess 1989, Merchant 1992). Human life is seen as but one element of a global ecosystem but one that is much more destructive than any other. Preservation of other life forms is a principal aim of sustainability, for any form of activity which results in the destruction of any species is deemed to be not ecologically sustainable. It also has spiritual dimensions concerned with individual and group experiences of, and feelings towards, nature (Adams 1995:95). Such an approach calls for a radical change in human activity and attitudes. It is a 'zero growth' approach – economic growth and population growth are seen to be inherently damaging. Furthermore, humans need a fundamental change in their attitudes towards the environment: they are part of nature and should not seek to dominate nature for their own development ends.

Sustainable economic development

Whereas ecologists lay stress on environmental systems and means of analysis to define and possibly implement sustainable development, economists not surprisingly use their tools of economic analysis. They bring a quite different perspective (Barbier 1987, Pearce *et al.* 1990).

Amongst economists there are conflicting views as to what economics can say about the environment and sustainable development. These views range from those who believe the environment is not a commodity and therefore economics cannot deal with environmental issues to those economists who freely turn the environment into a series of tradable commodities. For those arguing the latter, the previous failure of economics to address environmental concerns stems from the discipline considering the environment external to the economy. The solution for these economists is to incorporate the environment into their models, thereby taking account of environmental concerns and addressing the issue of sustainability. Others, however, have argued that environmental issues cannot be incorporated fully into economic models because the discipline deals largely with private goods (*The Ecologist*, 1993). More importantly, economics is not well equipped to place values on the environment for future generations.

In the media it is common to hear economists and politicians talking of 'sustainability' in relation to the economy but what they are talking about is 'sustainable economic growth'. This refers to a situation where an economy is growing over a period of time (measured by a continual rise in gross national product – GNP *per capita*) and surviving periods of relative recession. It also implies that the basic health of an economy (in terms of investment, productivity etc.) is good. Tied up with this is the idea of 'development' – the economy is growing because the institutions and infrastructures are being developed in the right way and there is a continual rise in the living standards of the population. Thus, to many economists, if an economy is growing year in and year out as a result of its own momentum, there is 'sustainable development'. This view is sometimes referred to as a 'cornucopian' perspective: nature is a cornucopia (an abundant supply of resources) to be used by humans for their benefit. It is also 'technocentric' in that it believes that humans have the technical capability to control nature and to achieve the best use of the environment (O'Riordan 1981:376). Yet what is talked about in this approach is 'growth' (a rise in GNP) rather than 'development' (a whole range of qualitative improvements in peoples' lives). The time horizons are also short. This view, centred on macro-economic policy, can realistically see only a few years ahead, rather than the decades or centuries needed for a view of true sustainability.

A related idea is that of project sustainability. Development planners and practitioners are concerned to ensure that the development projects they implement are 'sustainable' in that they can continue beyond the span of their own involvement and become independent of external support. This 'self-sustaining' objective of development projects, however worthy, does not constitute 'sustainable development' for it is narrowly focused on issues of funding and participation and does not necessarily involve notions of ecological maintenance. Sustainable development is not an objective that can fit neatly within defined development project cycles.

A second view presents the notion of ecological economics (Barbier 1993, Pearce 1993, Tisdell 1993). Ecological economics attempts to bring together environmental and economic concerns into one theoretical framework. Economic systems dealing with production and the question of distribution of goods and services are brought together with the ecological system comprising the natural environment and the living organisms within it (Common 1995:32). The ecosystem provides essential goods and services for production and consumption. These may range from the mundane but essential goods of clean water and fresh air to rare plant extracts for medicines. The ecological goods and services provided by the ecosystems are essential for the welfare of human beings, while the production and consumption that takes place in the economic system in turn has an impact on the ecosystem.

In an ecological economics framework the concept of sustainable economic development includes considerations of the economy as well as the environment. The economy will continue to maximise output with minimum inputs but in a manner that will not alter over time the stock and quality of natural resources. Ecological economics requires that sustainable economic development is achieved by using natural renewable resources at a rate less than or equal to the rate of regeneration and by producing pollution at a rate less than or equal to the rate it can be absorbed into the environment. Ecological economics has evolved into a major sub-discipline of economics with its own concepts, techniques and suggested mechanisms (such as resource accounting, discounting for future values, and 'green taxes') and there has been a considerable amount of theoretical work produced.

Sustainable societies

The sustainability literature has tended to be dominated by the ecological and economics perspectives introduced above. They have some areas of overlap but still represent two different broad schools of thought. They have been joined by a third perspective: that which stresses social structures and needs.

Unlike the ecological approach which puts the environment at the centre of sustainability, the social approach places poor people and their basic human needs first (Chambers 1986:10). It believes that development must be framed in a way that focuses on meeting people's basic needs (rather than concentrating on aggregate economic growth). This locally based and mostly small-scale approach allows for forms of development which do not compromise the environment and which use and modify ecosystems (without harming them) to improve economic and social well-being. It has some parallels with the mild ecological approach.

Growth is necessary, it is suggested, in order to meet basic needs but such growth need not be environmentally malign. Such a strategy aims to achieve not just environmental sustainability but also the sustainability of just and equitable societies. For if stable societies exist without poverty or injustice (in other words, people have a sustainable existence), then environmental damage should be minimised.

Another key element of the social approach is the emphasis on social equity, justice and liberation. Just as there are basic material needs for people, there are also fundamental social considerations of injustice. Unjust societies are not sustainable societies, because they rest on the exploitation or subordination of one group in society by another. Therefore, sustainable development is not possible within the context of an unjust society because that society cannot survive. The recent interest in ecofeminism has highlighted not only the similarities between patriarchy (the domination of women by men) and environmental degradation (the domination of nature by men) but also the importance of feminist environmental discourses (those which stress the nurturing and guardianship roles of women in the environment) (Shiva 1988, Merchant 1995, Mies and Shiva 1993, Salleh 1997).

This places stress on the removal of injustices and major inequalities within a society. Such injustices may take many forms, including, for example, the division of society by race, class or gender; the abrogation of basic human rights by rulers; or the existence of extreme inequalities in wealth. Dealing with these injustices and inequalities is, to the oppressed or poor concerned, the most pressing development need. Talk of sustainability is meaningless when such conditions persist. In a related way, the approach of ecosocialism emphasises the role of capitalism in establishing particular modes of resource (and human) exploitation and patterns of inequality (Redclift 1984:7–10, Pepper 1993).

One of the growing areas in development theory is the meeting of social needs and the achievement of sustainable societies. Two related concepts are worth mentioning at this stage. 'Participation' (sometimes otherwise referred to as 'development from below') embodies the key idea that poor people must be seen as primary participants in the development process, identifying and meeting their own needs, rather than merely objects for externally imposed projects or charity. It is crucial also for *all* people to participate, especially those otherwise marginalised in society (women, the poor, the disabled, etc.) (Vivian 1992, Chambers 1997). The second concept, 'empowerment', goes a step further, stating that development should occur by providing the means by which poor and marginalised groups can change their own lives for the better (Friedmann 1992). Empowerment is both a means and an end in itself of development and may involve profound political and social change. Thus, from this perspective, sustainable development must incorporate notions of social justice and be directed at achieving sustainable societies (in an ideal world free of injustice and major inequalities) as a precondition for environmental sustainability.

This brief survey of ecological, economic and social perspectives reveals that there is no clear definition of what sustainable development is, nor how it can be put into action, nor how it can be measured. In the plethora of definitions suggested, however, there are some common elements. There is a strong feeling that development is necessary to meet basic human needs, but an equally strong view that such development should not damage the environment so that future generations are unable to enjoy similar access to resources to meet their needs. Yet the definitions remain fairly vague – comfortable and non-contentious statements of principle – and there is a danger that an impasse has been reached whereby there is agreement on a common goal but no agreed way forward to suggest what it means in practice. Sustainable development, then, remains a flawed and vague theory even if it does constitute a worthy and vital guiding principle.

This book recognises the difficulty of defining sustainable development and putting it into practice but it seeks to contribute to the understanding of the concept in a number of ways. First, by presenting examples of what can be interpreted as sustainable development in practice, it is possible to highlight some of the many ways in which sustainable development may be achieved, rather than seeking any single general strategy. We are of the view that sustainable development practice may be best extended by learning from the multitude of current actions rather than seeking any way around the theoretical impasse. Yet, second, by placing emphasis on Pacific Island people, their cultures, resources, livelihoods and actions, the book tends strongly towards the social (rather than the ecological or economic) perspective and aims to increase our understanding of this, perhaps the least developed or accepted of the three theoretical perspectives. We see particular value in applying and extending the sustainable livelihoods approach of Chambers (1986, Chambers and Conway 1992) and placing emphasis on popular participation.

Sustainable Development in a Pacific Island Context

The Pacific Islands have not been prominent in the sustainable development literature or, when they have appeared, have been seen as small environments and communities inevitably caught up in the wider impacts of global environmental change (Pernetta and Hughes 1990).[1] It is generally recognised that these fragile environments will be amongst the first to experience – and indeed are already experiencing – the serious impacts of a rise in sea level, climate change or nuclear testing and dumping. It is an 'outside-in' view, one which sees Pacific Island communities as the environmental victims of largely Western-generated environmental change. This is a view promoted by international environmental organisations such as Greenpeace – and to an extent their local counterparts – which point to global warming and nuclear testing as the causes of critical changes in Pacific Island ecosystems (McDiarmid 1992).

[1] It is only recently that a book has appeared which addresses some of the issues of sustainable development in the Pacific Islands (Burt and Clerk 1997).

There appears to be some evidence to support this view. Pacific Island environments, especially small low-lying atolls, are extremely fragile. Their very small land areas, low altitude and very limited fresh water resources mean that even small rises in sea level, for example, will have immediate and deleterious consequences for human habitation there (Roy and Connell 1989). Similarly, because the Pacific Ocean is often perceived by industrialised powers as a vast empty space with potential to store their toxic wastes or test their nuclear weapons, and because small Pacific Island nations are not strong enough to resist such incursions, it is the six million or so Pacific Islanders spread across the ocean that will bear the impacts (Brookfield 1989, Ward 1989, 1993, Overton 1993a).

Yet it is wrong to see Pacific Islanders simply as helpless environmental victims, or to ascribe environmental change in the region solely to outside influences. People have modified the Pacific environment significantly from the time of first human settlement (Dodson 1992). Some of these changes have involved impressive adaptations to allow very restrictive environments to support human settlement – the giant swamp taro systems of Kiribati being one such example of productive and sustainable ecological adaptations. On the other hand, Pacific Island people have also been capable of major ecological damage – the rapid human deforestation of Rapa Nui (Easter Island) being now well recognised (Bahn and Flenley 1992). In short, there has been a history of significant and dynamic interaction between nature and humans in what are often very restricted environments. Nor should these Pacific Island environments be seen as static. Nunn (1993) has argued forcefully that 'natural' changes in climate and sea levels have wrought significant changes in the past, including the period of human settlement of the region. Environmental change is not solely anthropogenic.

Thus, we argue that there is a need to balance the 'environmental victim' perspective of Pacific Island environments with counter 'inside-out' views, ones which highlight the way local environments are being changed from within and the ways local people are adapting to these and global environmental and economic changes. In many ways, as this book will detail, people are 'acting locally' to initiate change towards developing more sustainable environmental and economic systems. They are often drawing on the experience and values of their ancestors but they are also adapting to new economic imperatives and opportunities. Furthermore, an 'inside-out' perspective recognises that changes within the Pacific Islands may have implications for elsewhere. This is not to argue that environmental changes on the islands can significantly change the global environment – with the possible exception of the deforestation of large areas of Papua New Guinea and other large

TABLE 1.1 • THE PACIFIC ISLANDS: AREA AND POPULATION

	Land area (km²)	Sea area (000 km²)	Population (1996 est.)	Population density (persons/ km² land)	Sea + Land density persons/ (000 km²)
American Samoa	200	390	58,900	295	151
Cook Islands	237	1,830	19,600	83	11
Federated States of Micronesia (FSM)	701	2,978	109,200	156	37
Fiji	18,272	1,290	800,500	44	612
French Polynesia	3,521	5,030	229,200	65	46
Guam	541	218	153,700	284	703
Kiribati	810	3,550	82,400	102	23
Marshall Islands	181	2,131	59,800	330	28
Nauru	21	320	11,200	533	35
New Caledonia	19,103	2,100	196,800	10	93
Niue	259	390	2,000	8	5
Northern Marianas	471	1,823	61,400	130	34
Palau	488	629	16,900	35	27
Papua New Guinea	462,243	3,120	4,141,800	9	1156
Pitcairn Island	5	500	54	11	0.1
Samoa	2,935	120	165,100	56	1343
Solomon Islands	27,556	1,340	395,200	14	289
Tokelau	10	290	1,500	150	5
Tonga	747	700	90,000	120	128
Tuvalu	26	900	9,800	377	11
Vanuatu	12,190	680	173,900	14	251
Wallis & Futuna	255	300	14,800	58	49
Total	550,772	30,629	6,793,754	12	218

Sources: Land area from South Pacific Commission (1995), sea area data from Crocombe (1992). Population data from South Pacific Commission (1998) – mid-year estimates, except Pitcairn Island (1994 census).

Melanesian islands – but rather that Pacific Island experiences of, and adaptations to, change may well provide lessons for other regions.

The Pacific Island region is also worthy of wider study and interest because its particular environmental, social and cultural contexts provide a unique stage for seeing how global economic and environmental changes are played out at the local level. It is a region that is marginal. It is marginal environmentally, because many of its islands are fragile and can only support human habitation with difficulty (others are much more benign). And it is marginal economically, for the small population sizes and the vast distances to be travelled mean that few economic activities are viable in a global market (Table 1.1). Being marginal, the region is amongst the first to feel the impacts of global change but it may also be amongst the first to offer new ways forward.

This book therefore has several aims. First, it seeks to examine sustainable development in a Pacific Island context. In this, it attempts to relate the general issues and theories pertaining to sustainable development to local Pacific Island circumstances – Pacific Island environments, societies, cultures, histories, economies and systems of governance. It recognises not only the similarities across the Pacific Island region but also considerable differences, and seeks to understand how the definitions of sustainability and strategies for its attainment may be shaped in such contexts.

Second, it aims to give prominence to local Pacific Island actions by using recent research in the region. The chapters that appear in this book focus largely on positive examples of change, on the way local people are not only reacting to change but also seeking to develop new (and old) ways to respond. These examples, in addressing such contentious issues as forestry, mining and tourism, and taking account of both restricted environments and diverse and dynamic cultures, provide some interesting lessons for the development of sustainable development strategies in other parts of the world.

Finally, the case studies examine the interplay of exogenous forces for change (both positive and negative) and local initiatives and responses. Global environmental change is certainly affecting Pacific Island environments and ways of life, as are local changes. Similarly – and more immediately – an increasingly globalised post-Cold War economy, together with dominant neoliberal ideologies, is fundamentally changing the shape of Pacific Island economies and political systems. And increasing global environmental awareness is beginning to affect the region through changing aid policies, market conditions and links to local environmental pressure groups. These represent the major shaping forces for sustainable development. Yet this book is concerned with the local outcomes of such forces. We aim to show that Pacific Island people are not simply being swept along by such global forces but are variously resisting, adapting to and initiating change. These actions, we believe, are of critical importance not only in the Pacific region but, potentially, elsewhere.

The authors involved in writing this book all have research experience in the Pacific Islands. Most are based in New Zealand or the Pacific Islands and much of the research presented comes from masters and doctoral projects involving extensive fieldwork. Thus, the book

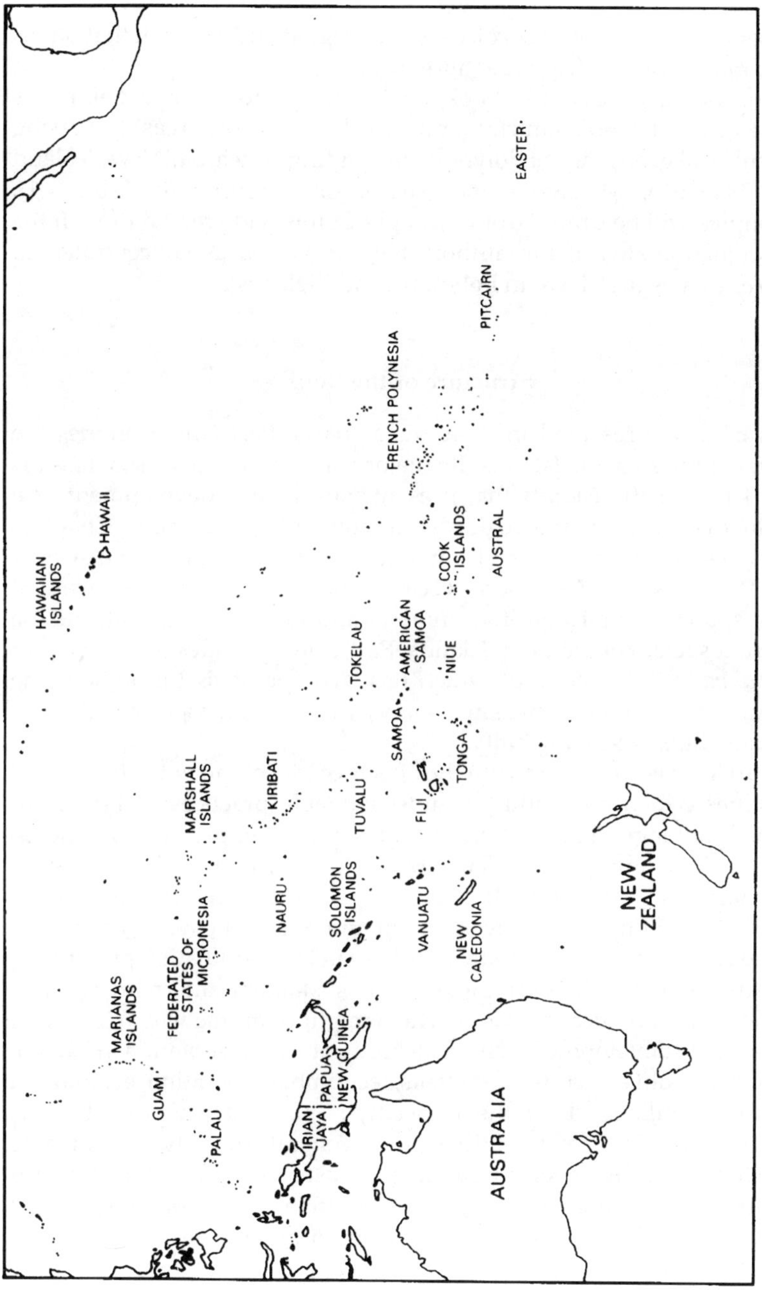

FIGURE 1.1 THE PACIFIC ISLAND REGION

presents a number of new voices on this region and research that otherwise might not reach a wider audience.

For the purposes of this book, the Pacific Island region is defined as those Pacific Island countries (and their land and sea areas) traversing the cultural groupings of Polynesia (excluding Aotearoa/New Zealand and Hawai'i), Melanesia and Micronesia (Figure 1.1, Table 1.1). Examples will be drawn from throughout this wide region though the research domains of the authors have not been as concentrated in Micronesia as they have in Polynesia and Melanesia.

Structure of the Book

This book is presented in three major parts. Part One examines the context of the Pacific Islands. Its major concern is to discuss what it is about the Pacific Islands that presents sustainable development as a distinctive issue in the region compared with elsewhere. Chapters cover resources and the environment, geopolitics, culture and society and Pacific Island livelihoods. Case studies to highlight these general ideas span the small atoll environments and societies of Kiribati and the migrant society of the Cook Islands. Part One concludes with a chapter on *vanua*, a Fijian concept which has close parallels throughout the region and which encapsulates many of the critical aspects and interrelationships of sustainability.

Part Two is concerned with the effects of 'development' – those local activities which are leading to unsustainable practices and environmental damage. The section includes the examples of logging in Melanesia, mining in Papua New Guinea, fishing, urbanisation in Polynesia and agriculture. It does not seek to be comprehensive in this survey of the impacts of development and does not cover all countries of the region, nor does it analyse issues such as population growth.

Part Three turns to examples of more sustainable alternatives, a few of the myriad of local activities which might point the way to forms of sustainable development. These include nature conservation in Samoa, recovery of old agricultural systems, 'ecotimber' operation, ecotourism and urban villages. Here the avowedly populist stance of the book is given expression, for we adhere to a general view that sustainable development, if it is ever to be attained, must emerge from the wide and diverse participation of all people, rather than solely from the planned implementation of the state, aid agencies or other external institutions and ideologies.

Finally, a concluding section attempts to draw together some of the major themes of the book, for it is important not to see these Pacific

Island examples as simply isolated, spontaneous and largely inconsequential actions but as possible exemplars for both implementing sustainable development and questioning its efficacy. Here we draw out the implications for development project planning, discuss the critical issues of participation, gender and livelihood strategies, and, finally, consider the global dimensions of such local changes.

Throughout we present a combination of specific case studies and more general and contextual discussion. Running through the three-part horizontal organisation of the book – spanning context, effects of development and sustainable alternatives – is an attempt to draw some vertical themes, notably the concepts of sustainable livelihoods and participation, and the special character and diversity of the Pacific Island region. It seeks to combine presentation of hopeful and positive examples of change with discussion of some thorny outstanding issues. In doing so, we hope to reinvigorate the debate concerning sustainable development in general.

PART I

Contextual Issues

CHAPTER 1 ARGUED that the Pacific Island region offers a unique perspective on the study of sustainable development. It is a region that offers a remarkable contrast in sizes: the sea area it covers (over 30 million square kilometres) is vast, the number of countries in the region (22, though several of these are dependencies) is similar to Latin America, yet its total land area is small (in the case of some states, minute) and its total resident population of around six and a half million is smaller than that of Los Angeles. Furthermore, the region is characterised by great diversity. Environmentally, it ranges from the large island of New Guinea, with mountains nearly 4000 metres high, to tiny atolls barely above sea level. Culturally, too, there are huge distinctions (though not a few similarities) and very different histories.

These questions of scale and the wide differences across the region frame the issue of sustainable development in quite distinct ways. The Pacific Island region is not just another part of the Third World. It might share with parts of Asia, Africa and South America common characteristics relating to colonial history, location on the periphery of the global economy, and often unfavourable development indicators. Yet in other ways it is quite different: average incomes are higher, there is a relatively low incidence of poverty and famine, there has not been large-scale alienation of Pacific Island land, and many Pacific Islanders have opportunities to migrate freely.

This section examines these broad parameters of Pacific Island environments, cultures, societies and politics. There are four major contextual chapters: the environment, in which the themes of fragility, diversity and change are emphasised; geopolitics, in which the changing place of the region in the world is surveyed; culture and society, where diversity and change are again apparent; and livelihoods, in which the main assets, constraints and opportunities of the peoples of the region are examined. There follow three shorter case study chapters. A village case study from Kiribati shows the complexity of both land tenure and related social organisation in an atoll environment. By contrast, the Cook Islands provides an example of profound social change as a result of migration and return. Finally, for Fiji, the concept of *vanua* is presented. This, with parallels across the region, offers an alternative set of potential environmental ethics that are based on existing and former customs and beliefs. This theme of the cultural and philosophical underpinnings of Pacific Island life, we contend, is critical to understanding the ways in which sustainable development might proceed in future.

This section provides an overview of the region, though one that is, of necessity, short. Readers wishing to learn more about the region are advised to consult some of the texts on its geography, society and culture, notably Crocombe (1992c), Brookfield and Hart (1971), Ward and Proctor (1980) and Campbell (1989). The French atlas of the South Pacific (Antheaume and Bonnemaison 1988) is also highly recommended.

CHAPTER 2

Resources and the Environment

JOHN OVERTON AND R. R. THAMAN

Contrary to the stereotypical image of Pacific islands as small, palm-fringed, low-lying and ringed with sandy beaches, there occurs an almost baffling diversity of island types, from geologically ancient continental islands to low-lying coral atolls. There is, similarly, great geographic and demographic diversity. Some countries, such as Guam, Nauru and Niue, consist of a single small island; others, such as Fiji, Tonga, and French Polynesia, are comprised of hundreds of large and small very dispersed islands. Total land areas vary from 10 square kilometres in the Tokelau Islands to over 460,000 square kilometres in Papua New Guinea. Great differences in climate, topographical features, soil types, mineral and water availability, and diversity of flora and fauna are also found in the area. Population densities for countries range from just over 7.7 persons per square kilometre in Niue to over 300 for Nauru and Tuvalu, and the range is much greater if individual islands are compared. Natural resource endowments contrast similarly from almost zero in the tiny coral atolls to the immense mineral, land and forest resources of Papua New Guinea. Nonetheless, the island states do have much in common: their tropical location, their relative isolation and their fragmentation. This chapter presents an overview of Pacific Island environments, stressing both common elements and diversity.

Habitat Diversity in the Island Environment

Pacific Island environments have been shaped by two major geological processes (volcanic and tectonic) and one major biological process (coral reef growth) (Nunn 1994). Superimposed on these have been the ongoing climatic and geomorphic processes, and human impacts that continue to shape the island environment.

The low islands: coral reefs and atolls

The growth of coral is responsible not only for the formation of coral atolls, but also for the extensive and diverse systems of barrier, fringing and patch reefs that encircle most tropical Pacific islands and are found scattered throughout the vast expanses of ocean in between. Most of the islands in the Marshall Islands, Kiribati, Tokelau and the Tuamotus in French Polynesia are low-lying coral atolls, but coral is present in all Pacific countries.

These massive living limestone structures are among the most biologically diverse and productive ecosystems on Earth. All coral reefs are built by diverse species of coral polyps and algae. Coral polyps are simple animals living up to 50m or deeper in sunlit tropical oceans, which provide the reef framework. The actual reef depends on the accumulated remains of the skeletons of secreting organisms, mainly corals, but also reef-forming algae. Where suitable reef-building organisms are present the type of reef developed depends not so much on the species of coral and algae but mainly on the topography (depth and shape) of the ocean floor, the recent geological history of the area, and the physical environment, especially temperature, light availability, tidal range, salinity and the degree of exposure to wave action and sedimentation (Veron 1986).

Although atolls are often referred to as 'coral atolls', they are in fact usually composed of one or a series of limestone islets and associated beaches encircling a central lagoon or are single 'table reef' islands (for example Arorae and Tamana in Kiribati) with no central lagoon. The limestone itself and the accumulated sand or debris is only partly composed of coral fragments. The bulk of the debris consists of mainly biogenerated sand composed of the remains of coral and algae, shell fragments, or the calcareous excrement of fish and other organisms. Coral debris, often consisting of large dead pieces of coral or entire coral heads, is washed in from the reef edge or reef flat, especially during storm events or tropical cyclones when the larger coral boulders and sand are deposited above the high tide mark. 'Land' is therefore normally highest at the beach ridge.

Behind the beach ridge, where the main coastal stand forest is found, there is often an inland limestone pavement, followed by deeper soils and more sandy substrate as one moves lagoonward. Human settlement is usually found on the lagoon (lee) side of the strips of land where the land slopes gently towards the lagoon and they are afforded slightly more protection from the potential damage of storm waves on the ocean side. As well as the strips of land built on coral debris, sand cays or *motu* (small sand-topped reef islets with sparse vegetation) may also be found.

The lagoons are a critical part of the atoll ecosystem. In most cases the lagoons are shallow expanses of water with some tidal replenishment. Some are open to the sea; others are only replenished through small channels through the fringing strips of land. On some atolls, access to the sea is completely closed off and in the lagoon area consists of brackish ponds or a completely infilled area of 'relic lagoons'. Lagoons and offshore reefs are major resources for atolls. They are rich in marine life. Finfish and shellfish species that inhabit the lagoons provide the major source of protein for humans and are easier to harvest than deep-water species outside the often dangerous reefs. Yet they are extremely fragile marine ecosystems, especially where the natural circulation of fresh sea water, so important for flushing and the provision of nutrients, is interrupted by causeway construction between previously separated islets. In such cases water temperature and salinity levels can be high and variable, often causing mortality of coral reefs, finfish and other marine organisms. As well as such natural variation and fragility, it is also important to note that lagoon ecosystems can be disrupted easily by human activity, for example through sewage disposal or over-fishing.

The climate of atolls varies greatly. Rainfall is perhaps the most important climatic element for human habitation. The islands of Kiribati and Tuvalu demonstrate this variability well: from around 3000 mm per year for the wetter atolls such as Funafuti and Butaritari to about 1000 mm for islands such as Tamana and Arorae. Kiritimati, with an annual rainfall of only 700 mm, is one of the driest islands in the Pacific. Whereas breadfruit and many other plants can grow luxuriantly on the wetter atolls, the drier atolls are too dry for breadfruit and many other common coastal plants to survive. Being very low-lying, they do not experience orographic effects.

Water resources on atolls are also extremely fragile and limited. Because land area is limited, there are rarely any non-brackish surface water resources, in the form of rivers or lakes. Rainwater collection can be important where rainfall is adequate and reliable, but in many cases humans have relied on critical sub-surface reservoirs. Rainwater on atolls collects in the ground and literally floats above the more dense salt water (atolls, it should be remembered, have very porous structures). This fresh water lens is shallow near the margins (sea and lagoon edges) but deepest under the middle of the land area. Capillary action from fresh water in the soil can support plant growth, such as breadfruit and coconuts, to a limited extent, though most plant species have to be tolerant of high saline levels. The lens can be tapped as a fresh water source but over-use or extended periods of drought can result in its rapid depletion or despoilation as a result of salt water infiltration. Humans have adapted to such conditions by having very low rates of fresh water consumption. Liquid intake comes from plants, such as the coconut, and the sea is used where possible for functions, such as washing, which do not demand fresh water.

Soils are usually very shallow, young and with very little natural fertility. They are excessively well-drained and calcareous soils, and are among the poorest in the world. They are almost devoid of soil macronutrients apart from calcium, and have little or no organic matter (Wiens 1962). A shallow organic layer may develop on top of the coral debris, but this is very restrictive in terms of plant growth. Biodiversity on atolls is thus very limited. Coconuts (*Cocos nucifera*) are extremely well adapted, for they are very hardy and can grow even if their roots lie in salt water. They form much of the terrestrial mainstay of atoll life, providing fibre, thatch, food, juice, firewood and an historic source of cash income in the form of copra. The sap of the coconut flower spathe also proves the nutritious drink ('toddy') that is almost a staple part of the diet in most atoll societies. Coconut trees are highly valued and sometimes one of the few individually owned items of property in a strongly communal system. The pandanas tree (*Pandanus tectorius*) is another valuable plant, supplying thatch, material for weaving and basket making, and edible fruit that is either eaten raw when ripe or cooked and made in to flour and confectioneries. On wetter atolls breadfruit (*Artocarpus altilis*) provides edible fruit and an alternative to root crops.

Despite the restricted water and soil resources, forms of agriculture are possible on some atolls. Elaborate systems of cultivation, using pits and mulching, are needed to maintain these scarce resources. They allow for the raising of root crops, mainly giant swamp taro (*Cyrtosperma chamissonis*), to provide much-needed starch and ceremonial food. Giant swamp taro, very carefully tended and hard to grow, is often the only ground crop that can be cultivated on dry islands. Where rainfall is more abundant, common taro (*Colocasia esculenta*) is favoured as it is easier to grow, better-tasting and of higher nutritional value. Other crops possible on moist islands include sweet potatoes (*Ipomoea batatas*), cassava (*Manihot esculenta*) and the greater yam (*Dioscorea alata*).

Coral growth is also responsible for landforms other than atolls. Reefs, reef platforms and coral beach ridges are found on the margins of nearly all Pacific islands and their ecosystems thus sit alongside those of the more diverse and productive high islands. In addition, coral atoll formation is responsible for 'raised limestone islands'. These islands (for example Niue, Nauru and most of the Tonga group) are atolls that have been raised above the surface of the ocean, as the result of either sea level fall or tectonic uplift. Atolls thus become islands with a steep cliffed margin (the former reef edge) – though a secondary coral platform may have developed – and a solid land mass, with the former lagoon entirely above sea level. Despite the greater land areas of such islands, they usually represent even harsher environments for humans than atolls. The steep cliff edges mean difficult access to the sea and a dangerous coast (though people are still dependent on fishing), the rough coral surface of the islands provides little better conditions for soil formation, and the sub-surface fresh water lens may lie at greater depths below the land.

To summarise, coral growth has created in the Pacific unique environments which, through an impressive set of adaptations, have become habitable. Yet they remain extremely fragile environments. There are very tight environmental constraints by way of scarce fresh water, very limited biodiversity, poor soils, small land areas, and little or no mineral resources. These environments can be upset easily, for example through pollution of atoll lagoons, depletion of the fresh water lens or over-fishing of shallow water species. The threat of climate change and sea level rise is also particularly serious in islands that lie only a few metres above sea level (Roy and Connell 1989, Nunn 1990, Wyrtki 1990). If significant sea level rise does occur, life on small atolls – even if they do not literally disappear beneath a rising ocean – may be compromised seriously by smaller groundwater resources (as saline intrusion increases) and susceptibility to coastal erosion. Human habitation is possible but tenuous.

The high islands: volcanic and tectonic landforms

Larger islands in the Pacific result from different processes and involve much more diverse environments (Brookfield and Hart 1971). Whereas the small atoll and raised reef islands are in evidence mainly in Polynesia and Micronesia, continental islands (resulting mainly from tectonic uplift) are found only in Melanesia, whilst volcanic islands are in evidence throughout the region. As larger and more environmentally diverse land areas, they support the majority of the region's population, by far the bulk of its commercial agriculture and nearly all of its mining, forestry and industry. They vary in size and origin. There are geologically ancient continental islands composed of sedimentary, metamorphic and igneous rocks of continental origin, such as New Guinea and New Caledonia; older andesitic volcanic islands, such as most of the islands in Fiji, Vanuatu, Solomon Islands, the eastern islands of Papua New Guinea, Guam and the Northern Marianas; and recent high basaltic volcanic 'hot spot' islands, such as the Samoas, the Cook Islands, Tahiti in French Polynesia, Pohnpei and Kosrae in the Federated States of Micronesia and the Hawaiian Islands

Vulcanism has been the most important geological process in island building. Tectonic weakness along plate margins has led to volcanic extrusion, often along distinct lines or chains. Islands have resulted when such activity breaks the sea surface and, thanks to coral growth, even when volcanic cones have subsequently eroded or subsided away. They vary from active or recent volcanic islands with classic conical forms, steep topography and sometimes high altitudes to old and eroded volcanic landforms with well-formed fringing coral reefs and relatively low elevations. Similarly, they vary in size from single cone systems to large multi-vent systems, such as the larger islands of Samoa. Vulcanism in the Pacific is rarely associated with the presence of valuable mineral deposits.

By contrast, continental islands are formed when blocks of land are thrust above the sea by tectonic action. These form the largest islands in the Pacific: those of Papua New Guinea and New Caledonia. Although primarily tectonic land masses, they may include volcanic processes in parts. Geologically, continental islands are very diverse, with old sedimentary and metamorphic rocks, often folded, faulted and eroded, and some volcanic overlays. They may be rich in mineral deposits, with gold, silver and copper much in evidence in Melanesia. As with volcanic islands, their margins are bordered by coral platforms, reefs and beaches, though their coastlines are also enriched with river deltas, cliffs and mangrove swamps. Their topography can span steep mountains, extensive valley or coastal flats, or rolling hill country.

The larger tectonic islands (and even a few of the larger volcanic islands) are sufficiently large to have climatic effects. Because most Pacific islands are within the trade wind belt, with the prevailing south-east (south of the equator) and north-east (north of the equator) trade winds, an orographic effect can be marked on the windward side of high islands. Conversely, a rain shadow effect is felt on the leeward side. It is therefore common to have wet and dry sides to high islands with marked rainfall and vegetation contrasts from one side to the other. Although seasonal drought can occur in the dry regions, the presence of rivers and the development of irrigation techniques often mitigate the effects of low rainfall. Another effect of topography is when high altitudes lead to temperature gradients with resultant altitudinal zonation of vegetation. Parts of the highlands of Papua New Guinea, for example, can experience frost – thus limiting the cultivation of many tropical crops – even though they are very close to the equator.

Soils in the high islands are similarly varied. Some of the more recent volcanic islands and areas of active vulcanism, such as the Gazelle Peninsula of north New Britain in Papua New Guinea, and the islands of Tanna and Taveuni in Vanuatu and Fiji, have very fertile young volcanic soils. Elsewhere, the alluvial deposits in the large river valleys and deltas have been able to support very intensive agriculture and high population densities. Natural soil erosion is a serious problem on most high islands, however, especially on older continental islands where soils tend to be thin and unstable on steep slopes, and severely leached and laterised on more gentle terrain (Ward 1980). Soil instability and waterlogging are additional problems primarily on larger continental islands. High humus content does compensate to a degree but soil fertility can be diminished easily when protective vegetative cover is lost.

In general, there is much greater biodiversity (Thaman 1993). Being much older geologically, larger, and with more favourable and diverse climatic and soil regimes than atolls, volcanic and, especially, continental islands have evolved great diversity in species of flora and fauna. Extensive humid tropical rainforests have developed in a number of places and much of Melanesia remains forest-covered despite recent forest clearance. There is a rich flora and fauna. For example, Papua New Guinea has about 100 species of mammals (mostly marsupials), 70 species of snakes, crocodiles, over 65 species of birds (including the rare birds of paradise and the cassowary which are of considerable nutritional and ceremonial importance), and, within its very rich insect fauna, some of the rarest and largest moths and butterflies along with dreaded malaria vector, the *Anopheles* mosquito. Agricultural cultivation is a much more straightforward task than on atolls, for favourable soils and climate mean that a great range of crops can be grown.

Thus, compared with small coral atolls and raised reef islands, the volcanic and tectonic islands of the Pacific present much more hospitable environments for human habitation. They have a much wider range of natural resources, there is greater diversity within and between island environments and they are home to over 90 per cent of the region's population – Melanesia alone accounts for 84 per cent. Yet, whilst more diverse and rich, these environments are also fragile. The islands may be large by Pacific standards but they are still islands and small on a global scale. Forest, fish, mineral and soil resources are limited and can be depleted or despoiled without conservation or wise management.

Resources and Constraints: Some Common Themes

Although diversity is a critical theme in any study of Pacific Island environments, it is also important to understand the features and processes which give the region unity from an environmental perspective.

Oceanic character

The Pacific Ocean gives the island states their essential character and integration and the 'way of the sea' is a critical element of lives and livelihoods in the Pacific region. Whilst, as Ward (1989) and Hau'ofa (1993) have observed, many foreigners have viewed the Pacific Ocean as vast, empty and foreboding, Pacific Island people have developed a quite different perception, seeing the ocean as a pathway, linking their islands and societies, and a storehouse, containing key resources for their survival. Marine navigation technologies developed by ancient (and adapted by some present-day) Pacific Islanders allowed them to explore a huge section of the planet's surface. The resultant settlement of the Polynesian triangle (bounded by Hawai'i, Rapa Nui/Easter Island and Aotearoa/New Zealand) represented not only a singularly impressive demonstration of the capacity of Polynesian navigation but also a high degree of cultural linkage and adaptation across a very wide range of environments (from the large and temperate islands of Aotearoa to the tiny atolls of the Tokelaus).

The closeness of Pacific Island people to the ocean has not diminished. Movements of people across the ocean (now by jet aircraft rather than ocean-going canoes) continue and social and cultural linkages span the whole region. In terms of livelihoods, the ocean is still critical. New sources of protein (tinned meat and fish, chickens, frozen meat) may now supplement fresh fish but fishing and reef gleaning remain important not just for food supply but also as a source of income. In addition, new marine resources, such as black pearls in the Cook and Tuamotu Islands or deep sea tuna, have been added to the range of income sources of Pacific Islanders. Similarly, the seagoing skills of some have found Fijians and i-Kiribati, for example, in demand as crew on international vessels.

The Pacific Ocean itself is perhaps the major economic resource of most small Pacific Island nations. Since international laws now recognise national economic rights over an exclusive economic zone, many archipelagic nations now have putative sovereignty over vast areas of the ocean. For nations such as Kiribati, with small populations but large numbers of islands spread over a great expanse of ocean, their territorial waters are huge. In one sense this represents a vast potential resource for it gives small countries, with few other natural resources, the right to lay claim to fish and mineral resources in their zone. Yet, such claims can be overstated, for a claim is not a capability. The costs of developing or protecting deep sea fishing are immense and well beyond the means of countries with a few thousand people. Furthermore, the open ocean is not nearly as abundant in marine life as the reef or lagoon ecosystems and there is no marine cornucopia in the deep ocean without expensive fishing technologies. At least in the short term, the land and in-shore fishing zones will remain the most important resources.

Natural hazards

As well as environmental resources and limitations, the Pacific Island region suffers from a large number of natural environmental hazards. These involve spectacular events, such as cyclones and volcanoes, and more insidious dangers, such as drought.

Cyclones are the most dramatic of climatic hazards in the region (Brookfield 1977). South of the equator the highest incidence of cyclones is between December and April and most of these originate around the Solomon Islands and Vanuatu, many then deepening and tracking, often erratically, in a south-easterly direction to hit Vanuatu, New Caledonia, Fiji, Samoa, Tonga and even, though less frequently, the Cook Islands and French Polynesia. In the north, the season is from April to December with the highest incidence in western Micronesia. Excessive flooding and hurricane-force winds, caused by tropical cyclonic activity, cause widespread destruction to crops, housing, tourist facilities, infrastructure and natural features throughout the islands. In the 30 years to 1976, New Caledonia experienced 36 tropical cyclones, Fiji 35, Vanuatu 25, northern Tonga 10, southern Tonga 16, Samoa and Niue 11 each, the northern Cooks 4, and the southern Cooks 15 (Keith-Reid 1986).

Drought is common on many of the small low-lying and equatorial islands, with islands such as Nauru, the Phoenix Islands, Kiritimati Island, and central and southern Kiribati experiencing severe droughts lasting several months. During such periods, rainfall may be as little as 20 mm per year (Carter 1981). Drought conditions are also common on the leeward sides of larger oceanic islands and in protected areas of continental islands. Even on the windward sides of high islands, which generally have abundant orographic rainfall, drought can occur due to the unreliability of rainfall. From mid-1977 through to February 1978, and again in late 1987, for example, drought conditions prevailed over an area of the Pacific from French Polynesia in the east to Vanuatu in the west.

Geological hazards can be as severe as climatic hazards. These include earthquakes and active vulcanism, and associated seismic sea waves or tsunamis. Tonga and Solomon Islands, for example, suffered serious earthquake damage, and, in the case of Solomon Islands, loss of life in 1976 and 1978 respectively. Active vulcanism is also a serious problem in many groups. In Papua New Guinea, there was a serious eruption of what was considered to be an extinct volcano, Mt Lamington near Popondetta, and there have been frequent eruptions of Manam (Vulcan) and Karkar islands off the north coast, which have led to loss of life. The town of Rabaul (with an estimated former population of 20,000 and the main town of the economically important East New Britain Province), has been evacuated several times in its history because of the threat from a nearby active volcano. Earthquakes and volcanic eruptions also cause seismic sea waves or tsunamis, which travel thousands of miles across the ocean and constitute serious hazards to coastal communities. In 1953, for example, an earthquake to the south-west of Suva caused a tsunami two metres high which inundated and caused considerable damage to coastal areas surrounding Suva, especially extensive areas of reclaimed land. Waves almost a metre in height were experienced over a hundred miles away in the Lau group to the east (Houtz 1962).

Humans have adapted to these hazards over the centuries but significant loss of life as well as damage to crops and property still result – and, unfortunately, many of the traditional coping mechanisms have been lost. There has been a widespread deterioration in the traditional capability to prepare for, respond to, and recover from natural disasters. This seems to be related to the increasing willingness of central governments and international agencies to rush in with relief supplies and material, before the severity of a given disaster is adequately assessed, thus inducing dependence and possibly paving the way for greater suffering in the future, when aid funds may not be so forthcoming (Thaman, Meleisea and Makasiale 1979, Thaman 1982, Chung 1988).

Isolation

Another common characteristic of the Pacific Island region is its relative isolation. The great distance from most of the islands to continental areas and centres of population (and thereby markets) imposes a key economic constraint on the islands' development. Although the Pacific Islands lie in an ocean between the major world economic powers of North America, East Asia (and to a lesser extent South-East Asia, Australasia and South America) they are not well integrated into the trade routes involved. Trans-Pacific shipping and airline routes often skirt to the north; when they do cross the region today's large bulk carriers, container ships or jumbo jets no longer need to stop to refuel and it is uneconomic to pick up small volumes of additional cargo (Kissling 1987). The costs of transport to and from the small scattered economies of the Pacific Islands (and, critically from one island to another) are very high, thus making uneconomic the trade in a number of potential export commodities (Brookfield 1984). It also means that shipping services are small-scale, have a relatively high cost per unit carried and are linked through a network of transshipment points (from the outer islands to Pacific ports such as Suva, Port Vila, Port Moresby or Apia) to more international centres, such as Auckland or Sydney (themselves on the margins of the global trading network). The Pacific Islands, therefore, present a paradox of being located in the middle of a major trading region yet, in practice, remaining on its periphery.

This view of isolation is one that, in a sense, looks into the Pacific Island region from the perspective of large developed economies on the rim; it stresses trade, economic development and transport, and is characteristically pessimistic in its prognosis for the economic future of the region. There is an alternative view. Drawing on the histories of the navigation and settlement of the Pacific Ocean, writers such as Epeli Hau'ofa (1993) have presented an opposite ('inside-out') view of isolation. The economic opportunities of the big Pacific Rim economies may lie outside but they are still accessible and Pacific Islanders, especially Polynesians, have proved adept at travelling to them and exploiting a wide range of economic and social opportunities. Transport connections do exist that allow for comparatively easy travel from the major islands of the Pacific to Los Angeles, Auckland, Sydney, Tokyo or Paris. Furthermore, the wide kin networks which link Pacific people 'at home' to migrants overseas have been likened to 'transnational corporations of kin' (Bertram and Watters 1985, Munro 1990) and it could even be suggested that their success in spanning a range of opportunities internationally mean that some Polynesians are perhaps model 'global citizens' (Overton 1998).

Isolation may not only be seen as a constraint. Distance – geographic and economic – from the industrial centres of the world can be desirable in many ways. It is what increasing numbers of tourists seek and pay well for. It allows Pacific Islanders themselves to maintain their cultures, to some degree, from the pervasive influences of Western cultural norms and to retreat to their own land and society when they wish. And it can protect, in part, the region from the negative consequences of industrialisation in the form of pollution, congestion, and social dislocation.

Fragmentation

A related issue is the fragmentation of the island nations into an often large number of small land areas over a very wide expanse of ocean. For example, Fiji has a population of over 750,000 but over 300 islands, 100 of which are inhabited. Its maritime economic zone extends over a very large 1,290,000 square kilometres. Even more extreme in this regard is Kiribati: a population of only just over 78,000 on 33 islands spread over the second largest maritime zone in the Pacific of 3,550,000 square kilometres (Table 1.1).

Such a spread of population over many islands and a large sea area has major consequences for development. First, because islands can be small, population densities can be very high, especially on the main islands where urban centres are located: over 21,000 of the total Kiribati population, for example, live in the urban area of Tarawa. This not only causes problems relating to land shortage and other environmental pressures on the limited land areas but also greatly increases the costs and difficulties of linking scattered populations in different islands. Again, the long distances and small populations involved mean that transport costs are high, services are necessarily few and the range of economic options for trade are limited. And, although the potential resources in the large maritime zones are very large, the ability of small populations to police, exploit and maintain these resources is greatly constrained. Alongside conventional measurements of population density (dividing total population by land area), in the Pacific Island context it is also useful to measure population density in relation to the total sea area (Table 1.1). What these two measurements reveal is that, for many of the smaller island nations of Polynesia and Micronesia, there is a paradox of high 'land-based' population densities (many over 100 people per square kilometre) and very low 'sea-plus-land' densities. Conversely the larger fragmented states of Melanesia have low land densities (some below 10 per square kilometre) but often higher sea densities. They reveal markedly different balances between population and terrestrial and maritime resources and differential abilities to manage and protect these resources.

Smallness

Smallness is one of the most frequently cited environmental constraints on Pacific Island development. A number of authors in the 1970s and 1980s saw in the Pacific Island region (and in similar situations in the Caribbean and Indian oceans) a problem emerging from the small populations and resource bases of island nations (Jalan 1982, Brookfield 1975, Connell 1988a, 1988b, Dommen 1980, Selwyn 1980, Ward 1967, 1982). They pointed to the diseconomies of small-scale economies, the lack of a sizeable domestic market to stimulate development and the high unit costs of servicing small populations. In the context of the emerging global economy, small size means that the Pacific Islands are simply not considered significant. Furthermore, it is paradoxical that in discussions of an Asia-Pacific economic community or the 'Pacific

Century' the Pacific Islands are largely excluded. 'Pacific' in these frameworks refers to the ocean that links the 'important' economic zones of the rim (usually north of the equator) rather than to the islands or people that live within the ocean.

A related issue concerns the political implications of smallness. Despite having small populations (only nine of the 22 states and territories listed in Table 1.1 have populations in excess of 100,000 and only one, Papua New Guinea, has over one million people) the 'microstates' of the Pacific often have to support the full edifice of nationhood (Bertram 1986). Thus, independent nations such as Tuvalu, Nauru or the Cook Islands may have total populations around the size of a small town in large countries but have to maintain the offices of a state: an executive, legislature, judiciary, bureaucracy, diplomatic service, military, customs service, international transport linkages, etc. The economic burden of statehood is considerable for such nations and it brings into question the viability of microstates as realistically independent entities.

Environmental Constraints on Sustainable Development

Thus, apart from supplying a unique set of resources, the varied environments of the Pacific Island region impose some major constraints on human activity. Critically, it is important to note the extreme fragility and vulnerability of island ecosystems to human-induced change (Fosberg 1965, Carlquist 1965). It is misleading to suggest that crude environmental determinism explains adequately the patterns of human activity and development in the region, for the catalogue of human adaptations to environmental hazards and constraints, and human modifications to the environment suggest a more complex interaction between Pacific Islands and their environments. When considering the prospects for sustainable development in the region, however, environmental constraints are ever present and limit the ability of present and future generations to survive and prosper.

Thaman and Ravuvu (1989) provide a useful summary of the constraints that face Pacific Island people (Table 2.1).[1] Due to the variety of habitats across the region, these are felt unevenly. As discussed above, some of the more important aspects of fragility and environmental constraints in the Pacific Islands include isolation and inaccessibility, small size and land scarcity, ruggedness or swampiness of terrain, drought, excessive rainfall and flooding, tropical cyclones and

[1] For other assessments of the risks facing the future of the region, see Brookfield 1989, Ward 1993, Overton 1993a.

TABLE 2.1 • ENVIRONMENTAL CONSTRAINTS IN THE PACIFIC REGION

3	severe or of serious concern
2	warranting concern
1	of localised concern in some areas

CONSTRAINT	Melanesia	Polynesia	Micronesia
Isolation and inaccessibility	3	3	3
Small size and land scarcity	1	3	3
Rugged or swampy terrain	3	3	2
Drought	1	2	3
Excessive rainfall/flooding	3	2	1
Tropical cyclones/strong winds	3	3	3
Mineral scarcity	1	3	3
Water scarcity/no surface water	1	2	3
Earthquakes and vulcanism	3	2	2
Poor or deteriorating soils	3	2	3
Poor or endangered biota	2	3	3

Source: Thaman and Ravuvu 1989

strong winds, mineral scarcity, water scarcity or absence of surface water resources, earthquakes and vulcanism, poor or deteriorating soils, and poor or endangered biota.

Thus, the environments of the Pacific Islands have much in common but also much that makes each island unique. Environmental resources, hazards and constraints differ markedly across the region. Yet, above all, the main distinguishing characteristics of the region are its fragility and vulnerability. Nearly all environments in the regions are under threat. Some of these threats result from global environmental changes (climate warming or sea level rise) but many are localised. Some are natural; others are human-induced. If these threats are not to become more severe and endanger the future of human habitation on the islands, it is imperative that changes will have to take place, both globally and locally, in current patterns of human activity.

CHAPTER 3

The Pacific Islands in the World

RICHARD WARTHO & JOHN OVERTON

The Pacific Ocean covers a third of the earth's surface area yet the islands that lie there have had but a minor role in the global economy and politics. They are typically perceived as being small, remote and of minor importance in the world order. Although settled from Asia from some tens of thousands of years ago, wider global connections, with Europe and the Americas, came much more recently, particularly in the last hundred years. What has emerged since is a region linked closely to the global economy through trade, aid and political relationships but one that is at the mercy of global forces and the often capricious nature of world politics and markets. This chapter examines the various ways in which the region is linked to the rest of the world. It begins with a brief examination of colonialism and decolonisation then moves to a review of the different types of economic and political linkages that do much to form the context of contemporary development.

From Colonialism to Democracy?

In the Pacific Islands political systems varied enormously before European intervention. Crocombe (1992a:8–9) contends that many Pacific Island societies, such as those of the southern atolls of Kiribati and the highlands of Papua New Guinea, were at least as democratic as the ancient Greek city states from which the word 'democracy' is derived. Conversely, most Polynesian and Micronesian societies, such as those of Hawaii, Tahiti and Yap, were extremely hierarchical as status was essentially ascribed: power was gained by accident of birth or military domination. Individual societies also varied in terms of political stability. In Tonga, for example, a unitary centralised system of political control was established in about the tenth century and remained for over 800 years (Campbell 1989:45). In Melanesia, traditional political systems were much more diverse in comparison with those in Micronesia and Polynesia (Hoadley 1992:15).

European contact with Pacific Islanders occurred as early as 1521 when the Portuguese explorer Ferdinand Magellan sighted the Mariana Islands. Spain went on to claim the island of Guam in 1565 but the first European inhabitants of the colony did not arrive until 1668 (Campbell 1989:128). Some attempts to convert indigenous inhabitants of the Pacific Islands to Christianity occurred from this time onwards, but it was only during the late eighteenth and nineteenth centuries, the period of colonial annexation, that Europeans began to have a significant impact on local political systems. By 1906, however, when France and the United Kingdom established a joint condominium over the New Hebrides, all inhabited islands of the Pacific Islands had been annexed or had become protectorates. Thus, by the dawn of the twentieth century, the region had become politically integrated into a world order dominated by European colonialism, although external influence in some localised areas such as the highlands of Papua New Guinea would remain absent for many years (Waiko 1993:88).

From the beginning of the eighteenth century until the 1950s, the countries of the Pacific Islands, with the exception of Tonga, were governed by colonial powers. The withdrawal of Germany following the First World War, Japan following the Second World War, and the Netherlands after the annexation of West Irian by Indonesia in 1960, left Australia, France, New Zealand, the United Kingdom, and the USA as the remaining colonial powers in the region. Various styles of colonial administration were implemented throughout the Pacific Islands which significantly affected future political developments. Australia, New Zealand and the United Kingdom, for example, utilised traditional political systems which evolved into advisory legislative councils and eventually into elected parliaments (Fairbairn *et al.* 1991:17). Alternatively, France, and to a lesser extent the USA, implemented policies of assimilation, and their colonies in the region underwent varying degrees of incorporation into the territory of the metropole.

The era of independence dawned at a relatively late stage in the Pacific Islands, although, with the exception of Samoa, universal suffrage had already been granted to all adults of the region. In most cases, however, the executive of government did not become directly responsible to the legislature until after independence or free associa-

[1] Free association' is a constitutional arrangement that allows countries to practice full internal self-government whilst voluntarily ceding responsibility to the metropolitan power for certain functions, such as defence. It also usually involves people having rights of citizenship within the metropolitan country.

tion (Larmour 1994:52–9).[1] The first sovereign state of the region, Samoa, achieved independence from New Zealand in 1962. Between 1968 and the end of the Cold War in 1989 a further nine followed and six more opted for free association with either New Zealand or the USA (see Table 3.1). France, however, was less willing to relinquish its colonial interests in the region. In the 1950s, universal adult suffrage was granted in New Caledonia and French Polynesia and limited self-government followed, although the national French government retained executive authority. Control of the New Hebrides was reluctantly renounced in 1980, owing largely to pressure from its condominium partner the United Kingdom, but France showed no intention of submitting to further requests for independence from the indigenous people of New Caledonia and French Polynesia, especially as people of European descent held, and continue to hold, electoral majorities in these territories and most oppose independence.

As parliamentary democracy developed elsewhere in the region, Tonga became the only independent country where the executive (King Taufa'ahau Tupou IV) was not responsible to the legislature. Thus, by the end of the Cold War, parliamentary democracy was already well established in the region; while seven countries remained dependent territories, only the tiny territories of Tokelau and Pitcairn Island lacked real self-government.

Political problems in the Pacific Islands have developed since the 1980s, most notably the 1987 military coups in Fiji, independence struggles in New Caledonia and French Polynesia, commoner unrest in Tonga and Samoa, constitutional challenges in Vanuatu and Palau, and a violent secessionist struggle in Bougainville. Yet the commitment to democratic governance has remained. For example, Fiji has gradually returned to a form of democracy following the 1987 military coups. A revised constitution was implemented in 1990 and elections held, though this constitution ensured political control by indigenous Fijians (Robertson and Tamanisau 1992:29). Since then, a Constitutional Review Committee has recommended, and the government has accepted, proposals for a new constitution which would be less discriminatory towards Fijians of Indian descent and more acceptable internationally. Elsewhere, there have been other democratic moves. In 1990 the government of Samoa extended suffrage from the traditional chiefly heads of households (*matai*) only, to all adults over 21 years of age, although this was not accompanied by a universal right to stand for election (Fana'afi Le Tagoloa 1992:131). The pro-democracy movement in Tonga, the Pacific Islands' only monarchy, gained momentum after 1987, although the King retains control over the executive of government (Helu 1992:145–9). In 1994 Palau, the last remnant of the

TABLE 3.1 • SOVEREIGNTY STATUS OF THE PACIFIC ISLAND STATES

Independent nation-state			Self-governing territory#			Dependent territory	
Fiji	1970	(UK)	Cook Islands	1965	(NZ)	American Samoa	(USA)
Kiribati*	1979	(UK)	Federated States of Micronesia (FSM)	1986	(USA)	French Polynesia	(France)
Nauru*	1968	(UK)	Marshall Islands	1986	(USA)	Guam	(USA)
Papua New Guinea*	1975	(Aust.)	Niue	1974	(NZ)	New Caledonia	(France)
Solomon Islands*	1978	(UK)	Northern Marianas	1978	(USA)	Pitcairn Island	(UK)
Tonga*	1970	(UK)	Palau	1994	(USA)	Tokelau	(NZ)
Tuvalu*	1978	(UK)				Wallis and Futuna	(France)
Vanuatu*	1980	(UK and France)					
Samoa*	1962	(NZ)					

Notes: # Level of political independence from patron state varies (see Hoadley 1992:19–21).
Dates refer to year of independence or self-government (existing or former metropolitan power shown in brackets).
* Denotes current membership of the British Commonwealth.

Trust Territory of the Pacific Islands (TTPI), finally signed a Compact of Free Association with the USA, allowing a greater degree of sovereignty.

Despite independence and democracy, however, challenges to the post-colonial order have come from outside. Continued colonial actions of metropolitan powers, particularly France and to a lesser extent the USA, have undermined principles of self-determination. While constitutional dependence is not necessarily an impediment to principles of liberal democracy (Crocombe 1992a:16), it can pose serious challenges, particularly in cases such as New Caledonia where the indigenous Kanaks are outnumbered by settlers from metropolitan France and its former colonies (Connell 1987b). While a relatively peaceful and politically stable period has followed the Matignon Accord of 1988, conflict is likely as the independence referendum scheduled for 1998 approaches. In New Caledonia, as in Fiji, questions about the representational rights of ethnic communities are likely to pose serious political challenges to legislators for many years.

The continued colonial presence of France in the region, particularly its nuclear testing programme, had become the major issue in regional politics by the end of the Cold War. This issue was reignited in mid-1995 following newly-elected President Jacques Chirac's announcement of a programme of eight nuclear tests, conducted at Mururoa and Fangataufa atolls in French Polynesia. Anti-nuclear sentiment from around the world quickly became entangled in the ongoing debate about the future sovereignty status of the French colonies in the Pacific Islands. Despite violent protests within French Polynesia, however, particularly in Papeete following the underground nuclear test in September 1995, evidence that local populations desired an end to French control of the territories remained contested. Following an end to the testing programme, France has begun a process of reducing its military presence and government spending in French Polynesia, and it is likely that the country will face a considerable reduction in its subsidy from metropolitan France in future.

Thus, the colonial era in the Pacific is not over. Although the transition to independent sovereign states with largely democratic systems of governance has dominated the politics of the region for the past 30 years, it is likely that a number of states will choose to remain quasi-colonies, with continuing close ties and support from their metropolitan patrons. What is becoming more apparent is not a simple wresting of political power from colonial masters but a more subtle process of negotiation in which the concepts of sovereignty, independence and dependence are open to varied interpretations. This is most clearly seen in the reformulation of economic relationships.

Economic Relationships: Patronage or Liberalisation?

Trade and migration routes crossed the Pacific Ocean well before the first Europeans visited the region and the Pacific Island tradition of voyaging and the search for new opportunities over the seas was well established (Hau'ofa 1993). Yet it was the colonial era that led to the incorporation of the region into the evolving global economy. Products from the region – copra, gold, coffee, sugar, nickel, timber and phosphate – were exchanged for the plethora of manufactured goods from Europe and North America. It is a pattern that continues to exist today, though global forces, particularly trade liberalisation and the end of the Cold War, may signal significant shifts in economic structures and relationships in the years ahead.

Present economic structures

The economies of the Pacific Islands vary greatly, although most are dominated by the primary sector and/or tourism. Increasingly, agriculture is not able to provide for the growing material aspirations of island people or their governments and new sources of income are being tapped, often those which plunder natural resources: minerals, forests and fish.

There has been a region-wide trend away from agriculture, the traditional mainstay of Pacific Island economies, due to depressed world prices and the increased availability of imported food (Overton 1993a:50). Subsistence agriculture is still, however, of great importance in much of the region. For example, in the Solomon Islands, Kiribati and Tuvalu about 75 per cent of households are economically still primarily dependent on subsistence agriculture (Ward 1993:9). In the countries associated with the USA, agriculture has barely survived due to factors such as the rapid monetisation of the economy and official neglect (Fairbairn *et al.* 1991:43). Commercial agriculture is well established in the larger countries of the region, particularly sugar in Fiji and copra in Papua New Guinea, the Solomon Islands and Vanuatu. In the smaller countries, opportunities for the development of commercial agriculture are restricted by shortages of land and isolation from international markets.

Mining is particularly important in Papua New Guinea and New Caledonia, accounting in 1991 for 76 and 90 per cent of exports respectively (Douglas and Douglas 1994:442, 548). In the past Nauru has relied almost exclusively on phosphate mining but supplies are now close to exhaustion. Whilst the Nauru Phosphate Company took control of the mining industry on independence in 1968 and profits were invested in a number of funds, controversy has surrounded the scheme (Hoadley 1992:145-7). In 1995, Nauru remains one of the world's richest countries *per capita* but continued prosperity depends on the future success of investments.

Secondary industry exists in the Pacific Islands but is not well established. Fiji, Tonga, Samoa and New Caledonia display the largest degree of diversification and in these countries manufacturing offers genuine development options for the future. The most notable manufacturing sector growth in recent years has occurred in the Fijian garment industry as a result of the Tax Free Factory (TFF) scheme.[2] Between 1986 and 1991 the value of garment exports rose from $A4.86 million to $A131 million (Douglas and Douglas 1994:187). Manufacturing has also been encouraged in Tonga but in 1989–90 it accounted for only 8.6 per cent of gross domestic product (GDP) (Douglas and Douglas 1994:640). Elsewhere in the region, however, isolation, lack of appropriate natural resources and shortages of investment capital discourage the establishment of secondary industry on a large scale.

Tourism is also of increasing economic importance. In 1993 nearly one million people visited the region, the majority travelling to the Northern Marianas, Fiji and French Polynesia (South Pacific Commission 1995). The scenic beauty and isolation which characterises the region makes this sector an excellent prospect for future development and most countries are pursuing tourism as a major development strategy. It is an industry that brings its own set of problems and constraints, however: tourist numbers fluctuate according to the economic health of source countries; the real returns on tourism development are constrained in countries which are highly dependent on foreign investment and imports of basic commodities; and there are cultural and environmental costs of which some Pacific Island societies are understandably wary.

The result of these different economic strategies and, in particular, of the different resource endowments of Pacific Island countries is wide disparities in income (Table 3.2). The differences in *per capita* income are very wide indeed, from $A600 in Kiribati to over $A22,000 in Nauru. There is some explanation for these disparities in the resource bases of the different countries: mineral- or phosphate-rich countries such as

[2] Fiji's Tax Free Factory Scheme was initiated following the 1987 coups in order to promote manufacturing sector growth. Under the scheme companies are offered a 'tax holiday' for 13 years provided that they export at least 95% of their output (see Chandra 1994:29).

Nauru or Papua New Guinea fare better than the resource-scarce atoll nations of Kiribati or Tuvalu. Yet the real contributing factor to the wide differences lies not in the inherent wealth of the countries themselves but in their external relations. Comparing Tables 3.1 and 3.2, it is apparent that those countries with continuing dependent status have much higher *per capita* GDP than most independent countries. Aid to New Zealand, French and American dependent territories is very high on a *per capita* basis and, along with remittances, is arguably the major determinant of the differences in incomes amongst the countries of the region. Clearly, political dependence is a critical factor in the economic development of many Pacific Island countries.

TABLE 3.2 • BASIC ECONOMIC DATA FOR THE COUNTRIES OF THE PACIFIC ISLANDS ($A)

	GDP *per capita* (year of data)	Government expenditure *per capita* 1991	Foreign aid *per capita* 1990
American Samoa	6,660 (1985)	na	2,117
Cook Islands	5,195 (1993)	2,389	912
FSM	3,400 (1993)	na	na
Fiji	2,716 (1993)	773	64
French Polynesia	19,622 (1992)	4,209	1,675
Guam	12,356 (1990)	6,208	878
Kiribati	600 (1990)	566	421
Marshall Islands	1,995 (1991)	2,624	1,386
Nauru	22,418 (1989)	5,592	27
New Caledonia	17,970 (1990)	3,832	1,901
Niue	3,946 (1991)	na	4,034
Northern Marianas	12,941 (1994)	3,700	na
Palau	4,163 (1988)	2,375	907
Papua New Guinea	1,882 (1993)	392	127
Pitcairn Island	na	na	na
Samoa	1,305 (1992)	743	160
Solomon Islands	947 (1993)	290	174
Tokelau	na	na	3,750
Tonga	1,815 (1992)	361	389
Tuvalu	1,256 (1990)	na	694
Vanuatu	1,678 (1993)	504	337
Wallis & Futuna	na	9,081	75

Sources: South Pacific Commission (1995), World Bank (1994)

The benefits of dependence: MIRAB economies, aid and preferential trade

In 1985, two New Zealand social scientists, Geoff Bertram and Ray Watters published a controversial article which argued that Pacific Island 'microstates' (including the Cook Islands, Niue, and Tokelau) did well from their close relationships with metropolitan countries, as dependent territories or self-governing states in free association. Their MIRAB model (migration, remittances, aid and bureaucracy) described the way small states derived much of their wealth by virtue of the aid that came from their patron states, which in turn supported a large public sector (the main source of local employment), and the remittances and savings that came from migrants, able to travel and work freely in the patron states and take advantage of much higher wage levels (Bertram and Watters 1985). Although such incomes from outside tended to raise the shadow price of labour and thus depress local development activities in agriculture, fishing and industry, it did allow for a good material standard of living to be sustained in countries where the local resource base, coupled with remoteness and very small-scale local economies, would not otherwise allow for more than a subsistence level of income.

Aid is a vital component of most Pacific Island countries and often the most important contributor to GDP in some of the dependent states. All countries except Nauru are dependent upon overseas official development assistance (ODA) to some extent. In 1990, for example, eight countries out of a total of 19 for which data is available, received ODA exceeding $A900 *per capita* and a further eight received over $A100 (see Table 3.2), making the Pacific Islands the most heavily aid-dependent region in the world (Connell 1986).[3] The aid programmes of the major donors to the region – Australia, France, New Zealand and USA – are overwhelmingly directed towards the countries with which historical ties are strongest. Over 75 per cent of Australia's Pacific Islands-bound ODA, for example, has been directed to Papua New Guinea as budgetary support, (Garrett 1992:22), New Zealand is the major donor for the Cook Islands, Niue and the Tokelaus (Crocombe 1992b:77) and the present and former territories of the USA in Micronesia receive very high levels of support (Ogden 1994:263). The relatively high dependence on foreign aid of most of the Pacific Islands, and the maintenance of old colonial ties, provides extra-regional

[3] Providing a comprehensive summary of aid to the region, however, is difficult, as 'internal' transfer payments from the USA and France to their territories do not technically qualify as ODA. Additionally, individual countries' shares of the increasing level of multilateral aid are difficult to determine.

powers with considerable opportunities to influence regional and domestic affairs. There have been marked changes in aid policies in recent years, however: budget support is being shifted at the behest of donors towards more project aid, the Pacific Islands region is receiving proportionately less of the aid of donors such as New Zealand (Scheyvens and Overton 1995), and whilst France and Japan increased their spending (Chand 1991:71–3), the USA and the United Kingdom have curtailed theirs markedly (*Pacific Islands Monthly* 1994:5).

The MIRAB model has been criticised for it seems to underplay the initiative of local people and their resources and paints a pessimistic picture of endogenous development, calling instead for continuing dependence (Hau'ofa 1993, Connell 1991b). Nonetheless, the model does portray accurately the way a number of countries owe their relatively high income levels to support from outside, from aid and from the remittances of their own people able to work abroad.

The model can be broadened, for it is not just the very small states which benefit from metropolitan patronage. Because of their small economies of scale and their remoteness from world markets, many of the conventional development strategies (industrialisation and commodity production) are not readily open to Pacific Island nations. Because of this situation, and because many world markets have been characterised by substantial trade barriers, patron states have bestowed preferential rights upon Pacific states in a number of areas. The Lomé Convention, first negotiated in 1975, offers preferential trade conditions in the highly protected European market to former colonies in Africa, the Caribbean and the Pacific (Ravenhill 1985). Under the Lomé III agreement the European Union provided ECU117 million worth of preferential trade access to the countries of the Pacific Islands between 1991 and 1996 (Fry 1993:238). The Fijian sugar industry in particular has been a beneficiary of this agreement, resulting in a boost to farmers of $F93 million in 1992 (Grynberg 1993:157, 1995b). Australia and New Zealand have also offered preferential terms to Pacific countries under the South Pacific Regional Trade and Economic Cooperation Agreement (SPARTECA) and this has helped develop the major manufacturing success story in the region, the Fiji garment industry (Chandra 1993, 1996).

The MIRAB model and the preferential trade agreements have thus been crucial elements of development strategies in the region. They are artificial arrangements, and may not survive global trade liberalisation (see below) but they have been sustained until now because metropolitan countries have been prepared to subsidise countries in the region, whether through a sense of post-colonial altruism or Cold War pragmatism.

The benefits of independence

Whilst high aid levels, the MIRAB model and preferential trade access point to the economic benefits some countries have gained by exploiting their close relationships with metropolitan powers, others have moved to gain advantage from their independent status. Statehood and international recognition as an independent nation have their advantages. In the Cold War era, some countries were able to use the threat of inviting closer relationships with the Soviet Union and China to attract more magnanimous treatment from Western aid donors (Campbell 1992, Overton 1994). More recently, other possibilities have been open, allowing some countries to compensate for their smallness and isolation by both overt and covert exploitation of their sovereignty (Connell 1988b, Bertram 1987).

The Cook Islands, Nauru, Samoa, Tonga and Vanuatu have attempted to establish international finance centres (tax havens). This has brought some income for government from registration fees and increased business for some local agents but it has also sometimes run these countries foul of their putative friends. For example, the questionable involvement of the Cook Islands government in the tax avoidance operations of several New Zealand companies, which came to light in the 'Wine Box' inquiry in New Zealand in 1997, led to a considerable backlash from some New Zealand politicians and fuelled calls for a reduction in aid.

Other dubious schemes have included the sale of passports. Countries such as Tonga have offered special passports (but not full citizenship rights) to those who can afford the high fee. This has proved popular amongst Chinese people in Taiwan and Hong Kong. Another scheme has involved waste dumping. The government of the Marshall Islands recently proposed utilising the geographic remoteness of its outer islands for the storage of nuclear waste. The government argues that, as the islands in question have already been contaminated by US nuclear testing in the 1950s, they are taking advantage of an already 'bad situation' (Rashid 1995:15). Despite international criticism of the proposal, the scheme may provide an opportunity for the Marshall Islands to attract much-needed foreign capital at a time when the long-term financial support of the USA remains in doubt.

Less controversial than these proposals has been the long-standing income derived from philatelic sales: small countries issue their own postage stamps which can be sold to collectors world-wide. Many more stamps are sold than are needed to cover the cost of the national postal services and there is a healthy net income for the state.

Perhaps the major economic benefit of sovereignty has concerned the fisheries resource. The rich fisheries of the Pacific Islands became more strategically valuable after the UNCLOS III, ratified in 1982, declared the 200-mile exclusive economic zone (EEZ). Pacific Island countries, though often very small in land area, command vast expanses of the Pacific Ocean and the marine resources that lie within them. Japan, Taiwan and South Korea, together with other countries, have subsequently negotiated access to the rich fishing grounds of the Pacific Islands through the Forum Fisheries Agency (FFA), established in 1979 to provide multilateral management of the resource (Bugotu *et al.* 1990:3–19). In May 1992 the island countries of the South Pacific Forum signed a fishing agreement with the government of the USA guaranteeing payment of $US180 million over a ten-year period (Fry 1993:236). As the traditional fishing grounds of the extra-regional powers such as the South China Sea, the North Sea and the North Atlantic become less productive, access to the rich ocean resources of the Pacific Islands will become increasingly important.

Changes afoot: the new world order and trade liberalisation

Whilst the above strategies, variously exploiting dependent relationships or national sovereignty, have resulted in relatively prosperous economic conditions for a number of Pacific Island countries, their future is uncertain. The end of the Cold War in the late 1980s and the subsequent diminished strategic value of the Pacific region has closed a number of options as metropolitan countries are less willing to subsidise countries that are no longer of value to them as testing grounds, military bases or votes of support in international fora. Concomitantly, moves to liberalise world trade are posing a serious threat to the trade preferences that have supported some of the few examples (apart from resource extraction and tourism) of apparently endogenous development in the region. The development strategies that have served the region well in recent decades may no longer be sustainable.

The post-Cold War world order is gradually changing the strategic and military situation in the region. Whilst Fiji and Papua New Guinea, and on a smaller scale, Tonga, have developed defence forces, military activity in the region primarily involves four metropolitan powers: Australia, France, New Zealand and the USA. France maintains a presence in the region for reasons partly related to reinforcing a 'major power' status (though this has lessened since the end of its nuclear testing programme), but the primary strategic concern of Australia, New Zealand and the USA is the security of trans-Pacific air and sea-lanes (Dorrence 1992:66, Thakur 1993:81), something that is not under threat at present. The demise of the USSR has greatly reduced the need for policies of 'strategic denial', although the long-term regional ambitions of China remain of concern to the Western powers. Only the need for peacekeeping in regional conflicts, such as Bougainville, and the programmes of military cooperation within the region maintain foreign military presence. Thus, military involvement in the region by the major powers is likely to wind down.

As military involvement lessens, so too have the aid programmes of major donors. Donors, most of whom have undergone major reform of their own public sectors, have turned their attention to their own ODA and are now much less willing to use ODA as a way of supporting what they see as inflated public sectors in the Pacific. They have moved away from blanket support of bureaucracies through budget aid and have put more emphasis on the private sector and targeted projects. The New Zealand ODA programme, for example, has undergone a major change in recent years (Scheyvens and Overton 1995). Although total volumes of aid have not fallen, there have been some significant shifts in policy and in the direction of aid. Projects which help to promote private sector development have been favoured (alongside those which address issues of sustainable development or gender inequalities) whilst there has been a reluctance to continue to support the bureaucracies of the Cook Islands and Niue. The New Zealand government refused to rescue the Cook Islands government from its debts in 1996–7 and, in effect, forced it to undergo a major restructuring of its public sector. The result was the shedding of at least a third of government employees. Australia is following suit, notably in Papua New Guinea, and the reduction in US aid to the region has been significant. No longer can Pacific Island countries rely on a steady stream of aid to support living standards and employment.

In terms of the moves to reform world trade, the countries of the Pacific Islands are not well represented within new trade organisations: Papua New Guinea is the only Pacific Island member of Asia Pacific Economic Cooperation (APEC) and is joined only by Fiji in the World Trade Organisation (WTO). Their small size in an economic sense may make them much less visible in a new open global economy. In other ways, liberalisation poses more specific threats. The South Pacific Forum countries are beneficiaries of SPARTECA which allows non-reciprocal preferential access to the markets of Australia and New Zealand. This agreement is of limited value, however, if moves toward free(r) trade continue, as the value of this preferential access will be progressively eroded as other countries – especially those in Asia – gain greater access to the economies of Australia and New Zealand under the APEC agreement. Of even greater concern, especially in Fiji, is the threat that the Lomé Convention may be significantly weakened or dispensed with altogether as a result of the gradual adoption of the free trade principles under the WTO.

Yet, whilst these changes and limited development options of the countries of the Pacific Islands have led analysts including Ward (1989, 1993) and Overton (1996) to question future levels of prosperity, moves toward greater trade liberalisation have met with some success. For example, a recent report reviewing the impacts of Fijian trade liberalisation reforms, implemented after the National Economic Summit in 1989, found the national economy had been positively influenced during the period up to 1994 (United Nations Pacific Operations Centre 1994:1). The report analysed a wide range of factors including price fluctuation, employment, business viability, manufacturing activity, trading controls and exchange rates, and found that in the five years since the reforms the range of consumer goods had increased, consumer prices had lowered, the number of businesses had grown by 5 per cent annually, employment had grown and levels of international competitiveness had strengthened.

Foreign investment has played a major role in the development of the national economies of the Pacific Islands (Fairbairn *et al.* 1991:44), and will continue to do so. Most countries have accordingly adapted relatively liberal trade and investment regulations, although some restrictions still exist. The local government of Tahiti, for example, imposes duties of 50–250 per cent on all imported goods (McShane 1995:5) and foreign investment in the Solomon Islands must be compatible with national development policies and be registered under the Foreign Investment Act (Economist Intelligence Unit 1994:60).

Many in the region believe that the countries of the Pacific Islands have opportunities to progress in the new international economic order, particularly when compared with many countries of Africa and East Asia, by such means as the development of tourism and fishing industries. The post-Cold War world order with its renewed emphasis on free(r) trade therefore presents an opportunity for the island countries to break free from the economic dependence that has been a central characteristic for many states in the post-independence decades. Yet what is not certain is the future of those economies and activities – dependent on aid or preferential trade agreements – that have evolved in the old world order and shaped the economic structures of many countries and the aspirations and activities of their people.

Conclusions: A New Pacific Order?

The political and economic context for development in the Pacific Islands region has fundamentally changed in the past decade. Much of the old post-colonial order rested on the assumption of an external threat – an albeit distant threat posed by the Soviet Union and China.

In this world, the countries of the Pacific Islands could, and did, find ways of exploiting their geopolitical situation. Their smallness and isolation were not major handicaps if they could be perceived to have a strategic value commensurate with the vast area of ocean they spanned. They could negotiate forms of sovereignty that gave them political independence yet continuing patronage. Those that remained dependent territories did best from generous aid programmes and liberal immigration laws. Others profited from preferential trade agreements. Behind the rhetoric of independence lay a subtle web of negotiated relationships that perpetuated a neocolonial order, in many ways mutually beneficial, as it traded strategic influence for economic benefits.

The old order is now disintegrating. The withdrawal of aid, military presence and economic support may be welcomed as a precursor of more meaningful political independence and a much more liberal global economy, but it will not be without major economic and social ramifications. Those that depended on the old order – the civil servants of the Cook Islands, the garment workers or sugar cane farmers of Fiji, the local workers on military bases in French Polynesia or the Marshall Islands – have much to be apprehensive about. Alternative development strategies may not be easy to find. Tourism, forestry and fishing offer possibilities, though these may put much greater stress on limited natural resources. Commercial agriculture and manufacturing may survive but only if wage rates are low by international standards or niche markets can be found. What is certain is that Pacific Island countries will have to forge a new place in the world, one that is less dependent on external support and recognises the particular cultural and environmental context of the region. It creates not only the urgency of finding new strategies for sustainable development but also the necessity of finding appropriate, diverse and autonomous paths.

CHAPTER 4

Culture and Society

REGINA SCHEYVENS

The introduction to this book noted: 'The social perspective still seems to be a junior partner in the sustainable development coalition.' This chapter tackles this anomaly directly by throwing light on the diverse and vibrant cultures and societies of the Pacific in order to show how cultural norms and practices of Pacific peoples are central to the achievement of sustainable development.

When considering ways of promoting sustainable livelihoods in the Pacific, much can be drawn from past practices and traditional knowledge about ways of utilising the resources of the land, forests and sea while maintaining the natural environment in good condition for future generations. There is also much to learn about effective social organisation which promotes cooperation, social order and harmony. In many Pacific Island communities, social sustainability is highly valued, as seen in the support for indigenous languages and cultural practices, and promotion of inter- and intra-generational equity (Young 1997:3).

This chapter does not, however, seek to romanticise past traditions and practices. Rather, it attempts to demonstrate ways in which the peoples of the region have evolved and adapted to change over the years: 'culture' is not static and unchanging (Pitt 1973/4:68). Over time Pacific societies have had to be dynamic and resilient in order to survive in a region which offers many challenges. Also considered are contemporary challenges to sustainable development, including social inequalities which have led to the marginalisation of sectors of Pacific Island societies. If development is to be truly sustainable, it must offer opportunities for all peoples – disadvantaged ethnic groups, overburdened women, peoples under colonial rule, disabled people, the poor and youth – to define and participate in strategies for change.

Cultural Diversity

While biodiversity is one main focus for many writers on sustainable development, much less attention is paid to the maintenance of cultural diversity as a strategy for sustainable development. Cultural diversity, it could be argued, is as much if not more under threat, as biodiversity. Distinct cultural differences can be discerned across the Pacific region. These differences are not well presented, however, in the sanitised versions of culture which tourists visiting the region, even those sleeping in thatched huts and attending cultural shows, are likely to observe (Howe 1997).

One way in which early navigators sought to categorise these differences was by dividing the region into three cultural areas: Polynesia, Melanesia and Micronesia (Figure 4.1). The supposed cultural traits of each area are discussed below.

Melanesia ('black islands') embraces countries of the South-West Pacific, notably Papua New Guinea, the Solomon Islands, Vanuatu and New Caledonia. In addition, the people from the western part of the island of New Guinea, which is presently under the control of Indonesia, are also Melanesian. Fijians are sometimes included in this category. As acknowledged by Crocombe (1989:20), however, while they have the bodies of Melanesians their cultural practices have more in common with Polynesians. Geographically, the large, mountainous Melanesian islands formed on the Indian continental plate and they are home to rich and diverse ecosystems because of their size and their closeness to mainland South-East Asia and Australia.

The islands and atolls of Polynesia and Micronesia consist of either the tops of volcanoes or coral outcrops which formed on now-submerged reefs fringing ancient volcanoes (Bodley 1997:152). The islands and atolls of Polynesia include the Cook Islands, French Polynesia, Niue, Samoa, Tokelau, Tonga, Tuvalu and Wallis and Futuna, which lie in a large triangle defined by New Zealand, Easter Island and Hawai'i. The atolls of Micronesia lie to the north of Melanesia. Micronesia consists of Kiribati, the Federated States of Micronesia, Palau (Belau), Guam, the Marshall Islands, Nauru, and the Commonwealth of the Northern Marianas. Helu (1997:1) explains how geographical factors have directly influenced cultural practices in the resource-poor atoll societies of Polynesia and Micronesia. In particular, there are certain traditions which seek to promote group welfare, as noted in the following proverb: *'Me'a si'i, femolimoli'i; mi'a lahi, takitaha kai'* (Food in scarcity you must always share; in abundance, though, you need not care).

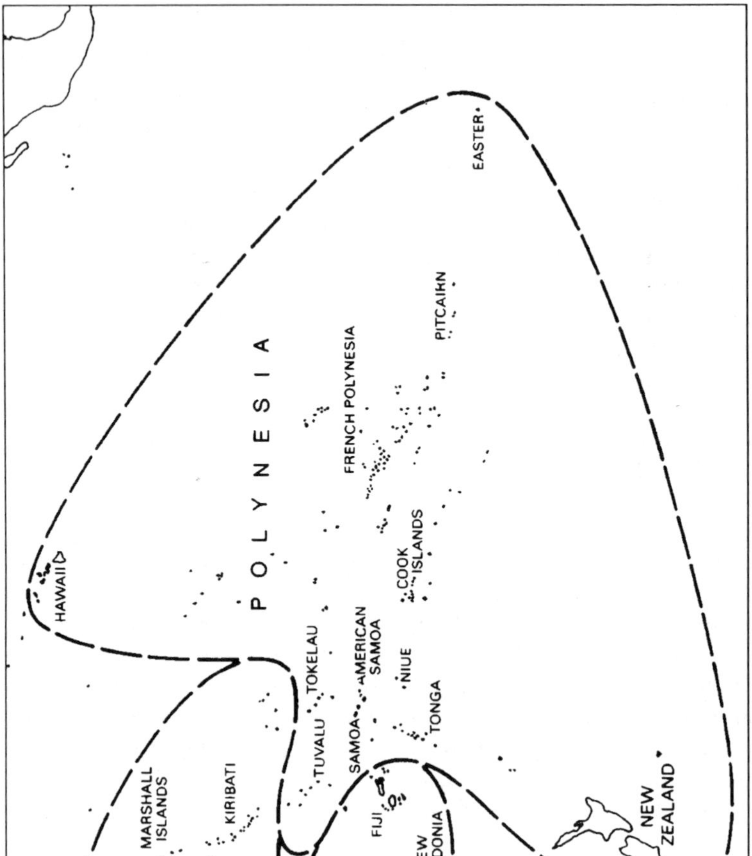

FIGURE 4.1 • ONE WAY OF UNDERSTANDING CULTURAL DIVERSITY WITHIN THE PACIFIC

Source: Valentine 1963.

Polynesians were regarded by early European explorers as being superior to Melanesians because they were more hierarchically organised (read 'more politically sophisticated'), and had lighter skin (read 'more attractive'). The head-hunting and cannibalistic practices which were associated with some Melanesian tribal groups were widely publicised in early colonial times, leading to assumptions that Melanesians were a savage and hostile people. The Polynesians, meanwhile, with their social organisations focusing on rank and status, were seen as more 'civilised' and akin to the hierarchical societies of eighteenth- and nineteenth-century Europe. Yet this idea of civilisation certainly did not equate with greater egalitarianism. In Polynesia, leadership was based on ascription rather than attainment. Thus genealogy had a major influence on personal rank and prestige (Bodley 1997). Such social order was, and still is, reinforced by traditions such as the *kava* ceremony of Tonga, whereby the roots of a plant from the pepper family (*Piper methysticum*), which has mild narcotic properties, are made into a drink and shared with others. This ceremony seeks to 'maintain or consolidate the power of the ruling elite', both through the way in which participants are positioned and the manner in which the *kava* is shared. Supposedly this should also be how other societal resources are distributed: 'Such rituals are object lessons or social theatre aimed at showing precisely where power lies' (Helu 1997:1).

Micronesian societies are similar in many ways to Polynesian structures, with hierarchies and status by ascription the norm. Many appear to involve much greater complexity in social ranking, however, and matriarchal descent is more prevalent. Custom survives but has been weakened by the heavy influence of colonialism since 1945. While monetary assistance from the United States has allowed many Micronesians to 'enjoy a material standard of living higher than at any time in the past ... this has altered their traditional cultural forms beyond all possibility of recovery' (Hezel 1992:219).

Melanesian societies are diverse and extremely fragmented, with people living in small communities often distinguished by language: there are over 1,200 distinct languages (Ahlburg 1996:4). Leadership was based on the demonstrated abilities of individuals. Leaders held on to their positions by continually proving their worth, especially through warfare, trade, manufacturing, and the accumulation and sharing of wealth. Kinship relationships were commonly cemented through flamboyant exchange systems. According to Harcombe (1993:28), 'Melanesian life is more democratic than the aristocratic and oligarchic system prevailing in Polynesian islands'. Even in the Polynesian countries, however, leaders in precolonial times typically had to prove themselves to hold on to a position of power. For example, if a *matai* (chief) in Western Samoa enforced traditional law in a way the extended family, the *'aiga*, was not happy with, it could over time withdraw its labour which would lead to a decline in the prestige and status of the *matai* and the village as a whole (Pitt 1973/4:69).

The cultural boundaries that separate Melanesia, Polynesia and Micronesia are not as clearly demarcated, however, as Figure 4.1 suggests. Recently these categories have been comprehensively criticised and systematically abandoned by some scholars who argue that they hide more than they reveal, brushing over significant differences within each area and also failing to acknowledge commonalties across the region (Howe 1997). As Bodley (1997:152) notes, 'These divisions make sense geographically but are anthropologically less precise'. Cultural diversity within the three cultural areas is easy to discern. For example, within Melanesia there are differences between 'knowledge cultures' whose politics are based around esoteric knowledge, and 'thing cultures' under which goods such as pigs and pearl shells are highly valued (Harrison 1993:139).

Cultural similarities can also be observed across the region, and derive largely from traditional similarities in the lifestyles of many Pacific Islanders (Crocombe 1989:20). Most engaged in subsistence agriculture, and foraging on the land and in the sea was an important activity in terms of finding foods to supplement the diet, plants with medicinal properties, or materials suitable for craft manufacture. Land was always held communally and most societies saw it as having spiritual qualities, especially where it was used as the final resting place of the deceased. The sea played an essential role in supplementing livelihoods in all but the most remote Melanesian societies based in rugged, inland areas.

For these reasons, the terms Polynesia, Melanesia and Micronesia are used throughout this book mainly as terms to distinguish geographical regions of the Pacific rather than, as originally intended, to categorise them as distinct cultural entities. These cultural entities can be discerned as Western constructs (Howe 1997), just as it can be argued that because of the arbitrary ways in which they were divided up amongst the colonising powers, the countries of the Pacific may best be understood as Western fictions (Macpherson 1992a:431).

Social Challenges to Sustainable Development

Despite these long-standing patterns of cultural diversity and similarity within the Pacific Island region, societies and cultures are changing. In most cases, these changes have resulted from the adoption of Western influences, in culture, commerce and politics. They have changed old forms of social organisation, sometimes removing old distinctions, at other times magnifying them. Emerging from these social transformations are new forms of inequality, new injustices and new groups of marginalised peoples, as well as benefits and opportunities.

From a sustainable societies perspective, issues of equity, justice and opportunities for all groups of people to participate in development processes are paramount when considering whether sustainable development is an achievable goal. It is when examining these issues that constraints on the achievement of sustainable development become more apparent. We are referring here, in particular, to inequalities which frame the marginalisation of significant groups within some societies. The following section discusses a selection of social inequities which currently provide a challenge for those hoping to build a sustainable future for Pacific Island countries.

Gender inequality

Gender inequities in Pacific Island societies typically prevent women from having the same opportunities as men to participate in and benefit from development processes. They also mean that the unpaid work of women is accorded less value than the work performed by men. As the economies of Pacific Island countries have become more monetised and men have taken on more paid work than women, women's contributions to development have not been accorded the respect they once received. In some cases, women are no longer consulted on important issues of resource extraction or development which will impact directly on their livelihoods (see chapters 9 and 10).

It would be wrong to suggest that there was gender equity in all traditional societies (Howe 1997). It is clear, however, that current social, political and economic structures reproduce and even deepen women's subordination in many contexts. To cite examples from the Solomon Islands, the education system enrols four times as many boys as girls in Form Six, the top grade in high school (MEHRD 1991), and the political system has produced only one woman member of parliament in 20 years. Furthermore, throughout the Pacific, development initiatives directed at women have often been limited in scope, making 'assumptions about gender roles which limit the aspirations and achievements of women' (Thomas and Hill 1987:106). Many focus on home economics activities even though, as noted by Women of Vanuatu (1983:3), this 'concentration on domestic topics fails to equip a woman to play a more dynamic role in the development process'.

Thus Jully Sipolo (1986: 8), a Solomon Islands poet, points out that for many rural women, life in their post-colonial, independent country offers fewer new opportunities than one might hope:

> MI MERE
> I am a woman, born in the village
> Destined to spend my life
> in a never ending vicious circle
> Gardening, child-bearing, house-keeping
> Seen and not heard....

There are discernible differences across the region, however, because while Melanesian women constitute only 15 to 20 per cent of the Melanesian population attending university, Polynesian and Fijian women students constitute 30 to 50 per cent of their respective university groups – and in the French and United States territories, women are the majority (Crocombe 1989:60). Similarly, more women have found paid employment in a variety of career areas in Micronesian and Polynesian countries than in Melanesia. In Tahiti, the Cook Islands and Niue, too, chiefly titles and the land rights which are associated with these titles are being conferred upon women more commonly than in the past (Crocombe 1989:110).

While some women have been able to take advantage of new opportunities, the progress of many other women has been hindered by their heavy workloads. As Lee (1985:233) writes with respect to Papua New Guinean women: 'It is ironic that ... women have been left behind in development, not because they are irrelevant, but because they are so central to production, so overworked and so burdened with responsibilities.' In addition, throughout the region, it appears that women, including those who have participated most fully in education systems and the cash economy, are suffering the consequences of men's disillusionment with change:

> Pacific men may be losing confidence as their traditionally dominant roles are eroded. They no longer have any significant defence role, and their traditional advantages are diminishing. The number of things that men can do better than women keeps contracting, and some men take refuge in high alcohol and drug consumption, body contact sports and violence against women, which is a matter for concern in most of the Pacific (Crocombe 1989:61).

Class and ethnic inequalities: the case of Tahiti

Social inequalities existed in many forms in precolonial societies but they have been magnified and transformed since, sometimes as a result of deliberate policies (the use of immigrant labour, 'divide and rule' strategies and the fostering of a ruling elite), at other times in response to changing social and economic circumstances. Different experiences of development in recent decades have exacerbated such inequalities and they are a feature of all Pacific Island societies today. Socio-economic and ethnic differentiation are different processes but their manifestations often overlap.

In Tahiti, a distinct class system which is closely related to ethnic affiliations has developed. After deciding that the Polynesian islands under their control would be an ideal place to test nuclear devices, the French government in the 1960s set about recruiting thousands of Polynesians from the outer islands to build the required bases, airstrips, wharves, hangars and roads. Many others found work in civilian construction and service industries. Most of them brought their families to Papeete, which saw the development of slum areas. There was a massive displacement of people from rural to urban areas, with over half the territory's population dwelling in the greater Papeete area by 1967, and a resultant dwindling in production of food for local consumption in rural areas (Finney 1992:360). A whole way of life had changed. Most of the indigenous labourers and their families chose to remain in Papeete when they were laid off after completion of the bases in 1970, and they came to constitute a new class of proletarians (Danielsson and Danielsson 1992:181).

Many French citizens followed the French troops out to Tahiti at this time, realising that business enterprises could thrive in this period of rapid investment by the French government. The nuclear testing programme which saw 44 atomic bombs exploded into the atmosphere and 131 bombs exploded underground in French Polynesia generated a great deal of money in the local economy. While French Polynesia's GNP *per capita* exceeded that of New Zealand in 1985, this income was very unevenly distributed. Most of the economic gains have been made by one third of the population consisting of the metropolitan French, the local *Demis* (those of mixed French and indigenous origins) and the Chinese. These people have been able to purchase icons of consumer society including VCRs and motorbikes. The indigenous people, *Ma'ohi* Polynesians, have been excluded from many of the benefits of development and are concentrated in semi-skilled labouring and service jobs, or are dependent on government benefits, but still have to cope with inflated prices for imported goods due to high import taxes instituted to make up for a complete absence of income taxes in the territory (Finney 1992:362). In the early 1990s, 18,000 people, mainly *Ma'ohi* and previously skilled farmers and fishers, were listed as unemployed. This amounted to almost 13 per cent of the population (Kelly 1993:38).

The slum population in Papeete has consequently grown, breeding an underclass of disgruntled citizens and dismantling traditional family structures:

> The psychological problems of these families, who live on small plots without a garden, or in European-style dwellings built by the government without any provisions for community life, are as serious as the material ones. Promiscuity often results in quarrels and fights. Since there is no room for grandparents and other old relatives – traditionally well-cared for by their sons and daughters – they are abandoned to themselves. For the same reason, countless teenagers leave home and join gangs of juvenile delinquents or become prostitutes (Danielsson and Danielsson 1992:181).

In this context, traditional support mechanisms often fail to operate: 'Traditional Polynesian values of sharing food and of rendering aid, so well adapted to rural living, are difficult to translate into meaningful actions in a way of life built upon wages and consumer purchases' (Finney 1992:363).

The indigenous poor are starting to make public their grievances with the rulers of the French colony, as evidenced in the riots of 1987, protests in 1991 and further rioting in 1996 which saw the burning of numerous cars and buildings. The problem for the future of this territory, however, is that the economy would be shattered by a direct withdrawal of French financial support (Finney 1992:370).

Cargo: the lure of Western material goods

Avoiding typical First World versus Third World divides, Durning (cited in Korten 1995) provides an interesting breakdown of the peoples of the world according to their lifestyles and consumption patterns. This argues that contrary to dominant perceptions, those people who live in houses made of natural materials, rely on public transport and use mainly unpackaged goods, should be seen as 'sustainers', not as the poor. Meanwhile, most Western peoples, commonly regarded as the rich of the world, are categorised as 'overconsumers'. This concept can be used to critique the idea that development equates with increasing consumption. In fact, increasing consumption is a significant development problem because of consequent exploitation of the earth's scarce resources. While many Pacific Islanders could still be seen as 'sustainers', there is a deep desire in Pacific Island communities to own Western goods. This offers a challenge to those wishing to promote sustainable development in the region in the future.

Perhaps the most fascinating representation of the lure of Western goods is the Melanesian 'cargo cult' which, in the past, led communities to discontinue their normal village work in order to build airstrips or wharves in preparation for the 'cargo' which they thought would be delivered to them at no cost (Trompf 1990, Worsley 1968). While cargo cults were in their prime after the Second World War, when unprecedented numbers of trucks, jeeps, military equipment and men carrying packs full of interesting items suddenly appeared on the islands' shores, they can still be detected today in areas such as Lihir, the site of the latest gold mine in Papua New Guinea (see Chapter 10). In isolated Lihir, which was a destination for one or two small planes a week a few years ago, within a matter of months from the start of mining operations, planes and boats laden with people and goods were arriving several times a day, a new township was constructed and work began on housing for over 1,000 workers. Supporters of the old cargo cult movements in the area turned to those who had scoffed at them in the past and said simply: 'See, we told you the cargo would come' (interviews, Masahet Island, April 1996).

Overton (1993a:50) sees the desire for Western goods and life in town as representing:

> a tendency to consumerism, individualism and materialism that are in contrast to 'traditional' values (even though these may be far from static). A related process is that of social transformation, the reorganisation of society based on new, primarily capitalist, social relations.... Accumulation and landlessness are two faces of the new Pacific society.

The suggestion here, therefore, is that a desire to emulate Western consumption patterns could lead to greater competition, rather than sharing, between peoples and a consequent rise in social inequality. Invariably, while some individuals and groups have found the means to accumulate money and goods, others, because of their gender, class, ethnicity, lack of education or other attributes, have been partially or wholly excluded from this process. Money does not necessarily provide the answer to improved quality of life in the Pacific.

The manipulation of tradition

Feinberg (1995:92) argues that, throughout the Pacific, 'Culture ... is self-consciously manipulated to promote a wide variety of personal and group agendas'. This phenomenon has spurred much academic interest in 'the politics of culture' (Linnekin 1990, Keesing 1989), or the '*invention* or *reinvention* of tradition' whereby 'contemporary identities ... [are] constructed by selective manipulation of cultural elements proclaimed as "tradition"' (Norton 1993:741,755). In this way, political customs can be used to oppress some sectors of society, while humanitarian customs can be used to exploit others (Helu 1997:3).

Some Pacific Island women, for example, have become frustrated with 'custom' being used to dictate what women will wear and how they will behave, while men are presumed to be able to dress and act as they choose. The following excerpt from a poem by Grace Mera Molisa of Vanuatu stresses this point:

> CUSTOM
>
> 'Custom'
> misapplied
> bastardised
> murdered
> a frankenstein
> corpse
> conveniently
> recalled
> to intimidate
> women ...
>
> (Molisa 1983:24)

Fiji provides a clear example of the manipulation of culture by indigenous Fijian elites. In Fiji, the two main ethnic groups are the indigenous Fijians and Indo-Fijians, the latter mostly descending from labourers who came to Fiji in the late 1800s and early 1900s. The labourers came to work on plantations and were either indentured labourers or free immigrants. The former received abysmal wages: in 1887 the average daily wage for a male indentured labourer was 7.28 pence, and for a female, 4.43 pence. The indentured labourers were housed in barracks like prisoners. High levels of suicide were evident amongst this group (Naidu 1992:157).

Despite several generations of Indo-Fijians being born and bred in Fiji, the governments of Fiji have chosen since 1987 to discriminate against them and privilege indigenous Fijians, supposedly on the basis of culture or tradition. Two coups occurred in 1987 after a general election which saw a win by a coalition of parties, dominated by Indo-Fijians but led by an indigenous Fijian. The coups were supported by

> an oligarchy of Ethnic Fijian chiefs, bureaucrats, and big business ... [which] had become the gatekeepers to Fiji's economic and political resources. They used the rhetoric of racial solidarity to defend 'Fijian traditions and institutions' which maintained them at the apex of Fiji society (Naidu 1992:199).

In Fiji 'tradition' is clearly being used to rationalise the undermining of the rights of Indo-Fijians (White and Lindstrom 1993:32). Fortunately, the situation has recently improved with agreement in 1997 to revise the discriminatory 1990 Constitution and allow for more, but not complete, political equality. Nonetheless, ethnic nationalism, 'tradition' and 'custom' will continue to play a major role in Fijian politics.

The Potential for Socially Sustainable Development in the Pacific Islands

Many of the problems and inequalities discussed above are partly the result of the application of Western models of development which prioritise economic growth and export-led production. These models were often first imposed during colonial times and have since been embraced, largely uncritically, by the planners and policy makers of many newly independent governments of the Pacific. Under such a narrow development ethos, it is not surprising that cultural and social considerations are accorded little priority, and that heed is rarely paid to the contribution which indigenous systems of knowledge can make, and have made, to development solutions in the region.

Despite the social constraints on sustainable development noted above, there is potential for sustainable development strategies to be pursued in the Pacific. Such optimism derives from an appreciation of the value of indigenous skills and knowledge, and an understanding of the effectiveness of Pacific Island peoples in adapting to change over time. Skills of adaptation to a range of new environments have been evident from the early years of settlement:

> The basic cultural requirements for the successful colonization of the Pacific Islands include the appropriate boat-building, sailing, and navigation skills to get to the islands in the first place; domesticated plants and gardening skills suited to often marginal conditions; and a varied inventory of fishing implements and techniques (Bodley 1997:155-56).

Incorporation into the global political and economic system does not necessarily lead to a complete displacement of traditional norms, values and methods of organisation (Macpherson 1992a:440); rather, there is evidence that Pacific Islanders have selectively incorporated aspects of change into their social organisation:

> By managing to carve out livelihoods and still create a satisfying way of life for themselves, many Pacific Islanders are effectively resolving the tension that has been evident in Western rhetoric over the last fifty years between the social and economic gains and losses of development (James 1993b:148).

BOX 4.1 • AN ETHIC FOR SUSTAINABLE DEVELOPMENT IN THE PACIFIC ISLANDS

Clarke (1990) suggests that three tenets of traditional wisdom that exist throughout the Pacific can be identified – integration, limits and beauty. These, he says, could provide an ethic for sustainable development in the region.

Integration refers to the fact that Pacific Islanders traditionally lived in systems in which physical, social and cultural systems are integrated. Thus the many components of the landscape were utilised in a careful manner based on the realisation that exploitation of one component could jeopardise the basic livelihood system a community relied upon. This sense of integration is also expressed through cultural concepts such as *vanua* (see Chapter 8).

Related to integration is the concept of *limits.* This may best be explained with relation to Dasmann's (1988) idea of ecosystem versus biosphere peoples. While biosphere peoples draw on ecosystems from all over the globe for their survival (for example, coffee from Brazil, wheat from Canada, butter from New Zealand) and are not particularly concerned with the condition of any given local ecosystem, ecosystem peoples need to be attuned to environmental conservation as they rely on careful use of local ecosystems for their well-being. If they persistently violate ecological rules, for example, by overfishing or by failing to maintain soil fertility, they will die. Pacific Island peoples, especially those living on small islands which had few opportunities for trade and exchange with outsiders, can be seen as ecosystem peoples who had to place limits on their exploitation of the natural environment: 'The famed characteristic of Pacific voyagers moving on to new lands rested in part on this recognition of limits in the original home island' (Clarke 1990: 247).

Lastly, the concept of *beauty,* according to Clarke (1990:248), relates to the way in which Pacific Island communities feel that they are part of nature, and that 'Nature needs attention, grooming, and care, as we ourselves do'. Thus plants are placed near to a village in such a way that they may be appreciated by those who pass by: they are not merely arranged for their utilitarian value:

> Anyone who has walked about in a traditional landscape with one of its older inhabitants knows the enjoyment felt at the arrangement of productive diversity all around. Medicine here, perfume there, fiber in the hibiscus stem, fruit, timber, edible leaves, and so forth. There is a strong aesthetic pleasure in these observations of utilitarian diversity (Clarke 1990:248).

Recently, there has been a rejuvenation of pride in tradition and a recognition of the value of traditional knowledge (see Box 4.1). No longer can all specialists called into the region be criticised for adopting attitudes of 'infallibility and cultural superiority', or for regarding traditional wisdom as 'inferior to imported knowledge' (Winslow 1991:504). From official reports by regional agencies to articles by academics, there is agreement that to work towards environmentally and socially sustainable societies in the Pacific, we must draw on traditional knowledge in addition to modern ideas (Clarke 1990:234, Winslow 1991:501).

Howe (1997) is concerned, however, that this interest in Pacific Islanders may romanticise indigenous traditions and cultures based, as it is, on post-colonial discourse which privileges the ideas and knowledge of the 'other'. It would be naïve to suggest that interaction with Western societies and technologies has offered no benefits to Pacific Islanders (as Macpherson 1992a:441 notes, the only people who mourn the passing of the thatched hut are those who have never thatched and re-thatched one), just as it would be naïve to suggest that all island societies were inherently democratic, communal and self-sufficient. Keesing (1989:29) is also quick to dismiss romantic notions about Pacific Island peoples being inherently at one with nature and each other: 'The imagined ancestors with whom the Pacific is being repopulated – Wise Ecologists, Mystical Sages, living in harmony with one another, cosmic forces, and the environment – are in many ways creations of Western imagination.' Perhaps the key issue here is to find a balance which does not, by default, allow Western institutions and values to dominate, and which recognises the potential for indigenous knowledge and practice to contribute to sustainable development solutions. It is not necessary for one culture to be subsumed under another, as recognised by Dr Karl Schmidt, who provided the following prescription for the mental health of people in the Pacific:

> Live your own culture
> Enrich it where possible
> Incorporate the best from other technologies without identifying with the cultures
> from which they stem.
> (cited in Crocombe 1989:62).

When paying heed to traditional knowledge, women's knowledge should not continue to be neglected. Where communities still rely on the natural resource base for their livelihoods, women commonly have a detailed understanding of the natural environment and are custodians of traditional knowledge. In Papua New Guinea, for example, women's specialist knowledge may include: how, where and when to grow starch crops; where to find wild foods which supplement the local diet by providing vital vitamins; and what plants are associated with fertility and childbirth.[1]

It is the strength of some traditional social systems and the knowledge and skills of the people that contribute to the adaptability and endurance of Pacific Islanders in the face of change. For example, despite the promises of aid and trade often failing Solomon Islanders in rural areas, communities continue on their path because they can revert to traditional activities and knowledge:

> There still is, for most Solomon Islanders, a fall-back position. If there is fuel for the outboard motor, you use it; if there is none, you paddle. If you can buy rice and tinned tuna and bread, you buy it; if you cannot, you eat your sweet potatoes and bush cabbage and coconut (Keesing 1993:52).

This testifies to the basic resilience and self-reliance of Pacific Island peoples, a different picture from that painted by those who suggest that Pacific countries are mostly dependent and inept at meeting their own needs: 'Ordinary Pacific people depend for their daily existence much, much more on themselves and their kin, wherever they may be, than on anyone's largesse' (Hau'ofa 1994:157).

Conclusion

Pacific Island cultures and societies are characterised by both great diversity and some strong threads of similarity. There were marked forms of inequality, injustice and conflict prior to European contact but these were rapidly transformed. Some unjust or unequal customs and relationships died, others flourished, and new forms appeared. Undoubtedly, the pace of social and cultural transformation has quickened as capitalist relationships have pervaded almost all forms of life and Western culture has become deeply embedded in the aspirations and daily lives of many. There have been negative and positive consequences. Some groups – women, youth, ethnic minorities – have become marginalised socially, or become more so, some inequalities have widened and poverty has become more common as customary support systems have broken down. Other groups have done well, cementing or promoting their position in the upper ranks of

1 Thirty-three such species have been recorded by scientists in Papua New Guinea (Mogina 1996) and doubtless there are numerous others which remain undocumented.

the social and economic hierarchy.

The dominant models of development employed in the Pacific Islands, almost exclusively borrowed from the West, have largely ignored these social dimensions of change, however, focusing instead on economic strategies for increasing production and national wealth. Social exclusion, poverty and injustice have become significant barriers to the attainment of socially sustainable development, for regardless of the benefits that many, or even most, might receive from development, the existence of significant groups who do not benefit, and whose position is made worse, creates a long-term challenge to any society. Thus, sustainable development cannot be achieved without addressing these issues of exclusion, marginalisation and inequality.

Participation, justice, equity and empowerment are the ways forward if Pacific societies are to work towards more sustainable futures. Rather than simply seeing participation as a means to improve project or programme results, participation should be seen as an end itself (Brohman 1995), which aims for marginalised groups to have the opportunity to participate effectively in society's political, economic and social structures, and to share in the benefits which should flow from this participation. All individuals should be empowered to feel that they have a valuable contribution to make to development, whether this means growing taro for their family's consumption, learning the craft of traditional canoe manufacture, caring for children and the aged, working at a rural health clinic, running a small store or being employed as a government official. If the predominant development discourse in the region proclaimed that Pacific Island peoples are important, they have valuable skills and traditional knowledge which can contribute to sustainable futures, they will be in a better position to draw on what is useful from the past and incorporate it with what is of value from the present, rather than being tempted to sideline their own belief systems for the sake of adopting the 'modern'.

CHAPTER 5

Pacific Islands Livelihoods

NICK PURDIE

As the work in this volume suggests, the quest for sustainable development in the Pacific Islands is a formidable task. In many respects this is a reflection of the nature of sustainable development itself, but is also indicative of the specific island contexts in which this goal is set. Small island states dispersed across a vast expanse of ocean, with limited land resources and limited means to exploit oceanic resources, present a wholly different set of constraints on development in the conventional sense. The suggestion, indeed necessity, that this development should also be sustainable in the long term works only to magnify these constraints. The general theme here is that due to these specific island contexts sustainable development in the Pacific Islands presents something of a 'special case', requiring an alternative approach to that employed in larger, more resource-rich countries.

While in general this may be the case, the commonly accepted constraints on development are also, in part, a product of how the Pacific Islands are perceived as a geographic region. The perception of the Pacific Islands as 'islands in a far sea' (Hau'ofa 1994:152) has important implications for how we perceive these problems and constraints, and the way we subsequently develop strategies to overcome them. There is, it would seem, a tendency to employ development blueprints constructed in and for contexts differing markedly from those in the Pacific Islands. Consequently, this chapter follows Hau'ofa's line of argument in which he suggests that by thinking of 'islands in a far sea' we necessarily invoke the problems of size and geographic isolation. Alternatively, if we conceptualise the Pacific Islands as 'a sea of islands' we come closer to the approximation of the oceanic environment which Pacific peoples have had themselves, in which the potential for livelihood, and the geographic realm in which livelihoods are sought, does not stop at the mean high-tide mark (Hau'ofa 1994:153).

The reconceptualisation which Hau'ofa suggests is at once a reassertion of the realities of people who are 'at home with the sea', but also contrary to that reality presented by the global economy: small scale and great distance equals less opportunity and higher costs. In this sense it is possible to discern two competing viewpoints with respect to the potentials and constraints of development in the Pacific Islands. One viewpoint sees the Pacific Islands as small and remote – an outsiders' viewpoint – and this immediately conjures barriers to trade and economic development. Although these barriers exist, there is still potential for involvement in, or expansion of, these economies, but often in a very exploitative sense, as is the case with logging in Melanesia, or the tuna industry throughout the Pacific. In this view, although these barriers to development exist, they must be surmounted as this is the only realistic avenue for development, and this often means foreign involvement in the exploitation of the resource base. The opposing viewpoint sees islands which are home, surrounded by ocean but not isolated – an insiders' viewpoint which frames the problems of development not in terms of the global, but of the local. This viewpoint sees development constraints as the problems which people confront on a day-to-day basis: the need for food, water and shelter; the need to provide education to children; and the need to interact with people as a fundamental need for social enjoyment and survival.

The supposition I wish to develop here is that a more sustainable development in the Pacific Islands, as indeed in most places, is one which embraces this insider viewpoint. Development must necessarily include more than simply economic precepts, and this involves the inclusion of individuals and groups as they live their daily lives, using and managing resources through social, economic, political and ecological institutions and networks. Although the management of a national economy is an important factor in this, it is indeed only one small part. In other words, it is argued here that the goal of sustainable development demands that we conceptualise development in the Pacific Islands in terms of the realities of people as they construct their daily livelihood. This alternative approach to development concentrates on securing viable and sustainable livelihoods for people as a means to tackle poverty and approach environmental sustainability. The reality for many people in the Pacific Islands is one of a continuing struggle to maintain a subsistence or semi-subsistence livelihood in a context of increasing population, urbanisation and growing material aspirations. Therefore, the essential characteristic of development in the Pacific Islands must be the continuing support and promotion of sustainable livelihoods as a fundamental basis for further economic growth and environmental sustainability.

Concepts of Livelihoods

The suggestion that all people, individuals and groups, should have a right to a secure and viable livelihood and that 'development' should actively promote and support this is not, of course, a new idea. In fact most development approaches, and particularly those in the post-Second World War era, have held this as their fundamental aim. The reality is that, even though there have been gains in macro-indicators such as GDP *per capita*, life expectancy and literacy, a great many people do not have access to sufficient resources with which to construct a secure and adequate livelihood. This is not simply an unfortunate consequence of development, with the implication that a certain section of society will always be marginalised by the development process, but is a breach of human rights and is contrary to the ethical and moral grounds upon which development is based. For, as Friedmann (1992:9) suggests:

> if social and economic development is to mean anything at all, it must mean a clear improvement in the conditions of life and livelihood for ordinary people. There is no intrinsic reason, moral or otherwise, why large numbers of people should be systematically excluded from development in this sense or, even worse, should become the unwitting victims of other people's progress.

In 1987 the Advisory Committee on Food Security to the World Commission on Environment and Development (Food 2000, 1987) suggested that the situation of increasing populations in developing countries, the vast numbers who live in poverty, and the processes of economic marginalisation which occur between rural and urban areas and between countries, means a future of increasing poverty and the further degradation of both livelihood and environment. The connection between poverty and environmental degradation is commonly, although not universally, accepted. People are often caught in a downward spiral of poverty and the need to degrade resources in order to survive, which in turn reinforces the poverty effects of a degraded environment. Conventional approaches to development, which focus on macroeconomic 'fundamentals' such as trade liberalisation, industrial and infrastructural development, market liberalisation, currency exchange rates and the overarching aim of economic growth, neglect the reality of a great many people. This is not to say that the management of a country's economy *vis-à-vis* the global economy – and particularly the impact of the global economic system at the national and local levels – is not important, but in many instances this approach does not account for the myriad ways in which people actually manage to survive, or indeed fail to survive. In other words, macroeconomic development strategies fail precisely because they ignore the realities of the majority of people whom they are supposed to assist.

In searching for an answer to this problem the Food 2000 report suggested that 'a new analysis' was needed which actively sought to support people, as front-line users and managers of resources, at the grassroots level (Food 2000 1987:3). There was a need to advance policies and action with this goal in mind, rather than simply promoting abstract notions of economic growth. These ideas form part of a general trend in development studies and practice towards more empowering and participatory approaches. The concept of a secure and sustainable livelihood gained further credence at the United Nations Conference on Environment and Development where it was suggested that one of the key goals for poverty reduction and environmental security was the achievement of sustainable livelihoods for all (Sitarz 1994). Subsequently, organisations who are involved in development work in the Pacific, such as the New Zealand Official Development Assistance Bureau (NZODA) and the United Nations Development Programme (UNDP) in Suva, have written livelihood principles into their programme documents (Ministry of Foreign Affairs and Trade 1995, UNDP, 1997:1).

Chambers and Conway (1992:7–8) provide a useful introduction to the concept of a livelihood as the means by which a people make a living:

> A livelihood comprises the capabilities, assets (stores and resources, claims and access) and activities required for a means of living: a livelihood is sustainable which can cope with stress and shocks, maintain or enhance its capabilities and assets, and provide livelihood opportunities for the next generation; and which contributes net benefits to other livelihoods at the local and global levels and in the short and long term.

This definition forms the basis for a livelihoods approach to sustainable development. The ability to derive a livelihood involves claims to particular resources, such as land, trees and water; the ability to access these in practice, which necessarily involves issues of local, national and international politics; the ability to store specific resources or forms of wealth as a hedge against risk (an aspect of the sufficiency of livelihoods); and the ability of individuals to apply their capabilities to carry out necessary activities required to derive a livelihood. Also central to this conceptualisation is the interplay between these factors in the process of livelihood construction. These principles are presented within an encompassing framework of sustainability, such that the activities of a livelihood should not impinge upon the efficacy of other livelihood strategies in other places or times.

A livelihood, then, is a complex of social, economic, political and environmental relationships which occur through space and time, the nature and process of which are governed by socio-political and cultural mechanisms. Although it may be necessary, in the interests of formulating policy, programmes and action, to define the exact nature of these relationships, their dynamic nature is of fundamental importance. Relationships and institutions which determine the nature, efficacy and longevity of livelihood strategies are neither static nor universal. They may be evident in one set of circumstances or in a particular place, and not in others. Additionally, they may only become evident in specific times such as those of crisis. In this respect a fundamental characteristic of livelihood strategies, and, therefore, of successful approaches to sustainable livelihoods, is their inherent flexibility and dynamism.

Although much work under the broad heading of livelihoods has been concerned with rural people (see, for example, Friedmann and Rangan 1993, Conroy and Litvinoff 1988), this definition applies equally to those residing in urban areas. The concern with environmental sustainability, destabilising processes such as rural–urban migration, and rural poverty has resulted in work focusing on rural resource managers. As we shall see, however, and this is increasingly the case in the Pacific Islands, there is also a need to focus on sustainable livelihoods in urban areas. Many poor people in cities do not, through necessity, restrict themselves to a single form of employment, and as Dey and Westerndorff (1996) indicate, the reality of life on the streets is often one of destitution, begging, chronic health problems and social, political, economic and environmental marginalisation.

Lawrence (1997) further suggests that the unitary concept of a 'job' is itself under threat in most societies.[1] Indeed, the suggestion that it has ever been relevant to poor people in developing countries is debatable.

1 Recent work in this area suggests a current trend towards 'flexible accumulation' (see Harvey 1990) in global capitalism, in which capital constantly restructures (including spatial flexibility) to maintain competitiveness. In this respect the notion of a 'job for life' is being replaced by the need for labour to constantly 'restructure' to remain employable, or alternatively to be employed on short term contracts. There seems little reason to assume that this is not the case in the formal sectors in the Pacific Islands. It would seem, in fact, that it is essential for individuals in most places to maintain as many options as possible for employment (in the widest sense of the word) as a means for livelihood.

In this respect simple 'job creation' strategies only go part way in securing livelihoods, and are based on assumptions that, first, a livelihood is synonymous with employment and second, that people are able to move easily into a particular industry without having a history in that industry, that is they have *capabilities* which are applicable. An interesting illustration of this in the Pacific is presented by Schoeffel (1994:35) who relates her experience of evaluating a fishing project that had failed. The conclusion she reached was that it failed largely because the people involved, although coastal dwellers, had no history of deep water fishing, having previously been reef fishers and farmers. In this respect it is naïve to think that because people live by the sea, they are necessarily able to exploit that resource in a global economic sense.

As Chambers (1997) indicates, the ways in which people construct a livelihood are complex and diverse, a situation which reflects the need to offset risk and potential contingencies. Commonly, a livelihood is a series of activities designed simply to produce income, either as goods or money, with which to sustain a livelihood. An individual's time often revolves around these activities but is not necessarily solely concerned with them. Activities which appear to be leisurely are often intimately related to the necessary social aspects of a livelihood which involves the maintenance of networks used for support in times of stress. Although an individual may not consciously regard these activities as necessary, their absence and the resulting social exclusion has a marked impact on the nature and success of livelihood strategies. Hence livelihoods have a very definite and fundamental social and cultural dimension.

A livelihood, then, is a lifelong process in which individuals position themselves as best they can with the resources they have at their disposal. The ability of individuals to do so, and the result of their efforts, is again dependent upon the social, economic, political and ecological contexts in which they find themselves. More important, though, is the interplay of these factors, and the extent to which the individual is able to exploit the opportunities they present. Consequently, a livelihood has a history, present and future which are intimately linked and which the individual determines through interaction with a socio-political and environmental milieu. Individuals work to construct their present and future livelihoods, but their ability to do so is largely dependent on their histories. Ultimately that livelihood is unique and differs from those around it.

Pacific Livelihoods

The Oceanic environment presents a unique set of constraints and

TABLE 5.1 • OCCUPATIONAL CLASSES IN SELECTED PACIFIC ISLAND COUNTRIES (%)

	Professional & technical	Administration & management	Clerical & related workers	Sales workers	Agriculture, forestry & fisheries	Production & transport	Not classified or unemployed
Cook Is.	15	4	14	6	15	28	7
Fiji	7	1	6	6	44	21	9
Kiribati	7	1	5	3	73	8	1
Marshall Is.	15	2	8	4	19	28	12
FSM	16	2	3	3	22	12	36
Palau	13	10	10	6	12	25	7
Samoa	13	1	5	4	63	9	1
Solomon Is.	4	0	2	1	83	8	0
Tonga	11	1	9	4	42	18	10
Tuvalu	13	4	10	5	40	19	3
Vanuatu	6	2	2	2	68	8	10

Source: UNDP 1997

opportunities for the people who inhabit it. Within this region there is a great diversity of physical, cultural and economic contexts. The following section presents some broad statistical evidence of the general nature of Pacific Island livelihoods. Although these suggest some common features and trends in the Pacific Islands, the entire livelihoods approach is framed upon the importance of difference and specific local level reality.

The larger Melanesian states exhibit greater land area and a larger endowment of natural resources and arable land which, as Ward (1993:2) suggests, presents a series of 'problems of a quite different order and kind to those of the smaller states'. At the opposite end of the spectrum countries such as Kiribati and Tuvalu are representative of a number of small atolls with high population densities and limited exploitable resources. Common throughout the Pacific, however, is the high proportion of people who continue to construct their livelihood by way of subsistence or semi-subsistence agricultural and fishing activities (Table 5.1). This, coupled with almost universally high population growth rates, suggests an increasing demand for, and pressure upon, the natural resource base, particularly arable land.

Although many countries in the Pacific are currently experiencing high levels of rural-urban migration and urban population growth (see Chapter 12), this does not necessarily relate to a decrease in pressure on rural land used for subsistence farming, given the need to provision urban populations through commercial agriculture.

Much of the increase in these urban populations, at least in its more visible manifestations, is accounted for by the increasing number of squatter settlements around urban areas (UNDP 1996:6). This process places increasing pressure not only on urban services, but also on available resources, particularly land, from which people can derive a livelihood. In broad terms, then, the context of livelihoods in the Pacific is one of transition from a predominantly subsistence base to an increasingly urbanised population. The process of urbanisation, in the broader context of high population growth, results in an increasing demand for formal employment which in turn stimulates a perceived need for economic policy focusing on this sector. As is the case in many countries, however, the formal job market is unable to meet demand, and the excess demand is often met by the informal sector (Table 5.2). As Allen (1996:36) indicates:

> The Papua New Guinea economy will be unable to provide wage employment for other than a very small proportion of this expanding population. In 1990 approximately 9.3 per cent of the population of Papua New Guinea aged between 15 and 64 were in wage

TABLE 5.2 • LABOUR FORCE IN SELECTED PACIFIC ISLAND COUNTRIES

	Potential labour force	Economically active	Formal employment	% of econ active	Informal employment	% of econ active
Vanuatu (1989)	79,638	65,400	17,000	26	48,400	74
Solomon Islands (1986)	150,300	136,200	24,000	18	105,700	82
Samoa (1991)	93,600	47,900	18,900	40	29,000	60
Fiji (1986)	446,200	241,200	89,000	37	152,200	63
Kiribati (1990)	57,900	32,600	11,200	34	21,400	66
Tonga (1986)	67,300	25,600	11,600	44	14,000	56

Source: UNDP 1997

employment. Although a mining boom will provide for a 3 to 4 per cent growth in wage employment (mainly in construction and utilities), it is estimated that labour force growth will exceed wage employment growth by 40,000 persons per year for the foreseeable future.

There is little evidence that the situation in other Pacific Island countries is any different other than in terms of scale. Although governments and aid agencies may wish to boost formal sector employment, the indication is that any success in this sector will still be insufficient to meet demand.

Table 5.3 indicates considerable variation between island countries with regard to their employment structures. A number of countries in the Pacific, and particularly the Cook Islands, Palau and the FSM, show an even spread across occupational classes, and Nauru exhibits no agriculture whatsoever. The figures for these countries are suggestive of fairly diversified, if small economies. The high concentration in the services sector is indicative, however, of the dominance of the government sector in these countries, a situation which is often the

TABLE 5.3 • AGRICULTURAL AND NON-AGRICULTURAL EMPLOYMENT IN THE PACIFIC ISLANDS (%)

	Year of data	Agricultural sector			Non-agricultural sector				
		1	2	Total	3	4	5	6	Total
Nauru	1983	0	0	0	69	0	4	6	100
American Samoa	1990	2	0	2	0	24	11	46	98
F.S.M	1980	2	0	2	0	1	11	60	98
Guam	1990	1	1	2	0	4	22	30	98
Northern Mariana	1990	–	2	2	0	22	13	26	98
French Polynesia	1988	–	–	10	0	7	14	29	90
Palau	1990	–	11	11	0	2	11	24	89
New Caledonia	1989	–	–	12	3	7	14	33	88
Niue	1986	–	13	13	0	3	8	34	87
Cook Is.	1986	8	10	18	0	7	17	31	82
Marshall Is.	1988	21	0	21	0	9	14	30	79
Kiribati	1990	23	0	23	0	6	12	41	77
Tokelau	1986	38	0	38	0	11	3	21	62
Fiji	1986	–	–	44	1	8	11	15	56
Tonga	1986	36	13	49	0	3	7	24	51
Western Samoa	1986	59	5	64	0	3	3	20	36
Tuvalu	1991	66	2	68	0	1	4	21	32
Vanuatu	1989	46	31	77	0	1	4	12	22
Papua N. Guinea	1980	76	6	82	0	1	1	4	18
Solomon Is.	1986	76	10	82	3	2	2	7	18
Wallis & Futuna	1990	73	9	82	0	2	2	4	18

1 Traditional agriculture
2 Commercial agriculture
3 Mining
4 Manufacturing
5 Commerce
6 Services

Source: Pirie 1994:52

result of a high level of foreign aid receipts. A number of the bigger countries, such as Solomon Islands and Vanuatu, show the continued dominance of the agricultural sector. This variation between island countries is further illustrated in Table 5.3.

These data indicate the continued dominance of 'traditional' agriculture in a number of countries, particularly in Melanesia where in Papua New Guinea and the Solomon Islands 82 per cent of the population are involved in this sector. The statistics are indicative, providing only a general sense of the situation in the countries presented, as differing years and collection methods in each country again make comparisons difficult. What they do provide, however, is an indication of the means by which people construct a livelihood in the Pacific Islands, and specifically the importance of land to this. Obviously subsistence agriculture and, to a lesser degree, commercial agriculture play a prominent part in many people's lives and are an important source of rural livelihoods. As has been the case with other developing countries, agriculture is the key sector with regard to possible development strategies:

> Change in the traditional societies of the South Pacific has been accelerating with growing exposure to the outside world, and it has become increasingly important to improve economic performance so as to meet the aspirations of the people.... The key economic issues are related to agricultural production and exports which continue to be the main source of livelihood for the majority of the people in the islands. (Cole and Parry 1986:1)

The suggestion that Pacific Island nations must export agricultural produce as a means of economic growth is nonetheless a contentious one. Integration into global agricultural markets presents as many problems as it solves, not the least of which are highly fluctuating prices in a general trend of decline (see Chapter 13). There is also a disregard for the lack of security that this engenders for very small producers. Economic insecurity is in no way conducive to ensuring that rural people have a secure and sustainable means of livelihood. This approach also disregards the reality of life on many Pacific islands, where high population densities and increasing urbanisation preclude much agricultural development. On Ebeye Island in the Marshall Islands, for example, there is a density of 32,000 people per square kilometre on 0.31 square kilometres of land (the population is approximately 10,000).

As Allen (1996) also suggests, the two possible means of increasing agricultural output, intensification or expansion, both have potential negative impacts on sustainability irrespective of whether or not they can be applied in Pacific Island countries. In this respect the dominant perception of development as economic growth through trade holds little relevance to the goal of decreasing poverty and increasing environmental sustainability. Knapman (1994:326) further suggests that even if the wants of Pacific populations remain static, economic growth will have to remain at something in the order of 2 per cent per annum to account for growing populations.

The continued importance of traditional practices in the Pacific does not, however, suggest that things have not changed or cannot change. There has been, over the last 150 years, a significant transformation in the political, social and economic spheres of life in the Pacific Islands (Ward and Kingdon 1995a:1). This has also been accompanied by a transformation in the physical environment and the institutions which govern it, and particularly those relating to land. Given the general dominance of agriculture, subsistence or otherwise, in Pacific livelihoods, and the concomitant importance of land to this, it is worth elaborating further on the systems of land tenure in the Pacific, and their relationship to development and sustainability.

Land Tenure

Almost without exception land is central to both society and economy throughout the Pacific Islands; this being so, land tenure systems play a fundamental role in determining livelihood strategies. The nature of land tenure systems differs from island to island, but in general complex tenure systems have developed over time to provide for the necessities of local populations with regard to their livelihood needs. These tenure systems are in a state of constant evolution, conditioned as they are by 'broader socio-political shifts' (Ward and Kingdon 1995a:6, also Crocombe 1994:1-2), but the common theme across the Pacific is the continued dominance of communal ownership systems. There has been continued pressure from both internal and external institutions to create freehold land in the Pacific, but this has often been met with resistance from owners, and where registration has been attempted the process is often slow (Crocombe 1994:2). Given the evolutionary nature of land tenure, however, the systems present today differ from those of the past and this is in part due to pressure from population, colonial government policy or the changing value of land in Pacific Island communities. The communal ownership of land, although central to Pacific Island societies, is also a contentious issue with regard to the development of that land. As agriculture is often seen as central to the development of Pacific Islands, so land and tenure systems become central to that development (Lutero 1994:19, Cole 1994:43), and lately to issues of sustainability also.

Debates concerning land tenure and development have often revolved around three broad issues: first, the ability of developers to attract investment to communal land (Crocombe 1995:19) and the hindrance which communal ownership presents; second, the issue of who benefits from the development of land; and third, what part communal ownership and use systems play in sustainable use. It has been suggested that in order to attract investment or credit, land needs to have a codified land tenure arrangement. Banks and other credit

BOX 5.1 • PAPER MAKING AND TRADITIONAL ART

Villagers from Balai on Malaita Island in the Solomon Islands set up a paper-making project with assistance from the Solomon Islands Development Trust, a local non-governmental organisation (NGO). Malaita is the most densely populated island in the Solomons group, and migration to Honiara, the capital city, has been a problem for a number of years. The project was set up to provide cash incomes for people in the village as an alternative to unemployment and homelessness in Honiara. The villagers use banana leaf, sugar cane and a variety of other tree fibres to make paper with low-tech tools. Using woodblock printing techniques the paper is then printed with traditional motifs. These are then sold to Honiara retailers for sale to tourists.

In the early stages of the project an exhibition was held at the New Zealand High Commission at which $5,000 worth of prints were sold with orders for more arriving and villagers struggling to meet demand. One print was purchased for the Museum of Contemporary Pacific Art in Noumea. The project impacts little on villagers' traditional lifestyle as they spend, on average, two days a week working making the prints, they make income from it, conserve their forests and record their traditional art and techniques.

Source: Hutching 1996

institutions are unwilling to lend money on communally owned or unregistered land, and foreign investors are unwilling to invest in the development of land when land rights are unclear. The benefits of land development which does occur are often appropriated by elites and the majority receive little benefit and are often doubly disadvantaged by resulting land degradation. Logging and mining are prime examples of this, as recent events on Bougainville in Papua New Guinea, and logging in the Solomon Islands and Vanuatu testify (see chapters 9 and 10).

Furthermore, as Crocombe suggests (1995:5), communal ownership does not necessarily correspond to sustainable use, either in the present day or in the past. There are a number of examples in the Pacific, in the past and at present, of widespread environmental destruction under communal ownership, whether as a result of logging or intensive agriculture. These examples, however, are largely the product of new

BOX 5.2 • SALE OF SEED FOR SUP SUP GARDENS

'Sup Sup' is the Pidgin word for mixed, and the sup sup garden is a common way for Solomon Islanders, particularly in Honiara, to provide for some of their daily food needs in an urban environment, and also excess which can be sold in the market.

The Honiara-based Women's Sup Sup Garden Credit Union was formed as a means to provide both seed and cash incomes for women in Honiara. Seeds are provided by the cooperative and the money from sales is lodged with the credit union and is available to members as loans for regular or emergency payments such as church and family obligations, school fees or uniforms. The cooperative is also involved in other income-generating schemes including catering for meetings and workshops, and it runs workshops on gardening techniques and child nutrition. There is evidence that the project has been beneficial to those involved, not simply in monetary terms, but in education and, as Hata puts it, 'in the healthy faces of their children'.

Source: Hata 1996

uses of land not suited to the context of communal tenure. Traditional tenure systems are not designed to deal with the sudden economic value of trees or other resources and there is a tendency for local landowners, or a small elite among them, to act in shortsighted ways.

These points do not mean, however, that land tenure systems need to be changed towards private ownership. There is, in fact, an argument for increasing and enhancing the security of traditional rights as a means to secure the benefits of land rights to livelihoods, which involves ensuring that all people with rights to use a particular piece of land are involved in the use decisions concerning it, and that the benefits from any development accrue to them. There is, of course, no assurance that this will result in sustainable land use practices, and land degradation may occur. In practice, however, this type of occurrence is rare and is more often a reflection of a select and powerful few, commonly men, making decisions in which the majority lose out. What is required in these cases is the promotion of visibly beneficial alternatives to destructive land use practices. Two cases from the Solomon Islands are instructive in this sense and have applicability, and indeed are occurring, throughout the Pacific (boxes 5.1 and 5.2).

Conclusion

Development is not simply an economic process but involves some form of intervention in the social, economic, political and environmental spheres of daily life, whether we intend it to or not. Consequently, sustainable development is not simply about ensuring that the ecological integrity of the resource base is maintained while an overall economic growth agenda is pursued. In many respects the qualifier 'sustainable', when added to 'development', demands that we re-interpret what we mean by development in the first place, in terms of both where we are and where we want to go. This chapter has suggested that the ongoing and dynamic support of people as they attempt to construct their livelihoods is of fundamental importance to any approach to development. The primary function of outside institutions, including the state, should be to ensure that these livelihood strategies are sufficient and sustainable. In this sense development which does not immediately focus on the well-being of the majority of people neglects the realities which they face on a daily basis.

There is no doubt that people in the Pacific Islands aspire to goods and services which must be imported, and this requires some form of economic development. But at the same time an approach which concentrates on this alone is destined to exclude a large section of the population, simply because their primary concern is to feed and house their families. The examples presented here suggest that a livelihood is a broad-based strategy for survival which involves the interaction of people with, and within, their immediate sociocultural and environmental contexts. This chapter has not dealt explicitly with migration and remittances, which play an important role both in people's geography and aspirations, and in the efficacy of local-level livelihood strategies. But for people living in a 'sea of islands', where a multitude of possibilities exists, these are merely a part of a broader whole. Migration may expand this realm of possibilities for some but not for others. In this sense our concern is with those people who live in the Pacific Islands, and survive through a multitude of tasks, networks and associations. In terms of development, the task becomes one not of expanding horizons through trade and economic expansion, but of increasing the density of the synergy which exists in these localities.

A livelihoods approach to development and sustainability in the Pacific Islands, then, means working at the local level to promote effective grassroots responses to an ever-changing world. It means promoting, for example, small-scale money-generating schemes, the potential for farmer-oriented agricultural improvement and diversification, and investigating, with local people, issues of environmental sustainability as they apply at the local level. Fundamentally, however, it means maintaining the ability of people to interact dynamically with the local environment in which they find themselves: on the inside looking out.

CHAPTER 6

Land Tenure and Atoll Society in Kiribati: The Case of Kuma Village

PETER S. KING

Land tenure has been widely recognised as one of the most important components of life and livelihoods in the Pacific Islands (Lundsgaarde 1974, Acquaye and Crocombe 1984, Crocombe 1987a, Crocombe and Meleisea 1994, Ward and Kingdon 1995a). It binds people to the land, to their history and to their society. Throughout most of the region, forms of 'traditional' tenure survive, though usually in much modified forms. As Pacific Island people cope with changing economic, social and cultural conditions, they have modified their land tenure systems or made changes in their residence, land use and social relations. Three critical issues have been observed in relation to these changes and their land tenure: new forms of inequality in landholding have emerged mainly as a result of differential population growth rates and commercialisation of agriculture; populations have moved in response to such inequalities in land endowments as well as changing economic opportunities; and customary forms of land tenure have adapted and accommodated new forms of commercial land uses.

Customary land tenure throughout the Pacific is characterised by strong relationships between kinship and land rights. Underlying this broad similarity, however, are considerable variations in the ways in which kinship, social status and land rights are articulated. These variations are based upon cultural, social, historical, political and physical differences throughout the region. In order to consider the connections between land tenure and sustainability, therefore, it is necessary to deal with individual systems of tenure in context. In keeping with that prescription, this case study focuses on land tenure and distribution in one Pacific Island village: Kuma village on Butaritari atoll in Kiribati. The case study discusses the contemporary pattern of land tenure and distribution with reference to the historical and social matrix within which it has developed.

Butaritari Atoll

Butaritari fits the coral atoll archetype of strips of land and fringing reef surrounding a lagoon. The atoll's position at the north of the Gilberts archipelago gives it a higher average rainfall, and hence soil fertility, than is experienced elsewhere in the group.[1] Like all atolls, Butaritari is low-lying, with its highest ground no more than four metres above the high-tide sea level. Thirteen islands and associated islets comprise the atoll's land area of 1,366.8 hectares (Statistics Office 1993:189). Of these, three are permanently inhabited: Bikati (pronounced 'bikas') to the north-west has an area of 55.97 hectares; the island running from Ukiangang village to Tanimainiku village has an area of 864.12 hectares; and the island running from Keuea village to Kuma village has an area of 376.30 hectares.

The island on which Kuma village is located is about nine kilometres long, with a maximum width of about 650 metres, a minimum width of about 100 metres and an average width of about 200 metres. In a practice common on Pacific atolls, the land area is divided among its residents in plots running across the width of the island from lagoon shore to ocean shore. This arrangement ensures that each plot incorporates all ecological zones, ranging from the exposed and relatively infertile ocean coast, through the central region where the water table is thickest and swamp taro (*babai*) most readily cultivated, to the sheltered lagoon-shore area favoured for residence and the cultivation of breadfruit. In the precolonial period, landholders' rights extended to the areas of lagoon and ocean reef projecting from each plot, but this is no longer the case.

Since the development of the copra trade in the nineteenth century, the planting of coconut palms has been widespread and palms now cover the atoll's dry land surface from the ocean coast to the lagoon coast. In village areas by the lagoon, the palms are interspersed with houses, breadfruit trees and banana trees. The central strip between village and ocean is a mass of pits dug to the water table, where *babai* is cultivated. Between the central strip and the ocean coast, on all parts of the atoll, coconut palms are interspersed with pandanus trees and hardy scrub able to tolerate the salt-filled air blown from the ocean.

[1] The mean annual rainfall on Butaritari and Makin is about 3,000 mm, whereas the southern islands, closer to the equator, are in a zone of much lower rainfall, with an annual mean in the vicinity of 1,500 mm (Burgess 1987).

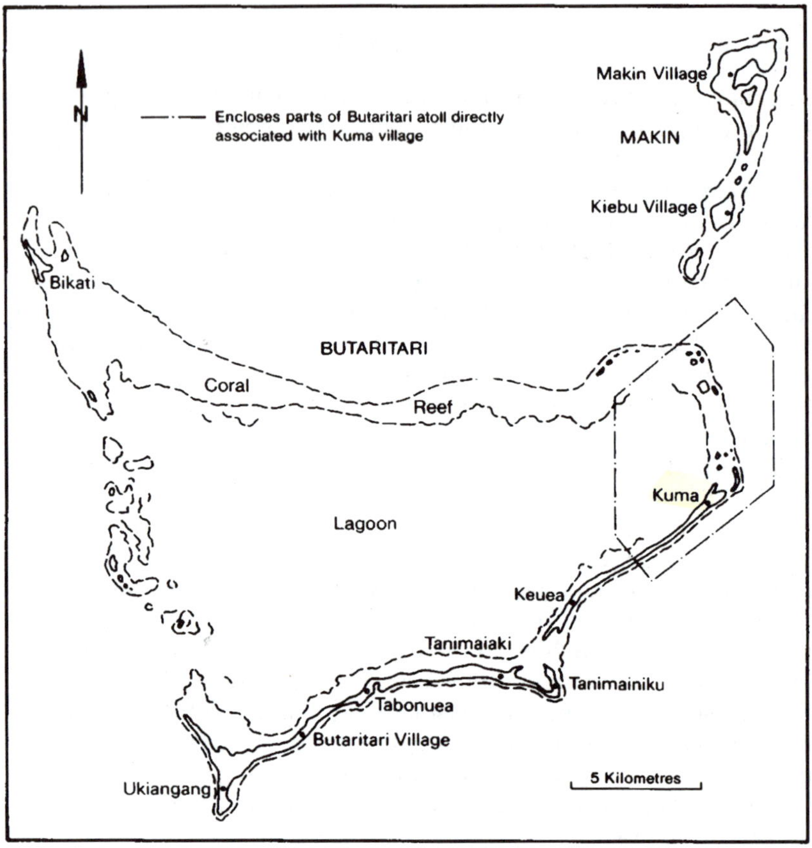

FIGURE 6.1 • BUTARITARI AND MAKIN ATOLLS

The Historical Context

Butaritari and the neighbouring coral island of Makin (see Figure 6.1) share a common history and culture which distinguishes them significantly from the other islands of Kiribati in terms of political institutions, land tenure, cultural practices and dialect.[2] These differences can be attributed, at least in part, to the geographical location of the two islands in the north of the group, where they were isolated from political changes introduced to the rest of the Gilbert Islands during a

[2] For discussions of land tenure in other parts of Kiribati see Hockings (1989), Lawrence (1983) and Lundsgaarde (1974).

series of invasions from Beru island during the seventeenth century (Maude 1963:14). The rule of single high chiefs was gradually replaced by village and island councils of old men, and land rights came to be controlled by ambilineal descent groups rather than high chiefs. On Butaritari and Makin, the High Chief retained political control and held supreme rights to all land on the islands, having the power to grant or remove land rights.

Under the precolonial system, land rights, apart from the absolute rights held by the High Chief, could be categorised as being either provisional or residual. The provisional holders of a particular land plot were those members of the non-exclusive ambilineal landholding descent group who lived on, or close to, the plot and were engaged in its cultivation. The residual holders were the members of the same landholding descent group who lived elsewhere, on other plots associated with the descent group to which they held provisional rights. After several generations residual rights lapsed so that the descendants of residual landholders no longer shared kinship ties or land rights with the descendants of the provisional owners. Through this process of disaffiliation from descent groups, the fragmentation of land plots and the rights to them were minimised.

A new system of tenure was introduced in 1922 by the colonial Resident Commissioner and Lands Commissioner, Arthur Grimble. This reform removed the absolute rights of the High Chief to all lands and gave him, instead, one quarter of each land plot. The remaining three quarters was shared between the aristocrats and commoners. The manner in which a typical land plot is divided is illustrated in Figure 6.2. Due to a misunderstanding, the new system did not distinguish between provisional and residual landholders and accorded the latter equal rights with the former. No redistribution of lands took place for over thirty years, during which time a proliferation of rights to individual plots occurred. The new system was accompanied by a change in residence practice as the residence of descent group members upon their land plots in large communal houses was replaced by village residence in smaller households based upon the nuclear family.

Between 1951 and 1956 a new Lands Commission undertook the redistribution of land plots, consolidating landholdings whenever possible and formally dividing the three quarters of each plot among the commoners and aristocrats who formerly had shared it. The High Chief's quarter of each named plot remained with him. The land settlement was completed in 1956 and formed the basis for the contemporary distribution of land plots.

The institution of High Chief was abolished by the British colonial administration in 1963 following the failure of the combined councils of old men of Makin and Butaritari and a section of the high chiefly family to agree on a successor to High Chief Uraura, who died in 1963. Even before its formal abolition, however, the importance of the institution of High Chief had undergone considerable decline. The land reforms instituted by Grimble had removed the High Chief's overarching rights to the land and, hence, the need for the payment of tribute by the aristocrats and commoners occupying the land. This had effectively removed the distinction between aristocrat and commoner because the functions with respect to the payment of tribute which defined the two groups had also ceased to exist. In contemporary Butaritari society any distinctions are further blurred by the prevailing egalitarianism which developed with the decline of chiefly influence. This egalitarianism had developed earlier in the southern islands following the declines of their aristocracies resulting from the Beru invasions mentioned earlier. People's connections to these former social status groups are revealed, however, when it is known to which land plots they share rights. This is because each land plot section is identified in the lands register according to whether it is High Chief, aristocrat or commoner land.

Contemporary Land Tenure

In common with islands throughout Kiribati, the rights associated with plots of land in Kuma village include residence and the cultivation and harvesting of coconuts, breadfruit and *babai*. Other fruits of the land suitable for firewood, building, mat weaving and roof thatching are freely available to all village residents from any land. Each plot has a name and is registered on a list of land plots, numbered according to its order in the sequence of plots beginning at the north-eastern end of Butaritari atoll and proceeding to the south-west. In contemporary Kuma, these plots are distributed among 95 descent groups.

Each plot is subdivided among the three social status groups that used to be a central feature of the Butaritari-Makin social system. Those were *uea*, referring to the High Chief and his children, *toka*, the aristocrats, who were descendants of a recent High Chief's younger siblings (Lambert 1963:49) and *rorobuaka*, the commoners, who worked on the land of the High Chief.[3]

[3] The commoners were formerly known as *Tabonibai*, which means finger or fingers, or *taan i makuri*, which means workers, but with the decline of the chiefly system those now demeaning terms were replaced by the more honourable term *rorobuaka*, which means warrior.

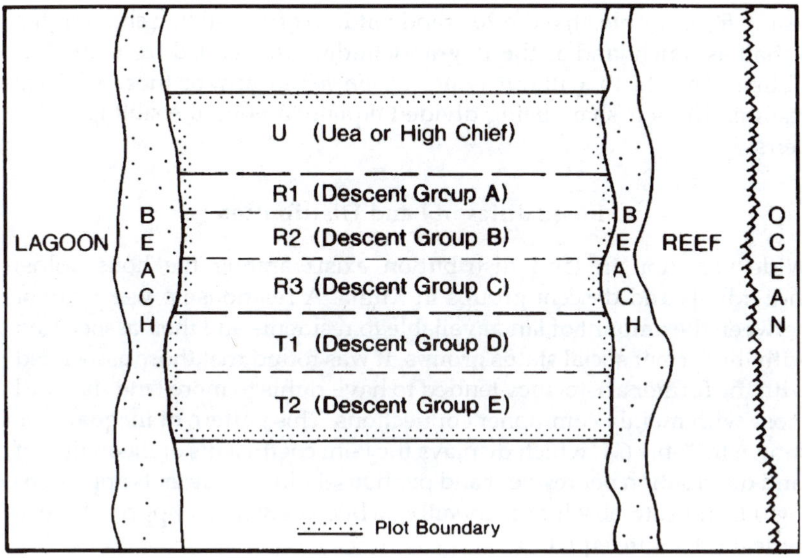

FIGURE 6.2 • DIVISION OF A TYPICAL LAND PLOT AMONG THREE FORMER SOCIAL GROUPS

Figure 6.2 shows the division of a typical land plot among the three former social status groups. 'U' indicates the one quarter of the plot allocated to the High Chief (*Uea*). Title to these 'quarters' is often still in the name of one of several now deceased high chiefs, although rights to them are now held by their descendants. 'R1', 'R2' and 'R3' indicate the divisions of one 3/8th of the plot among three commoner (*rorobuaka*) descent groups, 'A', 'B' and 'C'. 'T1' and 'T2' indicate the division of one 3/8th of the plot among two aristocrat (*toka*) descent groups, 'D' and 'E'.

In accordance with the ambilineal principle, people acquire descent group membership and land rights through both their parents. In contemporary Kuma, the great majority of land rights are registered in the names of groups of siblings who were the grandparents or great-grandparents of people now in their thirties and forties. The name of only one sibling was entered in the register with the qualification that his or her rights were held in common with his or her brothers and sisters. Each sibling held an equal share to the plots he or she was linked to in the land register. The descendants of each sibling inherited rights to the share of that sibling without regard to their number, with the result, for example, that the 20 grandchildren of one sibling share rights to half as much land as the 10 grandchildren descended from another sibling. The death without issue (*mwiin iti*) of any of those siblings resulted in their share being divided equally among the siblings with heirs.

Inequalities in Land Distribution

Wide variation in land distribution exists among the households, individuals and descent groups in Kuma. A relationship was evident between the amount of land available to residents and their association with the former social status groups. It was found that those associated with the former aristocracy tended to have rights to more land than did those with mainly commoner connections. This pattern of inequality is shown in Table 6.1, which displays the Gini coefficients of inequality of land distribution per resident and per household. Coefficients approaching 1.0 indicate absolute inequality, while coefficients approaching 0 indicate absolute equality.

TABLE 6.1 • GINI COEFFICIENTS OF LAND DISTRIBUTION INEQUALITY

	Rorobuaka (Commoner) land	*Toka* (Aristocrat) land	Total *Toka* and *Rorobuaka* land
Land per person	0.36	0.78	0.43
Land per household	0.52	0.80	0.54
Land per household per resident	–	–	0.48

Source: Fieldwork, 1994

All except five households had *toka* land included in the plots available to them. However, the ratio of *toka* plots to *rorobuaka* plots is mostly low. A clear distinction is evident between *rorobuaka* land and *toka* land per person and per household. At 0.36, the distribution of *rorobuaka* land among those with rights to it is relatively equitable. At 0.78, on the other hand, the distribution of *toka* land among those with rights to it is very unequal. At 0.43, the combined *rorobuaka* and *toka* land distribution is relatively equal. A similar pattern is evident in the distribution per household figures. The inequality of combined distribution per household is distorted by differences in household size, but when adjusted for household size, the Gini coefficient of 0.48 for households is very close to the coefficient of 0.43 for land per person.

This is significant because it shows that the inequality among descent groups is duplicated among households, the primary units of economic activity in the village. This indicates that the addition of lands available to residents through their spouses does not significantly change the pattern of inequality.

In one sense this pattern of inequality might seem unsurprising, given that it favoured those associated with the former aristocratic status group, because it might be expected that the numbers of commoners would exceed the numbers of aristocrats. That was, in fact, the case prior to 1922, before which time intermarriage between commoners and aristocrats was discouraged. The intermarriage which occurred subsequently, however, was such that the numbers of aristocrats and commoners were about equal by the early 1950s (Cartland 1953a:2). In view of the approximately equal numbers of *toka* and *rorobuaka* at the time of the Lands Commission hearings and the way in which the Lands Commission divided three quarters of each named land plot equally between them, the inequality observed is surprising.

The inequalities evident in the pattern of contemporary land distribution can be understood as being largely a consequence of differences in the residence practices of commoners and aristocrats. Commoner descent lines had tended to maintain a constant presence in the village, in contrast to aristocratic descent lines, which had displayed an intermittent presence. There was a marked tendency for the *toka* on Butaritari atoll to be concentrated in Butaritari village (Sewell 1983:81), the principal village on the island and the seat of the former High Chief. That tendency was also noted by Cartland when he visited Kuma in 1953 (Cartland 1953b). As a consequence, 83 per cent of the village residents were associated with commoner descent groups and only 17 per cent with aristocratic descent groups.

The differences between commoner and aristocrat descent groups are exemplified by descent group numbers 24 and 94.[4] Number 24 was a descent group linked to commoner land plots and had 131 members resident in Kuma. This was the largest single descent group and comprised 40 per cent of the 331 village residents who held rights to Kuma land plots[5] and 32 per cent of the total population. The area of the land plots held by this group totalled 7.06 hectares, or 0.054 hectares per

[4] These numbers are identification numbers for two of the 95 descent groups identified in Kuma. Once identified, the names of the founding ancestors were listed alphabetically and numbered from 1 to 95.

[5] The remaining 80 of Kuma's 411 residents, who were without land rights there were from other atolls and villages and most were married to Kuma landholders.

member. Descent group number 94 was linked to aristocratic land plots and had 13 members resident in Kuma. The area of the land plots held by this group totalled 15.77 hectares, or 1.213 hectares per member. While the members of descent group 24 had sufficient for their subsistence and basic cash income needs, the members of descent group 94 had more land than they could possibly use with the means available to them.

The significance of this inequality is mainly confined to the cash economy of the village because the rights associated with the legally defined land plots apply principally to the right to harvest coconuts. Apart from their subsistence uses, coconuts are the raw material from which copra is produced and this is the primary source of cash income for the villagers. However, the Kuma lands are relatively underutilised for copra production. Copra production for Butaritari generally is low in comparison with other parts of Kiribati. This can be attributed to the high rainfall, which makes drying the coconut flesh more difficult, and the rich subsistence economy that sees Butaritari people much more self-sufficient in food than people on other islands. Comparative consumption figures of subsistence foods are provided in Table 6.2.

TABLE 6.2 • MAJOR SUBSISTENCE FOODS CONSUMED ON FOUR GILBERT ISLANDS (% FREQUENCY)

	Butaritari	Abemama	Tabiteuea North	Tamana
Local protein	40.6	61.0	20.7	19.7
Babai (swamp taro)	36.6	5.8	1.8	1.0
Breadfruit	17.2	2.0	–	5.9
Pandanus	0.4	6.4	20.8	4.0

Source: Geddes 1982:40, Table 5.1.

Prospects

The question of absentee land rights is clearly linked to the inequalities of land distribution evident in Kuma. Under the precolonial system of tenure, the provisional rights held by absent descent group members would have become residual rights and these eventually would have been relinquished completely. But, as has already been noted, the reforms instigated by Grimble had the effect of removing the distinction between provisional and residual rights. This means that people absent for long periods retain rights to descent group lands.

If those absentees with rights to Kuma *toka* land plots were to return to the village, the population would increase by about 270 people (341–70 = 271), taking the total to about 680. According to figures from the 1990 Census only 61.2 per cent of people who named Butaritari as their home island actually lived there (Statistics Office 1993:104–5). Assuming that people with rights to Kuma lands are proportionally represented among the 38.8 per cent of Butaritari people living off the atoll, they would number about 260 people. If these people returned, they would raise the village population to over 900, more than double its present 411. This sort of population increase must be accepted as likely because the present growth of the urban population on Tarawa atoll, which absorbs the natural increase of the outer islands' populations, is unsustainable.

In view of the extent to which the lands are presently underutilised for copra production, such a population increase could probably be absorbed without a reduction in potential average cash income. In fact, increased population could lead to more efficient copra production because the pressure on space within the village would encourage the growth of smaller settlements between Kuma village and Keuea village to the south-west. This would allow many people closer access to their coconut producing land plots than they presently enjoy while residing in Kuma village, up to 5km distant from some Kuma land plots (see Figure 6.2). The precise source of any such population increase must be specified, however, when considering possible scenarios. For example, if the population of Kuma doubled as a result of return migration by landholders, the present degree of inequality would tend to decrease and the productivity of presently underutilised or unutilised lands would be increased. If, on the other hand, it doubled as a result of the natural increase of the present population, the degree of inequality would increase, with serious implications for the future sustainable use of the Kuma land plots.

In such a situation, addressing the question of absentee land rights would be crucial to the maintenance of sustainable land use in Kuma village, and Butaritari atoll in general. The present system of land registration lacks the flexibility of the precolonial system upon which it was imperfectly modelled, and it will be necessary for new mechanisms to be developed to effect the periodic redistributions of land which are required to maintain a balance between population and resources.

This case study has demonstrated the complexity of land tenure practices and changes in one village context. The customary land tenure system evolved in ways which reflected the social structure of the community and the particular atoll environment and ensured that every Kuma villager gained access to sufficient land and sea resources to ensure basic survival. The system has been gradually transformed, as a result of colonial laws, changes in social relations and migration. Important vestiges of the old system remain, though the legacy of colonial laws is particularly important in hindering the ability of the system to cope with issues of absenteeism. Commercial uses of the land, here based on copra, have been accommodated though they have not contributed to inequalities in landholdings. Kuma thus represents a unique configuration of society, economy and land tenure but the general issues evident there, of societal and cultural change, inequalities and the incorporation of migration and the cash economy, reflect many of the processes common throughout the Pacific Island region. Local manifestations of change – seemingly very different patterns of land tenure and land use across the region – result from contrasting historical, cultural and environmental contexts, yet the driving forces of change are very similar.

CHAPTER 7

Migration and the Cook Islands

KIRSTI HOOKER AND JUDITH VARCOE

Migrant Societies

Many Pacific Island societies are highly mobile. The greater part of the South Pacific Ocean, indeed, was explored and settled by Polynesian peoples over the past four millennia and this pattern of exploration and movement has been carried on through to the present day. People today use jet aircraft rather than ocean-going canoes but the process of opportunity-seeking is similar. Hau'ofa has countered the often pessimistic conclusions about the limited resources and prospects of the region by stressing the mobility and adaptability of Pacific Islanders in the movements across the wider Pacific region:

> Everywhere they go, to Australia, New Zealand, Hawaii, mainland USA ... they strike roots in new resource areas, securing employment and overseas family property, expanding kinship networks through which they circulate themselves, their relatives, their material goods and their stories (Hau'ofa 1993:10).

International movement is shadowed by internal circulation, often from villages to towns, and the result is a myriad of kinship-based chains of movement, linking home villages, local towns and international cities (Chapman 1991, Friesen 1993). People move, seemingly inexorably, towards the larger urban centres, yet there is considerable two-way movement along the chains. People return home, for holidays, for important family occasions such as marriages and funerals, and sometimes to retire. When they return they bring their savings and gifts as well as their new ideas, experiences and aspirations. Even without moving, their links to home are cemented in other ways, chiefly through the sending back of monetary remittances, or by hosting and looking after new arrivals overseas. They contribute not only to their immediate families but to wider social groups, notably the churches. Because kinship plays such an important part in these continuing linkages and because wider family units make decisions about movements, resources, investments and land, the term 'transnational corporations of kin' (Bertram and Watters 1985, Munro 1990) has been used to denote the economic and well as social dimensions of Pacific Island migration. In a study of market vendors Brown and Connell (1993) found examples of households in Tonga operating complex internationally oriented business operations through close kin networks. As Underhill (1989) concluded with regard to Manihiki atoll in the Cook Islands, movement was a socio-economic strategy for collective survival.

Such movement is not open to all people in the region. Those in countries with close ties to New Zealand, France or the United States can often move freely as citizens of the metropolitan country. Other countries, such as Tonga or Samoa, may have special agreements or historic ties to allow for more open migration to Rim countries. Even for countries that do not, such as Fiji, there is often a remarkable degree of movement by its citizens using a variety of international migration routes and qualifications (Bedford 1986, James 1991, Macpherson 1992b, McCall and Connell 1993). Overall, though, the immigration laws and enforcement policies of countries such as USA, Canada, Australia and New Zealand are critical in opening or closing opportunities for Pacific Island people.

There is considerable debate about the development implications of Pacific Island migration. The arguments stressing negative consequences centre on the fact that migration removes a disproportionate number of young, well-educated, and more highly skilled people from their home islands. A study of Tongans and Samoans moving to the United States concluded: 'Emigration results in the permanent loss of young, educated, skilled labour from the Pacific island nations. Skilled labour is in short supply and emigration probably hinders development' (Ahlburg and Levin 1990:84). Others point to a decline in agricultural production and increasing dependence on imported commodities (Curson 1979, Connell 1987a). Remittances are also seen as an unreliable source of income, inevitably declining over time and often frittered away on consumer goods rather than invested (Connell 1980). There have been other studies, however, which have taken a more benign view of migration. Following from the suggestion of Bertram and Watters (1985, 1986) of MIRAB Pacific microstates in which migration and remittances play a key economic role, Hayes (1991) argued that migration and remittances are key determinants of

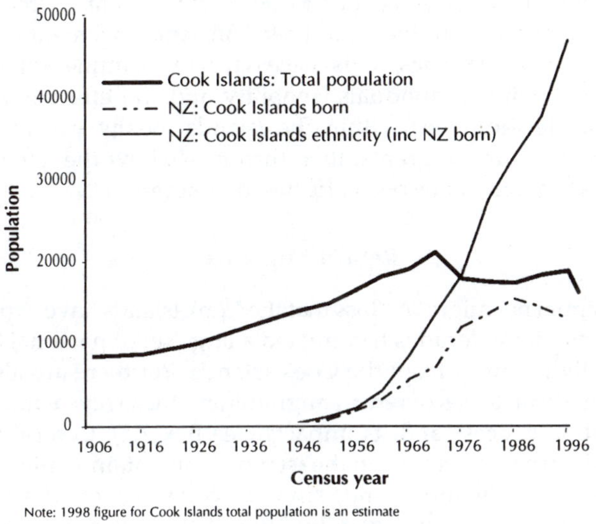

FIGURE 7.1 • COOK ISLAND MAORI POPULATION IN NEW ZEALAND AND THE COOK ISLANDS 1936-1996

Source: New Zealand and Cook Islands census data, various.

economic performance and welfare and a reason for the low incidence of absolute poverty in the region.

Little has been written, however, on what the implications might be for *sustainable* development of high mobility, beyond questions about the maintenance of remittances over time. The Cook Islands presents a good context in which to investigate this question. It has one of the most highly mobile populations in the Pacific Islands. With its special political compact with New Zealand, its citizens can enter the latter country with the rights of full citizenship (thence they can travel also to Australia). And with regular direct flights between Rarotonga and Auckland (since the mid-1970s – Loomis 1990a), large numbers of Cook Islanders have moved southward, so much so that there are now many more Cook Islands people resident in New Zealand than in the Cook Islands (Figure 7.1).

These data suggest a large net outflow of people from the Cook Islands, yet they disguise the degree of circulation. Not only have there been fluctuations in the volume and direction of flow – as following economic restructuring and rises in unemployment in New Zealand in the years after 1984, when many Cook Islanders returned home, or in the past two years when a similar neoliberal ideology led to a restructuring of the Cook Islands public sector and an increase in the opposite direction[1] – but there has been constant movement to and fro.

Beyond these statistics, it is necessary to examine some of the dimensions behind individuals' mobility and the effect this has on sustainable development within the islands. Below we analyse the experience of return migrants, then turn to see how the development experience of women has been affected by migration.

Return Migrants

The substantial net migration loss that the Cook Islands have experienced over the past three decades has created a large set of personal histories of people living away from the Cook Islands. Yet there are also many interesting life histories of return migrants and these reveal much about the migration process and its impacts (see Box 7.1). Central to many stories is the frequent return to the islands to maintain family contacts, to meet social obligations and, simply, to have a holiday amongst familiar surroundings and people. Two of the other important, and related, factors to come out of these histories, as studied by Hooker (1994), are education and land.

The pursuit of education and training is a major factor in Cook Islands migration. Traditionally, New Zealand has been an important destination but the growth of facilities in other states, such as the University of the South Pacific in Fiji, and the availability of scholarships elsewhere have widened the range of options overseas. Education can be seen not only as a cause of migration but also as a contributor to the underdevelopment of sending states, for it heightens the aspirations of the young and able within a population and leads them to employment and settlement overseas when they discover that they are able to acquire jobs and material wealth not available at home (Connell 1983, Bedford 1992). Others, however, have argued that the skills acquired overseas may, in fact, encourage a return home, for their education brings them both status and deference and high relative incomes at home (Marcus 1981:60). A study of return migrants in the Cook Islands by Hooker (1994) tended to support the latter conclusion. It is true that many Cook Islanders travelling overseas for higher education gained experience of travel and lifestyles, and skills, that encouraged them to stay away and earn incomes much higher than

[1] *The Cook Islands News* (1998) reported that 2,500 residents left the Cook Islands in 1997 and the net migration loss for the year was 1,137 out of a total estimated population in December 1997 of 16,500.

BOX 7.1 • TEVAI'S STORY

'In 1965 Tevai* was born in Aitutaki, one of the southern islands in the Cook Islands group. When she was old enough she went to school with the other children on Aitutaki. But Tevai didn't like school much and was sometimes naughty. Thinking she was a difficult child, Tevai's parents sent her off to live with some relatives in Tahiti. After about a year in Tahiti, Tevai was still unsettled and it was decided that she should go to New Zealand to live with some other relatives. Tevai didn't settle to life in New Zealand at all, and after three months the family sent her to Australia to live with her older brother and his family. It was hoped that the brother would keep a close eye on Tevai and make sure that she got a 'proper' education.

Tevai found a niche in Australia and, after finishing high school, went on to train as a nurse. Tevai had been working in Sydney as a nurse for six months when her father died and she was called back to her family on Aitutaki. The family asked Tevai if she would take over the responsibility of caring for her mother. Tevai agreed and for the next few years adopted a dual lifestyle, living alternately in Aitutaki and Australia. In Australia, Tevai earned good wages nursing and was able to send part of her wages home to her mother. While staying on Aitutaki she and her mother would lead a fairly subsistent lifestyle, living off the family land and contributions from other family members.

As her mother became ill, however, Tevai found it necessary to spend more and more time in Aitutaki. In 1991 she applied for a full-time nursing job at the hospital on Rarotonga. Having obtained an excellent reference from her former nursing tutor (who was holidaying on Rarotonga at the time), Tevai got the job. Although she considered her wage to be very poor compared with wages received in Australia, Tevai wanted to live closer to her mother.

Recently, after her mother's sixtieth birthday, the family had a meeting and decided that Tevai had done her share of looking after her mother, and that Tevai's sister would come back from Australia to take over. Tevai wants to go back to Australia in a couple of years to earn some more money but intends to return to Rarotonga eventually and build a house on the land given to her by her mother.'

* This is a fictitious name.

Source: Hooker (1994:1-2)

they could gain at home. Yet it is also significant that many qualified, skilled and experienced Cook Island people have journeyed back to the islands and been able to use their skills in a range of occupations, not only in the public service, hitherto the largest employer in the country. Thus, although education 'may encourage migration away from the islands, it also provides a way back' (Hooker 1994:66). Furthermore, many of the positions filled by the returnees, in government and in private business, are influential in shaping the direction of social and economic development in the country.

Another key element in the circulation of Cook Island people to and from the islands is land. There is no formal land market in the Cook Islands, beyond a limited supply of leases, mainly for residential purposes, and migrants who wish to maintain the option, at least, of a return home in the future are wise to gain an occupation right to customary land before they leave, and possibly build a house, or at least maintain their knowledge of land rights and cement their rights through continuing contact with fellow members of their families and landowning clan (Loomis 1990a:52).[2] Land is also crucial for it is 'both a symbol of identity and a source of economic and social security' (Hooker 1994:82). The need to maintain contacts, whether in the form of remittances or holidays home, has been a major factor in guiding the pattern of migration and in the resilience of kinship ties between the migrants and the families at home. Interestingly, also, it appears as if such ties are being kept by the younger generations, even those born overseas, for they 'seem just as determined to secure their rights to land in the islands as their parents' (Hooker 1994:873).

For the Cook Islands, at least, it is clear that international migration does not necessarily result in the permanent relocation of population, despite a net population loss to migration. Life history studies reveal that, although people leave the islands, some for long periods, many return and most retain social and economic ties of some sort. Whilst mobility gives Cook Islanders greater economic and social security, it has a more significant role than merely maintaining basic living standards. The relative ease with which Cook Islanders move to other places and return, bringing with them new ideas, skills and experiences, means that they are very much a part of the socio-economic transformation of the home society. The freedom and ability to be mobile provides them with added options for development. And this seems to be a sustainable process, for mobility and return are open to, and are being exploited by, succeeding generations. The whole process is

[2] Browne (1994) and Crocombe (1987b) have analysed the complex nature of land tenure in the Cook Islands.

dependent, however, on changing economic circumstances both in the Cook Islands and in destination countries (Loomis 1990b), these largely determining the volume and direction of the net flow.

Women Migrants and Development

If the long-term process of mobility appears to be durable and have benefits for Cook Islands development by adding new resources and skills, what does it do for changing attitudes and values? It could be suggested that the importation of modern and foreign value systems and lifestyles is inherently disruptive and, thereby, the antithesis of socially sustainable development. On the other hand, some of those new values may assist in the move towards a more just and equitable society. A study by Varcoe (1993) on the role of women in Cook Islands development offers some clues as to the social impact of migration.

Women are heavily involved in the migration process and, as Tevai's experience shows (Box 7.1), they are central in maintaining critical kinship links through social obligations. Women appear to be well represented in data on education, with girls having apparently equal participation rates with boys in education within the Cook Islands and scholarships to study overseas (Varcoe 1993:72–5). Thus many women are able to further their education overseas, gaining higher skills and valuable experience of work and life in a different society.

Within the Cook Islands, however, women's access to employment opportunities lags behind that of men. Men dominate the public workspace with nearly twice as many men as women in full-time work and an even larger ratio for employers and self-employed occupations (Booth 1989). In the political realm, women are very poorly represented: in 1993 there were no women members of Parliament nor any women on island councils (Varcoe 1993:81, Ingram 1991). These data and other indicators of domestic violence and rape, together with attitudes and practices prevalent in the law and the churches, led Varcoe (1993:94) to conclude that the Cook Islands was 'an essentially patriarchal society'.

Varcoe's interviews with women on Rarotonga, Aitutaki and Mauke, comparing their lives with those of their mothers, also revealed a noticeable perception of improvements in women's lives. Some improvements came from material goods, kerosene and electricity replacing firewood, for example; many from the opportunities provided by higher education and employment options; and some from modern health facilities (Varcoe 1993:97–100). Travel and residence overseas were strong factors underlying such changes. Mobility had clearly increased for women and many had gained experience of different social situations and practices. These experiences, often in societies where women were more active in the political and legal spheres and less likely to tolerate abuse and inequality, had allowed them to reflect on Cook Islands society. In many ways this seems to be leading to beneficial change, whether through women gaining independence and respect through their income-earning roles or their greater assertiveness. As well as change within households, there are some signs of new forms of collective change. There are many women's organisations in the country and most revolve around the churches or have relatively conservative aims, though nonetheless they allow women to come together. Others (such as the Cook Islands Business and Professional Women's Association) have an explicit manifesto for social change. And, whilst they might still be few in number, there are women who have taken on a prominent role in championing women's causes (Varcoe 1993:110–12). Interestingly nearly all have had access to higher education and have lived overseas.

It seems, then, that women in the Cook Islands are experiencing forms of emancipation. Material well-being has improved, there are more options open in education, employment and travel, and challenges have been mounted to the hitherto dominant ideas of male control. Mobility, through migration and return, has been central to these changes. A more just and equitable society is promised. Yet it is still far from being completely realised. Economic reversals and employment cutbacks, as in the past two years, can still turn back some of the gains and many patriarchal attitudes remain deep-seated.

Conclusions

The peoples of the Pacific Islands, for the most part, do not live in closed societies. For many, even if the opportunity to move overseas is not open, there is contact with the outside world through the media and there is the chance to move to towns and cities within a country. For others, such as those in the Cook Islands, international travel and resettlement is an important and almost commonplace aspect of the lives of most households. Such movement brings inevitable changes. 'Transnational corporations of kin' link people at home to those residing and working in other countries and remittances, gifts and visits bring new resources, ideas and interpersonal contacts that open the development options for others. Some of these changes may be harmful or socially disruptive, increasing dependence on imported food or challenging the authority of the social *status quo*, for example. Migration may also rob the islands of their young and most able, and it may increase the lifestyle aspirations of those that remain to well beyond what the local economy alone can provide. Yet, in the deliberate and informed decisions of individuals and kin groups, there is a clear recognition that benefits can be substantial, most importantly in increased opportunities for education and employment, and there seems to be a strong desire to maintain old contacts and ways of life which can both lessen the costs and problems associated with migration and maintain those social and cultural values and practices which people hold dear. Despite the perturbations of economic cycles and political decisions, Cook Islands people seem to remain largely in control of the process of migration. It seems durable, resilient and capable of significantly enhancing the development options for people, including traditionally disadvantaged groups, such as women. The maintaining of open-door immigration policies by metropolitan countries on the Pacific Rim, therefore, can be seen as a very effective form of development assistance, perhaps more so than aid in the form of capital or expertise.

The implications for sustainable development in such open societies are profound. Whereas some strategies for sustainable development may look to the past and the reconstruction of traditional values, relationships and practices, in open societies these are much less viable. People, rightly, will expect higher material standards of living, they will challenge some forms of tradition that conflict with their changing values, and they will look outside for alternative models of development. Sustainable development cannot be framed solely in terms of national perspectives on resources, society and culture, for many people are much more a part of internationally oriented kinship groups than they are constrained by national boundaries. The power of Pacific Island states in these circumstances to plan for, deliver or limit sustainable development is severely constrained.

Yet what the above analysis has shown is that this limited role for nation states does not mean that people instead will have recourse to some homogeneous, universal and globally focused development model. People respond to changing constraints and opportunities, they mix Pacific and Western lifestyles and they choose unique paths to, and goals of, development. Critically, Pacific mores of social and economic organisation and interaction remain, not unchallenged nor unchanging, but flexible, resilient and central to the world views of Pacific Island people.

CHAPTER 8

Vanua: Land, People and Culture in Fiji[1]

KALAVETI BATIBASAQA, JOHN OVERTON & PETER HORSLEY

Vanua and the Pacific Islands

The word *vanua*, in its regional variants, is one of the most widely used in the Pacific Islands. It is found in Fiji, it is part of the name for the country of Vanuatu and it is especially common in Polynesia, where the word appears in different guises:

> For example, in Cook Islands Maori, 'enua' means 'land, country, territory, afterbirth': in Futuna (Wallace) 'fanua' means 'country, land, the people of a place'; in Tonga, 'fonua' means 'island, territory, estate, the people of the estate, placenta' and 'fonualoto', 'grave'. We can see that in some Polynesian languages, proto-fanua is both the people and the territory that nourishes them, as a placenta nourishes a baby. (Pond 1997: 32)

Vanua is usually translated into English as 'land', though this greatly disguises the complexity of a concept that appears to have no parallel in the English language. In this chapter we examine the meanings of the term, with reference to Fiji, and consider how its lost meanings might be revived and used as an effective integrating concept for efforts to achieve more sustainable forms of development for Pacific Island peoples.

The Meaning of *Vanua* in Fiji

It is difficult to capture the essence of the word *vanua* in a foreign tongue. It has many different dimensions but these all coalesce around

[1] The authors acknowledge the useful comments and suggestions made by Peter Raine on the draft of this chapter.

a central idea of a bond between people and the land:

> It does not mean only the land area one is identified with, and the vegetation, animal life and other objects on it, but it also includes the social and cultural system – the people, their traditions and customs, beliefs and values, and the various other institutions established for the sake of achieving harmony, solidarity and prosperity within a particular social context. (Ravuvu 1983:70)

In Fijian, *vanua* may be best thought of as the environment in its totality, including both natural and human aspects. It *is* the physical elements that comprise the land – the earth, rocks, vegetation, rivers, seas and air – those things which form physical landscapes or 'nature'. This combination of natural elements form a series of unique environments and physical landscapes – ranging from small islands, to high hills and mountains in the main islands. They all form distinctive regional environments which inhabitants recognise, interact with constantly, and depend upon for survival. The earth, forests and sea have formed the basic resources to sustain human life in Fiji for centuries, and it is these elements that are at the heart of the concept of *vanua*.

But *vanua* is much more than the physical environment. *Vanua* can also mean 'people'. The word is used for an important level in the hierarchy of indigenous Fijian social units, a regional grouping of a number of *yavusa*, smaller than the *matanitu* (a large confederation and a word used as a translation for the government). This use of the word encapsulates the notion of people with a common territory and often a common dialect, history and cultural icons. It then becomes a part of terms such as *matanivanua* (a herald for the chiefs) and *vakavanua* (customary practices).[2]

Within these concepts, *vanua* also includes the idea of established customs and protocols that govern how people interact with each other and the land, and also the social structure through which these are carried out. Genealogy is an important element. Fijians are bonded to the land through their ancestors and guardian spirits. They 'inherit' the land from their ancestors and pass it on to succeeding generations. Knowledge of one's ancestors thus provides a vital link to the land – without kinship and without a genealogy, a Fijian has no identity as a Fijian nor any claim to communal land. Furthermore, *vanua* contains the history of one's ancestors in the trees, rivers and mountains where

2 *Vakavanua*, indeed, has gained usage in terms of contemporary land tenure, to denote practices which are in part customary and side-step the official laws and mechanisms (Overton 1987, Eaton 1988, Ward 1995b).

their spirits dwell. Fijians have traditionally recognised a strong spiritual dimension with gods and spirits embedded within nature and with power to influence both the physical environment and human activity. The spirit world overlapped the natural and human worlds and held dominion over both. While Christian and Western concepts have undermined these elements, they have not been lost from the Fijian psyche, and are still articulated in communal rituals and traditional religious incantations.

Combining these ideas of land, culture, history and beliefs, *vanua* can be suggested as an expression of Fijian values. It provides both a geographical and sociological point of reference and links the ecological, social, spiritual, and economic dimensions together. The Fijian language contains many concepts which express and develop these values (Ravuvu 1983 1987a, Tuvuki 1995, Raine forthcoming):

- *solevu, kerekere* (a distinctive economic ethic of reciprocity and mutual assistance)
- *veilomani vaka veiwekani* (a sense of kinship with fellow beings)
- *vakarokoroko taka/doka na yau bula* (a reverence for creation as a whole)
- *na kena taqomaki na yau bula me baleti ira na noda kawa* (a sense of commitment to safeguard all natural resources for future generations)
- *lewe ni vanua, gonedau, mataisau, Turaga ni vanua* (a sense of responsibility and stewardship for the way the gifts of nature are used)
- *na tabu kei na mana ni vanua* (a sacred regard for the whole of nature and its responsibilities as being gifts from God)

These values stress the bonds between people, the physical environment and the supernatural world. Each has a specific meaning and implication for human activity, but they are not incompatible with one another and they are all part of the overall notion of *vanua*. Indeed, these values might be considered the most critical element of *vanua* in terms of sustainability, for they govern how people see themselves and their environment, and how they make decisions that affect the world around them.

Vanua, then, is the physical composition and appearance of the landscape; it is the people that inhabit that environment and the Being of nature; and it is their values, customs and beliefs which determine how people interact with each other and the natural environment. Such a complex and multifaceted concept is not unique to the Pacific Islands but it has been lost from many Western cultures. The modern European idea that people are separate from nature, and have dominion over it, and that nature is divisible into a series of resources and commodities to be exploited and traded, is far from Fijian, and Pacific Island, views of *vanua*.

The Erosion of the Concept of *Vanua* in Fiji

Yet, whilst the concept of *vanua* might seem to offer a powerful, if complex, view of the relationship between people and nature, it should be stressed that it is a concept that has undergone considerable change in the past century or two. Although the word is still widely used, the substance of its meaning has been eroded. Gradually, different dimensions to the concept have been challenged, weakened and sometimes lost, largely as a result of contact with the commercial, bureaucratic and religious values of those who colonised Fiji.

The most dramatic change was the loss of land. Land alienation prior to the cession of Fiji to the British Crown in 1874 (and ratified soon after)[3] accounted for nearly 13 per cent of the land area of Fiji, including large portions of the most fertile land. Later, the leasing of 'native' land was allowed with secure 30-year leases granted. Whilst the colonial authorities succeeded in preventing large-scale alienation after cession and Fijians kept legal ownership of leased land, land became a commodity that was traded and transformed by the newcomers (and not a few Fijians themselves) so that landscapes were radically altered in many places. The British eroded the traditional power of the chiefs by transferring property rights to the *mataqali*[4] whose land boundaries were mapped. Registered *mataqali* 'owners' were then recorded and regulations drafted which limited the way land could be transferred. These attempts to regulate and ostensibly to protect Fijian land had the effect of freezing in time a system and a series of practices that had hitherto been flexible (France 1969, Chapelle 1978, Ward 1995b). *Vanua* became something that was written down selectively, interpreted and distorted by colonial authorities.

These colonial changes have continued since independence in 1970.

[3] The colonial authorities after 1874 stopped further alienation (with the exception of a brief period early this century) and investigated the claims of Europeans who had acquired land prior to 1874 (Ward 1969, France 1969).

[4] *Mataqali* is the term for the most important landholding unit in Fiji. Members of a *mataqali* are closely related through the partilineal line, they marry outside the group and land is allocated by the group to male members (Ravuvu 1983). The colonial authorities recognised the *mataqali* as the only landholding unit, though customary tenure had been much more flexible and involved both smaller and larger units in different locations (Ward 1995b).

The drive for modernisation and development has meant that colonial practices have been retained, land is even more a tradable commodity, and the natural world (especially its soils and forests) has become increasingly exploited as 'natural resources'. Critically, whereas in pre-modern times those resources provided for the welfare and livelihoods of the people by the production of subsistence goods on a largely sustainable basis, now people want to earn cash to satisfy rapidly rising material demands. This frequently results in resources being 'mined' through the removal of the natural forest cover or the loss of soil fertility.

Perhaps the major element to be lost has been the spiritual. Christian missionaries, despite slow beginnings, proved very successful in Fiji and now nearly all indigenous Fijians class themselves as Christians, albeit in a variety of denominations. The progress of Christianity led to an attack on pre-existing religions and beliefs. Christian missionaries expressed the view that there was one supreme God, not a series of spirits related to the physical elements of nature, nor to ancestors; this God was transcendent (and distant), not a part of the trees, rivers and seas; and people, through God, held dominion over nature. These were radically different views from what people had believed previously and the adoption of Christianity meant that a critical element of *vanua* was substantially weakened.

Finally, *vanua* has been weakened by the imposition of new governmental structures. *Vaka matanitu* (the way of the government) has superseded *vaka vanua* (the way of the land/people). A central government now makes the critical decisions about development for the country and passes laws that affect people's lives and their environment. Although customary chiefs might hold power within government structures, their influence as guardians of the people and the land has been weakened considerably. *Vanua*, as a set of protocols, practices and spiritual relationships, has become much less important.

Vanua as an Integrating Concept?

Although *vanua* has been diluted and distorted as a concept, its core components, given their long and successful application in village life, still have great merit and are worthy of reconsideration. Indeed, when viewed as a framework for the achievement of sustainable development in Fiji, *vanua* can provide a powerful integrating theme.

One example of the way *vanua* can be used is in the proposed *Vanua* Watershed Trust for central Viti Levu. This trust, which had its origins in discussions between landowners in 1994, aims to bring together landowning *mataqali* in the interior watersheds of the Navua, Waidina,

Wainimala and Sigatoka rivers to agree not to sign any further logging contracts – there has been pressure from companies and government to allow commercial logging of valuable remaining stands of timber in the area – and instead promote alternative economic activities in the villages and watershed areas such as community-based logging, agro-forestry, and ecotourism. The proposal depends on the agreement and cooperation particularly of traditional leaders in the villages and on a strong conservation ethic. It is being led from within the region and draws strongly on established kinship links, on traditional values and uses of the forests, and on the principles of *vanua* to guide appropriate development.

The example, however, also demonstrates some of the difficulties of using *vanua* as a set of principles to guide appropriate development. Firstly, it will draw the people of the region into conflict with government and with a dominant ethic of development based on resource exploitation. Despite attempts by the government of Fiji to promote sustainable development, it is still supportive of activities, such as logging, which can generate large incomes for government and those involved. Fijian political leaders, many of them of chiefly rank, feel that they are best placed to determine the development needs and strategies of rural people. Local *vanua* leaders arguing for local control and appropriate village-based conservation and development will meet stiff opposition.

Secondly, in a predominantly Christian society, recourse to traditional spiritual values may be unwelcome from some of the more rigid denominations, just as pleas for simpler, less materialistic lifestyles will be hard to accept for societies attracted by quick wealth and the promise of material goods. Thus, the *Vanua* Watershed Trust will have to tread a careful path, conscious of new societal values and cultural norms and ready to accept that forms of appropriate development will be necessary to generate incomes and balance the attractions of logging incomes. It will have to negotiate new concepts of *vanua*.

In any such reformulation of the concept, several key features must remain central:

- The valuing of land and the whole environment in ways other than as discrete economic resources. Such values would see the holistic and interconnected nature of *vanua*, not just of the physical environment but of humans and the environment.
- The view that humans are a part of nature rather than dominant over it and that customary land 'owners' have a responsibility to act as stewards of the land.

- The use of established communal and local modes of decision making, mutual assistance and the sharing of benefits and welfare rather than recourse to government-dominated agencies.
- Values which stress the stake that past and future generations have in the land.
- Values which place weight on community, stability and well-being rather than on materialism and 'progress'. This includes a strong element of spiritual well-being.

Such features draw heavily on essentially premodern ideas (the principles outlined above for Fiji) but they also recognise that societal values, practices and structures can and do change. They call for any development to dovetail effectively with local values and structures. As such they are consistent with a raft of recent NGO-based initiatives that focus on empowering local communities and developing appropriate education and training programmes for specific projects (Biodiversity Conservation Network 1996, 1997), and the emerging ecosystem management concepts (IUCN 1997). Indeed, there will be a major benefit to be gained in linking *vanua*-based organisations, such as the *Vanua* Watershed Trust, across the Pacific Island region so that expertise can be shared and mutual support gained. NGO networks could be crucial in providing a bulwark against attempts to undermine local initiatives.

Perhaps the greatest potential for the *vanua* concept, though, is not the complete recreation of old ways, but the development of an alternative set of values, based in the past but aware of the present, that can act as an effective counter to dominant ideologies of resource development and exploitation. The widespread use of *vanua*, and its local variants throughout the South Pacific, could provide the foundation point for a unique regional response that defines sustainable development in ecological, social, economic and spiritual terms, in ways that are appropriate to the living traditions of each island culture.

The acceptance of *vanua* as a central and integrating concept to guide sustainable development in the Pacific Islands, however, will not be easy. National politicians and planners will not wish to cede power and responsibility to the local level and many will perceive the idea as backward-looking and anti-development (even if some traditional leaders are ready to embrace alternative development ideologies based on *vanua*). Yet, unless there is a serious re-evaluation of the values, societal structures and customary practices, as well as the methods and processes that guide development and change, sustainability in the Pacific Islands will remain elusive.

PART II

Effects of 'Development'

AS THE INTRODUCTORY chapters to this book have shown, the South Pacific comprises unique and often pristine ecosystems and is home to a diverse range of cultures and societies, which rely upon the environment in varying degrees to meet their livelihood needs. Yet the manner in which 'development' is progressing in the region is disturbing:

> Here are mere periscopes of land peeping through the surface of the great ocean; island nations whose few acres cover the area of whole continents; seascapes of an almost painful beauty and fragility; truly remarkable people, bound together by extraordinary histories and perceptions, who imagined these places long before they found them with feats of navigation never since surpassed. A very special, precious place.
>
> So what do we propose to do with it? Why, dig it up! Drown it! Chop it down! Contaminate it! (Ransom 1997:10)

Development strategies that have been employed to date in the region have sought economic development above all. The stimulation of economic activity, it is hoped, will generate employment, earn foreign exchange to pay for rising imports, and create ripple effects through the whole economy. It is assumed that higher cash incomes, more formal sector employment and commodification of economic relations will be beneficial to society at large. The strategies have drawn on development 'blueprints' evolved elsewhere and adapted, albeit often in a cursory fashion, to the Pacific Island context. These have based economic development on one or more of four main approaches: resource extraction (minerals, timber and fish); the commercialisation of agriculture (to produce commodities for export or import substitution); tourism; and industrialisation. These have posed particular problems for implementation in the Pacific Islands, largely because of the small scale of local markets, the lack of natural resources in most countries, and isolation from world markets. Thus, the strategies have been supplemented by a range of special measures, with the support of metropolitan countries, to make the region more competitive internationally. These have included, in particular, trade preferences and aid. The former has allowed the products of the region a place on foreign markets that would be denied to them otherwise due to high costs of production and transport, whilst the latter has both provided incomes for those outside of the productive economic sectors and subsidised the development of economic infrastructure. The result has been the evolution of a particular configuration of economic activity, differing markedly from the resource-based strategies of Papua New Guinea to virtual aid dependence in the microstates of Polynesia.

This section uncovers some of the issues surrounding predominant forms of development which have been pursued in the Pacific Islands. In this regard, logging, mining, agriculture, fisheries and urban development are all laid open to critical scrutiny. The key question remains, therefore, do these activities contribute to, or undermine, prospects for sustainable development in the region?

CHAPTER 9

Logging in Melanesia

REGINA SCHEYVENS AND ROSS CASSELLS

While the Melanesian countries are economically poor according to widely accepted national accounting procedures, they are rich in natural resources such as minerals, tropical forest and marine life (Barlow and Winduo 1997:9). Furthermore, what makes them unique among their Asian neighbours is that local communities, rather than the state or private interests, own the legal rights to most natural resources (Lynch *et al.* 1995:100–1) and this is a necessary condition for social sustainability. An abundance of natural resources, most of which are owned by tribes or clans, should offer the Solomon Islands, Vanuatu and Papua New Guinea great opportunities for a self-determined, sustainable form of development, but this is incongruous with the type of development which has predominated in recent years.

This chapter focuses on the impacts of logging on the Melanesian countries. First, government policies and actual rates of logging in the region are examined in order to gain a better understanding of the extent of the problem. Later sections focus specifically on how logging affects local communities. The chapter ends by documenting recent responses by local communities to large-scale logging and considering whether there are viable alternative means of enhancing the livelihoods of rural communities.

Government Policy and Logging

For governments wanting to earn money in a hurry, the seemingly vast areas of tropical rainforest appear to be inexhaustible, a ready source of cash. As shown in Table 9.1, *per capita* forest cover in Melanesia is much higher than that of neighbouring Asia. Small wonder, then, that Asian and Australian timber companies, Melanesian politicians and landowners alike see the forest as a resource to be exploited. After all, at least from a Melanesian subsistence point of view, the forest has always been there to sustain one's needs, including food, building and handicraft materials. And now that the need for cash is paramount what else can one trade, other than the natural resources with which one has been so richly endowed?

TABLE 9.1 • *PER CAPITA* FOREST COVER IN SELECTED PACIFIC ISLAND AND ASIAN COUNTRIES

	Natural forests (ha)	Population	Natural forests *per capita* (ha)
Papua New Guinea	36,000,000	3,839,000	9.38
Solomon Islands	2,394,000	320,000	7.34
Malaysia	17,583,000	17,891,000	0.98
Indonesia	109,549,000	182,812,000	0.60
Thailand	12,735,000	55,583,000	0.23
Philippines	7,831,000	60,779,000	0.13

Source: World Resources Institute (1996), derived from data tables 8.1 and 9.2 using 1990 estimates

Rates of logging in Melanesia are high (Figure 9.1) and governments have come to rely upon the levies paid by foreign logging companies. A virtual doubling in the price of tropical timbers in 1993 provided a temptation to bolster floundering foreign reserves which was too difficult to resist. In Papua New Guinea, for example, average log export prices per cubic metre increased from $US88 in 1992 to $US171 in 1993, owing largely to bans on the export of tropical timber from South-East Asia and a reduction in timber supplies from North America (AusAID 1995:39). The logging industry's contribution to the economy is particularly high in the Solomon Islands, where timber accounted for nearly 60 per cent of total merchandise exports in 1993 (AIDAB 1994:6). The rate of log extraction was, however, several times the sustainable cutting level (*South Sea Digest* 1996:1). In 1995 the estimated sustainable annual cut for the Solomon Islands was 286,000 cubic metres, yet in 1994, almost 700,000 cubic metres was actually cut. This was at a time when the Australian-funded National Forest Resources Inventory recommended that the annual allowable cut be as low as 19,800 cubic metres in order to achieve long-term sustainability (Frazer 1997:63). As a result, this valuable economic and subsistence resource is likely to be exhausted in 10–15 years. The ongoing cost of this short-term gain will be paid for, however, by rural Solomon Islanders who will have to make do with depleted subsistence resources, a despoiled environment and, often, a legacy of social disruption. Similar problems are also likely to arise in Papua New Guinea and Vanuatu, as is shown by the number of logging licences issued in these countries (AIDAB 1994).

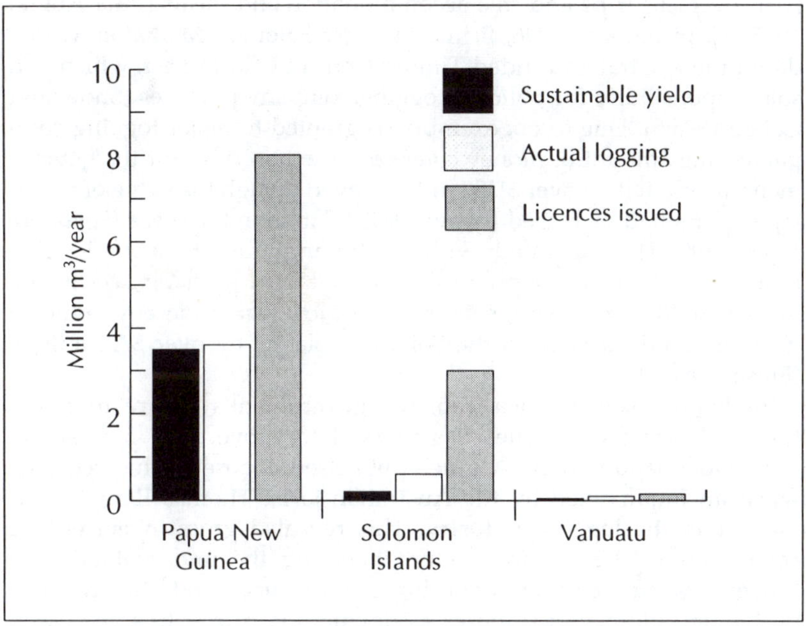

FIGURE 9.1 • RATES OF LOGGING IN MELANESIA

Source: AIDAB 1994: xvi.

In the Solomon Islands the unsustainable rate of logging has resulted largely from political decisions. Because of the importance of the logging industry to the national economy its resource needs have received priority over matters such as the interests of resource owners (Frazer 1997:40). While there is legislation which attempts to control logging, logging companies are not well policed in practice (Barlow and Winduo 1997:11). Compounding this problem is the fact that many government ministers have direct or indirect financial interests in logging activities. In 1993 and 1994 under the government of Francis Billy Hilly, a moratorium on the processing of new logging applications was declared and plans were made with the Australian government for a 'debt for nature' swap. Logging companies which failed to comply with Solomon Islands law were also suspended (*Times of PNG* 1994:4). When Hilly was ousted by Solomon Mamaloni, however, these positive initiatives were revoked. In 1995, seven government ministers went to court to face charges of accepting bribes from a Malaysian logging company (Rowell 1996:277). In addition to several million dollars in cash, the government ministers and senior officers were given cartons of beer, overseas trips and free accommodation and meals (Puia Angiki 1995a:1). In January 1996, Prime Minister Solomon Mamaloni closed down the Australian-funded Timber Control Unit Project, which had sole responsibility for policing logging company practices (Snow and Collee 1996:5). Due to tax exemptions granted to major logging companies, the amount of money collected as export duty for the government in 1995 fell by over $US3 million, even though the value of round log exports had increased by over $US4.7 million that year (*South Sea Digest* 1996:1). Frustrated with continuing unsustainable logging practices and the lack of political support, the Australian government, in 1996, withdrew its support for the forestry sector, thereby reducing its overall aid package to the Solomon Islands by over $A2 million (Fraser 1996:1).

In Papua New Guinea, too, the government's failure to police foreign logging companies has worked to subvert the interests of indigenous landowners. A much-publicised exposé of this occurred when an inquiry, led by the Australian jurist Thomas Barnett, was made into the logging industry. This revealed gross injustices and corruption in the logging sector, including the undervaluation of timber, transfer pricing, poor logging practices and the incorrect declaration of species in order to downgrade prices. In some cases, timber was undervalued by as much as 20 per cent and landowners were cheated accordingly. Barnett concluded that 'The share being received by landowners is ridiculously low' (Marshall 1990:178–9). The government was censured for poor enforcement of existing legislation and was reminded of the ecological and sociological disaster facing many rural communities which had allowed logging to commence on their land (Barnett 1989). There continue to be reports of under-reporting of export timber volumes as well as the undervaluation of timber prices as a way of reducing export duties and royalty payments (AusAID 1995:39). Furthermore, there are numerous unofficial reports of logging companies acting unethically in their attempts to ensure that local landowners sign logging agreements. Examples include 'treating clan leaders to airplane junkets to Port Moresby and the provision of cash hand-outs that rarely reflect the value of the timber rights purchased' (Lynch *et al.* 1995:103).

Despite policy moves by the government which favour foreign logging investors, the timber industry, as represented by the Forest Industries' Association (FIA), has continued to challenge the government for more support. The FIA has attempted to hold the government to ransom by saying that it will only cease exporting round logs and make greater efforts to develop a downstream timber processing industry, as government policies stipulate, if levies to be paid to landowners are relaxed (*The National* 1997). It is also pushing for greater incentives to be provided by the government, which already provides tax holidays, import duty exemptions on processing equipment and pioneer industry status to companies implementing downstream processing (Yadi 1997:23).

In Vanuatu, the government's position on logging has changed from one of supporting the interests of conservation and the sustainable utilisation of the forest resource to one which encourages large-scale logging. Vanuatu's Prime Minister, Maxime Carlot Korman, declared in 1994 that there would be a total ban on log exports and efforts to encourage companies to set up processing plants, stating that 'We will make the ban forever' (*Post Courier* 1994). The ban was approved as an Act of Parliament. This decision was repealed by the Council of Ministers in July 1997, however, and soon after five companies were given exclusive rights to cutting round logs.

Logging and Local Communities

When the European Union, a large aid donor to the Solomon Islands, criticised the government over the rapid logging of tropical rainforest, a government representative retaliated by saying that any person only had to fly over the Solomon Islands to see how green the country still was. There was, he maintained, no evidence of slaughtered forests and a naked landscape (Ueteri-Taasi 1996:7). While this may appear to be true due to the rapid revegetation so common in the tropics it cannot, to the trained eye, disguise the fact that many forests have been seriously depleted by logging. Large areas of secondary growth occur where species diversity has been reduced and vines and scrub with no useful function predominate. We need to understand what relatively undisturbed forests offer rural communities in Melanesia if we are to appreciate the often dramatic impact their destruction has had on people's lives and livelihoods.

Subsistence use of forests in Melanesia

The Solomon Islands, Vanuatu and Papua New Guinea are all countries where the majority of the people still live in dispersed rural settlements and depend on subsistence for their livelihoods. Subsistence primarily includes horticulture that is supplemented to varying degrees, according to the location, by fishing, hunting and gathering. People's survival thus depends on the integrity of the natural resource base. In all three countries land is communally owned by clans and although most people living in rural areas have a low monetary income, they are able to eat well and live fairly comfortably compared with many people in other developing countries because they can meet their basic needs from the natural resource base.

Changes, however, are taking place. Quite apart from the sudden and often traumatic changes brought about by logging, other more subtle changes are taking place as well. The situation that concerns many Solomon Islanders, for example, is the rapid increase of their population at the rate of 3.5 per cent per annum (Solomon Islands Government 1986). There is a fear that, in time, land resources will be insufficient to support an enlarged population. In many places land is starting to come under pressure. In a 1991 study on the island of Choiseul, Cassells (1992) found that garden fallow periods had been reduced to three or four years. This is insufficient to allow forest regeneration to occur and because forest litter no longer has time to accumulate, rejuvenation of soil fertility is unlikely. The distances villagers have to walk to new garden sites are also increasing because land close to the villages has already been taken up. Similarly, large trees such as *Gmelina moluccana*, which is suitable for building large canoes, have also been depleted in the vicinity of villages. If populations can be kept at the same level then subsistence production, as practised in the absence of logging, could continue to support rural villagers indefinitely. Population is likely to keep on increasing, however, so it is probable that even in the absence of logging, subsistence production will, at some point, cease to be sustainable (Cassells 1992:171–2). Logging, with its sudden depletion of the subsistence resource base, will only hasten this demise.

In one Solomon Islands community commercial logging led to a 15 per cent increase in average household income for a period of twelve to eighteen months (Frazer 1997:57). This may seem like a reasonable gain in income. In a 1991 comparison between the subsistence value of rainforest and logging royalties on the island of Choiseul, however, Cassells (1993) revealed that royalty payments for a logging trespass in the village of Kuku were worth only ten per cent of the subsistence value of the forest that had been destroyed through logging (Box 9.1).

Environmental impacts

The environmental impacts of large-scale logging of tropical rain-

BOX 9.1 • TROPICAL RAINFOREST: SUBSISTENCE VALUES COMPARED WITH LOGGING ROYALTIES

In a 1991 study to quantify the impact of tropical rainforest logging on rural village communities, Cassells (1993) spent some four and a half months recording and valuing the subsistence use of tropical rainforest. The field work was conducted in the villages of Nukiki and Kuku on the island of Choiseul in the Solomon Islands. The villagers were still heavily reliant on the subsistence use of tropical rainforest for their livelihood. Values calculated for these uses in Nukiki were quite substantial at $US3,195 per annum for the average-sized (seven-member) household.

Using information derived from Nukiki and applying it to the village of Kuku, where a logging operation had trespassed on village land, it was clear that the villagers had been severely disadvantaged when their forested land was logged. For example, one area of 41 hectares near Kuku village was calculated to have yielded 2,018 cubic metres in merchantable logs. The villagers were to be paid $US2.73 per cubic metre which would have given them a once-only royalty payment, to be shared amongst them, of $US5,520. Subsistence losses from the same area were reported to be 4 garden sites, 6 *ngali* and *sulu* nut trees, 21 betel nut trees, 346 sago palms and approximately 25 per cent of the villagers' other useful trees such as those used for house building, canoe making, medicine and food. This loss in subsistence production would be sustained over many years and was calculated to have a present value of $US53,682. The net loss suffered by the village as a whole was therefore $US48,161, or a substantial $US2,293 for each of the 21 households (Cassells 1993).

Note: All of the above rates in $US were converted from the Solomon Islands equivalents at the average exchange rate for 1994 of $SI 3.29 = $US1.00.

forests, especially where timber is clear-felled, are now well documented and widely recognised (Struhsaker 1997, Lamb 1990, Filer 1994). They include erosion of fragile rainforest soils, siltation or diversion of streams and rivers, loss of biodiversity, loss of soil fertility, pollution of lagoons and increased flooding. As noted by Baines (1989: 282):

> Logging liquidates a resource which may have served a lineage for many centuries, which harbours all of that line's historical links with the past, and which has traditionally been viewed as a resource borrowed from future generations.The logging of a landholding group's forests may be the most dramatic development impact they will experience.

Of particular concern are the implications these ecosystem changes have in terms of the welfare and livelihoods of local communities. In the Melanesian countries the majority of the people still live in rural areas and their lives are based around subsistence activities including horticulture, hunting and gathering. Thus their survival depends on the integrity of the natural resource base. Villagers in Bariki, Solomon Islands, have noted that since logging occurred in their area 15 years ago there has been an increase in pests that attack food gardens. The villagers consider that this is caused primarily by a reduction in bird numbers, the natural predators which, before logging, lived in the tall trees. Other villagers complained about a reduction in house-building and other construction material that had previously been readily obtainable from the forest. There was also an increase in malaria because ponding, which occurs in bulldozer tracks, allows more mosquitoes to breed (interviews, Western and Choiseul Provinces, March 1996). Collee (1995), who worked as a doctor in this area for several years, also noted that environmental damage in logging areas led to poor health among the population:

> Their fishing and gardens are destroyed, so we see malnourished children in the hospital. Their social structure is destroyed, so we see crimes of violence and venereal disease. Their water supply is destroyed, so we see skin infections and water-borne diseases. Their men become drunkards, their women turn to prostitution, their children buy cheap sugary drinks and rot their teeth. What the village gains in compensation is probably half a Korean executive's annual salary. What it loses is incalculable.

The social and cultural impacts of logging

As suggested in Collee's comment, in addition to the damage to the natural resource base, logging can also lead to widespread social decay. Fingelton (1994:20) argues that 'logging operations damage the very fabric of village society, leaving behind divided and demoralised communities'. In many respects the subsistence economy in Melanesia is in the process of being subsumed by the cash economy. Because the social norms associated with the two economies are often quite different, social dislocation is often symptomatic of this transition. This is thrown sharply into focus by logging. Well versed as they are in the economy of a subsistence culture, villagers are often ill-equipped to manage their affairs in the face of the somewhat predatory world of international business. Social disruption occurs with the monetisation of natural resources when seemingly large amounts of cash are offered to villagers for forest that hitherto had no cash value in their eyes. Divided in their approach on how to address the issues raised by this, splits and bitterness occur within these communities. Bewilderment and disillusionment are common sentiments in villages left in the wake of logging activities (Marshall 1990:180), a factor which may explain the increasing levels of stress and violence apparent in some households.

Disputes over land, the distribution of logging royalties, the conduct of logging company employees, increased alcohol consumption and the behaviour of village young people can divide families and villages, morally depleting these rural societies. Timber company officials must take some of the blame for encouraging dissent as they often circumvent traditional decision-making structures in their efforts to secure logging deals. By failing to allow extended group discussions, through which all landowners would have the chance to express their views on logging, they establish the grounds for conflict which occurs later within these communities (Marshall 1990:179).

In general, logging has improved the economic wealth of communities. This is a temporary phenomenon, however, and not all members of the community have access to royalty money. This can also lead to conflict within the community. Many Solomon Islands women who had lived in logging areas felt that where they had experienced economic benefits from logging, these were short-term and somewhat superficial. For example, money earned in the form of royalties was predominantly under the control of men and was often used to purchase consumables such as beer and radio-cassette players. As one woman noted, 'Royalty money is almost invariably all spent by the time the trees are gone' (interview, Sengighae village, March 1996). Rarely were funds spent on things which could benefit whole families, such as children's education. Women living in the logging camp of Moli, for example, listed toilet facilities among their three most immediate needs. They said, however, that while there were community development workers who could provide them with skills and knowledge on how to build toilets, there was no money to buy the materials. What money was being earned by their husbands was simply not being made available for such basic development activities (interview, Sengighae Village, March 1996).[1]

[1] All references to interviews in this chapter derive from fieldwork undertaken by Regina Scheyvens in Western and Choiseul Provinces in the Solomon Islands in March–April 1996.

Similarly, villagers do not suffer equally the negative impacts of logging. If logging destroys garden sites, food trees, firewood supplies, house- and canoe-building trees as well as customary medicine plants, for example, the loss incurred by the villagers can be very substantial. Often such losses are only partial and may not be spread evenly throughout the community (see Box 9.2).

BOX 9.2 • WEZIP ALOLOUM'S STORY

One of the most poignant tales of the harm forest destruction can cause was told by Wezip Aloloum, a villager from Joboto in the Madang District of Papua New Guinea (Aloloum 1982:217–20):

'I have strong feelings on this matter. Jant (logging company) came and cut down the trees and spoiled the spirits of my ancestors: they spoiled the places where my forefathers planted their gardens and the place where they took clay for pots. They spoiled these things but they did not help me properly in return with money or something. I asked them but they did not help me. Therefore I am sad and angry with the company and the Office of the Forests.

This is what happened to my land which the company logged. The machine dug up the ground and now the soil has lost its goodness. It's like the soil in Port Moresby now. If I plant banana, sweet potato or taro, they will not grow well. The leaves will be yellow. When we tried to make gardens in the cleared area it was of no use.

The main thing I am worried about is my clay pit for making pots. The spirit woman who looked after the pots and cooked the food in them has gone away.... That clay pit was like money to my ancestors. They ate pigs from their friends because of them.... It is now five years since the company cut the timber and spoiled this area. I have been watching but the clay has not returned.

Another problem is wildlife. Where they have cut down the forest there is no wildlife because there is no food for them. Even where the forest has not been cut down, there is still not very much wildlife. There are no goura pigeon, cassowary bird, bird of paradise and wallaby left. I would not like my grandchildren or their grandchildren after them to be short of wildlife, and to say: Father did not think of those of us who were coming later. He thought only of himself, and finished off all the birds and the animals, so that now I have none.'

Women often are hit particularly hard by the social impacts of logging. Many men, however, find that they are in a good position to enhance their status through employment opportunities or through the royalty payments they receive. Men have tended to take the lead in negotiations with logging companies, even in matrilineal societies where traditionally women's opinions would have been sought. Consequently women often feel frustrated that they are not consulted regarding logging agreements. A woman from Guadalcanal, Solomon Islands, complained that although women did attend meetings, men did not let them air their views: 'We cannot express what we feel about logging or any issues which affect our environment and our children's future. Women should not be treated as second grade copra' (Solomon Islands Development Trust 1991:11). Women's lack of influence over decisions and their consequent resignation is also reflected in the words of women of Poroporo village, where logging was occurring at the time they were interviewed: 'We do not want logging on our land, but we do not want arguments either, so we just let it be' (interview, Sengighae village, March 1996).

Women's social status, meanwhile, is further eroded as their work in subsistence production is not as highly regarded as the ability to earn cash. In many respects the dominance of men in planning and decision-making for the household as well as the clan, the village community and society as a whole, has become more entrenched. It is not surprising, therefore, that the great majority of women living in areas of logging feel unhappy with the changes going on around them. Of 51 women present at a regional women's group meeting on Choiseul in the Solomon Islands, many of whom had seen the effects of logging in their communities or in neighbouring areas, 50 said they were very unhappy with logging companies and their practices (interviews, March 1996).

The sexual harassment of women living in logging camps has also been a problem. When the case of a logging company official sexually harassing the wife of a company employee was made public in 1995, the company's manager threatened to sack union members and their colleagues who had reported the issue (Puia Angiki 1995b:2).

Do the Economic Benefits of Logging Justify the Costs?

As mentioned above, monetary rewards, especially royalty payments, are perhaps the key reason for local landowners allowing logging to go ahead on their land. Despite their attraction, the royalty payments made to landowners are actually very poor when compared with the value of logs and also the revenue collected by the government

(AusAID 1995:40; see Table 9.2). In Papua New Guinea, government export tax per cubic metre increased from $US5.02 in 1990 to $US42.56 in 1996, with actual export taxes reaching $US118 million in 1996, compared with only $US11 million in 1990 (*The National* 1997).[2] Over the same period, royalties for landowners increased from a net of only $US2.71 per cubic metre to $US7.22 per cubic metre. These, however, were the official figures. In practice, royalty payments of $US3-4 were more common in 1996 (Robie 1996).

TABLE 9.2 • BREAKDOWN OF FOB PRICE FROM NATURAL FOREST LOGGING, 1997

	Value of logs ($US/m³)
Average log price	118
Export duty	42
Royalty	14
Production cost	56
Earnings before interest and tax	6

Source: Solomon Star (1997), Wooff 1997

In Papua New Guinea, the logging industry continues to try to avoid, or keep to a minimum, royalty payments to landowners. Under pressure from the World Bank, the Papua New Guinea Minister for Finance, Chris Haiveta, introduced a graduated log export tax and royalty payment system in 1995. While the new export tax was implemented immediately, bringing direct benefits to the government, most logging companies simply refused to increase royalty payments to landowners. It was only in June 1996, when the World Bank withheld loans, that the Prime Minister finally forced the Minister for Forests, who had strong logging industry connections, to sign statutory notices which would increase royalty payments. In these notices, however, it was stated that landholders would only get $US7.60 per cubic metre, as it was felt that landowners were not sufficiently responsible to deal with large sums of money. Another $US9.88 per cubic metre would be designated as a project development levy, which could be paid in cash or through infrastructural development after an assessment was done

[2] These figures are based on conversions from Papua New Guinea kina. The average exchange rate in 1996 was K1.32 = $US 1.00.

of a logging project (Brunton 1997). In July 1996, however, the FIA threatened that logging companies would simply pull out of Papua New Guinea if they were forced to pay the extra $US7.60 per cubic metre to landowners (Robie 1996). By the beginning of 1997, only a minority of landholders had received the $US7.60 per cubic metre, and no project assessments had been done, meaning that no project development levies were paid in the previous year (Brunton 1997). Meanwhile, logging company officials continued to complain about the increased taxes and royalties, claiming that such payments have prevented them from spending money on community programmes, training and apprenticeships (*The National* 1997).

Another assumed economic benefit of logging is employment. Unlike mining, however, logging companies often only stay in an area for short periods of time. Consequently they rarely offer secure, long-term employment. Furthermore, supervisory or management jobs are concentrated in the hands of foreigners. Few women gain employment from logging, except those who have been recruited to clear and replant the land after it is logged over. Women living in Choiseul said, rather ironically, that they have no say about whether or not logging goes ahead and yet somehow they still end up cleaning up the mess (interview, March 1996).

Reaction to Large-Scale Logging

In the face of the devastating environmental impacts of logging, consequent social disruption and inadequate economic compensation, local communities have started to fight back against logging companies. Thanks largely to the work of several NGOs, villagers in Melanesia are becoming more politically aware and are learning how to respond appropriately to development initiatives which they feel run contrary to their interests:

- NGOs in Papua New Guinea picketed the Forest Authority Headquarters and demanded that the government investigate the timber industry after timber concessions were granted, in breach of environmental laws, in areas with a high biodiversity value (Joku 1997).

- Papua New Guinea landowners started their own lobby group, the Individual and Community Rights Action Forum. In 1996, to publicise the government's failure to implement the new landowner royalty system, this lobby group placed a full-page advertisement in a national newspaper stating, 'All forest landholders – you are losing millions of *kina*!' (Robie 1996).

- The Papua New Guinea Forest Owners' Association, angry at their failure to gain representation on the National Forest Board, threatened to destroy logging company equipment if this situation was not rectified. As noted by their president, Dominic Evera, 'Landowners have not been actively participating in the resource development for the past 15 years. We feel that we are just bystanders in our own land' (Nicholas 1997).

Considerable awareness raising has also been undertaken at the village level. The Solomon Islands Development Trust (SIDT), for example, tours villages making people aware of the long-term effects of unsustainable logging practices, among other issues. SIDT are supported by two theatre groups, one male and one female, which give powerful performances about the long-term social and environmental impacts of logging. One example is a play about the underhand methods company representatives often use to get logging agreements signed and the way in which men of communities typically exclude women from negotiations about such agreements. In Vanuatu, *One Smol Bag* put on similar performances around the country and there are also theatre groups operating in Papua New Guinea and Fiji (Barlow and Winduo 1997:12–13).

As a result of such awareness raising, rural people are more likely to react negatively to logging companies. In the Solomon Islands, protests have occurred publicly in the streets and, more covertly, through the destruction of logging company machinery and buildings (Frazer 1997:54). Resistance such as this from local landowners can paralyse company operations and have considerable economic costs. The Mamaloni government, however, has actively tried to suppress evidence of landowner dissent. In Pavuvu, for example, the government sent paramilitary forces to stop local protesters from interfering with logging operations (Frazer 1997:66). In Vanuatu the legal system has come out in support of the rights of landowners. A family which burned a bulldozer, after a logging company ignored a court injunction not to log their land, was acquitted of the charge of property damage. Chief Nalipo, head of the family concerned, said that the court decision was a victory for environmental conservation: 'This is not a case about money, rather it is about human and environmental rights and should set an example for those who want to exploit the people and resources of Vanuatu' (*The Trading Post* 1996).

The Search for Alternatives

The need to find alternative ways in which people can earn cash without destroying their natural environment has begun to receive greater attention from development agencies, church groups and aid donors in Melanesia in recent years. Various sustainable development initiatives have been tried and include ecotourism, butterfly farming, handicraft production,[3] plantation forestry, agroforestry, furniture manufacture, the marketing of sustainably produced timber and the harvesting of non-timber forest products (NTFPs) including nuts, aromatic oils, tan and orchids (Parnwell and Taylor 1996:269, Saulei and Aruga 1994). In this section some of the alternatives to large-scale logging are considered.

Donors need to support local communities by recognising the need to move beyond preservation of natural resources to supporting livelihood options (Grynberg 1994:12). In an interesting initiative, the Australian government aid agency, AusAID, has supported a project in Papua New Guinea which promotes natural regeneration of forests in areas where selective logging has occurred. AusAID pays local communities to select seedlings of useful commercial and subsistence species of trees, transplant them into gaps in the forest where necessary, and tend to them and clear vines and undesirable species from the demonstration plots. In addition to improving the income of villagers, this project will help to conserve the biodiversity of the forests and increase the number and quality of species with high subsistence or commercial value which will be available in the future (AusAID 1997:13–15).

Despite evidence of corruption and fickle support for sustainable development objectives with regard to the forestry sector in the past, Melanesian governments should not be regarded as incapable of supporting sustainable forestry. In 1995 the government of Vanuatu demonstrated its support for the conservation of tropical forests by signing a lease agreement which guaranteed traditional owners in part of Erromango Island payment in exchange for establishment of a reserve on their land. The reserve will protect the *kauri*, a prized tree species which was previously under threat from logging company operations in the area. Significantly, the government acknowledged the livelihood needs of the people by allowing activities such as subsistence agriculture and the collection of firewood and medicinal plants to continue within the protected area. The lease agreement pays the people slightly less than would logging companies; under this initiative,

[3] The New Zealand government is sponsoring a programme in the Solomon Islands which builds on a traditional skill in carving. Villagers are making paper out of plant fibres and then printing designs on the paper with intricately designed wood blocks. This is providing a reasonable cash income to those involved (see Box 5.1).

however, their subsistence livelihood needs are secure (Decloitre 1995: 28).

Hope for further change has also come by way of international organisations which have made efforts to support sustainable development initiatives. For example, in May 1997, after months of consultation with landowners, NGOs and government officials, the UNDP joined forces with The Nature Conservancy and the Department of Environment and Conservation in Papua New Guinea to establish a conservation trust fund for the country (Tobia 1997). Its aim will be to provide revenue streams for conservation rather than providing one-off project grants which cannot sustain a project in the long term. With the emergence of such new initiatives which seek to provide viable income-generating alternatives to landowners, it is going to be increasingly difficult for logging companies to convince landowners that logging will be good for them, especially when coupled with the awareness-raising work being carried out by NGOs in the region. Lynch *et al.* (1995:108), however, maintain that local communities still need more information about the nature of their property rights before they are pushed by the state, or commercial enterprises, to make decisions about potential uses of their land.

Political will is probably the most crucial factor necessary if sustainable forestry policies are to be enforced. The sustainable utilisation of forests should be seen as part of a broader development issue, that of sustainable rural development, which impacts directly on the lives of three-quarters of the population of Vanuatu, Papua New Guinea and the Solomon Islands. The forestry sector, then, is vital to overall strategies for sustainable rural development and, as such, it should be central to any plans for improving the livelihood options of rural communities in the Pacific.

CHAPTER 10

Mining in Papua New Guinea

LEONARD LAGISA AND REGINA SCHEYVENS

The Lure of Mining

Mining is an important industry for four Pacific Island countries in particular: Nauru (phosphate), Fiji (gold), New Caledonia (nickel) and Papua New Guinea (copper and gold). To the governments of these countries, the presence of significant quantities of minerals means there will be more investment, greater earnings of foreign exchange and a likely improvement in the country's economic standing, thus mining receives high priority on their development agendas (Connell and Howitt 1991:2). Countries faced with large trade deficits, rising national debts and heavy aid dependence feel compelled to exploit their rich mineral wealth (Emberson-Bain 1994:91), especially when minerals can account for up to 80 per cent of export earnings, as was the case with New Caledonia in the 1980s (Howard 1988:92).

Like all major resource development projects, however, mining projects cause extensive social and environmental disruption. Mining is an inherently unsustainable activity reliant, as it is, on extraction of non-renewable resources. If inter-generational equity is part of one's definition of sustainable development, it is difficult to see how mining could be seen as contributing to this development.

This chapter examines mining in Papua New Guinea from the point of view of its impacts on the lives and livelihoods of local communities. The brunt of the negative impacts which occur are invariably felt most by the local communities whose land is alienated and whose traditional resources are destroyed or degraded, while the benefits are spread more widely throughout a country and internationally (Hughes and Sullivan (1992:1).

The Mining Industry in Papua New Guinea

Economic rationale

Prior to the production of Papua New Guinea's first large-scale mining project in 1972, the colonial administration relied extensively on aid from Australia and other metropolitan countries for its development purposes. According to Auty (1993:204), Australian aid provided more than two-fifths of the government revenue and almost half of Papua New Guinea's foreign exchange in the early 1970s. Papua New Guinea became independent in September 1975, and a key aspect of the government's strategy to overcome excessive reliance on Australia was to develop the country's rich mineral resources, the discovery of which was seen as an economic blessing which could encourage the young country to progress and prosper. The main aim of the Papua New Guinea government in encouraging mining projects in the early stages of independence was the rapid raising of revenue which could then be used to achieve more desirable development aims (Jackson 1991:19).

The first of the large-scale mining projects was Bougainville copper mine at Panguna, which commenced operations in 1972. This was followed by Ok Tedi copper mine in 1981, Misima gold mine in 1989, Porgera gold mine in 1990 and the Lihir gold mine in 1997. The government is also in the process of developing approximately 12 other significant mineral deposits (Hughes and Sullivan 1992). Figure 10.1 shows past, present and potential future mine sites in Papua New Guinea.

Consequently, the mining industry has played a very significant role in Papua New Guinea's economic development in the last two decades. Papua New Guinea has a rich and diversified mineral resource base, and has become a significant producer of valuable metals in international terms. The development of the Bougainville copper mine, one of the largest open pit copper mines in the world, led the Papua New Guinea economy to grow rapidly in the 1970s with a GDP average growth of more than 8 per cent per year (Auty 1993:204). In the period 1973–4, the Bougainville mine alone was responsible for 64 per cent of the value of Papua New Guinea's export earnings (Howard 1988:109). In addition, the Papua New Guinea government was paid K466 million in taxes (excluding income tax from employees and import duties) from Bougainville Copper Limited's gross surplus of K980 million in the period 1972–85 (Jackson 1991:19).[1] Despite the closure of

[1] The kina (K) is the unit of currency used in Papua New Guinea. Its value has fluctuated markedly in recent years and underwent major devaluation. In June 1998 one kina was equivalent to $A 0.74 or $US0.48.

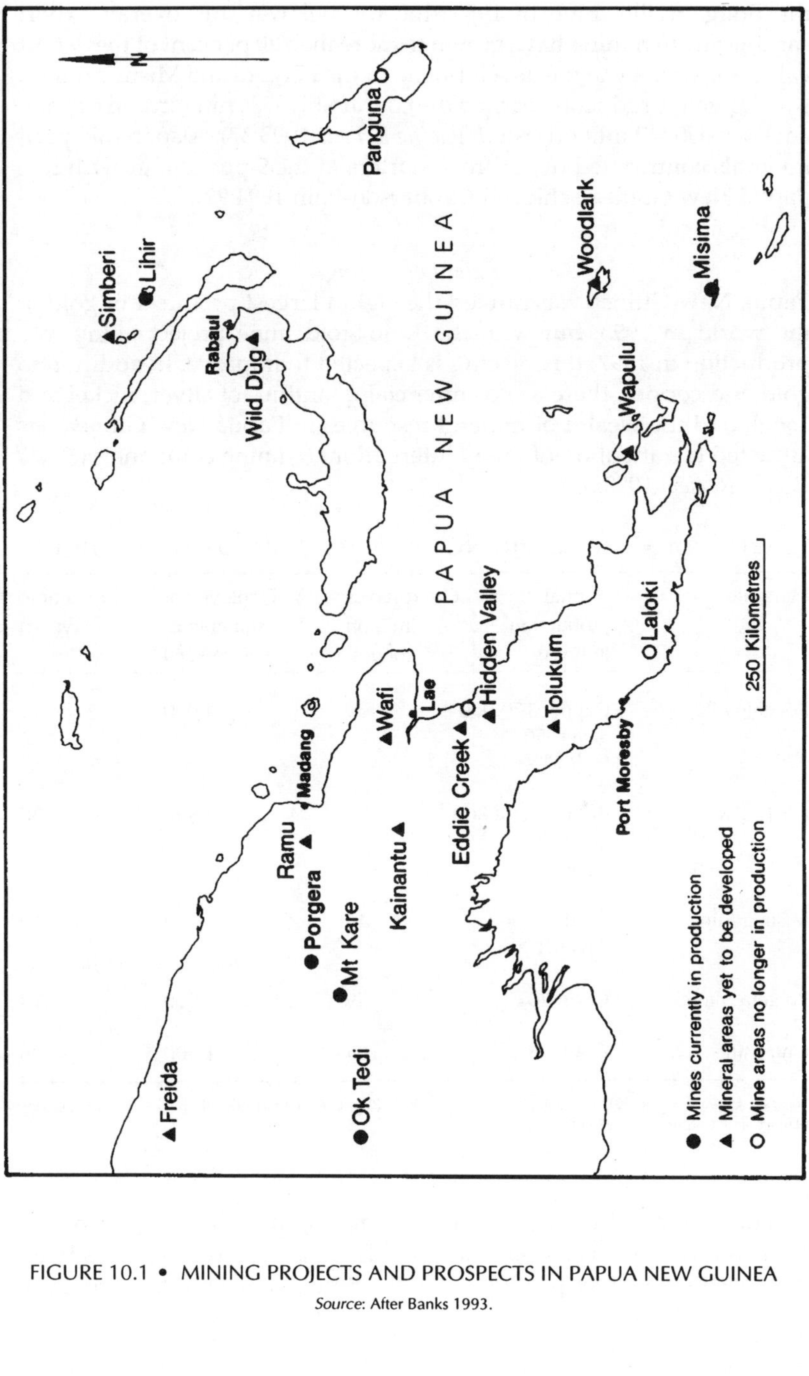

FIGURE 10.1 • MINING PROJECTS AND PROSPECTS IN PAPUA NEW GUINEA

Source: After Banks 1993.

the Bougainville mine in 1989 due to civil war, the overall export earnings from mining have grown to more than 70 per cent of the export value, due largely to the development of the Porgera and Misima mines. By 1991 gold production earned the country $US384 million and copper, another $US349 million (*South Pacific Review* 1993:37). Also in this year, minerals contributed over three-quarters of the 9 per cent growth rate Papua New Guinea achieved (Emberson-Bain 1994:92).

Extent of mining

Papua New Guinea was ranked the eighth largest producer of gold in the world in 1993, but with the Lihir gold mine project going into production in 1997, this placing is expected to improve. In addition to gold and copper, there are commercial quantities of silver, nickel and cobalt and the wealth of mineral resources in Papua New Guinea has attracted the attention of many international mining companies (*South Pacific Review* 1993:37).

TABLE 10.1 • MAJOR MINING PROJECTS IN PAPUA NEW GUINEA

Mine site	Annual production (tonnes)	Ore reserves (million tonnes)	Employment (number of workers)	Lifetime (years)
Bougainville Mine	Copper:170,000 Silver: 50 Gold: 15	900	4,000	30
Ok Tedi Mine	Copper: 200,000 Gold: 8 Silver: 13	137	2,500	30
Misima Mine	Gold: 6 Silver: 100	46	350	10
Porgera Mine	Gold: 26	59	900	18
Lihir Mine	Gold: 18	104	1,300	36

Sources: Howard (1988:98), Quodling (1991:4–5), *South Pacific Review* (1993:39), Banks (1996:223), Lihir Management Corporation (1995a:61).

The lifetime of the five large-scale mining projects ranges from 10 years for Misima to 36 years for Lihir (Table 10.1). There is a possibility of 13 years of further production at the Bougainville mine if a solution is found to the conflict on the island.[2] Employment in the mining projects ranges from 350 workers for Misima to the 4,000 workers who were employed at the Bougainville mine. Ok Tedi currently has the highest ore reserve with 137 million tonnes, mostly containing copper, while Lihir has 104 million tonnes, mostly containing gold (Banks 1996: 223).

Why local communities have allowed mining to progress

Governments and foreign investors are not the only proponents of mining development. For a number of reasons, local communities often welcome mining, especially in its initial stages. Mining projects in Papua New Guinea are located in what are considered some of the least developed, most remote areas of the country: the Ok Tedi mine and Bougainville mines are in rugged mountains, while the Misima and Lihir mines are located on small, remote islands. Thus many people in these areas where infrastructural development and economic opportunities were minimal were actually happy in the first instance with the prospect of mining development on their lands. They hoped it would bring them employment and business opportunities as well as roads, clinics and schools, services neither the provincial nor the national governments of Papua New Guinea had been able to provide adequately (Jackson cited in Banks 1993:321, Connell and Howitt 1991:1, Howard 1988).

Of the positive impacts of mining discussed, however, many provide only short-term benefits to local people. Over time, the enthusiasm of local people tends to wane and may turn into overt hostility towards the mining company as they start to experience disruption to their lives during operations and to perceive the long-term losses which they must live with when mining operations cease (Hughes and Sullivan 1992).

Negative Impacts of Mining

The physical development of large mining projects can occur very quickly and require rapid adjustment of the local community. There are often negative consequences of this change (Stayner 1992:5),

[2] In late 1997 an agreement was signed by members of the Papua New Guinea government, the interim government on Bougainville and the Bougainville Revolutionary Army at Burnham military camp, New Zealand, which promised to work towards a resolution of the conflict on Bougainville. Even if this positive step towards peace on the island becomes a reality, it is considered unlikely that future mining will proceed unless the needs and interests of local Bougainvilleans are respected.

particularly because most mining projects have not been successfully linked to the development goals of local groups of people (Connell and Howitt 1991:1). Commonly local people are marginalised and disempowered by mining developments. Barrow (1995) and Barbier (1987) suggest that sustainable development involves an overlapping of social, economic and biological (the physical environment) system goals, and each of these requires examination.

Impacts on the physical environment

Sustainable development goals relating to the physical environment include preservation of genetic diversity and ensuring biological productivity. The impacts of mining in terms of jeopardising sustainability goals are perhaps most easily apparent with respect to the physical environment because of the dramatic transformation of the landscape in a short period of time.

A significant factor about indigenous people in most developing countries is their attachment to land. For ToVagira (1990:6), 'Land for indigenous people plays a role in defining their selfhood and community, their being and belonging, their identity and identification.' In addition, land provides people with their basic livelihoods. They depend greatly on the natural environment, as did their ancestors before them, to provide food, materials for building, tools, weapons, artefacts and traditional medicines. The impact of mining on the natural environment thus becomes one of the most important concerns for local communities in Papua New Guinea. As expressed through the words of three Bougainvillean students during the early stages of mining in Bougainville,

> Land is our life. Land is our physical life – food and sustenance. Land is our social life; it is our marriage; it is status; it is security; it is politics; in fact it is our only world. When you (the administration) take our land, you take away the very heart of our existence. We have little or no experience of social survival detached from the land. For us to be completely landless is a nightmare which no dollar in the pocket or dollar in the Bank will allay (Dove *et al.*, cited in Connell 1991a:60).

The sudden changes wrought by mining developments on traditional land are usually very difficult for local communities to cope with, especially when the land is acquired for open cast mining purposes which cause massive destruction. The environmental impacts of large-scale mines include the direct loss of land (including the mine site, township and housing), land degradation, destruction of natural vegetation and ecological habitats, the loss of hunting grounds, the loss of water supplies and fishing areas due to contamination of rivers and sea, and noise and dust pollution (Banks 1993:322, Hyndman 1991:79). In Ok Tedi, for example, drinking water was contaminated by cyanide and in both Bougainville and Ok Tedi, tailings from the mines caused much destruction of aquatic life in the Jaba and Fly rivers, respectively, thus destroying important sources of food for the locals living along the rivers. In other areas, land shortages have led to shorter fallow times and consequent over-cropping. Population pressure has seen the depletion of wild animal populations traditionally used for food, including pigs, possums and flying foxes (Hyndman 1994, Connell 1991a:58).

Impacts on economic sustainability

From a sustainable development perspective, it is not the amount of economic growth promoted *per se*, but the way in which money is shared and spent which should be of critical concern. Clearly intra-generational equity, the sharing of economic benefits among people in the affected communities, and inter-generational equity, the goal of ensuring that future generations will continue to benefit from the economic gains from mining, are important considerations. So too is the satisfaction of basic needs and the reduction of poverty (Barbier 1987).

Rapid increases in monetisation of the local economy have occurred throughout major mining areas in Papua New Guinea through payments for employment, compensation, royalties and business opportunities created (Connell and Howitt 1991, Banks 1996). While many see this as positive in the short term, in the long term it undermines the largely self-reliant existence of local people who become increasingly dependent upon the mining company. In addition, 'the limited, unequal and discriminatory nature of the distribution of these benefits at the local level (with respect to workers, landowners and women) is a conspicuous anomaly' (Emberson-Bain 1994:104).

The exposure of locals, especially young people, to the monetary world and to a wide variety of Western goods sold in shops at mining townships, has undermined traditional lifestyles and customs. Why weave baskets when nylon or plastic bags are readily available, or why go fishing when the shelves of stores are stocked with canned tuna? Thus the desire for money has led local men, in particular, to disregard many activities which previously provided their livelihoods, including cash cropping and subsistence agriculture. As Banks (1993:322) notes:

> An economic dependence on the mining company can ... occur, with a corresponding neglect of other avenues of development. The much wider incorporation of the local population into the cash economy

can result in the loss of the subsistence component of the pre-existing economy.

In addition, when people are handed large sums of money they are not gaining a good grounding in the operations of the monetary economy. Money is given to them, rather than being earned, thus its value may not be appreciated.

While employment gained by local people at mine sites is generally seen as a benefit, it consists almost exclusively of unskilled jobs in which they earn low wages in comparison with others and endure difficult working conditions. New forms of social stratification have emerged at mining sites whereby the locals rarely gain supervisory and managerial positions which are typically reserved for the expatriate workers. Many protests resulted in Ok Tedi as local men complained about white men wearing white helmets to clearly indicate their authority while the unskilled Wopkaimin (the local indigenous people) workers wore yellow helmets (Hyndman 1991:85).

Multinational mining companies and the government have dominated in terms of gaining revenue from the mine. By virtue of their shareholdings mining companies usually make the biggest gains from mining profits (Table 10.2). In addition, a large percentage of the value

TABLE 10.2 • MINING OPERATIONS IN PAPUA NEW GUINEA: MAJOR SHAREHOLDERS

Name of Mine	Major shareholders	Percentage
Bougainville Copper Limited	CRA	53.6%
	PNG Government	19.1%
	Public	27.7%
Ok Tedi Copper Mine	BHP	30%
	AMOCO	30%
	PNG Government	20%
	Others	20%
Porgera Gold Mine	Placer	30%
	Highlands Gold	30%
	Renison	30%
	PNG Government	10%
Misima Gold Mine	Placer	80%
	PNG Government	20%

Source: Banks 1993

of extracted minerals leaves the country by way of a company's capital repayments, freight and transport costs, remitted wages, purchases of imported goods or services, or dividends. Most of the remaining earnings go to the government. In the case of Bougainville, when landowners' demands for a better share of the profits and other ancillary benefits were ignored by the national government and the mining company, civil unrest broke out and eventually all mining operations ceased. Local discontent was fuelled by the fact that compensation was unevenly distributed and that there was inequality in the distribution of employment and wages (Howard 1988:100, Hyndman 1991:86).

Although local people in Papua New Guinea have had better representation in decision making on mining operations than have other communities in Third World countries, there have still been inequities in terms of representation (Howard 1988, Filer 1995). Many traditional leaders have been sidelined from mining negotiations by more worldly and better educated younger men, and women are rarely represented in negotiations. While the younger men may be able to campaign successfully for greater compensation and economic benefits from the mining company, there is no guarantee that such benefits will be received by the majority of their people.

Impacts on social sustainability

With regard to mining developments it is important to consider whether all groups of people within a society have shared in the supposed benefits of the project, and to ensure that no group has had to bear the bulk of any negative consequences which may occur.

Because mining developments in Papua New Guinea have been located in remote and relatively underdeveloped areas, the associated social changes are always dramatic and often very destructive:

> Social impacts are often the most devastating, leading to what Filer ... described as the process of 'social disintegration' in the local communities. Certain processes internal to the local community contribute to mining 'time-bombs' – the self-destruction of local communities. These processes include the delineation of traditional communally held land for the purpose of mining leases, the uneven distribution of mining royalties within local communities, the subsequent stratification of the local population, and the problems associated with inheritance and succession within these communities (Banks 1993:322).

The social changes that commonly emerge from mining developments arise from an increase in the population of the area, greater social disorder, loss of power by traditional leaders, vandalism and criminal activities, and an unequal distribution of cash and other benefits of the mine (Jackson 1991, Gerritsen and MacIntyre 1991, Connell 1991a and Emberson-Bain 1994). Such changes are of great concern to many local people in mining areas and this usually leads to infighting as well as disputes between them and mining companies.

Dramatic increases in the population of mining areas occur when migrant workers, including expatriates and both skilled and unskilled workers from within the country, come looking for employment. In addition, locals living within the mining areas have been attracted towards the mining township thinking that they will find jobs; they abandon their villages and end up settling in squatter settlements, sometimes on indigenous land.

The presence of so many outsiders threatens local cultures, lifestyles and languages. The influx of mine workers, especially young single men, tends to result in the growth of prostitution, alcohol abuse and gambling (Banks 1993:323). Hyndman (1991:85) suggests that prostitution becomes more common as women's sexuality is alienated from themselves and controlled by men. Sexual harassment and rape have also reportedly increased in communities near mining areas (Hyndman 1994:117).

Many local people find it extremely difficult to cope with the combination of the loss of land, the entrenchment of a monetary economy and population change in mining areas. In this context, social disorder increases and acts of violence, both public and private, become more common. Frequent clashes between young local men and migrant workers have occurred at mine sites. Local elders have found themselves unable to settle these disputes because they no longer have the power and authority they once had (Connell and Howitt 1991). In the words of a prominent Bougainvillean, Leo Hannett:

> Our once-peaceful, non-violent living is now forever shattered: we are constantly harried by day and haunted by night with continual acts of violence in our midst. Where we once walked with our heads high, now we move around with our heads hanging low ... never quite knowing what to expect from these outsiders, heartless outsiders with their heartless machine slowly eating out like a cancerous growth the soul of our community; degenerating, humiliating, and dehumanising us with their 'development' at our expense. We are now made strangers in our own land (cited in Connell 1991a:60).

The negative social impacts of mining development that have been discussed 'underscore the depressing reality that mining by large-scale transnational capital, commonly supported by national political elites, is arguably proving to be one of the most destructive and violent forms of Western-style development' (Emberson-Bain 1994:56). While this statement is true for most of the indigenous people in mining areas of developing countries, the situation is worse for indigenous women.

Impacts of Mining on Women: The Case of Lihir

While there have been numerous studies on the impacts of mining in general, rarely have studies examined the impact of mining on indigenous women, even in cases in which their land provides the resource (Connell and Howitt 1991:2). In some Pacific Island communities, women were never consulted in the process of decision making and planning of a mine, even though they traditionally held ownership or usufruct rights to the land (Emberson-Bain 1994:49). When women's voices are absent from the outset, it is perhaps not surprising that many mining projects have led to what Bonnell (1994:162) describes as a decline in women's economic and social status relative to that of men. In examining the Lihir mining development, issues of the impacts on women's economic, social and political lives will be considered.

Mining in Lihir[3]

The Lihir gold mine, run by Lihir Management Company Pty Limited (LMC), is heavily supported by the Papua New Guinea government, which is keen to promote new mineral developments which promise to make up for the loss of revenue experienced following the closure of the Bougainville mine. One of four large-scale mines operating in Papua New Guinea, when production reaches its peak the Lihir mine will be the world's largest gold mine outside South Africa. The projected life of the project is 36 years, in which 226,000 ounces of gold is forecast to be produced yearly (Lihir Management Corporation 1995b:5). Ore will be extracted mainly from open pit mining in Luise Caldera.

Within Papua New Guinea, the Lihir island group is particularly isolated, lying to the north of New Ireland (Figure 10.1). It also has a small population of just over 8,000 people. Thus prior to the mining development it was very difficult for Lihirians to get involved in economic activities such as commercial agriculture and small-scale business projects. Government services to this part of the country were

[3] Leonard Lagisa carried out fieldwork at the Lihir mine site in February–April, 1996. All quotes in this chapter from Lihirians are translated from Tok Pisin (Papua New Guinea pidgin).

few and infrastructural development was poor. Until two or three years ago, therefore, the lives of most Lihirians were based on subsistence food production, a little cash cropping, hunting, fishing and cultural events. Traditional customs played a very influential role with regard to social structures and norms (Lagisa 1997).

As in most societies in Papua New Guinea, land is the most important asset for the people of Lihir. One elderly man explained the Lihirian's depth of feeling about the importance of land: 'Land is life and life is land. Without land a person is nobody' (interview, Lihir, April 1996). Although land is passed through the women's line in Lihir and children belong to the mother's *tumbawin* (clan), custom does not allow women to make decisions over land (Filer and Jackson 1989:48).

After several years of negotiations, an agreement was reached by representatives of Lihirian landowners which allowed mining development to progress. An Integrated Benefits Package, signed on 26 April, 1995, guaranteed Lihirians considerable financial compensation for alienation of land, damage to plants, and pollution of the air and waterways which would occur. In addition, landowners were granted relatively generous lease and royalty payments, and were provided with increased employment and business opportunities. Many men formed contractor companies which service LMC. It is generally agreed that, in economic terms at least, the Lihirian negotiators brokered a very good deal which was superior to deals struck at other mine sites in Papua New Guinea (Filer 1995:67).

LMC also established a Community Relations Office in order to promote social development in Lihir. This office has responsibility for the following: administering education scholarships and providing funding for local schools; improving health services throughout Lihir; providing better water supply systems and good housing to those in the directly affected areas; offering assistance to those who have been relocated; and running community development projects, with a particular mandate to assist women and youth.

The signing of the Integrated Benefits Package marked the beginning of rapid on-site construction and infrastructural development on Niolam island, the main island of the Lihir group. Main features of the construction phase of the Lihir development included: the relocation of some villages; building of a road around the island; a new port and an airport with the capacity to take international flights; the construction of camps which provide sleeping and eating facilities for over 1,000 mine workers from outside Lihir; and earthworks and building construction both at the mine site and the site of the new township where company offices have been built. Thus, although the Lihir gold mine only began production in June 1997, much disruption to the lives of Lihirians had already taken place by this time. A summary of some of the positive and negative impacts of the mining development, to be elaborated upon below, is provided in Table 10.3.

TABLE 10.3 • IMPACTS OF MINING DEVELOPMENT ON VILLAGERS IN LIHIR

Positive Impacts	Negative Impacts
• Improved education and health services • Improved transportation and communication networks • Increased business opportunities • Good employment opportunities and more money in pocket • Training opportunities and skills gained from work experience • Houses made of permanent materials (DA) • Better water supplies and sanitation facilities (DA) • Good compensation payments/royalty deals (DA)	• Social disorder • Increased alcohol consumption and drunkenness • Misuse of family money by adult males • Increased domestic violence • Increased pregnancy of young Lihirian women outside of marriage • Breakdown in respect for cultural values • Men have less time to engage in gardening activities, hunting, fishing, gathering, handicrafts, cash cropping and community work – thus women's workloads increase • Destruction and pollution of land and water (DA) • Less land for gardening (DA) • Women's dependence on men for money has increased (DA) • Decreasing church attendance on Sundays (DA) • Increased criminal activities (DA)

DA = directly affected areas, meaning those villagers living in direct proximity to the mine site, a number of whom have been relocated.

Source: This table incorporates the views of a variety of men and women in both directly affected and other areas of Lihir who were interviewed during fieldwork by Lagisa between February and April, 1996. The mine was in the construction phase at the time, and extraction of minerals had not commenced.

Impacts on women

Politically, women have not played a strong role in the development of the Lihir mine. Their views were poorly represented in initial decision making and negotiations about the mining development. While LMC did open up all public meetings to women, heavy workloads, cultural constraints and their own lack of confidence held women back from voicing their concerns. Most women have little personal autonomy.

Thus it is not surprising that their political power is weak. As one woman in Lihir confessed, 'We are under our men's authority. If they want us to cook, we will cook. If they tell us not to go to the garden, we will not go to the garden' (interview, Kunaie village, April 1996).

They did not participate in decision-making processes regarding the initial approval of the project, nor the detailed planning of its implementation, nor do they have a say in its long-term operational management.[4] In this context, men's dominance in planning and decision making for the household – as well as the clan, the village community and society as a whole – has been entrenched. As with other mining projects in the Pacific, the Lihir development has reinforced traditional controls over women (Emberson-Bain 1994:101).

As only men have been listed as leaders on LMC documents and agreements, official documentation now confirms and constructs women's marginalisation. Traditionally, when important issues concerning matters of clan livelihoods and future security were discussed, women were involved, at least informally, before men made their final decisions. While Lihirian negotiators brokered a good deal regarding economic benefits local peoples would receive, women were not put forward as representatives of the landowning clans, thus they do not control monetary benefits from the mining company. For Lihirian men, however, money and business are now key topics of discussion. As one old man described it, 'They talk money, eat money and sleep and dream of money' (interview, Lamboar village, March 1996). It is also becoming common for men to be referred to as owners of property or family wealth, whereas in the past property would have been said to have been owned by one's clan or family. Land is registered under men's names, regardless of traditions which prescribe that land is inherited through the woman's line. These factors impede women from pursuing business interests.

Following employment trends common throughout mine sites in Papua New Guinea (Emberson-Bain 1994:100, Robinson 1991:114), women comprise only ten per cent of the mining workforce in Lihir, including LMC and the contractor companies (Lagisa 1997). They are concentrated in low-paid, menial professions such as cleaning and labouring, or in subservient jobs such as secretarial and nursing work.

[4] Local landowner associations were formed to negotiate on issues concerning the mining development, but it has been difficult for women to participate in these associations as men say that it is not customary for women to take on leadership and decision-making roles. But, as Bonnell (1994:163) argues, 'There is nothing customary about a large scale mine. And there is nothing customary about landowner associations.'

Men dominate skilled and semi-skilled mine-related work. Married women who have found paid employment, including a few in high-status jobs, are experiencing pressure from their husbands to continue with their traditional tasks in addition to their new jobs. For example, in one situation a woman came home late from work and her husband was not happy because his meal was not ready at the usual time. He scolded his wife saying:

> What sort of work do you people do that you come home this late? Do you remember that we have children to look after? Tell whoever your boss is to remember that some of you are mothers and should come home early to cook for the family ... if you come home late again I will come and physically abuse you and your boss! (Lagisa, personal observation, Kunaie village, April 1996).

As seen at other mining sites in the Pacific, the engagement of Lihirian men in the mining workforce has caused two main problems for women: an increased workload as they have to take on village-based tasks otherwise performed by their menfolk, and disruption to family togetherness (Bonnell 1994:162, Gerritsen and MacIntyre 1991: 47). For example, men in paid employment spend from dawn till dusk away from their families, and may be required to work seven days a week, leading to a poorer quality of family life. Lihirian boys are missing out on the rich cultural knowledge that their fathers would have passed on to them in the past and some are becoming notably unruly. The money earned does not adequately compensate for men's absence as they tend to spend most, and sometimes all, of their pay packets at their discretion, and often neglect family interests. Heavy consumption of alcohol by some men has increased enormously, as is common at all major mine sites in Papua New Guinea (Emberson-Bain 1994:101, Connell and Howitt 1991). As one woman said:

> Sometimes when our drunken husbands come home and don't like the food we cook they will throw things around the place, chase us and our children out of the house, or even physically abuse us. We get very scared when they are drunk (interview, Londolovit village, March 1996).

While LMC have offered non-formal education programmes and training sessions for women, most do not have the time, energy or freedom to pursue these opportunities. Many Lihirian women stated that their greatest worry was violence in the household, and the fear of increasing their husband's anger prevented them from pursuing new development opportunities outside the household.

The sense of independence which many women had has been

undermined somewhat as they come to rely on their husbands to provide money for household needs. Women living in areas where land has been alienated, in particular, have to wait for housekeeping money from their husbands so they can buy food from the store, whereas previously they were largely self-reliant, producing food for their families from the land. Land is the major asset which Lihirian women have access to and to take it away is the same as stripping women of their status and identity. For example, a woman's status can reach a certain height if she produces a good harvest for a feast. Depriving women of land effectively deprives them of the opportunity to feel that they are contributing to society and are valued, productive members of their family and clan, as echoed in the following statement: 'Now we have nothing to do and we look like fools because we no longer have the land to make gardens and other activities like that' (interview, Londolovit village, March 1996).

Development cannot be seen to be sustainable when one group constituting 50 per cent of the population have seen their disadvantage entrenched and their contribution to society undervalued. Indeed, it is somewhat absurd that an activity which involves moving tonnes of dirt to extract grams of ore, leaving in its wake eroded slopes, compacted soil and silted waterways, is seen a as more productive and economically efficient activity than the work of women in producing food for their families' consumption in such a way that the soil will continue to yield a harvest for many years to come.

Conclusion

This chapter has examined the social, economic and environmental impacts of mining, showing that these impacts are most extreme around the mine site thus affecting the communities living in the locality of the mining area, while the benefits are more widely spread. Negative impacts include the degradation of natural resources, loss of land, increased dependence on money, social disorder and the disempowerment of some local people. Particularly evident is the severity of these impacts on women. Thus Emberson-Bain (1994:94) argues that:

> As a general rule, mining in the Pacific has probably proved to be one of the most destructive and unsustainable forms of foreign-initiated development ... the history of Pacific mining weaves a woeful tale of expropriation, social and cultural isolation, and environmental damage.

As noted in the introduction to this chapter, mining is an inherently unsustainable activity as it relies on the extraction of a non-renewable resource. The negative impacts of mining on the biological, social and economic systems were clearly spelt out in the course of examining mining in Papua New Guinea. It is vital, therefore, that before considering whether to allow this activity to be developed on their ancestral land, local communities are armed with information regarding the potential long terms effects of mining. There is a real need:

> to empower local communities so that they are better equipped to prevent the most harmful and destructive features of mining, to have a greater influence over mining policy, and ultimately, to help shape a more socially equitable and sustainable form of development. Otherwise, the bleak prospect of further conflict, violence and bloodshed may be the only alternative (Emberson-Bain 1994:107).

There have been no signs that Papua New Guinea people are becoming less concerned about the exploitation of mineral resources on their land over time – quite the contrary. Thus the interests of local people should be allowed to guide the nature of mining activities to a much greater extent than they have done in the past, ensuring that a holistic approach which caters for both social and economic development, and which minimises environmental disruption, is adopted.

CHAPTER 11

Marine Resources

SALOME SAMOU

In many parts of the Pacific the ocean is regarded as not separate from the land but as a part of it. As an extension of the land, the ocean and reefs are owned by communal groups who claim fishing rights and draw their sources of livelihood directly from them or through trading links exchanging marine products with inland dwellers for food crops. For atoll populations where land is scarce, the ocean is vital for survival. This chapter examines the problems and potential of fishing as a strategy for sustainable development. It begins with an analysis of traditional marine resource management then focuses on recent industrialisation of the industry before suggesting some alternative management approaches.

The Traditional Use of Marine Resources

In a pioneering study of marine tenure in the Marovo Lagoon in the Solomon Islands, Hviding coined the term 'customary marine tenure' (CMT) in which:

> 'Customary' refers here to a system that emerges from firmly traditional roots and has continuous and meaningful links with the past as it adapts to handling contemporary issues; 'marine' refers to the system as dealing with coral reefs, lagoon, coast and open sea and including islands and islets contained in this overall seaspace; and 'tenure' refers to a social process of interacting activities concerning control over territory, access to resources and regulation of their exploitation (Hviding and Baines 1994:16).

CMT systems are prevalent and exist in a great diversity throughout the Pacific. In most of the Pacific, with a few exceptions (in Tonga, for example, the reefs are owned by the monarchy), CMT comes under the jurisdiction of communities and traditional landowning units. This is particularly so in Melanesia. In general, CMT areas are demarcated by reefs, passages, bays, islands and other marine features. These designated areas are reservoirs of welfare for property-holding groups who control the resources and have rights and claims that include entitlements to fish in the same manner that they may garden or hunt on land. People fished in their traditional fishing grounds although access to other grounds was possible with permission or because of reciprocal rights with other groups. Marine boundaries also shifted and rights to fish in other groups' reefs or offshore areas were negotiated as the need arose.

Traditionally, resource use and management were intertwined with religious beliefs, which sanctioned or restrained people's behaviour in deciding when and which resources were to be exploited and for what purposes (Johannes 1977). Subsistence harvests of fish were small-scale and primarily for household consumption or ceremonial exchange. Offshore species, such as tuna, bonito and porpoise, had religious and mystical associations and ritual and ceremony surrounded their harvest. Fish expeditions were planned to coincide with seasons and cycles of food harvests or to mark important ceremonies such as rites of passage, funerals and births. Depictions of fish were carved on household and personal ornaments and fish were represented in songs, dances, stories and architecture, signifying also their daily importance.

Customs and ceremonies also regulated fishing practices (Johannes 1981, 1982). In Fiji, for example, following the death of a chief, a taboo was placed on a fishing ground to revitalise stocks in preparation for a funeral feast in his honour, both as head of his *mataqali* (land-owning clan) and *qoliqoli* (fishing grounds). More recently, and due to the demand for inshore products like trochus, periodic taboos were placed on a particular fishery or sections of the reef which were closed off for designated periods. Prohibitions were enforced for varying periods and they were lifted after certain ceremonies were performed. Religious beliefs and totem taboos included the prohibition of certain species of fish to be eaten by certain people, for example pregnant women, sick people, or men undergoing rituals. Also the reefs and shorelines were not only fishing grounds but also sites of historical and spiritual significance. In some areas, such as in the Marovo Lagoon (Hviding 1996), rock sacrificial shrines held skulls of ancestors of master fishermen and other sacred objects. They served as reminders of ownership and to ward off outsiders.

Moreover, although fishing was very important in the diets of people, fishing was not a daily activity and not done with such intensity as it is today. Fishing was conducted for a purpose and when that was accomplished people returned to other pursuits until another such occasion arose. Fishing methods and limited demand determined the amount of fish captured. The technology used was simple: line and hook or lure employed for fin-fish, reef gleaning, or free diving for molluscs and crustaceans. Plant poisons, wooden spears, arrows and fish traps were also often used, whilst fish enclosures trapped schools of fish to be scooped out with hand nets. Such practices, together with the smaller population involved, served as inherent conservation methods and fish stocks recovered readily.

Only men took part in deep-sea fishing and such occasions were preceded and concluded with observances of taboos and rituals performed by traditional priests. In some areas of the Solomon Islands, for example, the ability to catch a bonito was a demonstration of masculinity and a young male adolescent's passage into adulthood. Although women were excluded from deep-sea fishing, they were heavily involved in gleaning, diving and shellfish collection. Nor was fishing the exclusive domain of either gender. Women's knowledge of fisheries was not limited to inshore fisheries, though this was their primary area of expertise because of their constant involvement in gathering food for their households compared with men's more occasional and adventurous deep-sea fishing trips (Schoeffel 1985, 1996a).

Thus, in many parts of the Pacific, people's knowledge of the marine environment was as astute as their knowledge of gardens and forests. Knowledge of the physical and resource attributes of the sea and sensitivity to when and how much to harvest without harming stocks guided fishers' activities. They knew what could be safely harvested and when, the locations of the best fishing grounds (depending on lunar phases and currents) and what fish were to be caught and for what purpose.

Changes in Inshore Fishing

Whilst customary marine tenure, fishing methods and resource management practices have survived in many places, inshore fisheries have been transformed over the past century by greater commercialisation of catches. Inshore fisheries are very important for both subsistence and commercial activities (Wright and Hill 1993). A survey carried out on Viti Levu, Fiji, showed that over 99 per cent of the households surveyed consumed marine products at least once a week, with 9 per cent of rural households relying on fish as their main source of income. Some 45 per cent of rural Fijian women regularly fished and on average earned income of $F34 a week, a substantial amount by rural standards (UNDP 1997). Unfortunately many of the resources that have sustained these communities are now seriously under threat from over-fishing resulting from demand for cash and subsistence needs. One notable result is the reduced source of protein, largely derived from marine products, and the tendency to rely more on convenient tinned fish.

At the beginning of this century inshore marine resources, such as pearlshells, trochus, *bêche-de-mer* and giant clams, were being collected from all over the Pacific and processed for sale to Europe (predominantly Italy and Germany) as shells, or to Asia as gourmet food items. Much of this trade has continued but the rates of extraction have substantially increased for some products. Trochus shells, for example, are manufactured into buttons for fashion houses in Europe and the Pacific Islands produces some 59 per cent of the world's trochus demand (Gillett 1995). Demand has risen and the industry is now suffering due to the shortage of supply of trochus, attributed to the over-exploitation of the resource. In other cases, the increased demand for other shells used in local currencies and manufactured into curios for the tourist market has also contributed to their depletion in some areas. On Malaita in the Solomon Islands, for example, shells previously manufactured into local currency and exported to other Pacific Islands, like Papua New Guinea, have been over-fished and now have to be obtained from other islands. Turtle shells also continue to be exploited despite official bans.

The intensity of inshore fisheries harvesting has been exacerbated by an increasing demand for cash from rural populations with limited economic opportunities. There is growing demand for marine products, not only for export but also among rapidly increasing urban populations who lack ready access to the sea (Delana *et al.* 1988). Marine resources are targets of cash-earning activities, as most invertebrates are easily accessible and can be harvested throughout the year using relatively simple methods. Because of the absence of regulatory controls and the lack of public awareness of their vulnerability, however, inshore fisheries are particularly prone to over-fishing. Policing or enforcement of management and control regulations is often difficult to achieve due to the inadequate legal and administrative mechanisms. These factors have led to major increases in rates of exploitation of inshore fish species as well as crustacea (lobster, crab, prawns, etc.) and their consequent localised depletion (Swadling 1977, Johannes 1981).

Commercial inshore fishing now involves the use of introduced and, in some cases, destructive methods and devices. Spear guns, nylon fishing lines, lures and nets are now employed widely instead of traditional techniques, and motorised boats have replaced canoes.

Dynamiting, destructive to both fish and humans, has been used widely, despite being outlawed in some places. Scuba diving is now used, though it is considered detrimental because divers break off pieces of fragile coral when hunting fish. Fish nets that catch large amounts of fish are also commonly used along with plant poisons, such as derris root, a traditional method of fishing that kills indiscriminately. These methods have become more common as traditional taboos, marine tenure systems, and fishing regulations have been gradually abandoned.

Large-scale logging and mining are also contributing to the depletion of certain fish species through the overall degradation of the marine environment by silt deposition in bays, lagoons and rivers. Beaches and mangroves are used as dumping grounds for non-biodegradable and household pollutants, especially near urban areas. Overall, there is a major concern that inshore fisheries throughout the region may become so seriously depleted that they will not be able to meet local demands and alternative sources of protein will have to be found.

Industrialisation of the Fishing Industry

Large-scale foreign involvement in Pacific Islands fisheries began with the establishment of a cannery in American Samoa in the late 1950s. Since then, there has been increasing interest and involvement, resulting in the widespread industrialisation of the deep-sea fishery. Given the existence of customary property rights over inshore fisheries, and the relatively underexploited nature of the deep-sea fishery, foreign attention has been particularly in the pelagic (free-swimming) fishery, especially tuna. For many years, Pacific waters attracted boats from the distant-water fishing nations (Japan, USA, South Korea and Taiwan) seeking fish for the burgeoning luxury market for sashimi in Japan and the demand for canned tuna by North Americans (Doulman 1989). Pacific nations, however, received little or no benefit from these operations (Slatter 1994).

Following the Fourth United Nations Convention on the International Law of the Sea (UNCLOS IV) and international agreements over national ownership of the fisheries resources within their exclusive economic zones (EEZs – see Figure 11.1), new arrangements have been entered into which bring some income, if not full involvement, to Pacific Island nations in their deep-water fisheries development (Figure 11.1). Foreign fishers gained legal access to Pacific fisheries in return for licence fees and pledges to provide managerial, technical and marketing skills and training for islanders in such skills.

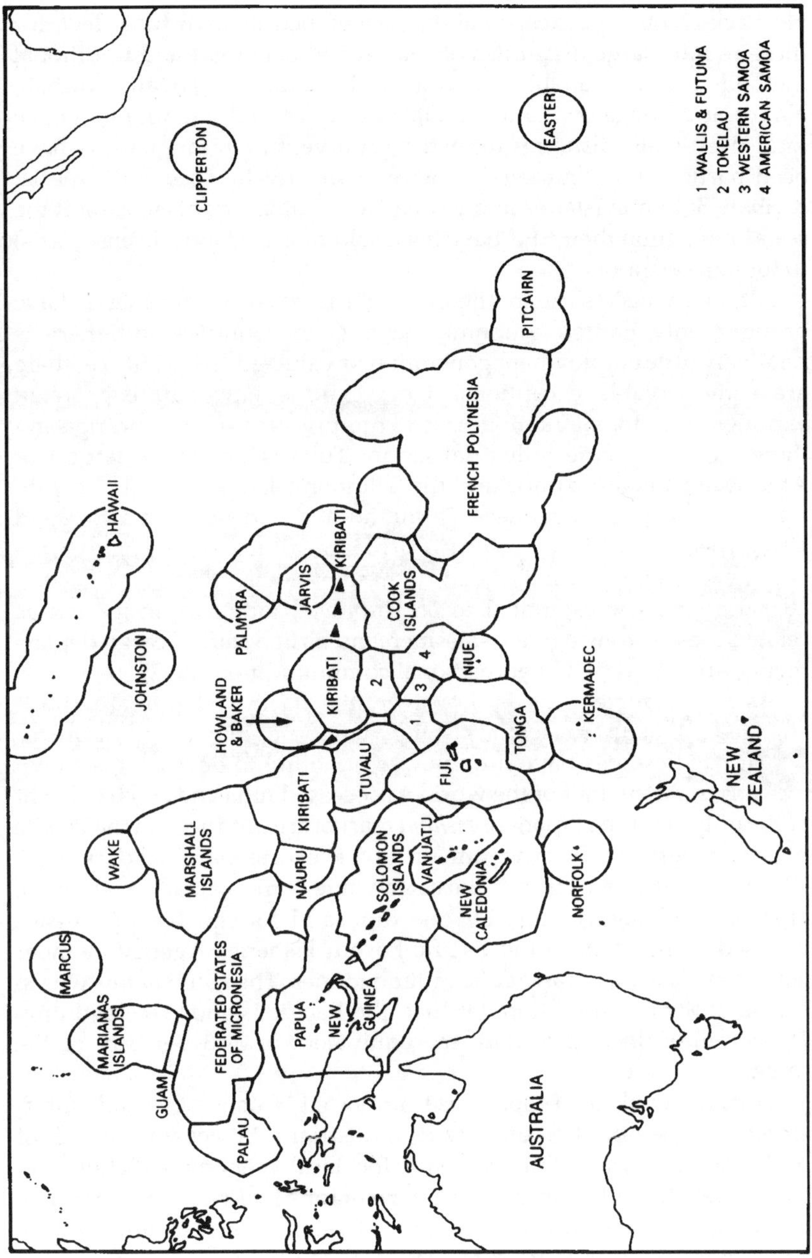

FIGURE 11.1 • EXCLUSIVE ECONOMIC ZONES OF THE PACIFIC ISLANDS REGION

No Pacific country, except Fiji, has developed its own tuna fleet, for these require large quantities of capital and expertise, and traditional methods are not suitable for industrial operations. Tuvalu, Kiribati, Nauru and Tonga own a few boats but not enough to mount a viable local deep-water fisheries industry. Joint venture arrangements have been particularly common. In the cases of Tuvalu, French Polynesia, Kiribati, Solomon Islands and Papua New Guinea, rights to exploit the resources within their EEZ have been sold or leased (on a license basis) to foreign operators.

Although necessary in the short term, such arrangements have brought only limited economic benefits to countries and there is relatively little employment generation or value-added profit. Yet there are some notable exceptions. Tuna exports now surpass foreign earnings from the plantation-based enterprises in some countries and there has been some industrialisation. Tuna is by far the largest of American Samoa's exports and the Solomon Islands and Fiji also gain significant export revenues. Throughout the region, an estimated 10,000 people work in factories, processing tuna or *sashimi*, or are employed on board foreign and domestic vessels. A further 10,000 to 20,000 people are estimated to be employed indirectly in numerous related areas – crew agents, salesmen and airline staff of cargo departments, and so on (R. Gillett personal communication, 1997).

As important as this is, however, the Pacific Islands are short-changed. The distant-water fishing nations dominate the industry whilst Pacific states have little power or ability to develop their own industries. About half of the world's processed tuna and 30-40 per cent of the output for the Japanese *sashimi* market are produced in the Pacific region. Benefits to the governments however, are marginal (Grynberg 1995a). In 1995, for example, the catch value of the skipjack, yellow fin, albacore and bigeye tuna by one thousand foreign fishing vessels licensed to fish within the Pacific Forum Fisheries Agency member countries' EEZs was put at one million tonnes. The value of this was in excess of $US1,700 million. Of that, the Pacific Islands received only $US60million in licence fees, the equivalent of 3.53 per cent of the catch.

Transnational operations use imported technology and infrastructure. They exist essentially as industrial enclaves with a lack of multiplier backward linkages with the local economies (Schug and Galea'i 1987). Whilst canning is important for American Samoa and Fiji, whole unprocessed fish exports far outweigh processed tuna. Whole fish exports may involve shore facilities for freezing, though this is more commonly carried out on factory ships, and local benefits are small. Furthermore, local processing is largely export-oriented, whereby the choice tuna meat is bound for foreign markets. What is consumed in the islands is often of poor quality, made from brown flakes (the part of the tuna product that ends up as pet food in some Western countries). Such products are nonetheless still a popular food item among Solomon Islanders because of the prohibitive price of the export grade.

World demand for tuna, combined with the pressure to intensify fishing because of diminishing stocks, poses a threat to the future of the whole fishing industry and its importance in Pacific economies. At a time when fisheries, as in the North Atlantic or Mediterranean Oceans, have become badly depleted, international demand for alternative fishing grounds makes Pacific waters a likely target of increased activity for a range of species. At the same time, fulfilling the demands of foreign markets for fresh and frozen whole tuna is also likely to contribute to the present threat. Moreover, the wide application of modern, highly mechanised boats that can remain at sea for long periods of time and have access to 'floating factories' could very well contribute to tuna's dire status (Grynberg 1995a). Already some species – the southern bluefin tuna, for example – are under threat from over-fishing. At its present rate of exploitation, it is estimated that by the year 2020 this resource will be history (*Fiji Times* 1997). One of the biggest dangers to fish stocks is the use of drift nets. This has been likened to 'oceanic strip-mining' and seriously threatens the long-term sustainability not only of the pelagic or oceanic fishery, but possibly also of the near-shore and inshore fisheries resources of Pacific states. It has been predicted that this technology, which utilizes fine monofiliment drift gillnets which can be from eight to 15 meters deep and 60 kilometers long, and which can catch fish, whales, turtles, ships' propellers and even birds, could, if continued at its current rate, cause a collapse of the rich South Pacific albacore fishery within five years (Thaman and Murti 1989).

Diminishing stocks will mean the loss of an important source of livelihood and associated knowledge. In many Pacific Island societies, such as the microstates of Kiribati, Tuvalu and Tokelau where tuna figures prominently, fishing is a major component in the economy, sustaining subsistence livelihoods as well as having recreational and cultural significance (Gillett and Toloa 1987, Meltzolf and Li Puma 1983). Exploiting fisheries purely for their commercial value diminishes people's knowledge of how to fish for self-sufficiency, and of the socio-cultural significance of fishing. Ultimately, the governments of the Pacific also stand to lose economically, as they become bystanders while foreigners exploit the region's richest resources.

Finding Alternatives

The above discussion has shown that, despite the considerable potential of both inshore and deep-sea marine resources as bases for economic development in the Pacific Islands, considerable doubts arise when considering the sustainability of this resource. Inshore fisheries are becoming depleted whilst deep-sea fishing is both diminishing the resource and limiting the returns to Pacific Island people. Both resource depletion and the economic returns suggest a need to seek alternative strategies.

Increasing local involvement

Given the lack of capital and technology within the Pacific Islands to run independent deep-sea fleets, one option for increasing returns to the region is to develop regional ports as bases of operation to reprovision and service the foreign fleet. The substantial amounts of money at present spent in their home ports could be fed into Pacific economies instead. For example, during four or five home port calls a year, a tuna seiner spends $US300,000 to $US450,000 – a total of around $US1.5 million. A *sashimi* longliner spends $US13,000 on a short trip; 60 vessels would generate $US8 million a year (Gillett 1997). What the 1,300 vessels that are currently licensed to fish in the region could generate is potentially enormous. Another option is to increase and encourage the employment of Pacific Island crews on the vessels. If the 1,000 longliners were to employ three or four Pacific Islanders each at the going rate of $US250 a month, this could earn $US9 to $US12 million a year.

Another possibility is the sale of fish to local markets. At present, fishing vessels often catch huge amounts of non-target fish, which are either thrown away at sea or sold very cheaply at ports. If these were marketed locally, they could generate employment and help ease the pressure on local inshore fisheries. There is then the problem, however, of displacing local artisanal fishers (Schug and Galea'i 1987).

Training is a further area that demands attention. Pacific Island government fisheries departments seem preoccupied with the tuna industry, engaging disproportionate resources in the administration, licensing and surveillance of foreign fishing vessels. While this might be justified, these much-needed resources could be better utilised in training local people in marine biology or in the control and management of the resource. Fisheries divisions commonly lack experienced Pacific Islanders with scientific and technical expertise. A trend in the 1970s was the recruitment of fisheries officers who acquired tertiary training and it was intended that they become counterparts to expatriate bosses, eventually assuming the responsibility of heading fisheries divisions. Many did, although many also left for the business sector or regional organisations where they are offered better monetary rewards (R. Gillett, personal communication 1997). The lack of dissemination of technical information or the acquisition of special skills, for example in management or marketing, does not seem to have been an objective of Pacific Island governments. Managed and run by personnel from foreign parent companies, local people's participation is largely limited to the provision of support services and cheap and unskilled labour on tuna boats and in the factories.

The South Pacific Forum Fisheries Agency (FFA)

Tuna is a highly migratory fish which is considered as belonging to a coastal country while it swims within that particular country's EEZ, but as it straddles national 'sea boundaries' and swims in international water, it is also considered common property (Doulman 1987). This makes international cooperation essential both for its exploitation and its conservation. As the world's richest tuna fishing ground, the Pacific region is a potential base for national economies and livelihoods if fisheries generally, but tuna in particular, are managed sustainably. Because of the islands' smallness and their incapacity to develop their tuna fisheries individually, regional cooperation is their best option. In response to UNCLOS III, which set out the rights and obligations of all coastal nations including the designation of EEZs, the leaders of the South Pacific Forum (formerly SPEC) formed the Forum Fisheries Agency (FFA) in 1979 (Herr 1990). It had the objectives of securing marine resources as a means of development, their conservation and 'managed utilisation', and the coordination of regional fisheries policies (Forum Fisheries Agency 1989).

The FFA is made up of 16 forum member countries, including Australia and New Zealand. It operates entirely on foreign aid, the bulk of which comes from Australia and New Zealand and the rest from the USA, Canada and Japan. The organisation provides scientific, technical and legal support, advice and training in the various aspects of its work, disseminating information on the latest developments in its field of competence. The agency cooperates and negotiates with the deep-water fishing nations in all matters relating to tuna dealings with member countries, securing of funds, obtaining licensing fees, maintaining a regional register of foreign fishing vessels and carrying out surveillance over the EEZs of the member countries. Under a patrol boat and aerial surveillance programmes, Australia and New Zealand assist the smaller members with surveillance of their own waters, a task which none individually has the capacity to undertake. Poaching is particularly problematic, as until recently it was almost impossible to track movements and activities of foreign fishing vessels and even more difficult to regulate their catches; the declaration of which so far has been done on a trust basis.

Fisheries development is inextricably linked to foreign aid. It can be argued that the Pacific Islands have compromised their national sovereignty by signing away their fishing rights in exchange for foreign aid and minuscule licence fees, especially in the cases of the USA and Japan. Interestingly, when Kiribati and the USSR signed a fishing agreement in 1980, there was an outcry from the West that baffled Pacific leaders. The USA was clearly keen to keep Kiribati from falling into the Soviet camp. Yet there may also have been economic reasons. In 1984 an American tuna fishing vessel, the *Jeannette Diana* was confiscated for poaching by the Solomon Islands government. In retaliation, the USA placed an embargo on Solomon Island tuna products – the USA was the country's biggest buyer. In these two cases was a clear illustration of the way the USA could interfere in the fisheries industry of the Pacific to safeguard its own economic and political interests. International law and Pacific sovereignty over their EEZs were secondary considerations.

Nonetheless, as aid diminishes, the FFA may need to accept or seek aid from outside the region and thus open itself to possible manipulation in exchange for access. It might entail, for instance, following the agenda of donors and the Pacific states might lose control of the organisation (Doulman 1987). Furthermore, in the 20 years of its operations, FFA continues to employ a largely expatriate staff with only one or two Pacific Islanders heading technical divisions of the organisation. While huge amounts of aid money support the agency's physical infrastructure and work programmes, there is relatively little 'trickling down' to the majority of rural Pacific Island fishers. In addition, the lack of local knowledgeable and skilled personnel, fisheries managers and researchers in the fisheries divisions constrain the work of the agency. Difficulties are created in coordinating efforts between the countries and the agency. Perhaps aid works to maintain this situation.

Communal property and co-management

The recognition and legal support of customary resource management practices and their potential in sustaining fisheries has been put forward by academics as a potential remedy for some of the present problems of the fishing industry and a means of promoting more equitable development (Hviding and Baines 1994, Hviding 1997). Since inshore fisheries are the property of communities, any management strategies need the involvement of their owners and users.

One area where communities could be involved is in regulation and policing. Community involvement is necessary because of knowledge of local situations and proximity to resources. Poaching, already a common problem, will only increase with pressure to intensify fishing, as more people need to be fed on top of the increasing need for cash. Because of the generally inadequate administrative frameworks throughout the Pacific, efforts by governments in this area have not been effective. The delegation of policing and settling of disputes to the community will be advantageous to both communities and governments: first, it will provide communities with a sense of regaining control of their resources and some traditional authority; second, governments will be spared the expense of spreading their resources thinly. An overall result of this is that communities will regain some legal control over their resources which they had lost through the centralisation of fisheries. Additionally, the revival of traditional knowledge will benefit fisheries managers, policy makers and aid donors.

Hviding (1989, 1997) suggests that property-holding groups could be the basis for future marine resource management, perhaps through fishing associations. These associations would form their own rules and management regulations, such as imposing quotas on the catch of certain species. They might also be able to overcome some of the most common problems facing small-scale commercial operators, such as transport difficulties and lack of refrigeration. Examples of successful communal fishing associations are available in Indonesia and Japan (Mantjoro 1996). Yet their use in the Pacific may be problematic. Schoeffel suggests that the failure of projects in the Pacific, in contrast to their success in Asia, is due to Asians not having other economic alternatives (Schoeffel 1996b). Pacific Islanders have other options, especially ready access to communal land, which acts as a safety net. For example, the Vanuatu fisheries development programme in the early 1980s, funded by the Asian Development Bank, had the goal of supplying the Port Vila market with fish, and creating employment and income for rural fishermen. It was assumed that ni-Vanuatu would fish regularly and in time become full-time fishers. Erratic fish supplies, transport difficulties and low returns resulted in the failure of the project. But what was not apparent to the project designers was that fishers had multiple other activities they were engaged in and more pressing needs, like securing enough food for their families, so that the low returns from the time spent on fishing were not rewarding (Schoeffel 1996b). Schoeffel also suggests that there are few incentives to work together in the Pacific, especially in the absence of a coercive authority.

To conclude, perhaps the most valuable asset that Pacific Islanders have for fisheries development is their knowledge of resources and the environment. Effective regulation of local fishing operations, as well as those of foreign corporations, requires government recognition of the traditional management systems backed by legislation. Similarly, the relative neglect of small-scale artisanal fisheries development, compared with the attractions of joint ventures with large foreign deep-sea operators, has meant that the region has gained little in terms of local food supply, employment and earnings from fishing. Unless there is a fundamental change in the way Pacific marine resources are managed, this most crucial of resources may not be able to offer even the most basic of livelihoods to Pacific Island people, let alone realise the great potential it has for future sustainable development.

CHAPTER 12

Sustainability and the Urban Pacific: the Case of Samoa and Tonga

DONOVAN STOREY

South Pacific Urbanisation

As part of the burgeoning of literature on sustainable development, much greater attention has been paid recently to Third World cities in which the important relationship between urban environmental issues and urban development has been noted (Burgess *et al.* 1997b:65, World Bank 1995). Discussion on urban sustainability includes a wide spectrum of issues such as water, sanitation, shelter and employment and a range of spatial considerations, including workplace, home, neighbourhood, city and regional issues and impacts (Hardoy and Satterthwaite 1989:146). This chapter will focus on the home, neighbourhood and city impacts of urban growth, while regional issues (urban 'footprints') are discussed in Chapter 18.

In this closer examination of Third World urban environments less attention has been paid to smaller Third World towns. Although small by international standards, Pacific towns are significant urban concentrations in relation to their hinterlands of country and the region. Indeed, they exhibit aspects of sustainability comparable with much larger urban agglomerations which are at the centre of scholarly attention. This chapter examines the 'sustainability' of the Polynesian towns of Apia (Samoa) and Nuku'alofa (Tonga). An inclusive definition of sustainability is employed: 'sustainability involves the interrelation of a wide range of environmental, economic, political and social components' (McIlwaine 1997:407), rather than just the 'brown' and 'green' issues of the built and natural environment.

Increasingly, the Pacific is also becoming an urban domain, though this has been a comparatively late phenomenon. Demographically, countries such as New Caledonia, the Marshall Islands, the Cook

Islands and French Polynesia have larger urban than rural populations, whilst smaller nations, such as Nauru, can be considered wholly urban. Atoll countries, such as the Marshall Islands, represent some of the densest urban areas anywhere in the world (Jones 1995:4). Throughout the region, annual urban growth rates of above 2.5 per cent are the norm and urban growth rates outstrip rural and national rates in all but a few places (Table 12.1). Consequently, the following century will be an urban one for the great majority of Pacific Island countries and peoples.

TABLE 12.1 • THE URBAN PACIFIC

	Main urban centre	Population of main town	% urban	Urban growth rate	National growth rate
Polynesia					
American Samoa	Pago Pago	10,000	48	8.2	3.7
Cook Islands	Avarua	2,000	58	2.4	1.1
French Polynesia	Papeete	108,000	57	2.2	2.5
Samoa	Apia	34,000	21	1.2	0.5
Tonga	Nuku'alofa	34,000	31	2.5	0.5
Tuvalu	Funafuti	4,000	42	4.8	1.7
Melanesia					
Fiji	Suva	160,000	39	2.6	2.0
New Caledonia	Noumea	100,000	71	2.7	2.6
Papua New Guinea	Port Moresby	225,000	30	4.1	2.3
Solomon Islands	Honiara	35,000	13	6.2	3.4
Vanuatu	Port Vila	40,000	18	7.3	2.8
Micronesia					
FSM	Palikir	n/a	26	2.6	1.9
Guam	Agana	2,000	38	1.9	2.3
Kiribati	Tarawa	30,000	37	2.2	1.4
Marshall Islands	Majuro	22,000	65	8.2	4.2
Northern Marianas	Saipan	12,000	94	3.2	5.6
Palau	Koror	11,000	68	3.8	2.7

Sources: Asian Development Bank 1996a:21, Bryant-Tokalau 1994:80–1, Connell and Lea 1993, 1995, South Pacific Commission 1996, United Nations 1995.

Despite this significant rise in urban agglomerations, global accounts have demonstrated a lack of interest in, and minimal documentation of, Pacific urban places. While there has recently been interest in notions of sustainability (Bryant 1993), planning (Connell and Lea 1993, 1995,

Jones 1995) and poverty (Bryant-Tokalau 1995), analysis of Pacific Island urbanisation lacks explanatory frameworks, models and detailed accounts (Jones 1995:2,11). While Pacific Island towns face similar problems to Third World urban centres, they also exhibit unique problems. Almost all capital towns and cities exhibit urban primacy, with many representing the only urban concentration within the country. High population growth rates have led to immense pressures on local environments, especially evident when urban development has taken place within the confines of fragile seafront, lagoon and mangrove boundaries (Bryant-Tokalau 1994:154). Additionally, atoll towns are constrained by geographical limitations on their size, disposal of refuse, access to potable water, and possible threats due to global warming.

Steady and, at times, rapid urban population growth rates have stretched the capacity of authorities to cope in terms of the provision of services and infrastructure. Melanesian populations are reproducing themselves (on average) every thirty years, with annual urban growth rates ranging between 2.6 and 7.3 per cent. For example, Port Vila (Vanuatu) will double its population every eight years at its current growth rate. This has led to significant issues of sustainability of these urban domains and beyond. Nevertheless, governments have been slow to plan for their urban futures, and perhaps this has been exacerbated by the value placed on Pacific Island countries as agrarian societies where urban lifestyles are considered 'foreign' and somehow 'unnatural' *vis-à-vis* rural traditions and histories. Urban decay and environmental degradation have stemmed from twin problems of a lack of national resources and insufficient investment, but they are also due to the 'generally uncontrolled and poorly regulated pattern of urban development and expansion' (Burgess *et al.* 1997b:65).

Official statistics of Pacific Island towns reveal a situation of adequate or good waste disposal facilities and access to potable water (UNDP 1994:75). The reality, however, challenges these official depictions. In the Pacific context, the most pressing problems centre on water, sanitation, and the use of land. Pacific Island towns, being primarily coastal and dissipated, face quite significant and serious issues of water pollution (through effluent dumping, industrial waste, faecal pollution), solid waste disposal, destruction of protective coral reefs, and degradation of mangrove environments (Dupon 1993). The principal neighbourhood environmental issues include the disposal of household and other refuse, drainage, sewage collection and the exploitation of marginal lands such as hillsides, river beds and mangrove swamps, particularly in informal settlements. As Reti (quoted in Bryant 1993:17) has noted:

> Sixty per cent of the region's countries have worsening water shortages caused by the overtaxing of groundwater supplies and the pollution of lakes and rivers. One-third of the islands are encountering problems of pollution and the destruction of soil and other resources caused by the intense development of narrow belts of coastal land ... More than 60 per cent of the islands have difficulty getting rid of rubbish and 90 per cent of them are in bad trouble with the disposal of liquid waste, particularly human waste.

Invariably, environmental costs are borne disproportionately by poorer households: 'a significant proportion of urban dwellers are living in marginal locations with inadequate garbage disposal, fresh water and sanitation' and evidence is that these conditions are worsening (Bryant-Tokalau 1995:119). In general, it is the poor who are more likely to live on marginal lands, in poorer quality housing, drink unsafe water, and have less access to efficient sanitation and services (Rakodi and Devas 1993:290, Hardoy and Satterthwaite 1989:156).

Polynesian Urban Growth: Apia and Nuku'alofa

Samoa and Tonga are still primarily agricultural nations and economies; in both instances close to two-thirds of people live and work in rural (mostly subsistence) spheres. Economic growth has been sluggish, with GDP growth rates averaging around 0–2 per cent in recent years, owing mainly to the low market prices paid for root crops, vegetables, copra and fruit, but also to a lack of internal and foreign investment, and to climatic disasters, particularly in Samoa.

Urban growth in Polynesia has developed steadily (if not spectacularly), and in increasingly unsustainable fashion. Indeed, recently Connell and Lea (1995:3) have argued that the 'pressures on urban services are as great in cities like Apia ... and Nuku'alofa ... where problems of water supply, sanitation, waste disposal and the supply of low-cost housing are already of concern, as they are in the larger Melanesian cities'. These pressures are likely to continue in the absence of serious government response. In both Samoa and Tonga urban areas are coming to play a much greater role demographically, but also economically with increased emphasis being placed on economic (and export-oriented) growth, incipient industrialisation and tourism.

Apia and Nuku'alofa are essentially post-war creations, though Nuku'alofa was settled in precolonial times and Apia did have a small European population in the late nineteenth century. Since the 1950s both Apia and Nuku'alofa have steadily increased their demographic significance with regard to their national populations (Connell and Lea 1995:35). Although national population growth remains low (being largely offset by emigration), urban growth has averaged much higher rates, leading Connell (1982:23, after Hauser) to describe demographic changes in the region as a 'population implosion'.

Nuku'alofa grew at an annual rate of 2.8 per cent over the 1986–96 period, with a significantly higher rate if its surrounds are included, and recently its population has been estimated at 34,000 (Connell and Lea 1995:33, Muller 1996:7). Over time, there has been a centralisation of population and services on the main island (Tongatapu) and the depopulation of outer islands. Additionally, Nuku'alofa is in the process of urbanising Tongatapu, where 68 per cent of Tongans now live (Statistics Department 1997:1). The main island is now interspersed with small towns and has an estimated density of 258 persons/km^2 (Statistics Department 1997:8). Tongatapu's annual growth rate of 5.1 per cent over the aforementioned period indicates that the 'main island' is considerably increasing its primacy, particularly when compared with the demographic stagnation of elsewhere, or, in the case of the Ha'apai group, the depopulation of nearly 25 per cent of residents from 1976–96 (Statistics Department 1997:1–2). Indeed, urban growth outstrips national growth at a ratio of five or six to one (UNDP 1994:33). The highest recorded growth in the last two censuses (1986, 1996 provisional) was in the peri-urban villages of Tofoa, which grew at 9.3 per cent (Muller 1996:2), and Kolomotu'a (9.8 per cent), on the western fringes of Nuku'alofa (Statistics Department 1997:i).

Similar trends are to be found in Apia, and in the relationship between the two main islands, Upolu and Savai'i (Government of Western Samoa 1993a:9). In the early 1900s, 57 per cent of the population lived in Upolu, but today the figure has reached 72 per cent. Urban growth is triple that of the national rate (UNDP 1994:33). Additionally, Samoans are increasingly choosing to live in the peri-urban agglomeration of north-western Upolu. The Apia and north-west Upolu strip doubled its population in the 1951–71 period (World Bank 1995:81) and now constitutes just under half of the country's population (Asian Development Bank 1996a:21). Today, the 40 km trip from Apia to Faleolo International Airport is one of continuous settlement. If these sprawling peri-urban areas are included in Apia's population, then using 1991 figures, the capital would comprise some 48,616 residents (Asian Development Bank 1996a:21). These trends are likely to continue. According to the Asian Development Bank, three-quarters of all national growth to 2011 in Samoa will occur in and around urban areas (Asian Development Bank 1996a:44). With current demographic trends, and even allowing for continued emigration and a modest national population growth rate of 1.5 per cent, Apia's population will rise to around 75,000 within 15 years (Asian Development Bank 1996a:36).

Much of this demographic growth has been driven by the increasing primacy of these towns and the 'main island' where secondary schooling, formal sector wage employment, hospitals and links to emigration routes are almost wholly centred. Apia is home to almost all secondary industries, which now account for 40 per cent of GDP and over 90 per cent of the country's paid employment. This economic, tourist, employment and educational primacy is also characteristic of Tongatapu.

In both cases this is a qualitative as much as a quantitative shift in human resources. Internal migration is not only a case of the rural poor relocating. Migration has also concentrated and urbanised the educated and entrepreneurial classes who may have otherwise have created employment and opportunities for school leavers in rural areas (Afeaki 1983:74–5, SPREP 1992:16). It also represents, in both instances, the shift of the economic, political, and educated elite and decision makers from the villages to the city (Thomas 1986:12-13), thus contributing to urban *qualitative* primacy.

The trends suggest that both Apia and Nuku'alofa are becoming the sites of more permanent, rather than circular or temporary residency. Government response, however, has been less than energetic. Neither countries have municipal authorities or agencies with jurisdiction either to plan or to implement urban plans. For example, in Apia 'there are no recognised urban plans ... and no legislative or administrative systems for preparing, adopting or administering any such plans' (Asian Development Bank 1996c:6). In both towns, there is an urban policy vacuum. National authorities with fragmented agendas and interests treat towns as they do villages or rural areas. With urban environmental and infrastructural pressures building, there has been minimal response from the authorities to curb increasing urban degradation and *ad hoc* development, and a reluctance to implement such plans and establish planning organisations.

Urban Sustainability: Key Issues

Urban poverty

The negative interrelationships between urban sustainability and poverty have been well made elsewhere (Hardoy *et al.* 1992). Both Apia and Nuku'alofa are becoming cities of the poor, a process which, in turn, is being driven and reinforced by a lack of formal and secure employment. As is the case throughout the Third World, there is a significant paucity of information on urban poverty. Bryant-Tokalau (1995:109) has noted that the term urban poverty is 'generally avoided and unwelcome' throughout the region, particularly with governments. Additionally, there are problems in conceptualising (Bryant-

Tokalau 1995:113) and measuring poverty (Satterthwaite 1996), with very few Pacific Island governments having established poverty lines (Bryant 1993:12–14) – despite the fact that it has been widely suggested that urban poverty (and poverty in general) has increased significantly throughout the Pacific in past decades (Bryant-Tokalau 1995:113).

To date, migration has played a significant role in shifting rural poverty into urban contexts. Unfortunately, expectations often outweigh opportunities and this has been a driving force behind international migration and national dependence on remittances. With private sector opportunites limited, most who find employment in Apia are likely to fill service and public sector jobs, although the latter are becoming increasingly scarce (Government of Western Samoa 1982:3). Indeed, only one-third of school leavers are able to find formal work each year (Department of Statistics 1996:2). Sixty-five per cent of Samoa's unemployed live in Apia and north-west Upolu, and most of them have lived in the area for more than five years, suggesting permanence and a reluctance to return to village and subsistence life, even in the face of urban hardship (World Bank 1995:82). Yet, despite these high official figures, a Samoan trade union leader assured the author that these barely touched the surface of actual un- and underemployment in the city (interview, 27 January, 1997).

In both Apia and Nuku'alofa those who migrate to the cities are principally the young with the primary motivation of access to education and the cash economy, or, in the case of many females, to help in the raising of younger (male) children. It has been noted that Pacific Island capitals are becoming home to a significant number of unemployed youth (SPREP 1992:17). With a significant movement of youth to Apia (more than 50 per cent of the population is under 25), the government is concerned about increasing unemployment and the resulting social implications (Government of Western Samoa 1993a:16). In a recent Urban Youth Survey, the young in Apia were found to be particularly vulnerable to suicide, drug abuse and unemployment (Department of Statistics 1996).

The Tongan government shares similar concerns (Central Planning Department 1993:9). In Nuku'alofa urban youth suffer disproportionately from a lack of access to land and employment and the informal sector has been the refuge of most (Connell and Lea 1995: 50–1). Unemployment rates of males in Nuku'alofa are officially below 10 per cent but are likely to be much higher, with female unemployment higher still. Indeed, youth unemployment rates have been estimated at 27 per cent for 15–19 year olds, and over 50 per cent for young females (SPREP 1993a:10). With marginally positive economic growth rates in the 1990s, a contraction of the agricultural sector, and tighter immigration laws in Pacific Rim states, urban unemployment may be expected to pose a significant structural and social issue in the future for both countries.

The built environment

Cities of the poor place inordinate pressure on social services and urban facilities, including access to shelter, health services (Connell and Lea 1995:55–6), education (Government of Western Samoa 1993a:20) and infrastructure (Bryant 1993:50). Both Samoan and Tongan governments are struggling to provide sufficient infrastructure and services for their urban citizens. This pressure is visibly pronounced in a steadily deteriorating housing situation. Urban housing conditions have been described as being generally inadequate and informal settlements now characterise Pacific Island towns (Connell and Lea 1993, 1995). Today, poor housing is evident in the low-lying areas and swamps encircling Apia and Nuku'alofa. A lack of available land, limited planning and unenforced housing standards have led to a proliferation of autonomous settlements in swamps and mangroves. Yet just three decades ago Kearns stated that housing in the Apia area was sound (Kearns 1965:50) and Walsh noted only emerging housing problems in Nuku'alofa (Walsh 1964). In recent years, however, Tongan authorities have recognised that many families now cannot acquire or rent decent housing (Kingdom of Tonga 1991:257). Presently, home finance is only available through commercial institutions. In Samoa, Housing Authority rates are too expensive for the poor, who have had to fall back on building *fales* (traditional Samoan houses) on customary land (Bryant 1993:49). In both cases, most residential shelter continues to be self-built and communally financed (Connell and Lea 1995:94–5).

Within these settlements, sanitation and drainage is inadequate, and preventable/communicable afflictions (especially diarrhoea, gastroenteritis and conjunctivitis) are generally high (Thomas 1986:10). With available urban land severely constrained, more marginal lands, such as mangrove forests and low-lying swamps, are being cleared and filled for housing. While offering a short-term shelter solution, these inferior sites remain prone to flooding and problems of sewage and drainage clearance (SPREP 1993a:23, Thistlewaite *et al.* 1993:44).

Nevertheless, both Tongan and Samoan authorities have been reluctant to become involved in the housing sector in any direct or significant way, or to develop residential zoning mechanisms (Connell and Lea 1995:112). As Connell and Lea (1995:105) note, 'commitment to housing policy formation and urban planning has long been absent', particularly in Tonga. In fact, Tongan authorities appear to have no clear strategy toward the future development of Nuku'alofa. In its Sixth

Development Plan it was noted that although 'more than a third of the population is urban, Government's policy towards urbanisation and human settlements in urban and densely populated areas has not yet been formulated'. The plan did note, however, that the absence of strategy hindered 'rational housing development', the affordability of shelter, appropriate land use patterns, and personal health and safety (Kingdom of Tonga 1991:257). Future emphasis in the housing policies of both countries appears to be twofold (with neither offering much promise): the encouragement of private sector initiatives in providing shelter and finance, and a reliance on communal and self-help initiatives, including a continued dependence on crowded peri-urban village communities to house increasing populations (Connell and Lea 1995:101). This is despite anecdotal and researched opinion suggesting that these social structures are at their limit of capacity in these regards (Monsell-Davis 1993).

The natural environment

The environmental repercussions of urban growth in smaller Pacific towns have been well documented by the South Pacific Regional Environmental Programme (SPREP) and others (Bryant 1993). The most pressing urban environmental and health issues in both Tonga and Samoa concern water, sewage and sanitation (Connell and Lea 1995). In particular, overcrowding, industrial pollution, marine destruction through urban effluent, and air pollution have been noted as established environmental problems in Apia (Convard 1993:79, Taule'alo 1993:34, World Bank 1995:88). Environmental damage around Apia has been described recently as 'severe' by the World Bank (World Bank 1995:85). The principal problems have been in waste management. Until recently, the city's garbage was dumped openly at Vaitoloa, one of the largest mangrove sites in Western Polynesia. Furthermore, it is reported that nationally, the 'majority of households dispose of their rubbish by throwing it down banks, into stream beds, or along the coast' (Taule'alo 1993:30–1).

The dangerous dumping of urban waste (both industrial and residential) has led to serious off-shore pollution in waters that in the past have acted as an important source of food and recreation. This also includes widely used tourist sites, such as Palolo Deep Marine Reserve, which, although highly contaminated, still attracts snorkelling, bathing and picnicking. In Apia itself, the main sources of spring and river water show high bacterial counts and sewerage contamination. These problems are compounded by the incapacity of government to regulate land use outside of urban boundaries. For example, one of Apia's most important water catchment areas, which is under village control, has been cleared and cultivated for communal and commercial use (Bryant 1993:34). At present these catchments are still an important source of urban potable water for Samoans who have one of the highest rates of use of water in the Third World (World Bank 1995:84). Likewise, demand for potable water consumption in Tonga has placed stress on the capacity of both government and the environment to meet demand which increased almost tenfold throughout the 1970s and 1980s, with the urban requirement doubling that of the rural (Thistlewaite *et al.* 1993:24).

As has been noted, it is the urban poor who suffer the most from environmental unsustainability. In Apia, the environmental 'hotspots' of most concern are the inner-urban swamps of Fugalei, Saleufi and Taufusi, where much uncontrolled and dense informal housing has been erected. Residents in these areas are most affected by problems of poor drainage, contaminated water supplies and problems of personal waste disposal (and reliance on pit latrines and septic tanks). These poorer socio-economic areas are also less served by the minimal urban services available, and residents are more likely to be exposed to unhealthy urban environments in and around the home (Hardoy and Satterthwaite 1989:147–62), and from their proximity to industry (a result of inadequate zoning). For example, residents in Vaitele regularly have crops damaged by falling soot and their water supply contaminated by industrial waste. Consequently, they are periodically forced to erect tarpaulins to protect themselves from pollution, or, at times they are forced to leave their homes for days at a time (World Bank 1995:87–8).

In Tonga, the concentration of population on Tongatapu has led to the clearing of forests, the parcelling of land into smaller allotments and the exploitation of sensitive marshes and mangrove swamps (World Bank 1993:31). Recently, it has been acknowledged that the proliferation of non-recycled garbage is also creating waste management concerns (Thistlewaite *et al.* 1993:28). For many years, garbage has been dumped by trucks into mangrove environments fringing the town, or directly into the sea (Thistlewaite *et al.* 1993:28). Refuse, combined with urban sewerage and run-off, has led to significant lagoon and ocean pollution. The resultant stresses on the marine environment have been noted by SPREP, particularly as the seafront continues to act as a fishing site for urban Tongans.

In Nuku'alofa overflowing septic tanks (which are used by approximately 70 per cent of households in Nuku'alofa) periodically make groundwater supplies unfit for drinking (Connell and Lea 1995:126). In Apia, there is no public sewerage system (Convard 1993:79). Human waste contaminates groundwater after flooding, thus threatening public health (Asian Development Bank 1996b:26). Little is known on the extent of marine pollution, but the effects of direct discharging of abattoir waste, oil refinery leakage and leeching landfills (particularly from the Vaitoloa site) are thought to be significant problems for the reefs and mangroves fringing Apia and the north-west coast (Klinckhamers 1992:39–40).

Urban land: the pressure for reform

Urbanisation is also placing a great deal of pressure on traditional land arrangements, which has led to the creation of an artificially scarce urban land market. To date, urban land issues have been a neglected aspect of urban and Pacific development studies, primarily due to the sensitive and highly politicised nature of debate (Ward 1997:8). Nevertheless, land is one of the more urgent issues facing Pacific Island countries, and it is a resource which is particularly vital for the poor.

To date, it has been land tenure arrangements that have dictated the nature of urban spatial growth and not national planning (Asian Development Bank 1996a:27). As Connell and Lea (1995:92) have noted, 'Apia and Nuku'alofa are towns still partially comprised of unplanned urban villages developed at low densities on communally held land.' Contemporary access to land is intrinsically linked to traditional control over it. Many present issues of urban land and land reform derive from systems initiated to suit pre-urban settlement. In the past, traditional land systems have played both a positive and constraining role in development. While traditional systems were originally conceived in order to promote/protect equality (Moengangongo 1992: 1–2), contemporary population pressures and neoliberal development trajectories may, however, be creating an opposite effect.

In both towns, urban land is administered no differently to that of rural or village property. Although two-thirds of urban land in Apia is 'freehold' (if predominantly church property), greater Apia, where the greatest need for land exists, is actually a collection of villages. Consequently, village elders can and do wield considerable regulatory and other powers over their land. Under the 1990 Fono Act, some 350 village councils in Samoa have powers over land use and contracting out for the development of village land (Asian Development Bank 1996c:5). Simply, authorities do not have the power or will to confront landowners (interview, 24 January, 1997). In fact, the *nu'u* (village) exercises legislative, executive and judicial functions even if these run counter to national law (Peteru 1993:102), thus acting, in effect, as autonomous political entities (Taule'alo 1993:29).

This is leading to an increase in the cost of land, and the growth of informal settlements. For example, one quarter-acre plot of poorly drained land in Fugalei increased in value from $S7,000 in the mid-1980s to $S70,000 in 1992, although it is still possible to buy 'suburban' land for $S15,000 (Connell and Lea 1995:87). With a shortage of freehold land, these prices are likely to escalate in years to come. Nuku'alofa, too, suffers from a critical land shortage. Good central land has sold for as much as $T150,000 for a smaller site, with outlying land selling for $T30,000 (James 1993a:224–5).

Likewise, Nuku'alofa is also essentially a collection of villages, though overlaying that is the role of the monarchy, which wields considerable power and control over land use. There are important land use differences however. While in Samoa land is owned and governed as communal land, under the 1882 Hereditary Lands Act in Tonga all males over the age of 16 are entitled to a plot of urban land (of 0.4 acres/0.16 ha), or *'api kolo*. Though still overseen by nobles, this land can be used for private purposes on the payment of a nominal yearly payment. Nevertheless, due to the intensive migration to Tongatapu over the past four decades, access to urban *api* is now increasingly elusive. Afeaki (1983:75), over a decade ago, put the figure of those unable to acquire *'api kolo* at one-third, while Sevele (1973:253) thought it was as high as 75–80 per cent. Walsh (1982:123) has noted that Tongan male landlessness (only males may normally inherit land) was most pressing on Tongatapu and Nuku'alofa.

The result of land shortages is visibly evident in increasing densities and poorer quality residences. In Tonga, the *'api kolo* is consistently being illegally subdivided, leased and sold to offset the shortage of land and alleviate landlessness. In a recent Samoan survey, urban youth noted that the greatest obstacle to their economic well-being was a lack of access to land (Department of Statistics 1996:29–30). This is leading to quite significant population densities within urban 'villages' and *fales*, or the alternative, which is to squat on unserviced and marginal land (Thomas 1987:242). Likewise, the government response has been to partake in environmentally destructive land reclamation activities to compensate for land 'scarcity', and this is likely to continue in both capitals (interview, 24 January 1997).

Urban land reform is an issue which has been increasingly highlighted as critical (Pauli 1987:239–40 on Tonga, Thomas 1987:243–4 on Apia). Recently this urgency has been recognised officially both in Western Samoa's Seventh Development Plan (Government of Western Samoa 1991:47) and Tonga's Sixth Development Plan (Kingdom of Tonga 1991:257). Still, given the strong traditional ties of Pacific Island governments and the continued power of traditional structures, norms and values, and given that present rural land tenure arrangements have offset deprivation and landlessness witnessed elsewhere, it is difficult to imagine how governments may alter urban land structures in any significant way.

Towards a Sustainable Urban Future?

Though still small, Pacific Island towns face environmental issues comparable with those of other Third World cities. Additionally, these issues are compounded by particularly limiting geographical, financial and cultural factors. The image of the Pacific Islanders living lives of subsistence affluence in idyllic environmental settings is passing. While depletion of natural resources is also occurring outside urban areas, urban sustainability will pose particular resource and political challenges to governments in the decades to come. With current global and national development trajectories encouraging shifts toward growth-first policies, both Apia and Nuku'alofa will increase their pre-eminent roles in national development, as will other Pacific towns and cities.

Bryant-Tokalau (1995:112) has noted that 'if issues such as population growth, environmental degradation, land distribution and tenure, as well as employment opportunities, are not urgently addressed, the future prospects for many Pacific Islanders are not good'. Nevertheless, government response has been less than compelling. Serious environmental action and funding has been conspicuous by its absence in both Samoa and Tonga. Sustainable urban futures will also involve more than developing environmental plans through consultancies, or tying the discourse of 'sustainability' to current neoliberal agendas which will serve to enhance the centrality and hegemony of Pacific towns (Burgess *et al.* 1997b:76–9) but limit their capacities to respond to environmental crisis, to provide services and to enact policies to ensure environmental and social sustainability *vis-à-vis* economic interests. Indeed, 'environmental management and planning is a much broader task which needs to involve communities, good local government, private enterprise and governmental and non-governmental bodies' (Bryant-Tokalau 1993:163). These linkages have been notable for their absence in urban growth-without-development in the Polynesian countries to date.

CHAPTER 13

Commodity Production and Unsustainable Agriculture

JOHN OVERTON, WARWICK MURRAY AND IMAM ALI

Agricultural Transitions in the Pacific

Agriculture in the Pacific Islands has been transformed enormously over the last century, although elements of continuity remain. In general, however, traditional – usually sustainable – agriculture has been replaced by modern commodity-based systems with a market (and often an export) orientation. These systems are causing concern given their characteristically non-sustainable nature. This chapter concentrates on the evolution of modern systems in Pacific Island agriculture and, through selected case studies, argues that urgent steps are required in order to secure sustainable agricultural development in the region. It develops the theme, to be taken further in Chapter 17, that the incorporation of selected elements of 'traditional' agriculture may go some way to achieving this crucial goal.

Despite their great diversity, pre-European agricultural systems in the Pacific were characterised by a number of features. They were based on subsistence production (though surpluses could be produced and trade for cash and barter did occur), they were marked by great diversity in terms of crops grown (notwithstanding the dominance of certain staples such as sweet potato or taro in certain places), they were low energy systems with little need for fertilisers (though fallowing and mulching were used), they were usually based on communal control of land, and labour inputs were relatively low, compared, say, with intensive wet-rice systems in South-East Asia. Some proved to be intensive, highly productive and stable, for example in the irrigated taro systems of New Caledonia, Fiji and Hawaii (Barrau 1958, Kuhlken 1994, Kirch 1977); others were low-density extensive, yet still sustainable systems, such as forms of shifting cultivation (Clarke 1971); whilst some proved ecologically damaging and unsustainable (Bahn and Flenley 1992, Spriggs 1986). Though rather simplistic, Fisk's concept of 'subsistence affluence' (Fisk 1972:24) does at least capture the general idea that Pacific Island agriculturists could in most cases procure food supplies without constant and heavy demands on their time. They were capable of modifying their environments, sometimes considerably and deleteriously, in order to extend and develop agriculture. Environmental impacts, however, were generally localised and temporary. When agricultural systems did prove impermanent, this was usually the result of social or political factors such as social conflict, population growth, or non-agricultural land and resource use.

By contrast, 'modern' (post-contact) agriculture has often proved to have major environmental impacts and it has involved fundamental changes in agricultural practices and associated social and cultural organisation. It has evolved in the Pacific Islands over the past century and a half, significantly changing rural landscapes and societies in its path. In addition, the notion of an agricultural economy has involved commodification not just of agricultural products but also of land, labour and technology. Such transformations were undertaken first by individuals and companies, and then, particularly since political independence, by governments who saw 'rural development' as a critical element of social and economic progress. Modern agriculture in the Pacific Islands has involved several general characteristics:

- Intensification of production: greater energy and labour inputs produce higher yields per hectare.
- Extension of production: more land is put under production of agricultural commodities.
- Market orientation and commodification: products are grown to be sold rather than primarily consumed by producers and both inputs (including land and labour) and outputs are traded on markets which increasingly integrate the 'farm' within the national and, notably, global economy.
- Specialisation: lower unit costs of production, captured through economies of scale and scope, are achieved by product specialisation and monoculture, and standardised agricultural commodities are produced across a wide area.
- Agricultural societies change from communally based villages to household-based farms in some areas.

Whilst such changes have been linked to 'development', 'modernisation' and 'progress' in the Pacific Island region, as elsewhere, doubts have arisen as to the long-term desirability and viability of such modern agriculture. These doubts concern not only ecological impacts but also the economic, social and cultural outcomes. Such concerns are especially salient in the context of the globalisation of agriculture and the shift towards export orientation which is becoming pervasive in the region. Increasingly, agricultural sectors are tied into a global complex over which they have little control, even less so than in the long history of copra production for world markets. Under such conditions, the impacts of wider change on localities are increasingly difficult to manage and have increased their vulnerability.

Evidence from research over the past few decades has shown that basing rural development in peripheral societies on globally oriented commodity-based production brings a range of costs and benefits (Shepherd 1998, Le Heron 1993). The benefits may include currency earnings, positive balance of trade effects, the attainment of higher material living standards in areas integrated into the system, 'demonstration' effects (the introduction of commercial and modern forms of agriculture can diffuse into other agricultural sectors) and forms of rural development that act as a counter attraction to wage employment in urban areas. On the other hand, costs include long-term declines in the terms of trade, price volatility, vulnerability to external political and economic change, ecological problems associated with monocultural systems, displacement of subsistence food production, exacerbation of income inequalities, higher demands for energy and other inputs, outflow of profits and dependence on a narrow range of products. Commodity production can be hugely beneficial, but only if managed effectively. If not, it has often been the case that such systems prove non-sustainable in the long run and tend to increase the very problems that they were implemented to ease.

This chapter examines the way Pacific Island agriculture has been transformed towards a globally oriented commodity production model. It recognises the advantages of such a transition but also questions whether the modern agricultural forms are sustainable. It covers two of the major agricultural commodities of the region – copra and sugar – and then examines a case study of smaller-scale production – squash – before drawing conclusions about the sustainability of these forms of agriculture.

Commodity Production: Rural Development?

The key feature of the transformation of Pacific Island agriculture in the past century has been the widespread adoption of commodity production, by small producers and large, for local, national and global markets. Commodity production has been the basis of development strategies by households, companies and governments. It has been seen as a way of generating incomes, especially through exports. It is seen as a vital element of rural development, bringing beneficial changes without widespread disruption and social dislocation. A plethora of initiatives, many small-scale and local, others large-scale and promoted by governments and aid agencies, have gradually transformed the Pacific Islands' rural landscape, ecology and economies. Commodity production has taken many forms, from quiet incorporation into village modes of production (retaining communal land ownership and customary modes of labour organisation) to major schemes to introduce new crops, new methods of production and new economic and social relations. It has involved a very large variety of products – copra, coffee, sugar, cocoa, livestock, taro, bananas, citrus and rice – and whilst some of these have failed, others remain as the cornerstones of rural development. Below we examine three examples – one widespread and the others country-specific – that illustrate not only the economic potential of commodities but also some of their social and ecological shortcomings.

Copra – the old king

Copra has been the most prominent agricultural commodity produced throughout the Pacific Island region in the past century. It has proved an ideal product for the region and its viability as a commercial product has only recently been called into question. Copra is the dried fruit of the coconut palm (*Cocos nucifera*). Its relatively high value compared with its weight and bulk, and its non-perishability, meant that it could be grown and dried in remote islands, then transported very long distances to ready markets in nineteenth-century industrial Europe. It suited the Pacific Island colonial economy. Local processing was minimal, apart from drying and packing, labour was mostly available (with the partial exception of the plantation sector) and technological requirements were minimal. It allowed the Pacific Islands to be linked to the industrial economies of Europe and provided a local source of income that could then be used to purchase consumer goods from Europe in return (Brookfield 1985, 1987, Knapman 1987, Lawrence 1983).

It was largely a sustainable crop. Because the coconut was virtually ubiquitous and required nothing in the way of extra energy or chemical inputs, it grew readily. It was a hardy tree, tolerating the very saline conditions typical of atolls and coastal margins, yet it could also be grown inland. It was relatively resilient to drought and hurricanes, though if destroyed it could be replaced easily and grew relatively quickly. Furthermore, because it was an indigenous tree crop, Pacific

Islanders knew how to grow and harvest the product, and copra production could be integrated easily into village modes of production. If not used for copra, the coconut tree provided a myriad of uses for people: food, drink, building materials and fuelwood. By the turn of the century, copra production was prolific throughout the region and it provided the main source of cash incomes for many village people.

Yet the progress of the industry has not been smooth nor without conflict. Whereas its integration into the village agricultural ecology and economy was straightforward, different issues arose when it was grown within a plantation mode of production. Attracted by high returns for copra in the mid- and late-nineteenth century, European planters established themselves in many parts of the Pacific, acquiring land, planting coconuts as a large-scale monocrop, and seeking a labour force removed from villages and committed to strict terms of employment within the plantations (Newbury 1972, Brookfield 1985, Bayliss-Smith *et al.* 1988). The loss of land and labour created immediate problems for villagers. Even when they agreed to release land for plantations, they normally had in mind not the permanent alienation of freehold title which planters sought (and obtained) but temporary use rights. Further to this, many men recruited to work on the plantations found that they did not like the harsh conditions and monotonous work often far from their homes, land and kin. As shortages of labour arose, planters recruited labour from further afield – Solomon Islanders, for example, working on the plantations of Fiji or Samoa (Bennett 1987) – and recruitment and employment methods sometimes bordered on deceit, coercion and quasi-slavery (Parnaby 1972).

Especially on plantations, but also in some villages where copra product was intensive, there was also an ecological impact, which Brookfield (1985) has termed the 'coconut overlay'. Lines of coconuts were planted on the best land available – usually the valley flats or small coastal plains of high islands, or the limited better soils of smaller and low-lying islands. Such coconut monoculture pushed village subsistence gardens outward, on to the poorer hill slopes or less fertile soils. This had two major consequences: poorer land meant lower yields and higher labour inputs in subsistence gardens; and distances to travel to the gardens were longer. Both these factors often impacted upon women rather than men; problems of land degradation increased especially where steeper hill slopes were cultivated; and the coconut overlay may have contributed to a qualitative change in village gardens and diets away from the nutritionally rich and diverse crops of the past to more low-input but poorer crops such as cassava.

Despite these problems, copra production has remained an essential element of Pacific Island village economies for the past century. At times copra prices have been favourable (for example during the two world wars or the 1950s) but, as with most bulk agricultural commodities, copra has experienced large variability in returns and an overall downward turn in the terms of trade against imported industrial goods. As new and cheaper sources of vegetable oils have replaced copra on world markets, Pacific Islanders have had to produce ever more bags of copra to pay for the same quantities of flour, cloth or kerosene, or to make the same donations to their churches or pay taxes. Such secular price falls hit the plantation sector more. Price variability and decline coupled with the rising cost of labour (and the difficulty of obtaining it as before) and the pressure from some independent Pacific Island states, such as Vanuatu, to recover alienated land, meant that large numbers of expatriate plantations have gone out of production or been sold as tourist resorts (for their secure tenure of land close to coasts has been highly sought after). Very few remain in operation today.

In the villages, too, copra is becoming much less of a mainstay. Its falling and unreliable value, the arduous nature of extracting, drying and packing the copra, and the rival attractions of wage labour or new cash crops have led villagers gradually to turn away from copra though still clinging to it as a source of income (Sofer 1985, Fleming 1986). Trees have not been replaced as they should have been to maintain yield and quality and many former coconut stands have been virtually abandoned, used only for local demands for coconuts. Today, villages rely on a wider range of income sources – fishing, tourism, kava, taro, handicrafts and remittances – and copra figures much less prominently. Copra is no longer king. It is hoped, though, that some laudable efforts to improve the quality of trees or introduce some appropriate forms of local processing (Wall 1986, Etherington 1988) come to fruition. This is desirable, for copra still retains many qualities of both social and ecological sustainability.

Sugar in Fiji – still sweet?

In many ways sugar can be regarded as the agricultural success story of the Pacific Islands. Grown in Fiji since the early 1860s, it has become a major and stable source of income for individuals and the state, a major source of employment and one of the principal reasons Fiji enjoys one of the highest material standards of living in the region. Furthermore, it is an example of how development can be endogenous, not reliant on aid or remittances, and more or less sustainable, being not dependent on one-off exploitation of natural resources as is the case with minerals. There are doubts about its sustainability, however, both in economic and ecological terms, and it is noticeable that its success has not been replicated in the Pacific region outside Fiji.

The industry developed from the start as a plantation mode of production. Foreign capital acquired land on the two main islands of Fiji, introduced the sugar-cane plant (*Saccharum officinarum*) and constructed an industrial infrastructure comprising sugar mills, a narrow gauge railway and ports. The high demand for plantation labour, coupled with British reluctance to recruit from (and thereby disrupt) Fijian villages, led to the importing of large numbers of indentured labourers from India from 1879 to 1916, thus (together with a stream of non-indentured migrants from the subcontinent) providing the basis of Fiji's dual ethnic population. The industry gradually rationalised. From a number of pioneering companies, a single powerful one emerged – the Colonial Sugar Refining Company (CSR) – which by 1926 owned all the mills in the country (Knapman 1985, 1987, Brookfield 1987). In addition, it was found that sugar cane grew best on the drier north-western sides of the main islands, thus leading to closure of two mills at Navua and Nausori on the south-eastern side. A further critical restructuring of the industry occurred in 1924. Before that time, CSR had run the industry on a full plantation basis, hiring labour, owning the land and controlling all field operations. But with the end of the indentured labour system in 1916 and the consequent rise in labour costs, and with the early 1920s slump in prices, CSR decided to withdraw from direct production to concentrate on oversight, milling and marketing (Ali and Narayan 1989). It granted leases to former employees and gave them contracts to grow cane. This shift to a smallholder basis for the industry in place of the plantations led to an apparently more equitable social structure (and one that has proved remarkably durable through to the present), though its monopsony position allowed the company to continue to exert very tight control over the new farmers and pass on price fluctuations directly to them. Whilst CSR continued to control the industry in Fiji, it oversaw a long period of relative prosperity – despite periodic price fluctuations – based on sugar cane. Smallholder farmers – nearly all of whom were ethnic Indians, though with some indigenous Fijians taking up contracts – could earn a reasonable basic livelihood and have a secure lease over their own 'farm'. Socially, it had become a lot more sustainable than the old plantation system.

Independence for Fiji in 1970, however, led to a second major restructuring of the industry. After protracted negotiations, CSR decided to leave Fiji and in its place a quasi-state organisation, the Fiji Sugar Corporation, took over in 1973. The basic structure of the industry remained the same, with its smallholder base. But with greater farmer say in the running of the corporation, coincidentally higher sugar prices on the world market, and guaranteed access to, and higher prices from, European markets under the Lomé Convention, the industry prospered as never before. The Fiji government, keen to promote rural development, and with new land tenure laws that allowed for secure leases to Fijian 'native' land, oversaw a major expansion of the industry. Whilst the CSR era was marked by production only on the better alienated land close to the mills and on fertile alluvial and coastal flats, the expansion of the 1970s and 1980s led to the opening of new lands for cane cultivation. Many new sugar contracts were offered by the corporation, the government opened new settlement schemes, such as Seaqaqa on Vanua Levu (Bayliss-Smith and Haynes 1988, Ward 1985), and the road infrastructure was improved to link cane production areas beyond the reach of the railway lines. In addition, fertilisers and other inputs were subsidised so that marginal land could yield the sought-after cane. Production increased markedly and the area under cultivation increased from from 47,309 ha in 1971 (CPO 1975:70) to 92,197 ha in 1985 (CPO 1985:46). Sugar began to dominate as it had not done before, not only moving onto surrounding hill country under Fijian *mataqali* tenure but also displacing important local complementary activities such as rice growing or livestock rearing by cane farmers (Ali 1988). Environmental consequences were soon noted, with accelerated soil erosion on the steeper slopes being a consequence of unwise expansion (Clarke and Morrison 1987). In addition, whilst cane cultivation had been carried on in colonial times with minimal use of fertilisers on fertile alluvial soils (fallowing had been widely used), the modern industry became more dependent on inorganic fertilisers (raising yields significantly with the use of fertilisers and cutting the need for fallowing). Other chemicals, such as paraquat, were also increasingly used to control weed growth and pest attacks. Since 1970, then, sugar has become a much more high-input, high-energy industry, dependent on increasing volumes of inputs not only to sustain its expansion but also its outputs from existing areas. In this sense, its environmental sustainability can be seriously called into question.

Yet what might more seriously condemn the sugar-cane industry in Fiji is its economic basis. Fiji is a relatively small sugar producer on the world scale and its small size, coupled with its location and fragmented pattern of mills and ports, means that it would be unlikely to compete on an open world market with lower-cost competitors, in the Philippines or Brazil for example. What has sustained the industry in Fiji is an effective and substantial price subsidy from Europe under the Lomé Convention.[1] This guaranteed access at higher than world prices

[1] There are also other agreements with the USA, China and Malaysia to supply a sugar quota, and favourable rates.

has amounted to a form of 'aid with dignity' (Taylor 1987) in recent years, in excess of the total amount of aid received from all other sources (Grynberg 1995b). There is mounting concern with global trade liberalisation that such trade preferences may disappear or be so whittled away as to become ineffective (Grynberg 1993, 1995b). Should this happen, the sugar industry may not collapse entirely in Fiji, but very large numbers of growers, not to mention government revenues and those employed in the mills or transport, will suffer significantly. A not improbable scenario is a retreat of the industry back to pre-1970 bounds with much lower profit margins, greater price fluctuations and a less prominent position in the Fiji economy.

Furthermore, there are other threats to the industry. In 1998 serious drought associated with the El Niño phenomenon led to considerable falls in yield, estimated by some to be as much as 50 per cent lower than normal and resulting in a loss of revenue of up to $F100 million (PacNews 1998). Political problems associated with land tenure are also on the horizon. Much of the expansion of the industry in the 1960s and 1970s was on land held under 'native' tenure, 'owned' by indigenous groups but leased on a 30-year basis to mainly Indian tenants. Many of these leases are coming up for renewal but landowners, after many years of receiving low rents (due to the rigid rent distribution formula giving a small share to resident *mataqali* members), are now pressing for the tenancies not to be renewed (Ward 1985, 1995b, Overton 1987, 1992a, 1994, 1995). This might result in a major decrease in production and considerable hardship for present tenant farmers. The industry's future, then, is very uncertain.

Squash in Tonga: the dangers of over-specialisation

Perhaps the most notable agricultural commodity boom of recent years in the Pacific Island region has been that of squash (*cucurbita maxima*) from Tonga. This small island country, at various times, has attempted to develop agricultural exports such as copra, vanilla and bananas with limited success (Fleming and Hardaker 1995, Hardaker 1987, Hardaker *et al.* 1986, Sturton 1992, Thaman 1976). In 1987, however, an explosion in the export of December pumpkins to Japan was initiated. This boom forms part of a wider trend in the region towards the export of non-traditional agricultural products[2] to 'counter-seasonal'[3] markets in

[2] Non-traditional agricultural exports may be defined as one of three following types: 1) items traditionally produced in a country but never before exported; 2) items not produced or exported from a given country before; 3) items produced or exported from a given country traditionally, which are sent to new markets (Barham *et al* 1992)

[3] The term counter-seasonal market is used to refer to the supply of produce

high-income northern hemisphere countries. This process has accelerated over recent decades, given the globalisation of the fresh fruit and vegetable complex and the shift to export orientation in many peripheral economies including the Pacific Islands (Murray 1998a, Whatmore 1995). The roots of the Tongan 'boom' are found in the private sector. Production was set up in early 1987 by a group of New Zealand entrepreneurs who spotted a three-week gap in the supply of squash to Japan (in between the Mexican and New Zealand supply seasons). Noting early successes, the government provided capital for growers to participate through the Tongan Development Bank (Tonga Development Bank 1993). Later, the state became involved in the issuing of licences to export companies in order to limit supply levels and maintain prices. Apart from these actions, however, the government has left the private sector to its own devices.

Growth in the squash export sector has been breathtaking. From a base of zero exports in 1986, by 1991 approximately 23,000 tonnes were exported (Kingdom of Tonga Statistics Department, various years). In terms of earnings, a peak of approximately 23 million Pa'anga was reached in 1993 – representing approximately 50 per cent of all export earnings (National Reserve Bank of Tonga 1997). In 1994, nearly half of all the farmers in Tonga (approximately 3,000) had plantations of squash (from less than one hectare to whole *apis* [plots] of 8 acres [3.2 hectares]). The socio-economic and environmental implications, especially at the micro scale, of the exposure to global economic forces have been profound. The boom has brought the country a range of important developmental benefits. On the other hand, a number of economic, social, political and environmental tensions exist which threaten the sustainability of the sector. If left unchecked, these problems promise to undo many of the gains afforded by the boom (Murray 1998b).

Undoubtedly, there have been benefits from the export boom. On the macroeconomic scale, foreign exchange earnings have helped to plug the export gap – a sizable trade imbalance traditionally filled by remittances – at least partially. Moreover, export expansion during the most favourable years has bolstered economic growth, which, in the absence of squash, would have been even more sluggish than it has been for the past decade. On both the macro and the micro scales, growth has brought important multiplier effects. Downstream effects, (in the retail sector) have been especially noticeable. There have been

to receiving markets during the winter/spirng months when domestic supply is not available. Increasingly, high-income northern hemisphere markets are being supplied by southern hemipshere production within the globalising fresh fruit and vegetable complex (LeHeron 1993).

further benefits more obviously observable on the micro scale. First, the demonstration effect of the widespread commercialisation has had the knock-on effect of raising productive possibilities in other agricultural products. Second, in those localities participating in the boom, and among those families which have been fortunate enough to be able to enter the sector, the increase in cash incomes has been large. This has raised material living standards for some. Finally, in the villages involved in squash production the opportunities for harvest and other linked employment has risen. This is especially important for women, who in many cases are entering their first paid employment.

On the other hand, it could be argued that the above benefits are being eroded and outweighed by a range of tensions which appear to be evolving in the sector. On the macro scale of resolution a number of serious problems can be identified. First, recent fieldwork suggests the development of an inverse relationship between squash export earnings and the level of remittances sent home from Tongans overseas. Thus, over time, the boom may have the effect of increasing the size of the foreign exchange gap which needs to be plugged. Second, squash exports have proved to be highly import-intensive: most of the materials and inputs – including the seeds – are imported, leading to poor upstream multipliers. Furthermore, there has been a notable increase in consumer imports which partly offsets the positive balance-of-payments implications of the boom. Perhaps most controversially, imports of second-hand Japanese cars have spiralled. In 1996, Tonga spent 50 per cent of squash export earnings (25 per cent of all export earnings) on such items. Third, over-reliance on one product for one market has developed (Japan is the sole market) – which has made the economy extremely vulnerable to price fluctuations and the whims of powerful receivers who can obtain supply from an increasing array of sources, including regional suppliers such as Vanuatu and Fiji. Finally, macro-geographical inequalities have been exacerbated. On Tongatapu (the largest island), due to both physical and locational factors, a concentration of successful squash growers is developing in the west. In the east of Tongatapu and on the outer islands, there has been relatively little squash development.

At the micro scale of analysis a further range of worrying trends is evident. First, not all growers are able to take part in the export system; many lack the collateral (or connections) to obtain credit to be able to move into export production – leading to an exacerbation in local differentiation. Often those farmers who do well in the squash sector expand through the leasing (illegal and legal) of land. This bears further negative consequences as relatively unsuccessful growers may lose subsistence plots and leased lands are farmed with damaging intensity.

Inequality is also highly evident in the relationship between the growers and the export companies. Low organisational capacity of the growers *vis-à-vis* the companies has placed them in a poor bargaining position. Thus, contracts are often not offered for squash, and minimum or guaranteed prices are not mentioned. Growers also have to pay considerable commission to the firms for their services and supply of inputs. An exploitative relationship quickly develops and has led, on occasion, to grower debt with the companies or the Tongan Development Bank. Second, the shift towards export production has led to an increase in monocultural practice on *apis*. This makes growers vulnerable in both environmental and economic terms. Traditionally, *apis* have been used for a mixture of commercial and subsistence production. By putting over a large proportion of land to squash production, many growers have lost access to a food supply. A further worrying development is the use of pesticides, fertilisers and other inputs – in quantities never seen before in Tonga. This is doing untold, and as yet unmeasured, damage to soil ecosystems. Third, although labour opportunities have increased, demand is seasonal in nature and therefore highly insecure. Thus displaced growers may have to travel into urban areas to find work in the off-season. Finally, the introduction of export cash crops is leading to the erosion of traditional social support mechanisms in the villages. Reciprocal relationships are being replaced by individualism, which involves successful families hiding the full extent of their wealth so as not to incur family 'responsibilities'.

Added to the above, a number of recent internal and external problems further jeopardise the sector's future: the Japanese are becoming increasingly concerned about the quality of the vegetables reaching them; competition from other islands and Japan itself is increasing and eating into the Tongan supply season; the Tongans have let the Japanese down more than once in terms of the volumes promised for shipment; and the sector is plagued continuously by political problems concerning the issuing of licences for export and allegations of corruption. It is – in the words of one of the advisers to the Minister of Agriculture – 'a niche market waiting to close' (personal communication March 1998). If the market does collapse, it will do unquantifiable damage to the thousands of individuals and the tens of localities which have become dangerously reliant on the sector.

At the root, the state is to blame for many of the sector's problems. The limited intervention which has taken place has been designed to further the interests of certain 'well-connected' export companies and interest groups in government. In other areas, where regulation is clearly required to temper the ill-effects of the exposure to global economic forces, the government has maintained a damaging 'hands-off' approach. This policy mix – which combines the worst of neoliberal economics and patronage politics – is precipitating a great deal of damage to social, economic and environmental systems and is prejudicing sustainable development.

The Need for A Reappraisal in Rural Development Thinking

This chapter has shown that agriculture in the Pacific Islands has been transformed fundamentally in the past century. Whilst the agricultural landscape might still contain significant elements of traditional crops and village gardens, the questions of what is grown, how it is grown and why it is grown now yield quite different answers. Agricultural commodity production, involving specialisation of production, higher energy inputs, greater market orientation and new modes of land, labour and technology organisation and exchange, has percolated deeply into plantations, farms and village gardens. The benefits of these changes are manifold: there are higher cash incomes (often leading to desired changes such as improved housing, education for children or the acquisition of consumer durables); there are profound social changes (many giving more independence and mobility to individuals and households); and there are the tangible signs of 'development' (roads, bus services, electricity, water supplies and schools). It could be argued that it is a model of development that has served some people well on the Pacific Islands, especially as it has come from the soil and sweat of its people, not from artificial and unsustainable external sources.

Yet, even if one accepts that the material and social benefits of such development are desirable (many might not),[4] the examples analysed in this chapter question whether such a model is sustainable. Agriculture is perhaps the most inherently sustainable of all human activities, using natural fertility of the land, sunlight, water and human labour to produce the basic necessities for survival. The model of commodity production now dominant in the Pacific Islands, however, has moved far from this ideal. There are ecological concerns as dependence increases both on inorganic fertilisers for an energy subsidy and on other chemicals for ecological modification, and land is being degraded through unwise land management and the imperative of increasing production on steep slopes or poor soils. There are social concerns as incomes from cash cropping are not spread evenly: some

[4] Some authors have pointed to problems such as social disruption from individualism, loss of traditional values, and money wasted on unecessary and harmful luxuries (Ravuvu 1987a, 1987b).

individuals profit from new activities and are able to invest and diversify elsewhere, whilst others, even if they gain a little, are often left with land that is less productive and incomes that fail to be maintained. And there are economic concerns as the changing global political economy threatens to diminish the viability of several key Pacific Island products. Governments are less likely to subsidise rural livelihoods given the trend towards deregulation within the neoliberal framework in the region. Furthermore, increased linkages into the globalising system are raising economic concerns as it is becoming increasingly difficult to predict and manage the local impact of political and economic change at higher scales of geographic resolution.

There is a pressing need to re-evaluate the dominant globally oriented commodity production model, something being suggested by writers working in other parts of the periphery (Shepherd 1998). From a sustainability perspective, the commodity production model is flawed. It has led to considerable environmental damage and often deleterious social changes and inequalities. The Pacific Island experience has had much in common with experiences elsewhere on the periphery but the impacts of globally oriented agriculture have also been localised and have brought particular cultural and environmental changes. Alternatives may, however, be hard to find. Perhaps they may lie partly in the past, in a rediscovery of the sustainable modes of precolonial times within the Pacific, or they may lie in the application of lessons from elsewhere, or in the introduction of new technologies (see Chapter 17). Whatever they are, they will have to address the issue of sustainability from not only an ecological point of view but also from an appreciation of the economic, social and cultural dimensions within the Pacific Islands.

PART III

Sustainable Alternatives

THE CHAPTERS IN Part II clearly demonstrated problems with exploitation of the natural resource base in the Pacific. The need for alternatives is critical. Whilst the immediate response of many environmentalists may be to argue for greater efforts to conserve the region's resources, this may not be a solution which would be supported by local people who depend on utilisation of the resource base for their livelihoods. It is just such a response which leads some to argue that the environmental movement is still a 'luxury for the middle classes of the rich countries' which has little relevance for countries desperately seeking development (Hadjor 1993:106).

Nevertheless, in recent years a significant amount of work has been undertaken by NGOs and aid agency personnel to spread the conservation message throughout rural areas of the Pacific, notably in areas under threat from logging companies. While many rural people have been receptive to such messages at first, they have tired quickly of outsiders who preach conservation of resources without providing any viable alternatives for income generation. Any attempts to implement conservation programmes without finding sustainable means for the local community to enhance their livelihoods will soon be jeopardized. As Ingram (1994:44) notes with reference to Papua New Guinea, 'conservation is only viable if it contributes to the resolution of conflicts over traditional tenure, if it produces badly needed cash, and if it provides a base for permanent jobs'.

Perhaps most significantly, much of the change that is already occurring in the region is the result not of government or NGO plans and projects but of the myriad of grassroots actions undertaken by individuals and communities. It has resulted from the desire to protect aspects of the environment and culture that people hold dear, as much as from the desire to increase material standards of living and improve the prospects of the coming generations. Most of these actions are not specifically 'sustainable development' projects – they are rarely if ever guided by considerations of the health of the global environment, nor do they seek to contribute to global change. However, often they articulate with outsiders – whether NGOs, tourists, consumers or government officials – who are imbued with those aims. It is this interplay of diverse everyday livelihood strategies with external and global forces that provides a fascinating, and often optimistic, outlook for sustainable development in the Pacific Islands.

The following section examines some of these activities. It looks first at changing nature conservation policies, where outside involvement has been strong, then moves to two critical sectors – forestry and tourism – where consumers are providing momentum for change but local response has been positive. Next, the quest for sustainable agriculture is examined largely in relation to a review of exemplars from the past that may offer models for the future. The section finishes by focusing on urban areas, where many of the problems of environmental sustainability are seemingly most intractable, and analysing the potential of alternative decentralised models of urbanisation.

CHAPTER 14

Nature Conservation and Aid in Samoa

NED HARDIE-BOYS

International aid is a common vehicle for transmitting both the practice and concept of sustainable development. In practice, sustainable development is often transmitted through nature conservation strategies in the form of protected areas. To be sustainable in Samoa as elsewhere, these protected areas must take into account particular socio-economic, political and cultural systems. This chapter examines case studies of three approaches to forest conservation in Samoa, providing an analysis of their appropriateness and effectiveness.

Nature Conservation Strategies

Nature conservation is an important strategy for achieving environmental sustainability. As such, it is a subset of sustainable development. It may even be regarded as a prerequisite for sustainable development. Protected areas are a common component of nature conservation strategies. Figure 14.1 depicts the major categories of protected areas as defined by the International Union for the Conservation of Nature and Natural Resources (IUCN). Each category of protected area is designed to meet specific objectives. The categories are presented in Figure 14.1 along a continuum, from those with strict protection objectives to those with multi-purpose objectives, including human use. In a general sense, this equates to a shift from a national park approach to conservation to an integrated conservation and development approach (McNeeley and Miller 1984:49–53, West and Brechin 1991:8–9).

An increasing number of protected areas are moving away from strict protectionist objectives to incorporate human use and resource development objectives. This temporal shift in emphasis, from national park approaches to what Wells and Brandon (1992:1) term 'integrated

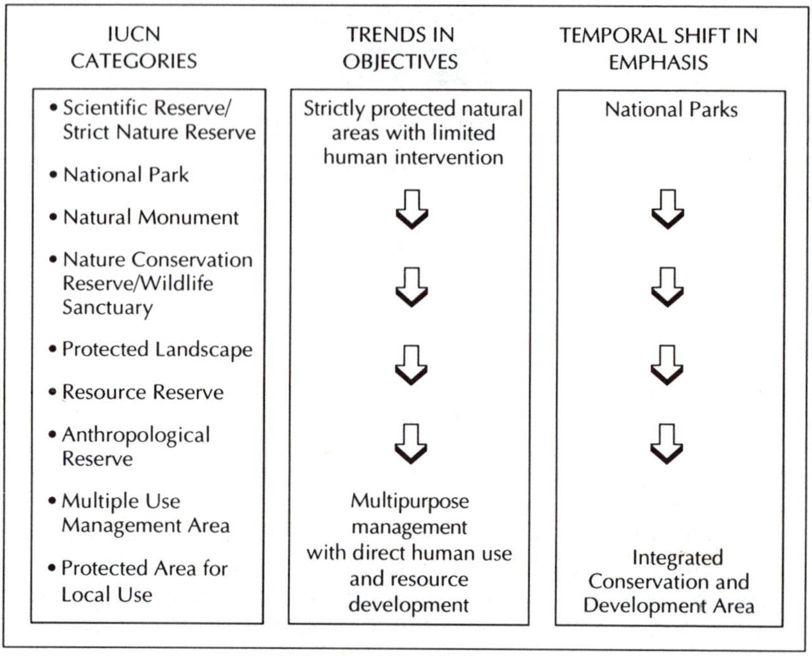

FIGURE 14.1 • CATEGORIES AND KEY OBJECTIVES OF PROTECTED AREAS

conservation and development' areas (ICDs), matches the evolution of sustainable development by including the objectives of people and societies.

National parks and conservation

The national park approach to nature conservation was initiated in the United States in the 1870s amid increasing awareness of natural resource limits. As these fears of limited resources eased in the West in the 1920s, the establishment of national parks slowed. In non-industrialised countries, however, as colonial powers perceived scarcity amongst resources such as large African mammals, national parks continued to be established during this period (Wells and Brandon 1992:1).

The national park approach flourished again in the 1960s and 1970s, in response to the reemergence of the politics of scarcity (McNeeley and Miller 1984:657, West and Brechin 1991:31). This resurrection of the approach coincided with the internationalisation of environmental concerns to include developing countries. As a result, there was a further extension of the national park approach into developing countries during this period.

It became apparent that such an extension required a shift in emphasis from the strictly protectionist objectives of the approach up to that time. The protectionist approach suited industrialised societies, where environmental management was separate from issues of livelihood. In developing societies, however, the national park approach confronted the socio-economic and cultural systems of people's livelihoods.

Integrated conservation and development

ICD approaches to nature conservation repackage protected areas using the rhetoric of sustainable development. Rather than seeing national parks as islands of antidevelopment, therefore, ICDs bring protected areas into the fabric of socio-economic and cultural development. Socio-economic development objectives are met by actively promoting development projects alongside conservation. Cultural development objectives are met by including local people in the process of establishing ICDs (Wells and Brandon 1992:42–7).

ICDs retain conservation objectives as their primary goal. Development objectives are incorporated as a means to achieve this goal (Brown and Wyckoff-Baird 1992:10). This distinguishes ICDs from environmentally sound development projects which have development as a main goal. Typical development projects within ICD approaches to nature conservation include the provision of social services to local communities and the establishment of appropriate enterprises, such as ecotourism operations. A key to a successful ICD project is clearly linking the development benefits of a project to the conservation action required. If this can be achieved, then conservation and development objectives are mutually reinforcing.

Development and Nature Conservation

Parallel with the evolution of sustainable development, consideration for the environment has become increasingly prominent in international development aid. This process has been referred to as the greening of aid (for example, Conroy and Litvinoff 1988).

The greening of aid

International aid first adopted a green face in the 1970s when environmental impact assessments were added to many development aid projects. During this period, however, environmental considerations were rarely more than special interest components of development aid projects (Carew-Reid 1989:41). In the late 1970s many aid agencies adopted environment-specific projects, including nature conservation projects. This approach was favoured by donors as it enabled them to allocate a portion of resources to tangible environmental projects, such as the establishment of national parks, while the majority of their resources could continue to be channelled along traditional development aid approaches (Carew-Reid 1989).

Following the emergence and acceptance of the sustainable development ideal in the 1980s, environmental considerations increasingly became integral components of development aid projects. The smudging of the boundary between environment and development has been matched by less distinction between environment-specific and traditional development aid. For example, a forestry management project could be classified either as an environment-specific project, or as a conventional development project with strict environmental impact assessment procedures.

The delivery of green aid

At the multilateral level, a number of separate agencies have been established to deliver green aid. These include the United Nations Environment Programme (UNEP) and the Global Environment Facility (GEF) under the administration of the World Bank. Similarly, within bilateral aid (government to government aid, also known as ODA – 'official development assistance'), governments have established separate environmental outputs. Examples of this include USAID's Biodiversity Conservation Network and New Zealand ODA's Environmental Support Programme (Biological Support Programme 1993, Ministry of Foreign Affairs and Trade 1994).

Increasingly, as aid takes on a green face, aid agencies are networking with NGOs in the delivery of aid to make up for the shortage of skills within many aid agencies. Within the delivery of this aid, NGOs themselves are forming partnerships between donor country NGOs and recipient country NGOs. For example, the Swedish Society for Nature Conservation (see the second case study in this chapter), networks with and supports 40 environmental organisations in developing countries. Furthermore, partnerships are forming between traditional developmental NGOs and environmental NGOs in the delivery of green aid. In this way, the Solomon Islands Development Trust, a traditional development NGO, has established networks with two environmental NGOs, including New Zealand's Maruia Society.

In respect of delivery, green aid retains a key similarity with traditional aid in that funds continue to be moved to developing countries. Often this is done with little debate as to whether the transfer of funds is necessary or desirable. Therefore, green aid faces the same risk as traditional aid of failing to recognise that the presence of capital is not the only condition for development (Bauer 1971:252).

Conservation in Samoa

Western Samoa (renamed Samoa in 1997) encompasses two main islands, Upolu and Savai'i. These islands are rugged and mountainous with slopes descending from volcanic crests. Forests in the interior of the main islands are increasingly replaced by plantations as the land descends to the coast. Approximately half of the coastline is bounded by coral reefs. The total population of Samoa is in excess of 160,000. Approximately 34,000 people live in the capital of Apia while the rest live in over 320 villages predominantly along the coastline.

Traditional social and cultural institutions are strong and driven by *fa'a Samoa* (the Samoan way of life). This traditional way of life is evolving, however, as it mixes with a new set of externally introduced behaviours and ideologies. This interaction between two ways of life is evident in the dual political systems (village councils versus Westminster-style central government), land tenure systems (customary communal land titles versus individual titles), economic systems (subsistence agriculture versus a monetary economy dependent on external aid and remittances), and social systems (the extended family or *aiga* headed by a *matai* versus the nuclear family). Strategies for nature conservation in Samoa must acknowledge these dualistic systems.

Within an environmental context, Samoa has a range of problems. As the following list of environmental damage (South Pacific Regional Environment Programme 1992) indicates, many of the environmental problems in Samoa are closely connected to deforestation:

1 Uncontrolled land clearing;

2 Watershed management problems;

3 Deforestation and loss of biodiversity;

4 Soil erosion;

5 Degradation of reefs by eutrophication and sedimentation;

6 Mangrove loss and pollution of mangrove stands;

7 Cyclone damage to forests, soil, agriculture, reefs and infrastructure;

8 Weedicide use;

9 Marine and coastal pollution; and

10 Nearshore overfishing and destructive fishing practices.

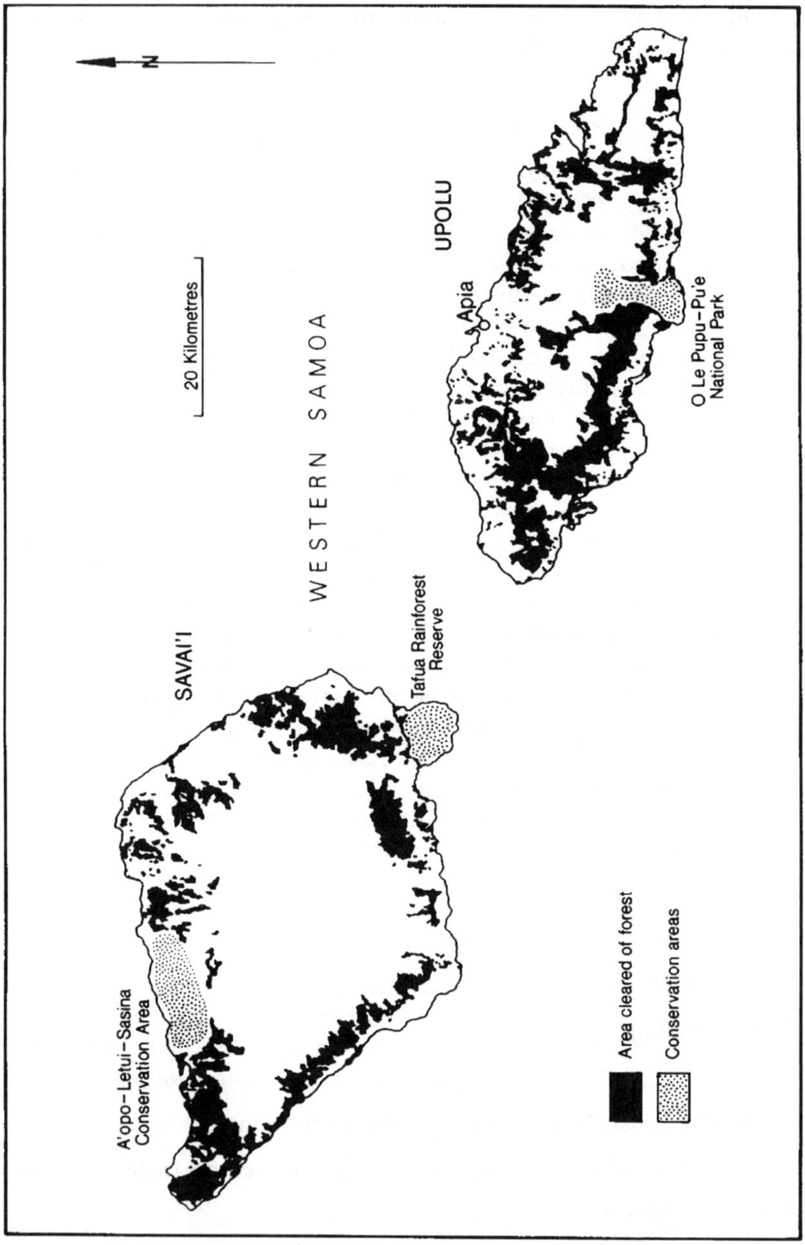

FIGURE 14.2 • AREA CLEARED OF FOREST (1954–87) AND LOCATION OF CONSERVATION AREAS

Source: After Ward 1995a.

Forest clearance in Samoa is attributed to commercial logging and clearance for agriculture. The latter has been crucial as a result of the way Samoans have cleared land to establish individual title to communal land (Ward 1995a, O'Meara 1995). Figure 14.2 indicates the area cleared of forests from 1954 to 1987. More recently, the rate of deforestation in Samoa was estimated to be approximately 3,100 hectares per annum (Government of Western Samoa 1993b:8). A land use survey conducted in 1991 showed 104,000 hectares of indigenous forest remained in Samoa (Government of Western Samoa 1993b:87). The majority of this (82,200 hectares) was non-productive and a further 9,400 hectares was protected through legal status or through village conservation agreements. These figures compare with the 96,100 ha of land used for agricultural purposes.

There is a clear need for forest conservation in Samoa. However, as the following case studies of conservation aid initiatives indicate, there is also a clear need to acknowledge the local context of Samoa's political, socio-economic and cultural systems within these conservation initiatives.

Case Study 1: O Le Pupu-Pu'e National Park

O Le Pupu-Pu'e National Park, in the south of Upolu, was established in 1978 following the enactment of the National Parks and Reserves Act 1974 and assistance from the United Nations Development Advisory Team in developing a national parks plan. New Zealand also provided technical assistance through its bilateral aid programme during the implementation of the park.

The 2,850-hectare park contains two low-quality walking tracks. Currently there is no visitor centre as this was destroyed by cyclones in 1990 and 1991. Visitor use in the park is concentrated around the grounds at the park headquarters and the adjacent swimming hole at Togitogiga Scenic Reserve. The park is administered by a ranger and 13 labourers.

The management plan for the park echoes the defensive ideology of the national park approach to conservation: its aim to 'erect and maintain boundary fences to ensure the boundary is adequately defined and protected as necessary against outside influences' (Mossman and Berg 1981:18). The National Parks and Reserves Act 1974 also reflects Western values of conservation including 'inspiration, aesthetic appreciation, enjoyment and recreation' (Department of Agriculture and Forests 1975:3). The success of the park is, to some extent, dependent on whether the values expressed in this national policy are common to the values of Samoans living in the vicinity of the park.

When O Le Pupu Pu'e National Park was established, it was

acknowledged that there was little awareness of its conservation or landscape values, even by the park staff (Mossman 1980:3). However, the park was to serve as an example to be used to create an awareness and understanding of the values of conservation and protecting natural areas.

Research in 1994 sought to gauge the understanding of the national park concept by the local people (Hardie-Boys 1994:75–85). In total, 30 people from 23 *aiga* were interviewed in three surrounding villages. The interviews focused on people's perception and use of the national park. Almost half of all respondents believed that the primary purpose of the park was tourism. Slightly over a quarter of respondents mentioned the ecological purpose of the national park while just under a quarter had no idea what its purpose was: 'I don't know the importance of protecting it.... It's a *palagi* [European] set-up' (interview, Iliili Village, April 1994).

During planning for the park, it was recognised that something was required to give some 'purpose' to attract visitors. In a sense, the Togitogiga Scenic Reserve adds this 'purpose' by providing an attraction of tangible use (a swimming hole and picnic area). From the interviews, it is evident that visiting the swimming hole was the primary 'use' associated with the park. A third of respondents never used the park because it restricted the uses that they valued, such as collecting nuts. A number of respondents stated that they occasionally hunted or gathered food and wood from the park despite the fact that these activities are not permitted there.

Despite the general lack of understanding relating to the purpose of the national park, there appears to be a certain respect and support for it. This support does not seem to have any ethical basis, however, and may be quite superficial. Without support for the park based on a greater awareness of its purpose and value, encroachments are likely to continue, particularly if pressure on resources intensifies. O Le Pupu Pu'e is still the only national park in Samoa. Alternative approaches to nature conservation, which include provisions for the local ownership and use of protected areas, are required on the 80 per cent of land that falls outside public ownership.

Case Study 2: Tafua Rainforest Preserve

Following O Le Pupu-Pu'e National Park, no new conservation areas were established in Samoa until 1989. In that year the village of Falealupo on the western tip of Savai'i signed an agreement with non-government foreign donors. The people of Falealupo agreed to preserve their lowland rainforest for 50 years in return for the donors paying off village debts which were at the time being financed by logging operations within the forest. This type of agreement was the basis for a similar agreement to protect lowland rainforest on the Tafua Peninsula in the south-east of Savai'i.

Logging companies were showing considerable interest in the Tafua rainforest at a time when adjacent villages were desperate for infrastructure. Two *palagi* scientists – Cox and Elmqvist (1993) – who were particularly interested in protecting the flying fox population within the forest, introduced the concept of a Falealupo-type agreement to the local villages. With the villagers showing an immediate interest in the concept, the scientists approached an environmental NGO, the Swedish Society for Nature Conservation (SNF), to raise funds to provide the necessary infrastructure for the villages. This was achieved and in 1990–1 three separate agreements were signed between SNF and the villagers, leading to the creation of the Tafua Rainforest Preserve.

In the case of Tafua village, the agreement restricted use of the forest to subsistence purposes for a period of 50 years in return for SNF providing specified development assistance. Initially, funds were used to build a primary school in the village. By 1994, however, funds from SNF had also been used for repairs and relief following Cyclones Ofa and Val, construction of a village canteen and experimental solar power unit, and cutting trails in the forest in anticipation of an ecotourism operation.

The people of Tafua continue to use the forest for a range of purposes, including gathering food, hunting pigs, collecting wood for housing and cooking, and collecting medicinal plants. In 1994, visits to the forest associated with ecotourism were still on a small scale, with just one or two official 'eco-tours' each week – though children of Tafua regularly receive small fees for guiding informal visitors through the Rainforest Preserve. With more recent funds in return for conservation commitments, the people of Tafua plan to harvest fruits, nuts and medicinal plants commercially and to develop a tourism project based on handicrafts and adventure-type tourism.

As part of a policy revision by the SNF, responsibility for administering and implementing projects resulting from funding was transferred to an NGO based in Samoa. This NGO, being based in Apia, was soon criticised by the three villages in the agreement as being unresponsive to their needs and a significant sponge on the funds which were meant for projects within the villages. It is estimated that less than 35 per cent of funds from SNF were reaching the three villages (Cox and Elmqvist 1993:10). As a result of ongoing conflict, the village of Tafua severed its relationship with SNF and the Apia-based NGO in 1993.

In 1994, SNF contracted a new NGO based on Savai'i with strong representation from Tafua, to administer and implement projects associated with the original agreement. The people of Tafua formally accepted the intermediary role of this new NGO. The political manoeuvrings concerning the rainforest agreement in 1990–4, however, had occurred at the expense of practical activities in the forest and villages. This was reflected in extensive previous research on local perceptions of the conservation agreement and the conclusion was further reinforced by interviews with a number of people living in Tafua in 1994.

It is apparent that the conservation agreement in Tafua was the result of a range of motivational forces. The conservation of biological diversity was clearly the starting point for the *palagi* scientists and the SNF. The fact that the village had recently objected to logging proposals indicates that some level of conservation ethic was also a motivational force for some of the people of Tafua. Evidence suggests that this was probably a spiritually based attitude to conservation rather than strongly linked to Western ecological conservation (Hardie-Boys 1994:98). Another obvious motivational force for the people of Tafua was the money that the agreement brought to the village.

The agreement was reached because the motivational forces for protecting the forest were compatible. The long-term success of the agreement and sustainability of the rainforest will require mutual understanding of each party's motivation. Research has indicated that some villagers believed that the conservation project belonged to the Swedish and there was some confusion as to why the Swedish would want to protect a small forest located so far from Sweden (Olsson 1992). Interviews by the author in 1994 indicated some level of understanding of the conservation values inherent in the forest but also some suspicion relating to what benefit preserving the forest brought to the Swedes. Many local people clearly related the conservation of the forest to the Swedish donors. For example, when asked why the forest was being protected, one respondent replied: 'SNF wanted to save birds, bats and trees for scientists to study' (interview, Tafua Village, May 1994).

The majority of people spoken to in Tafua were aware of the monetary benefits of protecting the forest and had some idea of the benefits of conserving the forest. The link between these two benefits, however, is often unclear, fostering a feeling that the villagers are getting paid to protect their forest. This may threaten the long-term protection of the forest or otherwise result in an expensive conservation regime. There is a need to link explicitly the monetary development projects in the village with the actual practice and management of protecting the forest.

Case Study 3: A'opo-Letui-Sasina Conservation Area

The conservation area at A'opo-Letui-Sasina, in the north of Savai'i, takes an ICD approach to achieving conservation. As such, socio-economic development is actively promoted so long as it is directly linked to the core objective of protecting the forest. This approach recognises that to be sustainable at a physical level (for the forest to be sustained) it is necessary for the approach to be sustainable at a socio-economic level (given that the forest is a source of livelihood for many of the surrounding communities). The approach was led by the government, international funding agencies and NGOs in collaboration with the villages of A'opo, Letui and Sasina.

At the time of field research in 1994, the development of a conservation area at A'opo-Letui-Sasina was reaching the end of its planning stage. The ecological basis for the conservation area was established following a survey carried out with assistance from New Zealand ODA. In recognition that the key to conservation lay in the acceptance and understanding of the local villagers, the survey actively involved the villagers in the collection and presentation of the survey results. This inclusion of local communities from the outset has been identified as critical to achieving village support and has assisted in gaining acceptance of conservation principles in general (Park 1992:8).

A forest use survey and a socio-economic survey were undertaken. The forest use survey was analysed to place a value on the resources currently being extracted from the forest so that the cost of obtaining these resources from elsewhere, if the forest were felled, could be quantified. The socio-economic survey established the livelihoods of the villagers and assessed what the villagers required and desired from the forests. A resource use survey was undertaken to establish sustainable yield potentials for the resources identified in the previous two surveys. Once again, the inclusion of the villagers in these surveys helped build a relationship and transfer a sense of ownership to the villagers.

As a result of the surveys, the economic development plan for the conservation area is based on carving, ecotourism and commercial harvesting of medicinal plants. Commercial logging, even on a sustainable basis, was excluded as an economic use because it directly conflicted with the policy of the international aid organisations involved with the project.

In line with the theory behind ICD approaches to conservation, it is also planned to influence behaviours and activities occurring adjacent to the conservation area. This includes teaching more sustainable practices on adjacent agricultural land to ease the pressure of expanding crop lands into the forest.

The initial political framework for establishing official conservation agreements with customary village landowners in Samoa is contained in the Lands, Surveys and Environment Act 1989. The Division of Environment and Conservation (DEC) was established to administer and implement this legislation. Outside of normal operations, which do not include establishing conservation areas, DEC relies on international aid to fund projects. The key funder of the conservation area at A'opo-Letui-Sasina is USAID through their Biodiversity Conservation Network.

The Biodiversity Conservation Network contracts the Biological Support Programme to implement the conservation area project. This organisation provides the funds to the government (through DEC) which collaborates with other organisations such as a local environmental NGO, village people and other government departments. In recognition that the villagers are the key to the future of the conservation area, Village Conservation Committees have been established and it is conceivable that in the future they will hold the budgets for the project under contract from government.

Presentations of the ecological survey to the villagers indicated that most villagers were not aware of the conservation significance of their lands (Park 1992:7–8). Nevertheless, during these presentations it appears that the villagers were generally receptive to the principles of conservation. Specific educational programmes and general liaison with villagers has further promoted conservation principles and knowledge.

Field research by the author in 1994 focused on interviews with key village figures including *pulenu'u* (village mayors) and *faife'au* (church ministers). The first impression gained from these interviews was that the villagers had been disillusioned with commercial logging following royalties equating to just $S301[1] per person for 2–3 months of logging. This realisation that logging was not the panacea for development fostered interest in the conservation proposal. Related to this, however, was the second impression gained: that DEC has nothing better to offer: 'The DEC will come again and ask all their questions but they do not offer anything in return' (interview, Letui Village, May 1994). The DEC acknowledged that a tangible benefit was required urgently if villagers were to maintain their commitment to the project.

The need for tangible benefits is partly due to the high expectations created by the conservation agreements at Tafua and Falealupo where villagers have received cash and infrastructure. Furthermore, A'opo had recently received $S112,000 from the SNF and an environmental NGO for 20-year logging rights for an area of midslope forest. This

[1] In 1994, $S30 equated to approximately $NZ21 or $US13.

forest was not in immediate danger of logging and of course SNF and the NGO have no intention of logging it. These types of deals can be very attractive compared with what DEC has to offer.

The ecological benefits of conserving the forest were often mentioned during interviews in the villages (Hardie-Boys 1994:105–20). These benefits were strongly related to the water-retaining characteristics of the forest as the area had an inadequate water reticulation supply. This recognition of the ecological benefits of the conservation area could be enhanced by providing villagers with direct socio-economic benefits from protecting the forest.

The approach taken by DEC promoted grassroots participation and in understanding of the conservation concept. This is commendable. The apparent confusion relating to DEC's motives, however, suggests a need for the department to declare its position. Too many questions were being asked while few opinions were being expressed by DEC. This certainly contrasts with earlier approaches to conservation and development.

Conclusion

Approaches to nature conservation in Samoa have evolved to recognise both the local socio-economic, political and cultural environment of Samoa and the global shift towards the concept and practice of sustainable development. The trend in conservation areas in Samoa has followed that depicted in Figure 14.1, that is, from the strictly protectionist objectives of national parks to the direct human use objectives of integrated conservation and development areas.

The national park approach of O Le Pupu-Pu'e established an 'island of anti-development in a sea of development'. It was deemed unnecessary to involve local people in the establishment of the park and this is reflected in current perceptions and understanding of the purpose of the park. Actions at a practical level totally outweighed changes in values and attitudes at a cognitive level.

The conservation agreement that established the Tafua Rainforest Preserve incorporated socio-economic objectives by providing funding for village projects. The projects were not closely linked to the conservation of the forest, and it is debatable whether the forest is actually any safer now than it was before the agreement. Once again, activities at a practical level have preceded changes at a cognitive level which are necessary to change destructive practices which threaten the forest. Linking funding initiatives directly to the conservation of the forest may be one means to influence behaviour at a cognitive level. Furthermore, unless projects actively foster ongoing local socio-economic development, the protection of the forest will continue to be dependent on aid.

The ICD approach at A'opo-Letui-Sasina has been more proactive in the promotion of socio-economic development. It has also taken a more inclusive approach to the cultural context of the villages in which it is being established. The approach was initiated at a cognitive level by trying to promote the values of conservation as a necessary precursor to changing destructive actions at a practical level. It would appear that a greater awareness and appreciation of conservation values are not sufficient conditions in themselves, however, to guarantee the protection of the forest at A'opo-Letui-Sasina. There is a clear need for real, tangible incentives to demonstrate the benefits of protecting the forest.

The case studies in Samoa provide an example of the emergence of the global concept of sustainable development within a local, practical context. The concept has come into practice through the vehicle of international aid. While this aid is subject to the usual motivations for giving and receiving aid, the application of the aid has become more responsive to the local village level context. This type of foreign assistance is likely to be necessary to encourage sustainable development practices under the current developmentalist ethos in Samoa. Enhancing the local understanding of the conservation benefits of these aid projects is a necessary but insufficient precondition for their success. The other necessary condition is direct socio-economic development benefits which enhance local livelihoods and are linked explicitly to the conservation projects.

CHAPTER 15

Sustainable Forestry Options in the Solomon Islands

ROSS CASSELLS AND REGINA SCHEYVENS

Chapter 9 showed how the lure of monetary rewards from logging is often very difficult to resist, for both rural communities and governments throughout Melanesia. This chapter moves on to consider direct alternatives to large-scale logging, alternatives which have the potential to enhance local livelihoods, to work side by side with the subsistence sector rather than undermining it, and which can be controlled or strongly influenced by local people.

According to Wijewardana (1995:45), 'Market opportunities for the future will increasingly be for sustainably managed wood.' While recent demand patterns of Western countries would tend to support this claim, the possibility of supplying sustainably managed timber is a topic which has attracted much controversy, with some conservationists claiming that there is no such thing as a sustainable timber yield (Rosoman 1995:9). In the context of Pacific Island communities facing considerable environmental degradation through large-scale extractive industries such as logging, however, the potential offered by sustainable forestry would seem to warrant serious investigation.

The Need for Sustainable Forestry

The Solomon Islands are a scattered archipelago of over 300 resource-rich islands which are home to almost 400,000 people, the majority of whom live in highly dispersed rural settlements (Figure 15.1). Most villagers rely to varying degrees on subsistence production for their livelihoods, and they are able to do this because 87 per cent of the land is still in the hands of customary owners (AIDAB 1994:13). The Solomon Islands are still largely forested. These forests are a major subsistence provider, be it as a location for shifting agriculture or as a source of food, medicine, and firewood or raw materials for building houses, canoes and handicrafts. In terms of the national economy, however, the forests are seen as a source of timber which generates much needed revenue. Chapter 9 showed how successive governments in the Solomon Islands have become dependent on the foreign exchange earnings the logging industry brings them, with log sales accounting for over half of the country's export revenue in recent years (AIDAB 1994:6).

While it is easy to blame successive governments for allowing the destruction of the forest resource, the bulk of forest land is under customary tenure and decisions concerning this land are actually the direct responsibility of the landowner (SPREP 1993b:55). As such it is often local landowning communities, rather than the government, who need convincing that there are other viable cash-earning opportunities available to them as an alternative to logging. Given the multitude of dispersed communities, however, and the need to communicate with and inform each community individually, this is difficult to do in practice.

It is on customary land that the future of the Solomon Islands forests will be decided, so if the government is to be more than a spectator then, in the words of the Solomon Islands National Environmental Management Strategy, 'greatly increased attention must be paid to the development of practical systems for environmentally acceptable forest management on customary land to the benefit of landowners and the broader community alike' (SPREP 1993b:56).

While some conservationists would like to see a complete halt to the harvesting of tropical rainforest this, simply, is not practical. Given that the imperative for continued harvesting of tropical rainforest is likely to remain, the challenge will be to try and ensure that commercial benefits are not gained at the expense of customary and subsistence values. The enhancement of local livelihoods should be at the centre of all sustainably forestry strategies. This chapter examines four options in which sustainability is considered achievable.

Forest plantations

The Solomon Islands timber industry as it currently exists has a limited future. Based on the unsustainable use of the indigenous tropical rainforest it is estimated conservatively that the merchantable forest resource will be depleted within ten years (Duncan 1994). The eventual depletion of the indigenous resource, however, has long been recognised and over a period of time considerable efforts have been made to establish forest plantations by the Solomon Islands government, development assistance programmes and, earlier, the British colonial administration. The problem with government reforestation, however, was that it was restricted to government-owned land and thus to a few areas. In the event, the momentum gained by the logging industry throughout much of the Solomon Islands reached such a level that the resulting deforestation of customary land totally eclipsed reforestation efforts by the government. More pertinently, the nationally significant combined plantings of the Government Forestry Division in the West and Kolombangara Forest Products Ltd (KFPL), a large joint venture project between the government and the Commonwealth Development Corporation located on the island of Kolombangara, are well short of the 65,000 hectares that is considered necessary to sustain a local forest-based industry. The solution to the problem of creating a sustainable forest industry, therefore, needs to be found on land under customary ownership rather than on government-owned land which, in some areas, may be returned to the original owners anyway.

Over the years, a lot of effort has been put into identifying the land use and reforestation potential of land in the Solomon Islands. Reports by Wall (1980) (North New Georgia), Fraser and Larsen (1981) (North New Georgia) and Shield (1992) (Solomon Islands general) provide such examples. While Wall, in particular, discusses socio-economic factors that could impact on land development, the social capacity of land owners to support large-scale reforestation has not been given the same level of attention in reports concerned specifically with reforestation. The social capacity of local communities is, however, as much a limiting factor to reforestation as is the physical capacity of the land to support it. In North New Georgia, for example, landowners have already shown a willingness to sabotage logging operations that displease them. In the 1970s they set fire to the Levers Pacific Timbers camp at Enogae, which resulted in Levers abandoning the logging concession they had in North New Georgia. In 1994 landowners also burned logging equipment belonging to Golden Springs International (SI) Ltd, a logging company that had taken over the logging concession previously granted to Levers Pacific Timbers.

Offset against these social concerns, however, is the fact that forest plantations can grow approximately ten times the volume of wood that can be produced in a similar area of well-managed natural forest (Wooff 1997). Without forest plantations, therefore, the Solomon Islands is unlikely to sustain any sort of viable national forest industry beyond the harvestable life of the existing indigenous forest. The incentives, then, to find solutions to creating economically, environmentally and socially sustainable forest plantations on customary land are only going to increase as the demise of the current and unsustainable logging industry draws closer.

In a 1995 social baseline survey conducted in North New Georgia to assess the social issues that were likely to affect a proposed large-scale reforestation project, it was found that there was considerable apprehension amongst villagers over a number of issues. The main concern was the need to retain adequate garden and subsistence reserves should a large-scale reforestation project go ahead. Villagers were self-reliant through subsistence but as the population was increasing rapidly this was beginning to place pressure on the land insofar as a greater area for gardens was required. Increasing demands were also being placed on the forest for other subsistence needs such as house-building material, medicine and food. The villagers were, quite wisely, reluctant to reduce the available subsistence area as it still provided them with their livelihood. It was also a form of social and economic security to fall back on when the cash economy could not support them. It would, have been disastrous, therefore, if villagers had lost their means of livelihood. This would have made them totally dependent on the cash economy which has very little chance of supporting them fully in the foreseeable future (Cassells 1995).

As a general rule the investors in, and managers of, a forest plantation are more likely to be primarily concerned with the operational side of forestry. On the other hand, customary landowners may see the forest plantation project simply as a means by which they can attain the benefits of development. Furthermore, in the small-scale fragmented societies of the Solomon Islands, it is very difficult to get people to form cohesive cooperating units (Schoeffel 1992). A forest plantation project – with its large area, multitude of landowners and relatively long time frame before benefits are derived by landowners – represents a fairly high risk for landowners and investor alike.

There are a number of ways of reducing this risk. First, it is essential to maintain the subsistence economy. Populations are expanding rapidly and more subsistence land will be needed just to survive. It would be fatal to lock up too much land in a forest plantation project. Adequate subsistence reserves, therefore, need to be set aside but will reduce the plantable area of a project, perhaps jeopardising the economic viability of some plantations.

The second way of reducing the risk of plantation project failure is to ensure good communication between investors, donors (where relevant), and the landowning groups. Given the difficulties caused by the diverse nature of Solomon Islands societies, it would seem wise to establish some sort of grassroots community organisation to deal with issues as they arise, whether grievances, disputes or the sharing of benefits. Although some communities may have run other types of projects successfully in the Solomon Islands, the concept of some sort of grassroots community organisation to carry a reforestation project has not been particularly well developed. Earlier top-down approaches, such as the North New Georgia Timber Corporation, have not been popular with landowners. Considerable investment may therefore be required by forestry plantation project initiators to nurture viable and effective community organisations that can both facilitate the smooth running of the project and ensure that landowners are not alienated from the management of the project, nor deprived of its benefits.

The difficulty larger-scale plantation forestry still poses for Solomon Islands landowners is that it locks up their land for a long period of time. Landowning groups are no longer able to use their land freely but, more than this, the planting of trees can also threaten land ownership itself. Under customary law a primary landowner may, for example, grant usufructural rights to a non-landowner for the planting of a garden, cocoa or coconut plantation. The life of a plantation, as compared with a garden, may span many generations and even if underlying land ownership is not overlooked, the original landowners are effectively denied the use of that land for an indefinite period. At present this is not a serious problem with small parcels of land such as are required for cocoa or coconut plantations. The problem does, however, become serious for large-scale plantations, particularly when population growth begins to place pressure on land resources. Small-scale woodlots may be much more compatible, therefore, with current customary land use patterns.

Household woodlots

The great attraction of small-scale woodlots (small blocks of privately owned forest) is that usually they are owned by a single household unit. Thus the potential for land disputes is diminished greatly. Woodlots may make good use of infertile land and abandoned garden sites. Although future subsistence production would be denied in these areas, at least for the duration of one tree crop, this may be acceptable to landowners if ownership and control is retained by them. In effect these woodlots would be a cash crop, the income from which would be used to support subsistence. Depending on the species planted, however, it can be a long time before an income is realised and this can be quite a disincentive for landowners who are thinking about planting trees.

A variety of introduced tree species have been planted in the Solomon Islands, ranging from quick growing balsa (*Ochroma lagopus* - 5 years to maturity) on Guadalcanal, *Gmelina arborea* (8–12 years) in the West, *Eucalyptus deglupta* (8–12 years) in the West and on Malaita, and teak (*Tectona grandis*), mahogany (*Swietenia macrophylla*) and *Cedrela odorata* (30 years). Obviously the quicker a return can be realised the more popular tree planting becomes, hence the attraction of faster-growing introduced, rather than indigenous, tree species.

In the early 1990s KFPL organised an outgrower scheme, whereby landowners were given assistance to grow trees for eventual sale to the company. It is interesting to note that after KFPL obtained a very good price for some *Eucalyptus deglupta* the outgrower scheme became very popular with landowners near the KFPL plantations. Using this approach larger-scale plantations could be supplemented by smaller customarily owned, or even joint venture, satellite woodlots. Similarly, on Guadalcanal, an English entrepreneur who had a market for balsa in Britain offered landowners a post-establishment grant of one dollar per tree if they would enter into a fixed price joint venture agreement with him. The grant, and the fact that balsa would yield an income in five years, provided a strong incentive for landowners and the joint venture balsa project, for a time, became very popular (Cassells 1996).

Projects such as the NZODA Customary Land Reforestation Project have also been instrumental in pioneering small-scale forestry in the Solomon Islands. Much of the effort, however, has been directed at training local forestry staff in extension and community forestry methods. Local staff, in turn, have worked amongst landowners to raise an awareness of the benefits of growing trees and to provide hands-on assistance in establishing small woodlots and, especially, in broadening attitudes towards forestry on customary land. Amongst landowners this has been to introduce the idea of sustaining the forest, be it by planting quick-growing introduced tree species for specific uses (cash-generating timber, firewood, fruit and nuts), or by encouraging regeneration in milled indigenous forest. This attitudinal change takes time but the interest generated in reforestation is likely to compound once participating landowners are able to reap an income and gain other tangible benefits from their existing woodlots.

Community woodlots

Between the household woodlot and the forest plantation is the community woodlot. Larger than the household woodlots, these small community forests have taken a number of forms. An early experiment in community reforestation on customary land was undertaken through the NZODA Malaita Customary Land Pilot Reforestation Project, located near Auki in Malaita. More recently NZODA were also involved in trying to establish a small plantation forest on customary land on the island of Kohinggo, in New Georgia. The intention at Kohinggo was to use a joint venture arrangement between an outside investor and the customary landowners but due to disputes over land rights, and the inability to attract an investor, the project failed.

The multiple ownership community woodlots are inherently vulnerable to land disputes. Management of these forests is not only logistically more complex. Depending on the size they may also require finance as well as good business and forestry management skills. These skills usually need to be introduced to the community and a benign development project is a good medium for doing this.

In addition to sound business and forest management skills, Solomon Islands communities often need assistance in forming cohesive operating units. A community organisation, a social infrastructure owned by the community, is necessary to carry these reforestation projects – yet, to date, very little work has been done in this area except, in a limited manner, on the Customary Land Reforestation Project. Community organisations have, however, been nurtured successfully on community projects in other developing countries, so good precedents exist. These might provide good insights into models that could be appropriate in a Pacific Island context and thus enable landowners to participate more fully in larger-scale forestry ventures in the longer term.

Ecotimber production

Ecotimber production is a system whereby natural forest is harvested on a very small scale. Ecotimber is a relatively new word which has yet to be defined clearly. As seen with terms such as 'ecotourism', the 'eco' label is now being applied to a range of products and services. To date, supplies of tropical timbers going under the name of 'ecotimber', 'good wood' or 'smart wood' have been produced in countries such as Brazil, Papua New Guinea, and Honduras. Ecotimber appears to have emerged as a marketable label which, its advocates hope, will give exporters of sustainably produced timber preferential entry into lucrative markets (Gilpin 1996): 'Environmentally conscious consumers the world over are now demanding credible "green" products and a greater level of information and certainty with these products' (Rosoman 1995:11).

As applied in the Solomon Islands, ecotimber production usually refers to sustainable small-scale portable sawmilling, or chainsaw milling, operations. Several NGOs operating in the Solomons have turned to ecotimber production as an alternative to logging which could, in both the short and long terms, earn a reasonably good income for those involved. At first, however, so-called ecotimber ventures were no more sustainable than large-scale logging operations insofar as forest management is concerned. Known locally as *wokabout somills,* portable sawmills that can be carried manually into the forest and set

BOX 15.1 • ECOTIMBER PRODUCTION: SWIFT

Solomon Western Islands Fair Trade (SWIFT) was established in late 1994 as part of the Integrated Human Development Programme (IHDP) of the United Church. The motivation behind SWIFT's formation lay in the church's desire to curb large-scale logging which was destroying forests and igniting social problems in Choiseul and Western Provinces. While church leaders had held village conferences to discuss problems with this type of logging, they were often greeted with the response: 'That's only talk: we need money.'

Requests from a number of village communities for assistance with the marketing and transportation of sawn timber had been received regularly by the church. This was seen as a viable industry which could provide a good return to villagers in a relatively short period of time and which gave it clear advantages over other development alternatives. Church leaders, therefore, decided that small-scale timber milling, carried out on limited areas of land at a sustainable rate, could be undertaken with a profitable return to landowners. It was hoped that the option of producing ecotimber would discourage villagers from opting for a short-term solution to their economic problems – that is, signing with logging companies. This was seen as undesirable from several perspectives: logging companies offer only a small financial return, their operations often lead to land disputes and they devastate local environments.

While the first aim of SWIFT is political, to enable people to say 'no' to logging company offers, its second aim is economic, 'to promote sustainable timber production for community needs and to facilitate earning a good cash income by selling these sawn timbers to the local and export market' (SWIFT Netherlands Foundation 1996:1). These aims are readily embraced by the sustainable livelihoods approach advanced in this text. SWIFT's key players in achieving these aims are producer groups, the 250 family, clan or tribal groups which have signed up to produce ecotimber to sell to SWIFT. Each producer group decides to put a small portion of their land aside for the production of ecotimber. SWIFT foresters help the producers decide which land to allocate to the project and together they draw up forest management plans (FMPs) for the pegged-off blocks. The FMP includes an inventory documenting the land and its resources, noting dominant tree species, and calculating how many trees may be cut in a one-hectare block over a five-year period. This is usually a maximum of four trees. It also lists forest regrowth monitoring details, silviculture measures for producers and areas which the producers are supposed to look after, including sacred sites and buffer zones around waterways. Any timber cut and sold to SWIFT has a number on it to identify the producer and the particular tree it came from, which can be verified by consulting copies of the FMP kept at SWIFT's timber yard.

SWIFT provides specific services to assist producer groups: loans to equip themselves with basic tools such as chainsaws, transport facilities for those in the widely dispersed islands who would otherwise not be able to bring their timber to the central yard, and training courses in forest management, timber grading and chainsaw maintenance. Perhaps the major service SWIFT provides, however, is access to markets. Through establishing an effective marketing structure and setting up a subsidiary company in the Netherlands to buy all exported timber, SWIFT has developed an excellent bargaining tool: it pays a very good price for timber which is produced in a sustainable manner according to the FMPs SWIFT has established. SWIFT offers up to $SI 1,200 per cubic metre for sawn timber, compared with around only $SI 35 per cubic metre which the logging companies pay for round logs. Through SWIFT a producer can, for example, earn $SI 5,000 a year by felling only two trees. To achieve the same income from logging royalties, 70–100 trees would need to be felled and the producer would have to wait around 200 years for the forest to regenerate (SWIFT Netherlands Foundation 1996:3)

In order to obtain credibility in international markets for the timber they buy from producer groups, SWIFT hired the Societé Générale de Surveillance to set up a timber certification system based on the standards set by the Forest Stewardship Council (FSC). The FSC is both a trade and NGO body whose mission is to 'promote environmentally appropriate, socially beneficial, and economically viable management of the world's forests' (*The Independent* 1996: 16). The key point here is that the FSC recognises that environmental, social and economic goals can be complementary if a project is managed in the right way, and they support the idea that local people should benefit from environmental projects. In addition to establishing and implementing a comprehensive FMP, SWIFT is required to monitor the activities of its producers regularly. As part of the certification system, producers must sign an Environmental Pledge and a Mutual Trust Agreement on which the traditional leaders or recognised representatives of a tribe or village are listed as trustees. Trustees commit themselves to developing their land and sea resources in a sustainable manner, while, in return, SWIFT agrees to provide services to enable that tribe or village to develop its resources over a 25-year period.

up next to the trees which are to be felled, were acquired by local communities and used at will. Rather than limiting the cut to just a few trees selected under the principles of sustained yield, trees which were easily accessible and had a ready market were felled, with the result that some areas of forest were decimated. Fortuitously, largely because earth-moving machinery is beyond the financial reach of most landowners, the environmental damage caused by this small-scale milling has only been a fraction of that caused by large-scale logging. The small size of these operations has also limited their environmental impact, and so has commercial viability: because small business management and machinery maintenance skills have often been lacking, many milling operations have collapsed before they could do much damage.

More recently, NGOs such as the Solomon Islands Development Trust and the economic and development arm of the United Church have begun to train Solomon Islanders in sustainable forest management practices as well as developing the infrastructure necessary to transport, reprocess, grade, package and ship this timber for export to sympathetic overseas markets. Certification procedures are also being put in place to verify that the timber is being produced sustainably and that an auditing mechanism to check this is in place. The idea of tapping into a premium environmental niche market allows organisations to provide landowners with a financial return which exceeds that provided by logging companies per cubic metre of timber produced (Box 15.1). Although entirely up to the landowners themselves, income could be used to supplement subsistence or provide a basis for further investment in the cash economy, with one possibility being the replanting of abandoned garden sites in woodlots, as discussed above. Certainly, if managed well, ecotimber production could provide a locally controlled, economically viable and environmentally sound alternative to logging.

The period over which an income from ecotimber can be sustained will, however, depend on how much forest area landowners have available. If the area is relatively small, which is often the case, landowners will only be able to cut a timber volume equivalent to the mean annual increment, or some multiple of this. Mean annual increment is the average volume of timber grown each year. If, for example, in cutting four trees a landowner removes five times the mean annual increment, he or she will not be able to cut trees in this area for another five years. The greater the initial cut, in terms of mean annual increment, the longer landowners will have to wait before cutting again. As a consequence, revenue gained from ecoforestry may only be intermittent and could even be limited to a single injection of capital for each generation.

Evidence of over-cutting has been found in the SWIFT ecoforestry project (Box 15.1) where unmarked trees have been felled in some areas. If forest inventories are well prepared, however, and the auditing of the milled area of forest thorough, then it should be relatively simple to detect such infringements. The care taken by producers to protect remaining trees when felling and cross-cutting also needs to be monitored. Long-term forest sustainability can also be affected by factors such as failing to disperse sawdust, which prevents regrowth in cleared areas. Armed with the skills and tools for milling, there is also concern that some landowners may withdraw from ecoforestry ventures to sell unsustainably produced timber to other buyers. As long as ecoforestry organisations can offer premium prices for the product they buy, however, this problem should not become a major issue.

Another concern relates to the dependence on international markets. While managers and supporters of projects such as SWIFT have done an excellent job of establishing sound markets for ecotimber in Europe and elsewhere, like any other primary commodity, ecotimber may be vulnerable to future international commodity price fluctuations. At present, ecotimber provides a more lucrative return on investment than, for example, copra or cocoa, but there is no guarantee that this situation will continue. It would seem wise, therefore, for projects such as SWIFT to diversify their market, preferably to adopt a broad livelihoods approach in which they look for ecotimber markets closer to home and at alternative uses of the timber, such that local communities can adapt to fluctuations in price without undue losses. In Papua New Guinea, for example, it has been established that the domestic market for ecotimber is very strong and thus most producers could sell all of the timber which they produced locally. In addition, an NGO working with a community in Morobe Province has made specific efforts to provide local people with training in unfamiliar building construction techniques so that they can use the timber they mill to improve their own houses (Rainforest Information Centre 1995). They have also learned a skill which may provide them with employment opportunities outside of their own village.

There is also the problem of land ownership. Whether this be primary or usufructural rights, the more landowners involved in an ecoforestry venture the greater the potential for disputes, or for the more rapacious members of the community to appropriate the revenue for their own benefit. Often it is left to the local Council of Chiefs to try and resolve landownership matters but, as with plantation forests and community woodlots, multiple ownership ecoforestry projects are likely to need a robust community organisation to carry the project, and to ensure that benefits are equitably distributed throughout the community. Women often fair poorly in this regard.

Finally, concerns about gender equity arise in relation to all forestry options. Plantations, woodlots and ecoforestry all tend to be initiated by men, who seem to be primarily interested in earning cash. The women, who have quite different needs (and high existing workloads) are usually asked to help, while not having any control and not necessarily sharing the benefits. This has also been the case in SWIFT's operations (Scheyvens 1996, 1997).

Conclusions

This chapter has examined in some detail four forestry options in which sustainability is considered to be achievable in the Solomon Islands. These options have differing impacts on local communities, both in terms of their livelihoods and their social structure. We can derive from these examples general findings which may give us insights into the potential and pitfalls of sustainable forestry in other Pacific Island states.

Plantation forests are ten times more efficient at producing timber than even well-managed natural forests, so if the Solomon Islands are to retain a nationally viable forestry sector then forest plantations offer a real hope of achieving this. The Solomon Islands can grow good quality timber, which can support a national industry, very quickly. On the other hand, rural Solomon Islands communities, with their customary land tenure systems and small fragmented social structures, have a limited capacity to support large-scale plantation projects which represent a big risk for them.

Robust community organisations with sufficient authority to influence plantation management, resolve land disputes and ensure the equitable distribution of benefits (and costs) amongst landowners will need to be actively nurtured if major social disruption and alienation of villagers from their land is to be avoided. Maintaining the viability of village subsistence economies in the face of forest plantation establishment is also extremely important. To do this, sufficiently large areas of intact tropical rainforest have to be reserved in order to maintain village subsistence livelihoods both now and in the foreseeable future.

Small-scale woodlots, on the other hand, are much more compatible with current customary land tenure systems and present land uses. There is a low socio-economic risk for villagers with woodlots, especially if they are owned by a single household unit. Woodlots can enhance household incomes as well as diversify the household economic base. As is the case with growing most species of trees, it can be a relatively long-term venture. Community woodlots, involving several landowners, represent a higher risk in so far as the potential for conflict amongst landowners increases in proportion to the number involved. But, as with the larger plantations, community organisations could be nurtured to reduce this problem.

Ecotimber can offer an alternative to logging by providing an immediate income. Although this income can be ongoing if sustained yield practices are rigidly adhered to, the revenue gained by individual landowners may only be intermittent and will depend very much on how much forest they own and how much timber is cut initially. Ecotimber thus can be interpreted as a good stop-gap measure. It provides an immediate alternative to logging and, ideally, should give landowners time to establish a more productive means of growing a sustainable wood supply.

In all of the sustainable forestry options discussed in this chapter, experience to date has shown that on the whole women have been marginalised in terms of their power to influence the direction and outcomes of forestry projects. In some instances minor sideline projects for women have been created but few real attempts have been made to weave the deeper issues of gender relations and roles, property rights and access to productive resources into the fabric of project planning, operations and management. Consequently, women have been unable to reap the maximum benefits from what should be a highly valued cash-earning opportunity for their families. Moreover, their existing knowledge of the forest is not being utilised and women are not being given the opportunity to learn contemporary forest management techniques. As a result women's influence over decisions regarding the use of communally held resources is likely to decline further. Managers of forestry projects could better draw upon women's knowledge and interest in preservation of the forests by, for example, employing them to conduct the ongoing monitoring of operations which is required in ecotimber production in order to meet criteria for certification.

Alternative, small-scale sustainable forestry ventures such as ecotimber production and the establishment of woodlots are vital if Pacific Island communities are to enjoy sustainable cash-earning alternatives to the more destructive exploitation of their natural resources, as occurs with large-scale logging, mining and some commercial fisheries. However attractive such alternative initiatives are, they should not be perceived as immune to some of the problems faced by development projects in general. Strategies which encourage local participation in development, complex as this may be within communities with fragmented social structures, are vital.

CHAPTER 16

Ecotourism

REGINA SCHEYVENS AND NICK PURDIE

Tourism in the Pacific

For decades the tourism potential of the Pacific region has been noted. The image of palm-fringed, sun-drenched islands with white sands, coupled with welcomes from smiling 'natives', has drawn a considerable number of visitors to the region. The growth of tourism in recent decades is particularly notable. Tourist arrivals in Fiji, the biggest single tourist destination in the region, increased from 15,000 in 1960 to almost 280,000 by 1990 (Haywood and Walsh 1996:117).

While such growth is significant, on a global scale the South Pacific region is seen as a small tourist market. It attracts only 0.15 per cent of the world's tourists (Hall 1994:148), and Fiji is the only country in the region which has over 4,000 tourist beds. Most of the remaining states have fewer than 500 beds (Sofield 1994:209). Yet as the region comprises only a very small share of the world's people and its land area, it is not surprising that the tourism occurring here can have dramatic environmental and social impacts. The tourism situation of Rarotonga highlights this point:

> In Rarotonga in the Cook Islands ... there were 39,000 visitors in 1991, 'hosted' by a local population of only 8,000. With an average length of stay of 10 days, there were at times up to 3,000 visitors on the tiny 32 square kilometre island and their presence was highly intrusive (Sofield 1994:210).

This chapter focuses, first, on the extent to which local communities participate in and benefit from tourism development in the Pacific, and, second, on the sustainability of tourism in the region. Those adopting a growth-oriented view of natural resource management would be likely to support forms of tourism which focused on the consumption, rather than preservation, of resources, while others adopting an ecocentric approach may argue that any activity, including tourism, should not interfere with the intrinsic value of the natural environment (Hunter 1995). Thus it is important that, in addition to scale, we consider the nature of the tourism activity and whether or not it is likely to contribute to sustainable development.

To date most tourism development in the Pacific has been resort-based. As large resorts are capital-intensive, they have generally required outside investment and thus they are mostly foreign-owned (Britton 1982, 1983). While they do provide some direct employment, the nature of the jobs available to local people is generally subservient and the wages are much lower than those paid to expatriate workers. Indirectly, local people may benefit from the sale of produce to the resorts and handicrafts to tourists (Milne 1990) but imports of food are substantial and there may be little flow-on to the local economy (Britton 1987, Dwyer 1989). In general, however, a number of negative environmental and social consequences have been associated with this mass, resort-based tourism in the Pacific, including, 'environmental degradation and cultural "bastardization" ... prostitution, commercialization of culture, the introduction of liquor and drugs, the breakdown of the family and increasing individualization' (Sofield 1994:209, also Baines 1987 and Lal 1984).

It is for such reasons that some governments and NGOs in the region have sought to find alternatives to mass tourism. Ecotourism has emerged as a key area of interest because of its reputation for being environmentally friendly and promoting participatory development (Rudkin and Hall 1996:203).

Ecotourism as a Sustainable Alternative

Tourism is one of the largest industries in the world and ecotourism is the fastest growing sector of international tourism, with an estimated growth rate of 10–15 per cent (Panos 1997). Ecotourism has been defined as:

> environmentally responsible, enlightening travel and visitation to relatively undisturbed natural areas in order to enjoy and appreciate nature (and any accompanying cultural features both past and present) that promotes conservation, has low visitor impact, and provides for beneficially active socio-economic involvement of local populations (Ceballos Lascurain 1996:20).

According to this definition, ecotourism can involve both cultural and environmental tourism and, in addition, benefits to the local population should be an integral part of the activity.

The demands of increasingly affluent Western consumers for 'remote', 'natural' and 'exotic' environments have seen an upsurge of interest in areas such as the Pacific Islands, which are seen as an ideal ecotourism destination. Of concern is the fact that it is precisely the more remote, less developed tourism areas that ecotourists seek which are most vulnerable to cultural disruption and environmental degradation (Cater 1993:89).

Many see ecotourism as offering opportunities for the conservation of important natural resources. For example, in East Africa the well known slogan is 'wildlife pays so wildlife stays' (Ziffer 1989:2), whilst in parts of the Pacific ecotourism is seen to offer an alternative source of income to communities which might otherwise sign logging agreements (Hall 1994:150, Weaver 1991, 1992).

While some writers emphasise the potential for ecotourism to promote the well-being of both local peoples and their environments (King 1992, McLisky 1992, Hvenegaard, 1994:27), others caution us against uncritically accepting ecotourism as a common good (Ziffer 1989, Boo 1990, Cater and Lowman 1994). As Cater (1993:85) notes, 'there is a very real danger of viewing ecotourism as the universal panacea, and the ecotourist as some magic breed, mitigating all tourism's ills'. Confusion has arisen because the term 'ecotourism' has been used by many operators primarily as a marketing tool (Thomlinson and Getz 1996), when they have little concern for the environmental and social outcomes of the activity. According to some authors, there are certainly problems with the way ecotourism has been applied in the Pacific:

> the concept of ecotourism in the South Pacific has been promoted within a particularly narrow band of conservation and business thought which has often failed to appreciate the role of social and political values within sustainable tourism development (Rudkin and Hall 1996:223).

It is important, therefore, to distinguish responsible forms of ecotourism from those operated by 'eco-pirates', whom Lew (1996:723) describes as 'people who copy existing responsible tourism products, but in a non-responsible manner – typically offering lower prices, inferior experiences, and detrimental environmental and social impacts'.

Ecotourism from a Livelihoods Perspective

A useful way to discern responsible ecotourism is to approach it from a livelihoods perspective, which considers social, environmental and economic goals, and questions how ecotourism can 'meet the needs of the host population in terms of improved living standards both in the short and long term' (Cater 1993:85–6). This perspective differs somewhat from those approaching ecotourism predominantly from an environmental perspective. Buckley (1994:661), for example, argues that ecotourism is based on nature tourism which is sustainably managed, includes environmental education and supports conservation. While Buckley helps us to understand that ecotourism is much more than just a product – nature – he fails to incorporate issues of local livelihoods and thus, from a development perspective, his framework is flawed. Helu Thaman's (1994:188) comments help to remind us of the importance of considering local livelihoods:

> In Western industrial societies, where large amounts of land are privately or state-owned, and where legislation can be enacted to promote conservation and wildlife protection, and prohibit resource degradation, tourism and conservation verge on the symbiotic. This (idealised) view of ecotourism becomes problematic in the context of Pacific Island societies, where economic livelihoods (20%–80% of real incomes) and cultural integrity depend on the continued use of ecosystems on a sustainable basis, be they forests, the sea, rivers, beaches, reefs, or agricultural and village lands.

Thus while 'communities do not want to destroy their environment ... they do need ways to maintain or improve their standards of living' (Theopile 1995:27). The need to consider social development and livelihoods, rather than just conservation or preservation, is well illustrated by the case of a proposed World Heritage Site in East Rennell, Solomon Islands.

Case Study: World Heritage Project on Rennell Island [1]

In 1989 the Solomon Islands government, in response to both domestic and international pressure, initiated a programme to gain World Heritage listing for two sites within Solomon Islands. The aim of the programme is to promote the conservation of Marovo Lagoon and Rennell Island as unique environments worthy of protection under an international conservation agreement. The World Heritage list is designed to 'provide for the protection of internationally outstanding natural and cultural heritage sites which were threatened by various kinds of development' (Nelson and Alder 1992:ix).

Rennell Island, of which only the eastern half is incorporated in the

[1] Nick Purdie carried out fieldwork on the World Heritage Project in Rennell in November–December 1995 and February 1996.

World Heritage proposal, is an upraised coral atoll lying approximately 250 kilometres due south of Honiara, the capital. It has been described variously as the largest and highest upraised atoll in the world, and the finest example of this landform anywhere (Maruia Society 1991:143). Over a period of one and a half million years Rennell has experienced five uplifts whereby it now rises to about 200 metres above sea level. Because of its isolation, the island is the habitat for a number of unique species and subspecies including sea snakes, bats, birds and an endemic orchid. It is this unique flora and fauna which make Rennell a possible candidate for inclusion on the World Heritage list.

The aim of the World Heritage Project is to gain a listing for Rennell Island and to promote the area internationally as an ecotourism destination. Developmentally, it is expected that local people will benefit from the project by way of the expected influx of tourists and the provision of goods and services to them. In this respect an ecotourism/small business scheme is being implemented to support the development and exploitation of entrepreneurial opportunities by local people, both those associated with the tourist market (such as the provision of accommodation, food, transport and guiding) and those separate from it (beekeeping and handicrafts are being investigated). In this way it is suggested that the project can both conserve the environment on Rennell and at the same time ensure that local people benefit from that conservation.

In early 1997 the Rennell Island project was at the stage where the nomination document to be forwarded to UNESCO in Paris was close to completion, and there were initial efforts by local people to develop some form of tourist infrastructure. There were signs, however, that local people were becoming discontented with the way in which the project was being implemented and with what they perceived as the lack of benefits. Participatory rural appraisal (PRA)[2] surveys carried out in 1996 in two of the five villages associated with the project suggested that development and livelihood needs as perceived by villagers have not being taken into account in project design (Purdie 1996). Problems associated with local livelihoods include:

- A lack of potable water, particularly during dry periods;

[2] Participatory rural appraisal can be described as a menu of methods for the collection of information concerning local level livelihoods, resource use and knowledge systems (see Chambers 1994a, 1994b, 1997). Far from being solely a research methodology, however, it is designed to construct a two-way learning process of research such that both the researcher and local people can gain insights from that process.

- A lack of suitable building materials for dwellings, particularly given the frequency of cyclones in the area;
- A need for improved sanitation and waste disposal facilities;
- A decrease in the quality and amount of food provided by gardening activities due to introduced pests;
- A perceived lack of diversity in the local diet;
- A lack of adequate cooking and laundry facilities; and,
- A decrease in the quality of food and water in the lake.

Although these problems have been identified by local people as being important to the livelihood strategies that they have at their disposal, and were having a negative impact on both the effectiveness and sustainability of these, they were given only cursory attention by the World Heritage Project. In this respect local people were concerned with the short-term needs of day-to-day survival: to provide food and shelter for themselves and their families. Conversely, both the design and implementation of the development project tended to exhibit a longer-term view of an overall conservation and development strategy. Local people, however, had little concern for the conservation of internationally important flora and fauna when their crops of taro, the key staple in their diet, were being destroyed by an imported insect pest. The consequence of this was that increasingly local people were losing interest in the promise of the development project and were thinking of alternatives, such as timber milling, crayfish and coconut-crab harvesting and hunting, to support their livelihoods and, more specifically, to earn cash. Ironically, these activities may also prove to be unsustainable in that they are undertaken to earn cash with which to buy livelihood goods, rather than for direct consumption. This immediately opens up the possibility of over-harvesting for pure financial gain, or simply out of a need to do so to secure a livelihood.

Similarly, at Lauvi Lagoon, also in the Solomon Islands, a proposed ecotourism development was supported by local elites, government officials and foreign donors (Rudkin and Hall 1996). The proposal appears to support principles of nature conservation, yet local people were concerned that it would jeopardise both their physical and social quality of life. First, they were worried about the cultural disruptions tourism would bring. Second, they were unconvinced about the economic benefits they would gain from ecotourism. And third, as local representatives stated, the project had the potential to undermine their livelihoods by preventing them from accessing the resources of the lagoon and surrounding land:

> We are concerned that the site indicated is our main fishing ground. Our ancestors were using the land as we are and our generation will be using it. We will fish for food, collect shells, crabs, cabbages and [do] gardening etc. etc. without fear because we own it rather than foreigners restricting rules over the area [where we presently] roam freely (cited in Rudkin and Hall 1996:217).

The project's supporters had no interest in alleviating existing livelihood concerns of the local community, including the community's lack of access to a regular and safe water supply, their need to control agricultural pests and their need for seeds and tree crop seedlings (Rudkin and Hall 1996:220).

Lessons for proponents of ecotourism

These examples suggest that governments, donors and NGOs promoting ecotourism which is based upon the protection of environmentally significant areas need to incorporate the urgent necessity of immediate and secure livelihoods into their action plans. At the very least this is required to gain the long-term support of people for their projects.

It is understandable that many communities may lack motivation to become involved in ecotourism if they perceive that this will impinge upon their participation in livelihood activities and social institutions (de Burlo 1984:298). Key concerns for ecotourism proponents should, therefore, include whether ecotourism will undermine existing activities by diverting labour and resources from them, whether the rewards justify such diversion, and whether ecotourism can be organised in such a way that it will compliment existing livelihood activities. Such issues are important in societies reliant for their physical well-being on the subsistence economy, including gardening and fishing, and dependent for their spiritual well-being on involvement in social institutions including cooperative associations, churches and traditional organisations.

In some cases it may be necessary for the organisation encouraging ecotourism development to compensate communities for forgoing livelihood strategies. For example, on Wotho atoll in the Marshall Islands the community has agreed not to harvest certain marine species and birds because, in exchange, they will receive technical support and capital so that they can establish their own small-scale ecotourism ventures (Valentine 1993:112). Similarly, Tacconi and Bennett (1995), in their study of the establishment of a protected area of rainforest in Vanuatu, conclude that local people should essentially be paid to 'do' conservation. The people they refer to live in a relatively isolated village and have few opportunities for earning cash. Yet offers from logging companies have been directed at them and thus, the authors argue, if the Vanuatu government wants to create a protected area in this location they should arrange a lease agreement with the local people which would ensure them a regular income over the long term. In this way local livelihoods would be enhanced and the people would have a stake in ensuring sustainable management of the protected area.

The Value of Community-Based Ecotourism

Viewing ecotourism from a livelihoods perspective allows us to focus on how ecotourism can work in with the needs and desires of local communities. Some writers have suggested that the term 'community-based ecotourism ventures' should be used to distinguish those initiatives which are environmentally sensitive, but which also aim to ensure that members of local communities have a high degree of control over the activities taking place, and that a significant proportion of the benefits accrue to them (Liu 1994:98, Cater 1993:85). This is in contrast to ecotourism ventures which are controlled wholly by outside operators, and it is also distinct from contexts in which most of the economic benefits of tourism accrue to the government (Akama 1996:572).

The notion of control is important. An outside operator making token concessions to local culture is not handing over control:

> I encountered few instances of social and cultural factors built into the design of tourism enterprises in Vanuatu. There were usually – even in the case of joint ventures – only the ideas of using local produce (rather than imports), hiring and training local staff, and a token 'island' architecture. These tourism schemes are indicative of the sort of thinking that considers cultural factors to be 'constraints' (de Burlo 1984:294).

Yet as Sofield (1991) has shown, since then the *naghol* (land dive) in Pentecost, Vanuatu, has been turned into an economically successful and relatively unintrusive enterprise for local people because they have retained control over it. In the *naghol*, men jump from a high platform with vines tied around their ankles so that their fall is broken just short of the ground. Local chiefs established their own tourism council which consults ancestors in order to decide on the sites for the jumps, the number of jumps (eight were allowed in 1988) and who will participate in them. A maximum of 50 visitors is flown onto the island to watch each jump and they are flown out on the same day, thus minimising cultural disruption.

Other factors which may help to retain cultural integrity in communities vulnerable to cultural disruption include limiting visitor involvement in the private spaces of local people by building accommodation a little distance from the local community (Sofield 1993:745), or limiting the frequency of visits and the time visitors spend with the community (Sofield 1991). Some Aboriginal communities in Australia have stated that they do not want direct involvement in any tourism activities, and would prefer to earn an income from tourists indirectly by making craft goods or sharing the entry fees to environmentally distinctive areas (Altman and Finlayson 1993). This may also be a good option for Pacific Island communities who feel that entertaining and accommodating tourists may interfere with their participation in important cultural occasions, such as birth or death ceremonies, and for those who only want to participate in ecotourism at times when other seasonal activities are slack.

Lovoni Village, Fiji

An example of a community-based ecotourism initiative which is entirely reliant upon local resources, and in which local people have retained control, is the Lovoni village initiative in Fiji. Overton (1993b, Overton and Purdie 1997) visited this operation in 1992 and reported on a thriving small-scale venture.

The enterprise operates out of the town of Levuka on the island of Ovalau, Fiji. It is not widely promoted and depends for its customers on a sign in the local museum and word of mouth. It mainly involves a guided walk from Levuka over an old crater rim through bush to the village of Lovoni. Lunch is provided, along with some relaxation in the village, and a truck ride back to Levuka. It is operated by one household but involves others as contributors such as in the preparation of food and transport back. It is a small-scale operation with a maximum of twelve tourists per day, no overnight stays, and little impact on the village. Yet it does provide employment and income, and the involvement of local adults and children as guides is crucial – they are able to recount the history of their village and details of the natural environment. It is educational, then, for tourists but also demonstrates to villagers that others are interested in their environment and history. In short, the Lovoni ecotourism venture seems a model for village-based sustainable development. It is environmentally based, preserves resources, provides income, is sensitive to the local community and minimises disruption to it.

A feature of the project is the high percentage of income retained by the village for guiding and local foods used in the lunch. Of the $F12 cost to tourists, perhaps at most only $2 went immediately outside the village (an estimated share of the petrol cost for a scheduled truck/bus trip back to Levuka, Overton 1993). The income may have been used for the many necessities that demand cash in a Fijian village: education costs for children, basic goods (such as garden tools, kerosene etc.), and transport. In Lovoni there was also a village electrification project based on solar power and plans for other 'development wants' such as television and video sets.

It appears, however, that the operation has not progressed smoothly. Although rated now as one of the tourist highlights on the island of Ovalau, a rival operator from the village has commenced business and is offering a similar tour in open competition (Jones and Pinheiro 1997:235). It seems as if the success of one household's venture has opened up conflicts within the village and this community may not be agreed on the best way of running ecotourism, nor sharing in its benefits. In addition, there are concerns about the way income from the ventures might be spent. Whilst much of the income undoubtedly is used for essential items, some is devoted to consumer goods and the meeting of new aspirations stimulated by an expanding culture of Western-oriented materialism (Weaver 1994).

Constraints

While the rhetoric suggests that there is much support for community-based ecotourism ventures, it is difficult to find successful examples of this in practice. Recent studies suggest that local elites, particularly men, often coopt and come to dominate community-based development efforts and monopolise the benefits of tourism (Akama 1996:573, Mansperger 1995:90, Rudkin and Hall 1996, Sindiga 1995:53). Mansperger (1995:90), for example, describes how one village chief in Yap, Federated States of Micronesia, kept all of the entrance fees to his village for himself. This led some community members to feel that: 'Money is making people stingy and therefore harming community spirit.' In the Lauvi Lagoon example from the Solomon Islands mentioned above, a local 'big man' tried to initiate the ecotourism development with minimal consultation with others in the community, thus resulting in considerable dissension (Rudkin and Hall 1996).

It seems, therefore, that the assumption that communities can share unproblematically in the production of the tourism product and the benefits deriving from this is excessively romantic (Taylor 1995:487). Taylor notes that there is much acceptance of the idea of community participation but little understanding of the complex mechanics which may be required to make this a success in practice. Much may depend on the initial cohesiveness of a community, or the extent to which competitiveness and individualism are evident (Taylor 1995:488). Clearly in all communities there are inequalities which may be exacerbated by the introduction of a somewhat lucrative industry to which all will not have access. Thus, in determining the success and sustainability of an ecotourism venture, the distribution of economic benefits from ecotourism is just as important as the actual amount of benefits a community may receive (Wilkinson and Pratiwi 1995).

Environmental constraints may also stand in the way of communities wishing to promote ecotourism. The fact is that not all environmentally significant areas are sufficiently 'scenic' to attract the casual visitor; thus it is important not to overestimate the potential for ecotourism to contribute to the long-term conservation of natural areas. This may only be possible in a small number of areas which are attractive to the outside eye yet which are also not too difficult to travel to and where adequate infrastructural services can be provided for visitors. Though ecotourists may be more 'down to earth' than the average traveller, they are still likely to want access to a toilet and bathing area, at a minimum.

The assumption is that small-scale operations are an important aspect of the ecotourism experience (Blamey 1997:120). Thomlinson and Getz (1996) argue that while small-scale tourism is perceived to fit in well with the philosophy of ecotourism, in practice mass tourism may be the preferred option because it brings in more money to local communities and can be more easily restricted to certain locations, thus minimising harmful cultural impacts. Communities may, for example, prefer busloads of tourists coming to them on selected weekdays – for a cultural performance and to buy crafts, before returning to their hotels – to the more culturally invasive ecotourism experience, in which outsiders live with them and 'share their lives'.

At the level of government, there is clearly a need for redirection of policy and practice if community-based ecotourism is to be encouraged and supported. Most Pacific Island governments have encouraged resort-based tourism because of the hope that it will bring in much-needed foreign exchange. There have been few serious efforts by governments to promote alternatives to mass tourism through which major economic leakages, both for imported goods and services and through repatriation of profits, occur. In Papua New Guinea, for example, the Tourist Office operating in the early 1980s offered no support at all to guest house owner-operators, choosing instead to refer visitors to large-scale, Western-style hotels (Ranck 1987:165). Furthermore, the government has a responsibility to regulate tourism development. Tourism will only proceed in a sustainable manner if it is controlled by the public sector at the local level: 'Local authorities, through the production of integrated plans and development control powers, are best placed to assess the characteristics of the local environment and the priorities, needs and attitudes of local people to tourism' (Hunter 1995:92).

Complementarity between government policy and practice is also important, as Sofield (1993) points out, because in some cases government policies which support involvement of local communities in tourism development are impeded by legislation. For example, in the Solomon Islands, building codes are based upon Western standards, making it very difficult for small-scale tourism ventures to be developed. Using traditional construction methods and materials, local artisans cannot meet the requirements of the building code. It has been estimated that if building regulations were adhered to, a small-scale tourism venture would cost around $US100,000, a sum which very few villagers could raise (Sofield 1993:737). In addition, over 80 per cent of land in the Solomon Islands is under customary ownership, but this land cannot be used as collateral in securing a bank loan, which may be needed to fund tourism development, unless the land is registered. Land registration under the Solomon Islands Lands and Titles Act is a lengthy and often expensive process which frequently provokes counter-claims. Furthermore, where customary land is registered for commercial purposes, the Commissioner for Lands takes over title of the land.

> An appropriate path for village-based tourism in Solomon Islands must be sought. If not identified, then Solomon Islands faces the prospect of foreign domination, local elite control, and/or government institutionalization of the tourism sector, as has occurred in many other small developing nations (Sofield 1993:747).

Sofield moves on to describe a Malaitan community which flouted the above legislation and established small-scale tourism ventures utilising traditional houses and based on tourists' involvement in aspects of local community life, such as fishing and manufacturing craft goods. They have been successful in terms of both promoting small financial gains and retaining cultural integrity: 'it remains as a low key operation entirely dependent upon word-of-mouth for visitors, and (because of its "illegality") firmly under the control of the local community' (Sofield 1993:739). Similarly, guest houses in Tufi, Papua New Guinea, have also relied on local materials for building and local foods for meals, as the villagers simply could not afford to buy the commercial equivalents. What has emerged is a highly satisfactory arrangement, however: guests get a more 'authentic' village experience, and the local communities have been able to finance their ventures without outside assistance, thus retaining ownership and control of the tourism occurring in their area (Ranck 1987).

Finding an Appropriate Path for Pacific Island Tourism

This chapter has examined the potential, and present reality, of ecotourism initiatives in the Pacific. Is criticises present mass tourism trends in the Pacific on the basis of their lack of effectiveness in promoting community-based development and lack of equity in terms of the distribution of benefits. It also warns, however, that ecotourism is not immune to these problems. Principles for equitable ecotourism development in the Pacific have been compiled in Box 16.1.

From a livelihoods perspective, it is critical that local communities benefit directly from ecotourism:

> Ecotourism is not a panacea for economic or environmental woes in the United States or overseas, but if integrated with larger strategies it can be a valuable tool for sustainable development. Empowering local communities to evaluate the tradeoffs and strike this balance for themselves is at the heart of any successful ecotourism venture (Theophile 1995:27).

Akama (1996:573) would appear to concur with Theophile, suggesting that communities need to be empowered, both socially and economically, in order to decide what forms of tourism development they wish to pursue, who will bear the costs and who will share in the benefits of this development. In practice it is important that local stakeholders, who may include church groups, women's groups, trustees of communally owned lands or local NGOs, all have the opportunity to voice their opinions on ecotourism development (Sindiga 1995:48). Too often women, in particular, have not been consulted on such matters (Kinnaird and Hall 1994). Further, even if some Pacific Island communities decide they do not wish to be involved in tourism enterprises, they should be encouraged to be involved in decision making and planning concerning tourism development in their areas. This is particularly important in contexts where, for example, the community lives adjacent to, or within, a protected area such as a national park or World Heritage site.

In order to maintain local control over ecotourism initiatives, it may be best to keep the initiatives small in scale. Advantages of small-scale schemes include local ownership and control, the use of local businesses (with associated multipliers such as use of local labour and materials), the local retention of profits, and the provision of an alternative to unsustainable local uses of the environment, such as logging

BOX 16.1 • PRINCIPLES FOR EQUITABLE ECOTOURISM DEVELOPMENT IN THE PACIFIC ISLANDS

1. Indigenous ownership or part-ownership.
2. Indigenous control through appropriate structures and organisations.
3. Community support, based on consultation and involvement in decision-making processes.
4. Mechanisms to ensure that younger generations are taught the appropriate cultural norms and skills so that the activity can be continued in the future, if they desire.
5. Prior education for tourists about the local culture and appropriate behaviour.
6. Small scale of operations (e.g. keeping visitor numbers relatively low).
7. Government policies to promote indigenous participation in tourism and provision of government support structures (e.g., technical expertise, coordination of marketing of special events).
8. Equitable system for distributing benefits among communities.
9. Avoidance of major capital works that would require bank loans and outside involvement, wherever possible. Use of intermediate technology wherever practical (e.g., composting toilet systems rather than flush toilets requiring imported components and trained plumbers to maintain them).
10. Ecotourism should be part of a broader, integrated development strategy which sets up training programmes for local people and involves other possible sources of revenue, for example, harvesting and marketing of non-timber forest products and sustainable farming practices, and which does not undermine important subsistence activities.
11. Ongoing monitoring and evaluation of social, economic and environmental impacts, with findings being widely discussed with all stakeholders.

(Based upon Sofield 1991 and Ziffer 1989)

(Panos 1997). As noted in the section on constraints, however, small-scale initiatives may not always be seen as serving community interests: while 'small is beautiful in the context of ecotourism ... small is also vulnerable' (Thomlinson and Getz 1996:197). Thus support structures must be created to assist local communities who choose to follow the ecotourism path. Governments, in particular, must be prepared to assist community-based ecotourism, rather than enforcing impediments to this, including inappropriate legislation. We may hope that the demand from tourists for authentic cultural and environmental experiences is reversing the perceptions of government officials who see accommodation based on traditional housing and experiences based on traditional skills and activities as 'primitive' or 'inferior' (Sofield 1993:742).

CHAPTER 17

A Future in the Past? Seeking Sustainable Agriculture

JOHN OVERTON

Towards Sustainable Agriculture

The search for more sustainable forms of agriculture in the Pacific Islands has become pressing since the recent recognition that changes in the sector have created threats to the ecological and social future of rural areas (Chapter 13). Dependence on a narrow range of crops with uncertain markets, increasing use of chemical inputs and energy subsidies, and new forms of social inequalities have accompanied the move to a model of rural development based on the specialised production of commodities. The search for sustainable alternatives is not straightforward. Sustainable agriculture requires not only a strong concern for ecological integrity but also a recognition of the need to minimise social and cultural disruption and be labour-intensive, yet simultaneously meet the livelihood demands of both rural producers and increasing numbers of urban consumers.

In discussions of sustainable agricultural options in the Pacific Islands, a number of strategies have been suggested, including the application of new appropriate technologies (Clarke 1978) and other means to intensify agriculture. Yet it is the old systems of production, proven to be sustainable in the centuries prior to European contact, that appear to attract most attention. Though careful not to romanticise such systems – for there were many examples where indigenous agriculture proved far from sustainable – the geographers Clarke (1977, 1990, 1994, 1996), Brookfield (1972, 1986), Thaman (1978, 1984a, 1993) and Bayliss-Smith (1985, 1997), together with anthropologists and prehistorians such as Kirch (1994, 1997) and Yen (1974), have argued that there was much to commend certain systems. It has been contended that these could be the basis for present and future rural development strategies (Clarke 1978, Overton 1993b).

Despite the promise of the past, there is much that stands in the way of a revitalisation of old sustainable systems of agriculture. Much has been lost: techniques, genetic material, and the social and cultural milieu within which production was organised. Much has also changed: material expectations have risen above mere subsistence, many Pacific Islanders are no longer primarily producers of food for themselves and their households, and most would not accept the high levels of coercion from their chiefs that previously was required to develop 'landesque capital' (Blaikie and Brookfield 1987:9, Bayliss-Smith 1997:148). Furthermore, there is heightened pressure on land in many places, so that a simple extension of the land frontier, especially when using extensive land use practices, is no longer feasible (Ward 1985). Land tenure has become increasingly individualised, despite the common retention of *de jure* communal tenure systems (Ward and Kingdon 1995b), thus making it harder to employ communal means of production. And the history of inappropriate land use practices (mostly recent but also ancient) has lowered the carrying capacity of many rural environments through soil erosion, loss of fertility or destruction of forest cover (Clarke and Morrison 1987). In short, a simple return to the old subsistence methods of production and the social structures that facilitated them is not a viable option.

Before discarding the potential of pre-modern agricultural systems in the Pacific, however, it must be noted that there are some advantages to be taken from the modern era. Though it may have underpinned the rise of high-input, high-energy and ultimately unsustainable agriculture across the globe in the past 30 years (mainly through the Green Revolution), modern agricultural science has provided much to guide a move to more sustainable agriculture: more is known about the physiology of plants, animals and pests; environmental impacts can be better monitored; and new technologies need not automatically involve Green Revolution industrial modes of production. In addition, the colonial legacy often led to a situation where people's locational choices (and thereby agricultural landscapes and productivity) were less guided by the need to avoid malaria or invasion by enemies than before. And, though far from perfect in application, modern systems of food preservation and transport mean that less agricultural endeavour has to be devoted to guarding against periodic crop loss and famine. Clearly, there is scope to use these modern advantages whilst rediscovering and reutilising what is beneficial from the past:

To achieve sustainable development today we must devise land

> use practices which absorb improvements and so encourage re-investment, but preferably in the context of existing cultural norms and agricultural practices, rather than being imposed from the outside. This may require a synthesis of the old and the new (Bayliss-Smith 1997:152).

This chapter examines the possibility of achieving a greater degree of sustainability in agricultural production by learning from the past. It starts by discussing the difficulties and potential of recovering knowledge about past systems, then moves to analyse ways in which some systems can be built upon and made workable in the present context. Finally, it considers the extent to which such approaches can provide a viable strategy for sustainable rural development in the Pacific.

Recovering the Past

The major difficulty in reassessing premodern agricultural systems in the Pacific, let alone reintroducing them, is the lack of knowledge about them, in whole or in part. There are very few if any remaining working examples of any agricultural systems that have not been radically transformed in the past century. Technology, markets, population change, new aspirations, social change, religion and the availability of substitutes have all conspired to alter significantly, and often remove entirely, systems of production that existed a century and more ago. Agriculture today, even if involves 'traditional' crops, customary land tenure and minimal use of modern technologies, bears little resemblance to the substance, if not the form, of what it was. To a large extent, what is left for us to learn about the past is fragments from the archaeological record, oral history or aerial photography. Yet in a few places, there are examples of systems and societies that have retained in part the essence of pre-modern agriculture. There is evidence of some very impressive and, to a large extent, sustainable systems of agriculture – ones which modifed the environment in ways beneficial to the long-term well-being of people. Terracing of hillslopes (Wright 1962), agroforestry (Clarke and Thaman 1993) and irrigation (Kuhlken 1994) all provide examples of essentially sustainable agricultural 'development'. Learning from these may provide clues to the nature of what was (or, indeed, was not) sustainable agriculture in the Pacific.

The Rewa Delta, Fiji

The Rewa Delta in south-eastern Viti Levu, Fiji is a large low-lying alluvial delta, often flood-prone, cross-cut by distributaries of the Rewa River and bordered on its seaward margins by mangrove swamps. In this unpromising environment emerged one of the most intensive and productive agricultural systems in the Pacific. The record of this system has been uncovered by John Parry (1977, also 1981, 1987) through an examination of aerial photographs corroborated by historical accounts and some present-day field observations.

To combat the swampy conditions, the people of the area (no doubt cajoled by their chiefs) constructed a landscape and developed practices which allowed for major intensification. Ditches were dug, usually in a circular shape, and the earth was piled into ring mounds. There is evidence also of substantial drains being built (Bayliss-Smith 1997:162–3). The ring ditches had a threefold effect. The ditches themselves provided an ideal watery environment for the cultivation of both giant swamp taro (*via kana* – *Cyrtosperma chamissonis*) and taro (*dalo* – *Colocasia esculenta*), and very high yields could be gained, no doubt helped by mulching and flooding to replenish nutrients. Secondly, the raised mounds formed not only drier residential sites but also drier garden sites for the cultivation of less swamp-tolerant plants. Thirdly, because the ring ditches formed a very elaborate series of mazes and the *via kana* plants grew over two metres in height, the system provided a very effective defensive mechanism in an area otherwise difficult to defend: attackers got lost in the mazes, local residents could 'feel' them coming through the spongy earth, and they could hide, flee or ambush their foes in response.

Although there is some debate over the estimates Parry made of population size and densities (Overton and Chung 1988), it is clear that this was a system that supported a large population, probably well in excess of what it is even today and with one of the highest population densities in the whole region. Parry estimated a total population of around 30–40,000 people with an average density in excess of 260–300 persons per square kilometre (Bayliss-Smith 1997:163). Although taro and *via kana* were the mainstay of diets, the proximity of the mangrove swamps and the sea provided valuable protein, whilst the valued stands of trees and bush on drier areas provided food, building materials and many other items. It was a remarkable agricultural system: one that had modified the environment, allowed for very intensive agriculture and settlement, was adapted to a particular social and military context, and exhibited many of the hallmarks of sustainable agriculture.

Unfortunately, little remains of this system beyond what can be seen from the air. Land development, in the form of rice cultivation projects and older attempts at sugar cultivation (Overton 1988, 1989), has led to a levelling of the ditches in many places and much of the land is in fallow or unused. Only from the air, when the texture of the ditches and the ring patterns of cultivated trees are apparent, can some idea of the intensity and extent of the system be gained. Taro is still being grown, but through more dry-field methods and with greater recourse to lower-intensity crops such as cassava (*tavioka – Manihot esculenta*) and xanthosoma taro (*dalo ni tana – Xanthosoma spp.*). *Via kana* is present but not as a significant foodcrop – its slow growth, high labour demands and less favoured flavour consigning it to a secondary role as a mainly ceremonial crop.

The Magic Gardens of Tanna, Vanuatu

Whereas in Rewa we may find evidence of what was grown and how, there is little that remains in these localities of the way practices of cultivation linked to social structure or religion. Bonnemaison's work in Tanna gives some clue to this. Working in what are still regarded as 'pagan' villages, where the spread of Christianity is not yet as pervasive as in other parts of the archipelago, Bonnemaison (1991, also 1984, 1994) studied 'magic gardens'.

The magic gardens of Tanna are ones that are still cultivated in some villages by people who eschew the new religion and new agricultural techniques. The gardens they tend are governed by an intricate web of beliefs and practices that govern nearly all aspects of cultivation: when, where and what to plant, who does what and when in the garden, and how the products are distributed and consumed. Agricultural technology is inextricably linked with animist religion and social customs. They represent remnants of an agricultural system that existed much more widely on Tanna – and probably elsewhere though with undoubted local variations – for many centuries before the coming of the missionaries, administrators and traders.

The design of the gardens provides a means to understand, at least in part, their structure and relationships. At the centre of the garden are the most sacred plants – yams (*Dioscorea alata*). These are tended very carefully and are symbols not just of the health of the garden but of the community and the potency of the men that grow them. They have very high ceremonial value when harvested and there are strict rules and taboos about their planting, tending and harvesting. Women have little role to play in their cultivation and are prohibited from entering the centre of the garden at certain times. Towards the periphery of the garden are the plants of more lowly status, firstly taro, then the newer introductions, such as cassava. Outward from the centre of the garden, rules relax and the sexual division of labour becomes less marked. The foods of the forest obtained through hunting and gathering could also be regarded as an outward extension of the gardens, though they are governed by a different set of rules and beliefs. Again, this was a largely sustainable system. There was long-term stability, there was strict observance of resource management practices, the gardens provided well for the subsistence needs of people, and culture and environment were closely integrated.

Although this appears as a remarkably intricate and intensive system, Bonnemaison has noted how it is declining. The maintenance of the gardens is not just a matter of cultivation practices but a whole social order and a religion. As pagan gives way to Christian and as the young move away from the village (or even go to school) the complex technologies of the system are lost. Without the knowledge or the commitment to the beliefs and social relationships that maintain them, the magic gardens become secular.

Taro Cultivation on Puluwat atoll, Micronesia

Whereas our knowledge of the examples from sites such as Rewa is dependent on the prehistoric record and the magic gardens of Tanna seemingly are in decline, there are a few examples of systems which are surviving and may even be undergoing a slight revival. Robert Kuhlken, for example, has conducted research on remnants of irrigated taro terracing systems in Fiji, a few of which, as in Kadavu, are still in operation (Kuhlken 1994). Yet some of the most striking cases of irrigated taro cultivation are still extant in some of the least likely environments – the atolls of Polynesia and Micronesia. Here, the poor soils and absence of surface water has led to the evolution of practices which involve the digging of pits into the subsurface fresh water lens and the growing, with intensive mulching, of taro in the artificial swamps. Known as *babai* pits in Kiribati (see Chapter 6), they have provided the staple food for atoll dwellers for many centuries.

Manner's work on Puluwat atoll (Manner 1994) in the Federated States of Micronesia provides an excellent example of how some of these systems remain. Freshwater depressions have been excavated to allow for the growing of taro (*Colocasia esculenta*) and giant swamp taro (*Cyrtosperma chamissonis*). The technique is known as *maa* and involves artificial islets within the pits. 'The islets are made by anchoring coconut and pandanus trucks in excavated depressions to form a roughly oval base, which is then filled with organic matter' (Manner 1994: 80). Soils are created with decomposed vegetation and coconut fronds act as a mulch and keep down weeds.

> The *maa* epitomises the Puluwatese understanding of the physical factors that affect their way of living. Specifically, the *maa*, by virtue of its location near the centre of the islet, takes advantage of the hydrostatic equilibrium between salt water and fresh water.... As

> these depressions are surrounded by natural and planted vegetation, damage to the *maa* by salt spray and storm wave inundation is lessened. Other traditional knowledge represented by the *maa* includes normal tidal ranges, physical and chemical properties of organic spoil and composting (Manner 1994:80–1).

There is a close relation between the *maa* and settlement, for the residents are close to the gardens, perhaps reflecting the recognition of the heavy labour requirements of the gardens, especially for women, who undertake most of the garden work. Yet the *maa* are not the only source of food, the sea and the trees of the atoll's interior being important sources for proteins, vitamins and medicinal plants.

Lessons learned?

These three case studies demonstrate the relevance but also the difficulties of using former agricultural systems as a basis for sustainable agriculture in the present and future. Perhaps most importantly, even if they cannot be resuscitated they do demonstrate a long history of agricultural innovation in the Pacific Island region. There has been innovation, profound change, intensification (and disintensification) and a close link between agriculture and the well-being of Pacific Island people. The examples tell of indigenous 'science', of the ability to adapt practices, modify environments, experiment with plants, and accept change. If nothing else, they should dispel the myth that the only route to rural development is through the progressive application of Western scientific models and the greater industrialisation of agriculture.

An interesting illustration of this is the perception of swamps. Whereas many of the most intensive and complex ancient systems of Pacific Island agriculture involved swamps – indeed the artificial creation or manipulation of swamp environments (Spriggs 1985) – European agricultural history has involved a tradition of draining and destroying swamp environments to allow for dryland agriculture.

The case studies also show that Pacific Island agricultural history is not automatically associated with environmental sustainability, for environmental change was pervasive and sometimes extensive. Although there has been a very close association of Pacific agriculture, social organisation, religion and culture, and many examples of ethics which protected and conserved key environmental resources, often the extent of environmental modification and damage was limited only by available technology:

> The early inhabitants [of the Pacific Islands] did not avidly practise a conservationist ethic that preserved their habitat as an unchanged

> paradise until the Europeans brought major disturbance and degradation. Instead, the Islanders did what all peoples, especially pioneers, do: in their efforts to make a living, they actively manipulated, modified, and, at times, degraded the ecosystems in which they lived, producing environmental changes that in turn required ecological adaptations and social adjustments (Clarke 1994:15).

Nor was there always 'subsistence affluence' (Fisk 1972:24), in which subsistence food requirements could be met easily, leaving free time for social and cultural pursuits. Whilst root crop cultivation was usually less demanding of labour time than, say, rice, the agricultural systems of Rewa or Puluwat required a major investment of labour to construct and maintain the landesque capital involved. And the labour demands, often on women, in the sweet potato gardens of the Papua New Guinea Highlands were far from light. The need to develop and maintain these systems, and the reproduction of the knowledge to manage them, required intricate 'social technologies' – ways of organising labour, managing environmental resources and transmitting knowledge – just as they demanded complex agricultural technologies. They represented holistic systems whereby agriculture was closely integrated into the social, cultural and religious web of daily lives. When the means of social organisation and control broke down, so too did agricultural systems.

To recover these systems, what is needed is not only the relearning of past agricultural techniques and the preservation of genetic material but also an appreciation (if not a readoption) of the social and cultural context within which they operated, including social structures, religious beliefs and gender relations. It requires a recognition of indigenous science and, more difficult, an appreciation of the values and ideologies that created and reproduced that science. This latter task is difficult, for many former practices and beliefs (for example, regarding gender relations or the great power of some traditional leaders) are now anathema to present values.

'Progressing with the Past'

It is one thing to rediscover old systems of agriculture that had many of the virtues of sustainability; it is quite another to revive them and have them as viable systems meeting the requirements of present economic demands and social conditions. Clarke (1978) suggests the notion of 'progressing with the past' whereby the use of old energetically efficient forms of agriculture could be used as a basis for modern rural development, especially when combined with some modern techniques.

This approach argues for a melding of old systems and some aspects of modern science. It could be added that the notion of 'progressing' with the past is preferable to a 'recreation' of the past and the automatic acceptance of old ways of life that are now considered inappropriate. Thus, it should encapsulate ideas of social sustainability alongside the pursuit of environmental sustainability.

There are many examples of how this is occurring in practice, such as the revival of traditional crops to supply new urban and international markets (see Box 17.1), but what is not happening is any systematic or substantial attempt to make these enterprises more overtly sustainable. Farmers producing taro for the market are inherently no less likely to use chemicals, clear bush or diminish soil fertility than those who grow squash or ginger (Chapter 13). How, then, might agriculture be turned towards a more sustainable path? Below are some possibilities, as yet largely unrealised:

- *'Green' export markets:* One of the major changes in international produce markets in recent years has been the substantial rise in demand for organic produce. Consumer awareness of the health risks of chemical additives and residues in produce has created a substantial demand for certified organic fruit, vegetables, grain and meat not only in small health food outlets but also in major supermarket chains. The demand is most pronounced in North American and European markets and producers there have been quick to respond. There is virtually no evidence, however, of any response by Pacific Island producers, still mainly producing fruit and vegetables for less discerning (or more complacent) Australasian markets. There is also a difficulty in producing chemical-free organic produce for such markets when those countries have stringent import regulations to prevent the introduction of pests and diseases. Yet there should be considerable potential for developing such an industry, not only for organic citrus, bananas, papaya and pineapples, but also for organic tropical vegetables such as aubergines, okra or beans. Developing such an industry would have the advantage of using the international image (if not the reality) of the Pacific Islands as having clean, unpolluted and unspoilt environments, thus allowing for careful niche branding to associate a particular product with a certain location. Small-volume, relatively high-value production for specific markets might compensate for the disadvantages inherent in exporting produce from the Pacific: high transport costs (especially for perishable goods), poor economies of scale, and intense competition from other tropical producers. It would require a monitoring system, however, to authenticate the organic methods used that would be acceptable to consumers internationally.[1]

- *Local awareness:* Much agricultural production is aimed now at domestic markets within the Pacific Islands, particularly with many urban dwellers not growing their own food. Whereas such consumers are very discerning with regard to quality, freshness and origin of the produce they buy, there is much less awareness about the health risks of chemical residues in food, especially as there is little or no regulation of what is grown and sold locally. Vegetables, root crops and fruit purchased in urban markets throughout the Pacific may well contain highly dangerous levels of chemicals because producers use chemicals as a major labour-saving device to control weed growth, insects and fungus and they often use inorganic fertilisers to boost production. When such chemical use is by the untrained – apocryphal evidence abounds of ready availability and indiscriminate use of agricultural chemicals in Fiji and elsewhere – not only is the food produced potentially unhealthy but there are harmful ecological consequences for the land on which it is produced. Government regulation may help, but with limited budgets this is a low priority. Governments have also been prone to encourage and subsidise chemical use to boost overall production. What may be more efficacious is education, not only of producers (education about the dangers of use and storage of chemical and the risks of selling contaminated produce, especially overseas) but also of local consumers (the dangers to their health). When local consumers, perhaps backed by official regulation or organic certification, begin to discriminate in markets between taro that has been sprayed with pesticide and that which has not, then there will be a major impetus towards more organic and sustainable agriculture.

- *Expatriate Pacific Islanders:* One of the main markets for Pacific Island agricultural exports is the large number of Pacific Islanders resident overseas. The world's largest Polynesian city is Auckland, and Sydney, Honolulu and Vancouver also have substantial populations of people of Pacific Island origin. These are people who seek to buy taro, yams, breadfruit, kava and mangoes and they often prefer produce from their island of origin – there are marked preferences for, say, Samoan taro or Fijian kava. They comprise a large and stable

[1] In New Zealand, for example, the 'Bio Gro' label is used for producers who meet a very stringent set of regulations governing organic production and lack of chemical residues. It is recognised by the International Federation of Organic Agriculture Movements (IFOAM), the international umbrella organisation for organic agriculture (see internet http://ecoweb.dk/ifoam).

market for Pacific Island fruit and vegetables and for 'traditional' crops. Given that these crops and the techniques used to grow them (high chemical use notwithstanding) are more grounded in local environments and knowledge, they offer considerable advantages over the mainstream commodities – copra, coffee, cocoa, and sugar – which face more volatile and vulnerable markets and which often involve more energy-intensive, higher-input techniques.

- *New technologies and agricultural extension:* The modern era has been associated with agricultural innovations based on sciences and practices which encourage industrial methods of production: specialised uniform products, energy-intensive methods to increase productivity, interventions to minimise damage (through pests and diseases for example), and economies of scale. Yet there are many examples of scientific advances which have not followed this path and, indeed, which have sought to remedy the ecological damage caused by such approaches. The list of such advances is long but includes techniques of low-input farming, integrated pest management, biological controls, plant breeding to build in pest and disease resistance genetically, and soil conservation strategies (Myers 1994). Some are overtly 'organic', others merely seek less ecologically harmful ways to increase production. Many evolve from an appreciation of the capacity of farmers themselves to innovate and develop locally appropriate techniques and cultivars (Richards 1985, Shiva 1989). If these diverse and non-industrial approaches to sustainable agriculture are to gain ground against the solutions derived from the small number of prestigious international research centres and the vigorous promotion of their products by international agrochemical companies, then a profound change is necessary in the way agricultural extension work is carried out. 'Farmer first' approaches to extension work (Chambers 1997) seek to develop change only after an appreciation of farmers' needs, resources, expertise and aspirations. They do introduce new ideas when appropriate but they do so in a way which does not belittle local knowledge and they try to minimise the disruptive effects of change.

Therefore, it may be possible to bring about changes in Pacific Island agriculture which will turn it towards a more sustainable path. To a large extent this can be informed and built upon an appreciation of the virtues of old systems of agriculture that existed in the region prior to European contact and which had many of the attributes of sustainability (stability of food supply, the integration of society, culture and agriculture, and modification of the environment that was more 'enhancement' (Spriggs 1985) than destruction).

BOX 17.1 • IRRIGATED TARO CULTIVATION ON RAROTONGA

Near the inland road (*Ara Metua*), that partially encircles the island of Rarotonga, and in some of the valleys that reach towards the interior of the island, there has recently been an increase in the cultivation of taro. It is still on a fairly small scale, for there is much more land under fallow, trees, other forms of cropping and residences, but it does now appear as one of the main forms of agricultural endeavour on the island. Its growth may be explained by recent economic conditions in the Cook Islands, where cuts in public sector employment and expenditure have turned more people towards agriculture as a means of livelihood. It might also be the result of an opening of export markets for taro – the Samoan taro blight has meant that the market for taro, especially in New Zealand, has offered opportunities to new exporters.

This increase in taro cultivation, along with parallel increases in vegetable production (for the local market) is in marked contrast to the remnants of former rural development efforts, mainly the ageing citrus trees that stand nearby, a testament to the failure of this industry in the 1970s (Bellam 1980). The apparent burgeoning of the taro industry represents the revival of an established staple crop and old production methods to meet new economic and social conditions with the assistance of some new techniques.

There appears to be a reversion to old, if modified, methods of production. Irrigation is being used to boost productivity. This varies in type from plot to plot. In the valleys behind the town of Avarua, old (but not ancient) irrigation channels and inundated plots are in operation, with taro (*Colocasia esculenta*) being grown in small ponds. With the exception of the occasional concrete water race and gate, these appear to be similar to the old irrigation systems described by Bellwood (1978) which draw water from the streams that flow through the valleys. Elsewhere there is also irrigated taro but in the form of planted mounds separated by ditches of water. Some of these plots are interesting for the form of mulching used. Whilst coconut fronds and other organic material are used, also noticeable is the use of black polythene sheeting, an effective and labour-saving device to control weeds. And yet elsewhere, where water supply from streams is not so readily available, more dryfield cultivation is employed, though here irrigation is also apparent, this time in the form of polythene hoses which allow water to be drip fed to the rows of taro.

Whether the industry is sustainable is questionable. Much will depend on the vicissitudes of economic conditions – the recovery of the Samoan industry, for example, could have a major effect on export returns. It is also not a fully organic crop – chemical sprays are used and the extensive use and disposal of polythene sheeting could create some environmental problems in the future. Yet, it is a relatively low-input crop, one that draws on established expertise and revives some old techniques and infrastructure. It does not seem to disrupt social organisation – indeed, provides a safety net and an expanded range of livelihood strategies for some people facing economic dislocation. Whilst it shows promise, however, the industry has yet to prove itself sustainable.

Yet caution is necessary if old systems are to be revived. The form of traditional agriculture may be evident, yet the substance has been eroded. The crops may be the same, or similar, but much else has changed: chemical inputs have increased, inorganic fertilisers have taken the place of fallowing, monoculture has displaced diversity in many gardens, and the social and cultural context of reciprocity and communalism has given way to individualism and the commodification of land, labour and product. The science of traditional cultivation, embedded in the beliefs, customs and stories of generations of Pacific cultivators, has been progressively devalued, modified and lost. Moreover, even if it was possible to recover old knowledge, many people today might baulk at returning to practices and forms of social organisation that would today be regarded as harsh, unjust and even despotic.

There is also much in the way of the revival of old systems to meet present needs. Population growth and urbanisation have created a demand for substantial surplus food production from the countryside, well beyond what former subsistence systems were able to produce. A simple return to old systems would not satisfy such basic food needs, let alone new material wants. Agriculture, unfortunately, is no longer a prestigious occupation and it is often associated with poverty – able young people seek careers in higher paid urban-based occupations and there is a real danger that the knowledge base of agriculture may be eroded if there are not enough members of future generations committed to its continuation. Finally, there is, as yet, no strong ethic of sustainability in Pacific Island agriculture, at least not one that is capable of understanding and dealing with the dangers of modern agrochemicals and the loss of biodiversity. That requires a programme of education for producers and consumers. And it may necessitate a fundamental shift in values away from the now dominant concepts of progress, materialism, individualism and domination of nature, and back perhaps to some older concepts of communalism, intergenerational responsibility and guardianship of the land.

Yet the prospects for using modified forms of old systems as models for future sustainable agriculture are good. Knowledge about these systems has not been entirely lost and some are still in operation, albeit in changed form. The staple crops of the old systems, particularly root crops, tree crops and vegetables, are still central to the diets of Pacific Islanders at home and abroad. And the advantages of the systems for sustainability are still apparent: low environmental impact and use of organic farming methods (compared with modern high-energy and high-input agriculture), low social impact (within existing social and cultural contexts), and a stable base of production and consumption (compared with the production of global commodities). The challenge is not to recreate and return to the past but to learn from it, add to it what modern technology can offer, and develop new agricultural systems to meet new needs, if not spiralling modern material desires.

CHAPTER 18

Sustainable Urban Footprints

JOHN OVERTON AND DONOVAN STOREY

Urban Ecological Footprints

Despite their relatively small size, urban areas in the Pacific Islands nonetheless have begun to experience mounting urban environmental problems. Such problems (as outlined in Chapter 12) have included air and water pollution, solid waste disposal, congestion and destruction of nearby marine and mangrove ecosystems. Environmental impacts have been particularly severe, even when the absolute size of urban centres has been small, when towns are located on atolls or other fragile environments. Environmental problems loom large in discussions of the future of Pacific Island urban areas (Bryant-Tokalau 1993, Connell and Lea 1995). This chapter explores possible ways to face and mitigate some of the more severe urban environmental problems in the Pacific Islands. It first presents and extends an alternative conceptual framework – urban ecological footprints – for analysing such problems and their solution, then moves to examine two alternative models of urban form in the Pacific – compact and decentralised. On this basis, it looks in more detail at two types of informal activities – autonomous housing and urban home gardening.

Dealing with urban environmental problems has followed a not unfamiliar trail of attempted regulation and control, weakened by lack of administrative resources and occasional official lassitude. Such measures have attempted to deal with the symptoms of environmental problems – cleaning up the mess or limiting the activities of polluters – but they have often done little to address the underlying processes of environmental changes in urban areas. In order to understand how urban environmental problems might be analysed or dealt with in other ways – and in some cases are already being dealt with by citizens if not city officials – alternative conceptual frameworks may be useful.

To a large extent, conventional frameworks have implicitly involved what Girardet has termed a 'linear metabolism' model (Girardet 1992). This model involves a view of a city as an organism which receives inputs, such as energy, water, raw materials and human labour, processes them to generate industrial products, food and services, then generates waste in the form of air and water pollutants. In this framework the policy implications for improving the urban environment are, mostly, to limit the volume of the most harmful forms of waste production, or at least make waste disposal more efficient or less visible. There is little effort to focus on inputs or production methods, for these are associated with supposedly beneficial processes of economic growth and would involve greater, and more unpopular, forms of government intervention in industry – something which is likely to be less common under neoliberal agendas (Burgess *et al.* 1997a). Government – national and municipal – is seen as the most likely (in some cases the only) agency capable of restricting waste generation and legislating for improvements in the urban environment.

An alternative framework to this linear model is provided by extending the growing body of literature on 'ecological footprints'. Rees (1992, 1996), Wackernagel and Rees (1996) and others (Girardet 1992) have undertaken studies which have shown how countries and cities extend a very large ecological 'footprint' over their surrounding hinterlands. For these authors, the footprint of a city can be conceived of as the hypothetical area needed to sustain human life and activities within that city. They have calculated and compared what such areas might be, including areas required for food production, energy generation and carbon sequestration. Such work has illustrated the dramatic impact cities have on their surrounding environment: London alone, for example, has a footprint equivalent to the entire area of the United Kingdom (Girardet 1992).

Another aspect of the footprints literature is the promotion of an alternative, or 'circular' metabolism (Girardet 1992). A circular metabolism is one in which a city derives more of its inputs from within (ores from recycled materials, oxygen from trees within the city, nutrients from efficient sewage treatment, food from urban gardens) and seeks to lower its production of waste materials (by efficient public transport, clean technologies and effective recycling). In short, a city becomes more ecologically self-sufficient, with less dependence on its surrounding areas for inputs or disposal of outputs, and with a much smaller ecological footprint.

What this footprints literature can also do is suggest different ways in which this more circular metabolism can be achieved (van Diermen and Overton 1998). Ecological footprints can be thought of as not just a single hypothetical area required to produce inputs and absorb waste, but a real set of overlapping spatial realms for different types of inputs (for example, materials produced in the nearby hinterland or acquired from the global economy) or outputs (local, regional and global environmental impacts of urban pollution). Furthermore, each of these spatial realms may involve different types of governmental agency, ranging over community, municipal, regional, national or even international forms of involvement. For relatively wealthy Western cities with strong local authorities and low population growth, the clue to achieving a more circular metabolism may lie in greater urban concentration and regulation. Thus, efficient public transport, sewerage and water reticulation and waste disposal and recycling services can go hand-in-hand with high urban population densities and more compact urban form. This more compact urban model leaves more room for green spaces, in turn for recreational spaces, trees and less encroachment on the surrounding countryside. Although local governments in Western cities may not be able to intervene strongly in the economy,[1] characteristically they do have a strong rating base and good technical and legislative resources and enjoy support from their citizens to control the worst excesses of urban pollution. A compact, smaller-area city with well-defined and effective governmental structures to regulate environmental impact and promote environmental improvements is, therefore, a supposedly effective means of lessening a city's ecological footprint.

Yet this approach, though implicit in some planning approaches to urban environmental problems in the Pacific and elsewhere, is often inappropriate in developing countries. Though some Third World states may have putatively strong central governments, their municipal counterparts are frequently weak, poorly funded and overwhelmed by the pace of urban growth. Rapid urbanisation not only stretches municipal services beyond breaking point but also complicates the capacity of urban authorities to act, as settlement and industry spill over into surrounding areas. Not only are urban authorities not able to act in the same ways as Western cities do but they face problems of greater magnitude: the relative poverty of many of a city's inhabitants (and therefore of its government), very high growth rates, rapidly changing consumption patterns and the propensity of people to act, often through necessity, in disregard of poorly-enforced or non-existent environmental laws.

[1] Political and economic reforms in the West since the 1980s have seen a diminished role for the state in the economy and a distrust in many quarters for government regulation and taxation.

What has emerged is something different to the compact model: what might be called a 'decentralised' model (van Diermen and Overton 1998). This involves lower density of settlement as autonomous settlements sprout on vacant land, more individual and community-oriented actions to deal with things such as water supply, waste disposal and even crime (in the place of municipal government), and more local provision of inputs (through gardening and recycling, for example). Conventionally, squatter settlements, communal rubbish dumps and urban sprawl (which can be elements of a decentralised model) are perceived as unsightly, uncontrolled and environmentally malign. Yet, it can be argued that rather than being indicative of more severe urban environmental problems, this model may, in fact, provide a positive alternative for many cities. It does not depend on the presence of a strong local government, it builds on people's and communities' initiatives and it recognises the efficacy of factors such as home gardening, communal tenure and informal recycling of waste. It leads to cities that are not as neat as in the compact model – they may have low densities and cover a very large area by comparison[2] – but they do have much higher levels of internal/circular production and (re)processing of goods, they may be associated with more green spaces (though often in the form of productive food gardens rather than recreational parks) and, to be realistic, they may be the only alternative for rapidly growing and poor Third World cities.

What follows is an exploration of these two models – compact and decentralised – in the Pacific Island context. We recognise that both are in existence and both are necessary, yet because most official action has centred on the compact model, we tend to stress the need to recognise and encourage the positive aspects of the decentralised model.

The Compact Urban Model

Few, if any, Pacific Island cities could claim to be compact, other than in terms of having low populations. Despite the application of some Western town planning techniques in cities such as Port Moresby and the presence of well-defined and laid-out colonial cores, recent rapid urbanisation has created cityscapes marked by suburban sprawl, autonomous settlements, and urban services (roads, public transport, drainage, sewerage and water reticulation) seemingly unable to keep

[2] McGee (1995, 1997) has noted the growth of very large urban agglomerations in the developing world and coined the term 'extended metropolitan regions' (1997:35) to describe 'mega-urban regions' which extend their influence well into surrounding rural areas, with high population densities.

pace with growth. Urban population densities are low by world standards (as are total urban populations) and multi-storey buildings confined to the central business districts of a few Pacific Island cities (Suva, Port Moresby and Noumea).

Yet it is the compact model, apparently, that has governed urban environmental planning in the Pacific Islands. Urban authorities have attempted to plan and manage urban environments in ways which have sought to improve the efficient mass distribution of services (roads, water, sewerage and electricity to planned and zoned residential subdivisions), restrict the encroachment onto surrounding farmland, and separate incompatible land uses, such as heavy industry and residences. They have allowed, even encouraged, higher-density housing and multi-storey buildings nearer town centres, they have tried to promote infilling of vacant land, and they have zoned for parks and other recreational spaces within urban limits. Yet they have struggled to provide services at the same rate as urban growth. Traffic congestion has appeared, electricity shortages and cuts have arisen and water and sewerage reticulation often do not reach newly settled areas. The high cost of such services is often beyond the resources of municipal authorities.

To a large extent, this compact model rests on a particular type of land tenure and landscape. Urban land in most (but not all) Pacific Island countries has involved individual and usually freehold or secure and transferable leasehold tenure. This has evolved from colonial times, when towns were populated by expatriates and urban land markets developed. Residents, as landowners or lessees, live in houses or apartments that have discrete titles and areas. Suburbs have developed in the formal housing areas with bungalows or semi-detached buildings separated from others by fences or hedges. Each has its garden and each needs connection to water, electricity and sewerage. Most such suburbs – like their Australian and New Zealand counterparts – are low density. Even the autonomous settlements of the Pacific Islands exhibit this general characteristic: not jammed together like the *barrios* of Sao Paulo but more akin to their formal sector suburban neighbours. Whilst these individual urban land tenure systems do facilitate collection of rates, they increase the cost of service provision and socially they promote a more individualised and isolated mode of living in contrast to the communal base of many Pacific rural villages. Thus crime is seen as being a matter for the state (in the form of the police) rather than the community, children are cared for and watched within households (albeit by often extended families) rather than within a wider village environment, and social interaction is configured increasingly by workplace and neighbourhood rather than (or as well as) by village and kinship.

Suva is a city that perhaps best exemplifies the compact model in the Pacific Islands. It is recognised as having one of the most efficient municipal authorities in the region, with good services including rubbish collection, domestic water supplies, and sewerage. Although low-density suburbs predominate, within its boundaries also lie some experiments in higher-density housing, with the low-income housing blocks at Raiwaqa as somewhat bleak testimony to the application of old Western planning techniques. There are autonomous settlements in many places within Suva (Bryant 1990:177), but there are also attempts to limit these and rehouse their inhabitants. Suva, however, is also the scene of major environmental deterioration. Marine resources have been stripped from most of the nearby reefs and inshore fisheries, and rubbish is still routinely disposed of by dumping in the sea. Little has been done to control air pollution from automobiles and factories and many local creeks are heavily polluted. Clearly, it is questionable whether either the Suva City Council or the Government of Fiji have the means or strong desire to promote a more sustainable urban future for the city.

The Decentralised Model

Whereas many local authorities in Pacific Islands have struggled to implement measures to plan and regulate their urban environments, large numbers of their residents have gone about fashioning their environments to meet their own circumstances and needs. Where the provision of housing and basic services has been deficient, people have obtained their own; where government planning and regulation have been non-existent, people have acted freely, though not without regard for the wishes of their neighbours and communities; and where land has been seen to be available, they have built their houses and planted their gardens to form green, low-density settlements. This is a decentralised urban model. Rather than rely on mass provision of services or central city planning, communities spring up on and within the urban boundaries and often function as quasi-independent communities, sometimes with wide-ranging powers of sanction explicitly supported by national legislation (for example in Samoa's Fono Act of 1990). Though they may still be subject to central regulations, law enforcement and planning guidelines, on a day-to-day basis many individual households and communities are primarily responsible for their own urban environments.

These are what can be regarded as 'autonomous' forms of urban transformation, for they are often undertaken outside of any legislative or regulatory frame and by residents themselves (even if there are forms of sub-leasing and a *de facto* housing market in existence). They are also, in many cases, 'communal' actions, for not only is the land on which they settle frequently controlled by local communal kinship-based units which accord rights to settle on their land to tenants, but also the residents often act in concert to develop their own services, agree on boundaries of gardens or keep a protective eye on each others' children and property. It may be too much to describe autonomous urban settlements in the Pacific Islands as urban villages (for the strong kinship base that binds residents together is usually lacking) but they often do operate in ways which imitate the strong communal character of rural villages.

Indeed in Apia and parts of Suva, there are villages which retain some of their original character as they have been enveloped by the expansion of the towns and as they have absorbed newcomers from other areas (Rutz 1987). The urban villages of Apia, for example, are very much 'towns without fences' with recognisable village form, common land rather than individual titles and sections, and no fences separating houses and household plots. In Melanesia, the control and use of *kastom* (custom) land is determined by the needs of families and groups at, and for, a particular time (Larmour 1984). In situations of both expanding and contracting extended families, this flexibility of tenure allows land to be distributed by *kastom* authorities to those in most need. Through these flexible land arrangements, land is essentially 'borrowed' for family/clan use and its custodianship is renegotiated at a later date. This communal ethos of group assent for individual actions, and the use of traditional means for dealing with outsiders (for example, the granting of rights to settle on communal land), are still in evidence in parts of the urban Pacific.

What is important about these autonomous settlements – and, indeed, much of the formal sector suburban housing – is the urban environment they form. They are low-density settlements. Households, whether separated into sections by fences or grouped together around a common village centre, have land attached. This land is important: to provide space for children's play, privacy or social interaction; to give aesthetic value with decorative plants and trees; and to provide an important economic supplement to households, with food gardens and fruit trees supplying a high proportion of many households' food requirements. Indeed, it is common in Pacific Island urban areas to see land which may otherwise be considered 'waste' or 'vacant' planted in taro, cassava, or sweet potato gardens and papaya, banana and coconut trees.

Low-density settlement also means that households can deal with other important matters such as waste and energy. In the absence of sewage systems, 'long-drop' toilets may be constructed; in the absence of piped water supplies, people may rely on rainwater collection; and where electricity is absent or deemed too expensive, trees may provide energy through fuelwood. Community action may be evident also: recognised walking tracks instead of roads, illegal tapping of electricity lines or water pipes, and efforts to deal with local petty crime. In short, low-density settlement can relieve considerable strain on centralised urban services.

But, lest it be thought that such low-density autonomous settlements form a complete answer to urban environmental problems in the Pacific Islands, or elsewhere, it must be noted that there are also many shortcomings. There can be a 'tragedy of the commons' effect, for example, where dumping of rubbish on common ground mounts over time to become a serious local problem for which no-one is responsible. Effluent disposal can quickly foul local creeks. Fuelwood demands can lead to a destruction of mangrove swamps and other treed areas. And rather than relieving the burden on municipal services, illegal tapping of water pipes or electricity lines can increase the cost for legal users and magnify the overall problems of mass distribution for the central agency. Furthermore, local communities are not the best agencies for providing public transport,[3] building roads or dealing with powerful private companies.

In pre-existing villages absorbed by urban expansion, it may also happen that the impact of increasing numbers of migrants from outer islands breaks down previously cohesive social structures in which the roles and ranking of members were known and respected. Urban proximity may also act to break down traditional structures through the introduction of monetary exchange and urban values (Griffen and Monsell-Davis 1986) and the impact of urban lifestyles, in the form of fast food and non-recyclable goods such as tinned food and plastic bags, may place greater stress on health and the environment. The decentralised model may offer some advantages in moving towards sustainable urban environments but it also creates a particular set of problems that still require some form of state or municipal involvement.

The physical expansion of Pacific towns is occurring without the emergence of clear policy support or urban development models. This has allowed Pacific Islanders to retain rights and access to land for housing and subsistence even when their incomes are low. Housing in many peri-urban and urban village environments reflects both the old and the new. Certainly, houses made from traditional materials have long been replaced by those constructed from more permanent

[3] The example of the Cautata village cooperative bus company in Fiji (Tukai 1988) however, suggests that this may be possible to a limited extent.

materials, such as tin and concrete, which are perceived to be of higher status and more able to withstand hurricane damage. Nevertheless, as with the urban villages of Apia, houses retain the traditional *fale* design: in many instances they consist of roofs over several beams with no walls. The house is, in fact, open to the community. There is little evidence of any significant problem of property crime, as traditional controls remain strong and, under the Fono Act, Samoan village chiefs have considerable powers of sanction and punishment. In contrast, in Suva and Port Moresby, houses are almost always heavily fenced, many with barbed wire, and windows are secured. Property crime and break-ins are frequent, and social anomie is widespread. It is apparent that such social breakdown correlates with the breakdown of communities and ethnic ties, including the declining role of chiefs, as evidenced in the experiences of National Housing Authority estates in Raiwaqa, Suva (Monsell-Davis 1986). Indeed, where housing authorities have attempted to provide public housing, as in Suva, they seem unable to meet the demands of the poor and have catered more for the middle class (Walsh 1984). On the other hand, where self-built environments have predominated in and around Pacific Island towns, they have often provided a much more pleasant and sustainable form of housing, catering better for the needs of the poor, than that which meets official standards.

There will come a time, and for some places it has already come, when urban boundaries have been reached and all urban land has been filled. The urban village concept then has some appeal as an alternative form of urban expansion. Nevertheless, there are important considerations which may act as an impediment to this (outside of government lassitude). The question of land and migrant access to land remains a difficulty which any decentralised model would need to deal with. Often, particularly in Melanesia, urban boundaries are areas of strictly delineated freehold land. Outside, land tenure is exceedingly complex and under constant dispute among various parties. Because of the increasing cost of urban land, rapidly increasing urban populations have mostly settled in peri-urban areas which dot the landscape beyond the urban boundaries. In essence, they are dormitory suburbs (Overton 1992b), but they are also along the lines of the decentralised model where gardens are maintained and *kastom* laws are predominant. For many this is an effective way of minimising costs. Growing urban populations are increasingly not from nearby regions, however, and outer islanders do not have the right of access to land. This has meant a proliferation of tenuous and exploitative renting taking place, in which unscrupulous 'landowners' exploit desperate migrants. There are also problems for urban authorities. For example, most of the growth in Port Vila's population is outside the urban boundaries, and thus outside of revenue collection and the provision of services to these communities. It has also often been the case that *kastom* land owners have blocked the implementation of basic sanitation and other services to these communities for fear that government involvement may weaken their control (Storey 1998).

Certainly, efforts to plan Pacific Island towns tightly to mimic their Western counterparts have failed. Municipal and other government offices throughout the Pacific are littered with numerous copies of (typically foreign-authored) planning exercises, often referred to as 'dust catchers' or 'door stoppers'. Partly the failure of urban planning is to do with the reluctance of Pacific Island governments to establish potentially strong (and thus, to them, rival) municipal authorities, and partly it is a reflection of the general incapacity of Pacific Island governments to enact laws and regulate change in urban settings. It is also appropriate, however, to question the relevance of many of these plans. Perhaps it is time to pursue alternative urban options based more on local realities.

This includes the concept of an 'urban village' model for Pacific island towns, as favoured in recent reports on the future of Port Vila. In these, Paul (1993) and Royds Consulting Ltd (1997) have demonstrated an interest in pursuing the urban village concept to deal with the problems and future political and social fallout from the continued growth and expansion of Port Vila into surrounding *kastom* lands. Paul, in his 1993 report, noted that if somehow the village environment could be transferred to an urban context, then it might be possible to reap the benefits of both environments. He noted that the quality of life of those ni-Vanuatu living in villages near Port Vila was superior to that of those living in autonomous settlements closer to town, or inside the urban boundaries. This was attributed to a more healthy and spacious environment, and easier access to the sea and gardens. It was also coupled with a stronger relationship with custom and traditions, greater access to communal meeting places, and more involvement of local chiefs. While it may not be possible to reproduce these environments completely within town boundaries, certain key features may be replicable to improve urban conditions. It may be an area for future planning which deserves greater attention and research.

Another model for urban development may lie in the encouragement of urban home gardening (Box 18.1). This phenomenon is widespread throughout most Pacific Island urban areas but, despite its productivity and environmental benefits, it is usually conducted without official support and (because it usually takes place on unoccupied ground) sometimes falls foul of the law.

BOX 18.1 • URBAN HOME GARDENING

The phenomenon of urban home gardens in the Pacific Islands has not received much recognition and appreciation other than in the work of Thaman (1984b, 1988). Urban home gardens are a critical part of the urban landscape and household economies of many urban areas in the Pacific and world-wide, but they are often neglected, being seen as 'merely' part of the subsistence sector and more as a sideline activity for households rather than a crucial part of their livelihood strategies. They should also be recognised as having a potentially major role in helping to create more sustainable urban environments. At present, though, they are threatened by a desire to increase urban infilling and the increasing costs of urban land which can result in the selling or subdivision of garden plots for housing or commercial enterprises.

In the Pacific Islands, home gardens are much in evidence in many urban areas. Thaman's (1988) surveys showed a very wide range of crops being grown but some important regional differences in crop compositions. Root crop staples – taro, cassava and sweet potato – are particularly in evidence, as are tree crops, principally bananas, coconuts and papaya but also breadfruit, jackfruit and mangoes. These tree crops are important not just as sources of food but also as fuelwood and building materials. Vegetable crops, herbs and spices are also grown, as are plants with medicinal uses. Livestock, particularly poultry and occasionally pigs, may be kept by urban households and these can prove useful to dispose of some household waste. Urban gardens also include plants for decorative purposes and a noticeable pride is taken in the appearance of household gardens in many parts of the region.

Food gardens are critical for the welfare of many poor urban households. They save households the expense of buying staple foods at the market, they provide a fresh nutritious diet and, in some cases, surplus production can be sold to earn a little extra cash. In addition, the crops grown are familiar ones: they can be grown with existing knowledge, they do not require high inputs (though the use of chemical herbicides and fertilisers in urban home gardens is not uncommon), and the variety of crops provides a mostly steady source of food throughout the year.

What urban food gardens lead to is a situation where the urban landscape is green, with open land separating mostly low-density housing, but the open spaces are filled not predominantly with parks and recreational facilities as in planned Western cities, but with gardens and tree crops as well as some common recreational spaces. These are not planned or zoned but the boundaries of, and *de facto* property rights over, gardens and trees are recognised locally. It is a very productive landscape compared with the green spaces of Western cities but one that is equally – if not more so – valuable in improving the aesthetic appearance of the city and improving the carbon sequestration of polluted air.

Towards Sustainable Urban Areas in the Pacific?

Pacific Island towns are small by world standards and their environmental problems seem of little consequence by comparison. Yet, for their inhabitants – a population likely to continue to grow rapidly into the next century – the issue of working towards a more sustainable urban environment is no less pressing. Pacific Island towns and cities will continue to grow, they will continue to encroach on larger areas of their often fragile hinterlands, they will continue to face the problem of poverty at both the micro (household) and macro (local government) level, and they will continue to cast a larger environmental shadow on their surroundings, through demands for inputs, land and waste disposal.

In the search for a more sustainable urban future, the concepts of urban footprints and metabolisms may provide some important insights. Developing smaller ecological footprints, by moving towards a more circular metabolism, is achievable. To a large extent it is being achieved already in features such as home gardens, urban villages and self-help service provision. Decentralised, partially self-sufficient communities can be, and are, an important component of any sustainable urban environment. And it also requires continued effort and will on the part of urban authorities to plan, promote and regulate for urban environments less prone to pollution, congestion and unmanageable waste generation and disposal.

Finally, any move towards sustainable cities in the Pacific Islands must consider what is appropriate for the region. Centralised, compact, 'modern' cities with mass uniform systems of service provision are not viable in places that lack the resources, the political and physical infrastructure and the cultural values to mimic Western approaches. And they are simply growing too fast to allow for a uniform, controlled and managed response. Centralised urban planning and regulation alone will not work. Central authorities, however, have been reluctant to allow effective and meaningful decentralisation of their roles and influence to occur. While decentralisation is often touted in development plans and political platforms (Larmour and Qalo 1985), it has rarely gone further than lip-service. In fact, the trend since independence in many Pacific Island states has been towards increasing centralised control, and the primacy of the 'main' island and town. It is time to take the rhetoric of decentralisation more seriously.

What it lacks in resources, the Pacific region may compensate for in other ways. The small size of its urban centres is an advantage, for towns with populations measured in the tens or even hundreds of thousands, rather than the millions or tens of millions, are more straightforward entities to deal with. Furthermore, it is argued here that present urban centres in the Pacific – with evidence of nascent urban communities, low-density settlements and often considerable degrees of internal/circular production and processing of products and waste – are already some way towards developing an alternative and more sustainable urban environmental future.

CHAPTER 19

Conclusions: Achieving Sustainable Development

JOHN OVERTON, REGINA SCHEYVENS
AND NICK PURDIE

This book has examined the issue of sustainable development in the Pacific Island region: not only its challenges and abject failures but also its potential and quiet successes. It has argued strongly that the region is unique and that it demands a fresh set of perspectives, ones which require an understanding of the particular environmental and cultural setting of the region. It has analysed the ways conventional development strategies have usually led to unsustainable bases for development with unequal and sometimes destabilising social outcomes. More positively, it has shown that there are alternatives, many of them apparently sustainable, and these are being implemented, modified and extended mainly by the autonomous actions and initiatives of local residents, though often in concert with external agencies. Throughout, the underlying theme of the close relationship between culture, society and environment, encapsulated in the concept of *vanua*, has presented itself strongly.

This chapter suggests a number of themes and implications that emerge from the substance of the book. It begins by reviewing the precarious nature of present development strategies and suggests that their future is seriously in doubt as they are overtaken by wider processes of global economic and political transformation as well as by local environmental change. Secondly, it extracts examples of more sustainable (and some not so sustainable) activities that are evolving separately from the mainstream development paths. It argues that these provide important lessons for future moves towards sustainable development in the region, not just because they prove that forms of sustainable development are possible but also because they reveal some of the key elements of apparently successful 'development': a concern for human livelihoods as well as the environment; the participation of all groups in society; the importance of maintaining sovereignty over land and other resources; and the way local people and outside agencies can interact in mutually beneficial ways, especially if capacity building and empowerment are integral components of their cooperation. The chapter then moves to suggest some implications for sustainable development on a wider stage. Development practice, we believe, can be enhanced by some of the lessons from the Pacific Islands. These involve a critical analysis of 'development projects' and 'project cycles' as well as a strong argument for the centrality of a livelihoods perspective. Finally, there are ways that sustainable development theory can be reassessed in the light of the findings of this book. Here we argue that the social perspective needs further attention, particularly with regard to issues of enhancing livelihoods and social inclusion. Yet we also suggest that there is a cultural dimension to sustainable development theory that has been neglected and which is vital if the direction of development is to be challenged and changed and the substance of sustainable development is to be attained.

Questioning Development Blueprints

For the past 50 years the Pacific Islands have been part of a grand 'development project' (McMichael 1996). At first this involved (and sometimes still does) colonial administrations and then independent governments struggling to meet the overarching objectives of 'development': increased material standards of living, improved education and health, and greater use of capitalist relations of production and exchange (Norgaard 1994). Until recently, the nation state was seen to be central to this cause. Aided by foreign donors, advisers and investors, it aimed to increase economic activity and accelerate social 'progress'. The policy tools used were varied but most came to the Pacific Island region as a result of ideas and experiences elsewhere. They were 'blueprints': policies, practices and systems that were seen to work in one place and were therefore expected to be successful in the Pacific. Thus came a procession of such strategies: agricultural modernisation, import substitution industrialisation, regional development, five year plans, tax free zones, export orientation, urban planning and many more. They were usually conveyed and implemented by foreign experts or local people educated overseas. They promised much, they changed much, but development has remained elusive.

Out of the chequered history of development practice in the Pacific Islands emerged the realisation that the local context *did* matter. Local markets were too small and often too poor – and the costs too high – to justify the doubtful returns on programmes of import substitution industrialisation. Economic planning and forecasting was fraught with difficulties when the price of commodities on the world market could vary wildly in a short space of time. Commodity exports faced often crippling transport costs and fickle markets. In response, new approaches were sought, though these aimed to modify and bolster the blueprints rather than seek alternatives. Thus, in the past 30 years, independent Pacific Island states were able to exploit their strategic importance to attract aid and other concessions, such as preferential access to otherwise restricted metropolitan markets (Chapter 3). These measures allowed the development project to proceed with even higher levels of state involvement and support, from within and outside, even though the foundations of such development were shaky and its impacts uneven.

Four major development trajectories were followed. First there was resource exploitation. For those countries with natural resources to exploit (gold, copper and trees in Papua New Guinea; nickel in New Caledonia; phosphate in Nauru; and fish and trees in the Solomon Islands) the returns could be very high. In Chapters 9 and 10 it was shown how mining and logging have brought sudden and substantial riches to governments and landowners alike. Such development also involved a heavy loss of autonomy, however, for foreign companies have controlled the industries and profited most, while local landowners, especially, have found that quick riches are both short-lived and inadequate to compensate for the permanent loss of resources. The fishing industry (Chapter 11) has also exhibited these trends of resource depletion and foreign control. Furthermore, the social impacts of such development have involved widening social inequalities: between men and women, between regions, and between the elite and common people.

A second strategy involved export-oriented industries growing under the protection of preferential access to markets. This had two sides: industries producing for local markets protected by import tariffs and export industries with preferential access (with quotas and/or guaranteed prices) to overseas markets. Fiji has taken this strategy further than any other Pacific Island state. On one hand the expansion of its main industry, sugar, was supported by the substantial benefits it received from access to Europe under the Lomé Convention (Chapter 13) and its rising star, garment manufacturing, was aided by the SPARTECA agreement with Australia and New Zealand (Chapter 3). On the other, it protected some of its own industries, dairying and rice (Overton 1988) among them, from foreign competition. The result was an improvement in incomes for those involved in the industries –

significant for sugar cane farmers or garment manufacturers, doubtful for garment workers on very low wages (Slatter 1987, Chandra 1996) – but costs for others, with rice consumers facing higher prices. The system worked quite well to even out market price fluctuations and it did spread the benefits of economic growth perhaps more effectively and widely than, say, localised and short-term resource exploitation. Furthermore, as a form of 'aid with dignity' (Taylor 1987) it avoided some of the pitfalls of aid dependence and manipulation of aid by both donor and recipient governments.

For countries with few natural resources and limited potential for industrialisation and export trade, there was a third alternative: dependence on foreign patrons for high levels of aid and access to overseas labour markets. These became the MIRAB states (Bertram and Watters 1985). They were countries that found it difficult to establish a stable economic base, either in local resource extraction or in viable industries. Export earnings were well below the cost of imports and the deficit was made up by aid, the remittances of Island people working in New Zealand, USA or Australia, and small incomes from such sources as philatelic sales (Connell 1986, 1988b). In addition, aid provided the means to support a bureaucracy that typically became the country's largest employer and a source of employment for those who received higher education. This, together with the relative ease of earning high incomes overseas, tended to inflate local wages and further diminish the prospects of an export-led economy. It also accelerated the rate of urbanisation (Chapter 12). Despite these problems, MIRAB economies did seem to be secure and appropriate forms of economic organisation for small island states. They resulted in high average incomes for the region; they opened opportunities for a wide range of people, either locally or overseas; and were more stable than reliance on a narrow range of commodity exports.

Finally, there was tourism. This is a strategy that has been followed by nearly all Pacific Island states, though to varying degrees of intensity and success. The major tourist destinations in the region – Fiji, Tahiti, New Caledonia and northern Micronesia – have mainly opted for 'mass tourism': a high-volume, resort-based and import-dependent industry that has brought foreign exchange and employment but also resulted in substantial leakages through imports, high degrees of foreign ownership and questionable cultural and environmental impacts (Chapter 16). Other countries have attempted to follow suit, though some have been more cautious. There have been undoubted economic benefits and, despite fluctuating tourist arrival numbers, the industry has proved one of the few examples – perhaps the only major one – to secure a solid, and generally growing, economic return based on physical characteristics (smallness, isolation, tropical marine location and climate) that have otherwise constrained economic activity.

These four strategies, then, have evolved in the Pacific in response both to wider economic and political forces and the exigencies of local environmental and social contexts. With the possible exception of tourism, all are under threat and they are now highly questionable as bases for sustainable development into the next century. First, large-scale resource extraction can never be regarded as sustainable. The current dominant forms of mining, fishing and logging are seriously depleting resources – some of which, such as the phosphate of Nauru, have already all but disappeared – and there is little sign that current income is being invested wisely to secure continued income after the resources are gone. In addition, resource extraction – in mining and logging – is leading to substantial local environmental damage, through poisoning and silting of waterways, accelerated soil erosion in the hills and loss of biodiversity. These are often irreversible changes that will affect the ability of future generations to gain livelihoods from the land.

Second, threats have arisen from changes in the global political and economic order. The end of the Cold War has lowered significantly the strategic value of the region: no longer is it a potential scene of conflict between the superpowers, nor is there a pressing need to test weapons of mass destruction. Aid has fallen and there is less willingness on the part of patron states to subsidise living standards in the Islands. Instead, there has been a significant shift towards a new economic development blueprint – neoliberalism (Brohman 1995, 1996), which for the Pacific has involved a new set of policies being imposed by experts: free trade, substantial cuts in the public sector and the dismantling of internal and cross-border subsidies. This new blueprint has the potential – sometimes the explicit aim – of overturning the second two economic strategies, those of export orientation within preferential trade agreements and MIRAB. MIRAB economies may survive but without the aid and bureaucracy components being so dominant. Significantly, whilst neoliberalism advocates freer trade in commodities, financial services and intellectual property, it has not expanded to encompass free movement of labour across international boundaries, one change that might open up opportunities for Melanesian countries that already exist for some of their Polynesian counterparts.

Neoliberalism is leading to a situation where the 'development project', based on economic nationalism and state intervention, is being replaced by the 'global project' (McMichael 1996). In this case, the power of states to guide the development of their citizens is being consciously weakened and, indeed, states are being pressured to relinquish their own sovereignty in order to bring their countries into line with new international laws and conventions which further open up boundaries for global capitalism. It has been observed that neoliberalism poses serious challenges to the progress of sustainable development world-wide (Burgess *et al.* 1997). We believe it has particularly serious consequences for the Pacific Island region. Tourism might survive, and even prosper, but the export of agricultural commodities, manufacturing and an aid-supported public sector are all likely casualties. The 'global project' is already forcing a major reassessment of the development strategies of the region. The critical challenge is to ensure that these will be more sustainable than those which evolved in the past 50 years.

Finding Exemplars of Sustainable Development

Whilst the main development strategies of the region may be questionable, it is apparent from the studies in this book that there are many alternatives. Furthermore, some of these alternatives may offer a more sustainable future for island environments and societies. They do not, in general, follow external blueprints, though blueprints have been used in examples such as the national park approach to nature conservation in Samoa (Chapter 14). Instead, they result from a multitude of individual and group actions. They represent attempts by people and organisations primarily to secure a better material standard of living and a more secure future for coming generations. They are not, for the most part, dominated by considerations of global environmental change. Yet, they are in many cases more inherently 'sustainable' in character because they are in accord with local conditions, are small-scale, and draw on people's desires to preserve the elements of local environments and cultures that are important to them.

Yet, although these activities have evolved quietly from within the region, they often involve links with the outside world, with consumers, conservation organisations, aid agencies and tourists. It is this articulation between local initiatives and outsiders that is central to the progress of sustainable development in the region. Outsiders bring critical elements to the process of sustainable development: cash, ideas, commitment, skills, and awareness of the wider implications of environmental change. Such features are not, by any means, absent locally but there is a synergy between local and outside views, for one cannot operate effectively without the other. Ecotourism requires not only village-based operations which protect and celebrate local natural environments and cultures but also foreigners prepared to travel to them, pay well and behave in appropriate ways (Chapter 16).

Sustainable agriculture depends not only on farmers growing produce organically but also on consumers in Suva, Auckland or Los Angeles being able to recognise the worth of such products and willing to pay more for them (Chapter 17). Conservation requires villagers to agree to protect their flora and fauna but also agencies such as the Swedish Society for Nature Conservation (Chapter 14) to provide funds to help meet basic local needs. Ecotimber schemes depend on the integrity of local forestry and milling practices as well as the integrity of Western consumers to seek out and pay a premium for certified timber products (Chapter 15). And sustainable urban environments require not only the functioning of viable neighbourhood communities and 'urban villages' but also the willingness of government to facilitate the empowerment of such communities through decentralisation (Chapter 18).

Three related themes can be suggested from these examples as having particular importance in determining their success or failure. First, to draw on the work of Hau'ofa (1993), it is vital that Pacific Island people are seen not as passive recipients of outside resources, nor as being incapable of autonomous development, nor as victims of forms of development or environmental change that are imposed upon them. Rather, it is apparent that much of the groundswell of activity that is leading to more sustainable development is coming from within. Just as they have been able to negotiate constraints and exploit opportunities in the past through migration, education and employment, so too has there been significant initiative, awareness and assertiveness on the part of people who have sought to develop new development strategies. This is not to deny that many have engaged in activities that are socially destabilising, which exclude others or damage the environment. But, by maintaining concepts such as *vanua* (Chapter 8), incorporating new ideas and skills from education or following experiences of living abroad (Chapter 7) and starting their own enterprises, there is considerable evidence of positive change and of a plethora of grassroots sustainable development strategies (Ghai and Vivian 1992).

Second, in analysing the way such activities have developed, it is apparent that a livelihoods approach is critical (Chapter 5). People have changed their economic activities, and often their forms of social organisation, in response to new economic constraints and opportunities and to changes in the basic 'assets' from which they develop and maintain their survival strategies: their land, social relations and their skills. Certain characteristics of a sustainable and secure livelihood stand out as essential: the ability to diversify, modify and transform the structures and activities of everyday life; to access and make use of necessary livelihood resources, including land, water and educational opportunities, in situations of changing needs; and to do this in the face of adversity or out of desire to improve standards of living. Associated with these abilities is the synergy and dynamism which exists at the local level, seen in the ability of people to take stock of their situation and organise to make improvements relative to that analysis. Understandably, people are more likely to be swayed by evidence of local environmental change (destruction of mangroves and other food gathering grounds, pollution of streams, and soil erosion in their gardens) than by talk of possible future global warming. There is, however, a need to ensure that local people have the capability to confront the local level manifestations of global level processes, including environmental change and the changes in the global economy. It is at this local nexus that these processes become evident and impact most forcibly, and this is why the local is the context for change.

Third, sovereignty is critical. The discourse of sovereignty in the region has hitherto been dominated by the struggles for political independence in places such as New Caledonia or regional separatism in, for example, Bougainville. There has also been a strong vein of ethnic and nationalist assertiveness, as in Fiji in 1987. These all represent struggles to gain, or retain, control over resources and, ultimately, livelihoods. Yet the issue of sovereignty goes much deeper, and the political relationships are much more complex than straightforward decolonisation or political independence. In many places in the region, the most fundamental issue of sovereignty is ownership of land, and, in this, there is no great struggle involved. One of the benefits of being colonised late and not having resources that were coveted, at least in the colonial period, by global capitalism, has been the preservation of indigenous and communal land tenure. Compared with many other parts of the globe where indigenous land rights were extinguished through land alienation and communal systems of land tenure were replaced by systems of individual tenure, most Pacific Island societies have retained ownership of their most important physical asset, their land. This has been critical in providing a basis for survival and development. Control over land has allowed a more subtle form of sovereignty to be exercised. As long as long-term ownership is recognised, many communal landowners in the Pacific have been willing to accommodate outsiders in joint ventures or as tenants. More complex land tenure arrangements, based on 'traditional' ownership and practices (Ward and Kingdon 1995a), have opened new opportunities for individual and group benefit. Similarly, once forms of independence have been reached at the national level, states have been able to negotiate terms of engagement with metropolitan powers that have ceded some elements of national sovereignty, in return for economic benefits, but not changed the fundamental nature of their right of self-determination. Sovereignty, then, is at the core of livelihood strategies at both the local and national levels, but it is a flexible and negotiable asset.

Implications for Development Practice

Having explored some of the themes to emerge from the studies in this book, it is now possible to suggest some wider implications for both development theory and development practice. The implications for development practice are ones that, in part, concur with recent changes in practice towards more participatory approaches (Chambers 1983, 1997) but in other ways argue for a re-evaluation of the structures and philosophies involved in the development activities of government agencies and NGOs. Four themes emerge: the need for diversity; the need for participation; the deficiencies of the project cycle approach; and the deficiencies of modernist strategies.

Diversity is an inevitable outcome of development strategies that emerge from the everyday actions and ideas of ordinary people rather than the programmes of planners and politicians. This book has emphasized the diversity in environments (Chapter 2) and cultures (Chapter 4) across the region. As a result, there are very wide differences in the ways people's livelihood strategies evolve at the local level (Chapter 5). Such diversity, we argue, should be seen as a virtue rather than an indicator of chaotic and uncoordinated development. We further suggest that it is this diversity which development needs to maintain as a strength and essential characteristic of sustainability. As such, effective and sustainable development strategies must be developed according to the context of people's lives, their resources, aspirations and values.

Participation is also a key element of sustainability. Too often, conventional development strategies have brought rewards for some (individuals, regions, social and ethnic groups) but costs for others. Participation is a key principle, for it contends that all people affected by a development activity should be involved in its conception, implementation and evaluation, and share in its rewards. For development practice, participation means more than just consultation and it must involve empowerment in terms of handing over control and ownership of activities to those most involved and affected. The substance of ownership must be palpable so that people can control the pace as well as the nature of change. Furthermore, participation must involve the ability *not* to participate (should people so desire), or not to be adversely affected by development. The reality of participation in practice, however, is much more complex and contentious. It involves mechanisms of power which exist at local, national and global levels. In addition, communities are rarely homogeneous, power is rarely shared evenly amongst all and participation can become another tool by which powerful groups exploit others (Rahnema 1992). Nevertheless, if the principles of inclusion and participation are uppermost in the minds and practices of development agents, methods to ensure participation of those who by virtue of their race, class, gender or age are often excluded (Chambers 1997) can be very effective in promoting more effective and socially sustainable activities.

Projects are the most evident means by which outside agencies participate in development activities, largely because they allow for a clear definition of the goals, methods and responsibilities involved. Project planning cycles help define accountabilities and targets and promote project efficiency. The priniciples of sustainable development have been incorporated into the goals and general policy outlines of development agencies. Yet at a fundamental level we believe there is a need to question the reliance on projects and, in particular, their ability to deliver the goals of sustainable development. In the first place, the notion of a fixed timespan for sustainable development projects seems contradictory to the concept itself, which demands a very long time horizon. Thus the quantitative outputs of a project – those indices used to evaluate its success or failure – will be unable to capture the essence of change, the long-term impact of which may take generations to become evident. In addition, as we suggest below, many of the substantive elements of sustainable development are concerned with attitudes, values and beliefs which define the nature of that development and the outcomes it promotes. These are qualitative dimensions which cannot be captured adequately in short-term data on outputs. There is a further philosophical objection to the project approach: the very idea of a 'project' suggests that the society, economy or environment to which it is applied is bounded in space and time, and that it can be managed and controlled as a system. Given the great complexity and diversity of societies, cultures and environments, the widespread networks and interactions people have as a livelihood necessity, and the apparently seamless contiguity of social and ecological life, we believe this assumption is seriously flawed. Additionally, 'management' implies a certain degree of external control which runs contrary to the principles of participation and empowerment outlined above. Certain interventions and outcomes may be guided, measured and regulated within the project cycle but the impacts, especially those beyond the intervention phase of a project, cannot. Instead, there is perhaps a case for interventions to be much less controlled, to be able to evolve and change as impacts – both planned and unforeseen – are assessed and as people's aspirations and circumstances change.

We concede that projects are a necessary aspect of development and in particular aid delivery where they provide an acceptable vehicle for external donor involvement and accountability. A 'project' can help coordinate activities between disparate groups at the local level and new interest in 'sustainable projects' may help ensure that external intervention has self-sufficiency and independence as clear goals. Consequently, we advocate an iterative and adaptive approach to project design, which necessarily involves integrating local opinion into the planning and design process, and ensuring flexibility throughout to account for contingencies and changing circumstances. At a fundamental level we suggest a move from seeing 'the project' as a bounded object, to viewing it as a process which is only a small part of the broader process of change and adaptation at the local level.

Finally, this book contends that sustainable development must break free of modernist approaches to 'development' and 'progress' (Norgaard 1994). We have seen considerable merit in the rediscovery and re-evaluation of the past: in concepts of human-environment relationships (Chapter 8); in agricultural systems (Chapter 17); and in natural environments and traditional cultures (Chapter 16). This is not to suggest that such ways of life should, or could, be recreated in their entirety just because they proved sustainable in the past. They, too, were suspect – social injustice and inequality and environmental destruction were not unknown – and there is, perhaps, little value in reconstituting and crystalising the past as a means of securing the future. What it does propound, however, is that the past can offer an antidote and be a complement to the modern. Sustainability, if not implying no change, does at least question the inevitability or desirability of constant change. Progress demands change, whereas custom, tradition and history – strongly incorporated into Pacific Island notions of identity, social interaction and veneration of ancestors – are concepts that are more in accord with long-term stability and inter-generational responsibility. Instead of development implying inevitable increases in economic activity and wealth, sustainable development must be a more basic and diverse notion of improvement and well-being, even if this involves minimal change and merely the maintenance of existing livelihoods. Ideally, it allows people the option of combining and adapting what they regard as the best of old and new. For development practice, this requires a much more passive and facilitative role for outside individuals and agencies, compared with the all-too-common role of provider of skills, resources and power.

Implications for Development Theory

Development theory is presently undergoing a major change (Schuurman 1993, Edwards 1993). Partly, this has resulted from the challenge of postmodernism, questioning the very concept of development itself (Sachs 1991, Escobar 1995, Rahnema and Bawtree 1997), but an associated catalyst for this has also come from a gradual realisation that existing development theories have not served development practice well. There have been confusing changes in paradigms, blindness to environmental and social impacts, and preoccupation with meta-theories of social and economic change. Similarly, theories of sustainable development are of questionable worth as long as they allow such a broad range of interpretation and suffer the same philosophical deficiencies as the concept of development itself does. Such critiques of development should encourage us to be more open to 'multiple interpretations and 'solutions' to development problems' (Marchand and Parpart 1995:12).

This book began with the suggestion that the Pacific Island region was a worthwhile focus for the study of sustainable development, first, because it is likely to be one of the first regions to suffer the consequences of global environmental change; and, second, because it may offer some early lessons on the way in which people have developed strategies for sustainable development. It is from this practice in the Pacific, developed and presented throughout the substantive chapters of the book, that we wish to draw some implications for the way theories of sustainable development might be sharpened and extended.

The observation in Chapter 1 that the social perspective was the least developed in sustainable development theory, relative to the ecological and economic spheres, can and should be re-emphasised. To date, work on the social dimension has been concerned largely with aspects of social inclusion, justice and equality and has built on contributions from feminist and Marxist theories. The central argument of this work is that unjust and inequitable societies, which exclude or exploit significant and specific groups, are not sustainable. This book, in presenting examples of the marginalisation and exploitation of women (chapters 4 and 10), is in accordance with this view. Similarly, the exclusion of youth, the poor and ethnic or regional minorities are indicative of the belief that social instability will continue in the short term at least. We also see a number of potential avenues for extending the social perspective, particularly at the micro-level (individuals, households and communities) where there is a definite need to understand the local complexities of access to resources, decision making, and maintenance of physical and social assets. These considerations, extended in the analysis of the livelihoods approach (Chapter 5), are critical in the way people's livelihood options are formed, extended or constrained. Socially sustainable development must involve the maintenance and expansion of options, whether they be the ability to simply derive a subsistence living, or the potential to derive income, whether it be from an ecotimber venture, a Sup Sup garden or from culturally and socially supportive handicraft manufacture, to invest in the education of the next generation.

There is also a case for extending the three perspectives on sustainable development to include a fourth: culture. In the Pacific Islands we have seen that beliefs, values and protocols are central to the way people's daily lives are conducted and integral to their sense of self-esteem and dignity. Yet indigenous culture has been often ignored, and sometimes suppressed, by outsiders in ways which work to undermine the pride and stifle the initiative of Pacific Island peoples (Hau'ofa 1993). Custom has been vital in the past in providing a way of explaining and regulating human relationships with nature (Chapter 8) and has been manifested in social phenomena such as the magic gardens of Tanna (Chapter 17) or the land tenure systems of many islands. As cultures have changed, as with the replacement of animist religions by Christianity, or the spread of individualism in place of communalism, so too have the ways in which people have interacted with their environments. Cultural change has been a driving force for environmental change. Thus, in sustainable development theory, there is a place for the study of culture – of religion, beliefs in the supernatural, aesthetics (Clarke 1993), language and genealogy – as much as there is a place for botany and economics. Cultural integrity and village autonomy should also be valued as contributing to sustainable development (James 1993b:147). For the Pacific, there is much to be gained from a closer appraisal of concepts such as *vanua*, with its associated concept of stewardship, as possible alternative philosophical and cultural bases for sustainability.

To conclude, we suggest that the way sustainable development is conceived may need questioning. The environmentalist motto 'think global, act local' is a powerful and worthy metaphor. It calls on people to be guided by considerations of global environmental change and seek to implement a multitude of small-scale everyday actions – recycling, minimising waste, taking care with what we buy and how we vote, planting trees, etc. It is these actions which can achieve greater sustainability at the local level and which, it is hoped, will aggregate into beneficial change at the global level. There may be, however, an equally strong case for the reverse: to 'think local, act global' (Overton and Purdie 1997). This book has demonstrated that there are numerous examples of local actions within the Pacific Island region that are helping to achieve forms of sustainable development. These are not driven solely by global awareness and in most cases the impetus for them rests on the way people assess their local situation: their resources, their ambitions and their culture. Given the potential effectiveness of a new cultural perspective, it is apparent that 'thinking locally' is essential in order to capture the necessary richness which this perspective entails. Alternative cultures, concerns, values and skills are worthy of exploration, understanding and support. They can be as powerful as global awareness, if not more so, in stimulating action and they will lead to quite diverse strategies and goals.

Furthermore, 'global action' – though perhaps difficult and contentious – is still essential. Although action may be directed at global agencies (corporations, multinational institutions, and NGOs), just as critical is the need to challenge the global culture, particularly that which is concerned with progress, materialism, consumerism and individualism. The pervasiveness and rapaciousness of this worldwide culture is in evidence in the most remote parts of the Pacific. It presents itself on radio, television, newspapers and films, through advertising, the examples presented by tourists, and the experience of living overseas. This global culture is part and parcel of the wider phenomenon of globalisation and represents the 'thickening' of a global consciousness. Its impact at the local level, and the subsequent unsustainability that this engenders, can be combated only through a concerted effort to 'thicken', that is reassert, the local culture, and the more intimate relations this implies. Events such as the Festival of Pacific Arts work to reassert the Pacific culture as an equally, if not more legitimate, form of cultural expression than that presented from the global level. Through this reassertion of local culture and an allied strengthening of local civil society, people are better able to assert themselves in the face of encroachment from powerful external forces, including that of the state, and thereby to cement a basis for the self-determination and participation which this book propounds. Fundamentally, this is an assertion of the insider viewpoint, a recognition that the local does matter in all its diversity and richness of culture, society, economy and environment.

Bibliography

Acquaye, B. and Crocombe, R. (eds) (1984) *Land Tenure and Rural Productivity in the Pacific Islands.* Institute of Pacific Studies, University of the South Pacific, Suva.

Adams, W.M. (1990) *Green Development: Environment and Sustainability in the Third World.* Routledge, London.

Adams, W.M. (1995) 'Green development theory? Environmentalism and sustainable development' in J. Crush (ed.) *Power of Development.* Routledge, London and New York, pp.87–99.

Afeaki E. (1983) 'Tonga: the last Pacific kingdom' in A. Ali and R. Crocombe (eds) *Politics in Polynesia.* Institute of Pacific Studies, University of the South Pacific, Suva, pp.57–78.

Ahlburg, D.A. (1996) *Demographic and Social Change in the Island Nations of the Pacific.* Asia-Pacific Population Research Reports, East-West Center, Honolulu.

Ahlburg, D.A. and Levin, M. (1990) *The North-East Passage: A Study of Pacific Islander Migration to American Samoa and the United States.* National Centre for Development Studies, Australian National University, Canberra.

AIDAB (1994) *Melanesian Forestry Sector Study.* International Development Issues No.36, AIDAB, Canberra.

Akama, J.S. (1996) 'Western environmental values and nature-based tourism in Kenya' *Tourism Management* 17 567–74.

Ali, I. (1988) 'Specialisation leading to increasing vulnerability on sugar farms in Fiji' in J. Hirst, J.D. Overton, B. Allen and Y. Byron (eds) *Small-Scale Agriculture.* Commonwealth Geographical Bureau and Department of Human Geography, Australian National University, Canberra, pp 111–26.

Ali, R.A. and Narayan, J.P. (1989) 'The Fiji sugar industry: a brief history and an overview of its structure and operations' *Pacific Economic Bulletin* 4,2, 13–21.

Allen, B.J. (1996) 'Land management: Papua New Guinea's dilemma' *The Asia–Pacific Magazine* 1 36–42.

Bainer, G. B. K. (1987) 'Manipulation of islands and men' in S. Britton and W.C. Clarke (eds) *Ambiguous Alternative: Tourism in Small Developing Countries.* University of the South Pacific, Suva, pp.16–24.

Banks, G. (1993) 'Mining multinationals and developing countries: theory and practice in Papua New Guinea' *Applied Geography* 13 313–27.

Banks, G. (1996) 'Compensation for mining: benefit or time-bomb? The Porgera gold mine'in R. Howitt, J. Connell and P. Hirsch (eds) *Resources, Nations and Indigenous Peoples: Case Studies from Australasia, Melanesia and Southeast Asia.* Oxford University Press, Melbourne, pp.223–35.

Barbier, E.B. (1987) 'The concept of sustainable economic development' *Environmental Conservation* 14,2 101–10.

Barbier, E.B. (1993) *Economics and Ecology: New Frontiers and Sustainable Development.* Chapman and Hall, London.

Barham, B. Clark, M., Katz, E. and Shurman, R. (1992) 'Nontraditional agricultural exports in Latin America' *Latin American Research Review* 27,2 43–82.

Barlow, K. and Winduo, S. (1997) 'Introduction' *The Contemporary Pacific* 9,1 1–24.

Barnett, T. (1989) *The Barnett Report: A Summary of the Report of the Commission of Inquiry into Aspects of the Timber Industry in Papua New Guinea.* Asia-Pacific Action Groups, Hobart.

Barrau, J. (1958) *Subsistence Agriculture in Melanesia.* Bernice P. Bishop Museum Bulletin no.219, Honolulu.

Barrow, C.J. (1995) 'Sustainable development' *Third World Planning Review* 17,4 369–86.

Bauer, P. (1971) 'Foreign aid: necessary? useful? damaging?' *New Scientist* 527 252–7.

Bayliss-Smith, T.P. (1985) 'Subsistence agriculture and nutrition in the Bimin Valley, Oksapmin sub-district, Papua New Guinea' *Singapore Journal of Tropical Geography* 6,2 101–15.

Bayliss-Smith, T.P. (1997) 'From taro garden to golf course? Alternative futures for agricultural capital in the Pacific Islands' in B. Burt and C. Clerk (eds) *Environment and Development in the Pacific Islands.* National Centre for Development Studies, Australian National University, Canberra and University of Papua New Guinea Press, Port Moresby, pp.143–70.

Bayliss-Smith, T.P. and Haynes, P. (1988) 'Land settlement as a rural development strategy' in J.D. Overton (ed.) *Rural Fiji.* Institute of Pacific Studies, University of the South Pacific, Suva, pp.123–45.

Bayliss-Smith, T.P., Bedford, R.D., Brookfield, H.C. and Latham, M. (1988) *Islands, Islanders and the World.* Cambridge University Press, Cambridge.

Bedford, R.D. (1986) 'International migration in the South Pacific: a New Zealand perspective' *New Zealand Population Review* 12,1 32–48.

Bedford R.D. (1992) 'International migration in the South Pacific region' in M. Kritz, L. Lim and H. Zlotnik (eds) *International Migration Systems: A Global Approach.* Clarendon Press, Oxford, pp.41–62.

Bellam, M. (1980) *The Citrus Colony. New Zealand – Cook Islands Economic Relations.* New Zealand Coalition for Trade and Development, Wellington.

Bellwood, P. (1978) *Archaeological Research in the Cook Islands.* Pacific Anthropological Records, No.27, Bernice P. Bishop Museum, Honolulu.

Bennett, J.A. (1987) *Wealth of the Solomons.* University of Hawaii Press, Honolulu.

Bertram, I.G. (1986) 'Sustainable development in Pacific micro-economies' *World Development* 14,7 809–22.

Bertram, I.G. (1987) 'The political economy of decolonisation and nationhood in small Pacific societies' in A. Hooper, S. Britton, R. Crocombe, J. Huntsman and C. Macpherson (eds) *Class and Culture in the South Pacific*. Centre for Pacific Studies, University of Auckland, Auckland and Institute of Pacific Studies, University of the South Pacific, Suva, pp. 16–29.

Bertram, I.G. and Watters, R.F. (1985) 'The MIRAB economy in South Pacific microstates' *Pacific Viewpoint* 26,3 497–519.

Bertram, I.G. and Watters, R.F. (1986) 'The MIRAB process: earlier analyses in context' *Pacific Viewpoint* 27,1 47–59.

Biodiversity Conservation Network (1996) *Annual Report 1996: Stories from the Field and Lessons Learned*. Biodiversity Conservation Network, Washington DC.

Biodiversity Conservation Network (1997) *Annual Report 1997: Getting Down to Business*. Biodiversity Conservation Network, Washington DC.

Biological Support Programme (1993) *The Biodiversity Conservation Networks Grants Programme for Asia and the Pacific: Requests for Proposals and Application Guidelines*. World Wide Fund for Nature, Washington DC.

Blaikie, P. and Brookfield, H.C. (1987) *Land Degradation and Society*. Methuen, London.

Blamey, R. (1997) 'Ecotourism: The search for an operational definition' *Journal of Sustainable Tourism* 5,2 109–30.

Bodley, J.H. (1997) *Cultural Anthropology: Tribes, States, and the Global System*. Mayfield, Mountain View.

Bonnell, S. (1994) 'Dilemas of development: social change in Porgera 1989-1993', unpublished report to Porgera Joint Venture, Subada Consulting Pty. Ltd, Cairns.

Bonnemaison, J. (1984) 'The tree and the canoe: roots and mobility in Vanuatu societies' *Pacific Viewpoint* 25,2 117–52.

Bonnemaison, J. (1991) 'Magic gardens in Tanna' *Pacific Studies* 14,4 71–89.

Bonnemaison, J. (1994) *The Tree and the Canoe: History and Ethnogeography of Tanna* (translated and adapted by Josee Penot-Demetry). University of Hawaii Press, Honolulu.

Boo, E. (1990) *Ecotourism: The Potentials and Pitfalls*. World Wildlife Fund, Washington DC.

Booth, H. (1989) 'Cook Islands: a statistical profile of men, women and children', unpublished report, Pacific Mainstreaming Project UNDP/ UNIFEM, Suva.

Britton, S.G. (1982) 'International tourism and multinational corporations in the Pacific: the case of Fiji' in M.J. Taylor and N. Thrift (eds) *The Geography of Multinationals*. Croom Helm, London, pp. 252–74.

Britton, S.G. (1983) *Tourism and Underdevelopment in Fiji*. Development Studies Centre, Australian National University, Canberra.

Britton, S.G. (1987) 'Tourism in Pacific Island states: constraints and opportunities' in S.G. Britton and W.C. Clarke (eds) *Ambiguous Alternative: Tourism in Small Developing Countries*. University of the South Pacific, Suva, pp. 113–39.

Brohman, J. (1995) 'Universalism, Eurocentrism, and ideological bias in development studies: from modernisation to neoliberalism' *Third World Quarterly* 16,1 121–40.

Brohman, J. (1996) *Popular Development: Rethinking the Theory and Practice of Development*. Blackwell, Cambridge.

Brookfield, H.C. (1972) 'Intensification and disintensification in Pacific agriculture: a theoretical approach' *Pacific Viewpoint* 13,1, 30–48.

Brookfield, H.C. (1975) 'Multum in parvo: questions about diversity and diversification in small developing countries' in P. Selwyn (ed.) *Development Policy in Small Countries*. Croom Helm, London, pp.54–76.

Brookfield, H.C. (ed.) (1977) *The Hurricane Hazard. Natural Disaster and Small Populations*. UNESCO/UNFPA MAB Population and Environment Project in the Eastern Islands of Fiji. Island, Report no.1. UNESCO/UNFPA MAB/ Development Studies Centre, Australian National University, Canberra.

Brookfield, H.C. (1984) 'Boxes, ports, and places without ports' in B.S. Hoyle and D. Hilling (eds) *Seaport Systems and Spatial Change*. John Wiley, London, pp. 61–79.

Brookfield, H.C. (1985) 'An historical and prospective analysis of the coconut economy and the coconut districts of Fiji' in H.C. Brookfield, F. Ellis and R.G. Ward, *Land Cane and Coconuts*. Department of Human Geography, Australian National University, Canberra, pp.91–215.

Brookfield, H.C. (1986) 'Intensification intensified' *Archaeology in Oceania* 31 177–80.

Brookfield, H.C. (1987) 'Export or perish: commercial agriculture in Fiji' in M.J. Taylor (ed.) *Fiji: Future Imperfect?* Allen and Unwin, Sydney, pp. 46–57.

Brookfield, H.C. (1989) 'Global change and the Pacific: problems for the coming half-century' *The Contemporary Pacific* 1/1&2 1–17.

Brookfield, H.C. and Hart, D. (1971) *Melanesia. A Geographical Interpretation of an Island World*. Methuen, London.

Brown, M. and Wyckoff-Baird, B. (1992) *Designing Integrated Conservation and Development Projects*. Biodiversity Support Programme, Washington DC.

Brown, R.P.C. and Connell, J. (1993) 'The global flea market: migration, remittances and the informal economy in Tonga' *Development and Change* 24,4 611–47.

Browne, T.P. (1994) 'Traditional rights and customary usage in the Cook Islands' in R. Crocombe and M. Meleisea (eds) *Land Issues in the Pacific*. MacMillan Brown Centre for Pacific Studies, University of Canterbury, Christchurch, pp.205–19.

Bryant J.J. (1990) 'The acceptable face of self-help housing: subletting in Fiji squatter settlements – exploitation of survival strategy?' in D. Drakakis-Smith (ed.) *Economic Growth and Urbanization in Developing Countries*. Routledge, London, pp.171–95.

Bryant, J.J. (1993) *Urban Poverty and the Environment in the South Pacific*. Department of Geography and Planning, University of New England, Armidale.

Bryant-Tokolau, J.J. (1993) 'What future Pacific cities? The challenge in managing urban environments' in E. Waddell and P.D. Nunn (eds) *The Margin Fades: Geographical Itineraries in a World of Islands*. Institute of Pacific Studies, University of the South Pacific, Suva, pp.151–65.

Bryant-Tokalau, J.J. (1994) 'Our changing islands: Pacific urban environments' *The Courier*, 144, March–April, 80–82.

Bryant-Tokalau, J.J. (1995) 'The myth exploded: urban poverty in the Pacific' *Environment and Urbanization* 7,2 109–29.

Buckley, R. (1994) 'A framework for ecotourism' *Annals of Tourism* Research 21,3 661–69.

Bugotu, F. et al. (1990) 'A review of the achievements of the Forum Fisheries Agency in its first decade of operations' in R. Herr (ed.) *The Forum Fisheries Agency: Achievements, Challenges and Prospects*. Institute of Pacific Studies, University of the South Pacific, Suva.

Burgess, R., Carmona, M. and Kolstee, T. (eds) (1997a) *The Challenge of Sustainable Cities: Neoliberalism and Urban Strategies in Developing Countries*. Zed Books, London.

Burgess, R. Carmona, M. and Kolstee, T. (1997b) 'Contemporary urban environmental strategies and policies in developing countries: a critical review', in R. Burgess, M. Carmona and T. Kolstee (eds) *The Challenge of Sustainable Cities*, Zed Books, London, pp.65–88.

Burgess, S.M. (1987) *The Climate and Weather of Western Kiribati*. New Zealand Meteorological Service, Wellington.

Burt, B. and Clerk, C. (eds) (1997) *Environment and Development in the Pacific Islands*. National Centre for Development Studies, Australian National University, Canberra and University of Papua New Guinea Press, Port Moresby.

Campbell, I.C. (1989) *A History of the Pacific Islands*. Canterbury University Press, Christchurch.

Campbell, I. (1992) 'A historical perspective on aid and dependency: the example of Tonga' *Pacific Studies* 15,3 59–75.

Carew-Reid, J. (1989) *Environment, Aid and Regionalism in the South Pacific*. National Centre for Development Studies, Australian National University, Canberra.

Carlquist, S. (1965) *Island Life: A Natural History of the Islands of the World*. American Museum of Natural History, The Natural History Press, Garden City.

Carter, J. (ed.) (1981) *Pacific Islands Yearbook*. Pacific Publications, Sydney.

Cartland, B.C. (1953a) 'Land settlements: Butaritari and Makin', Unpublished memorandum (GEIC 2, F 48/2/1), Kiribati National Archives, Tarawa.

Cartland, B.C. (1953b) 'Diary of the Chief Lands Commissioner 1953', unpublished MS (KNA 29/IV, item No. 11), Kiribati National Archives, Tarawa.

Cassells, R.M. (1992) 'The valuation of subsistence use of tropical rainforest on the Island of Choiseul, Solomon Islands: a comparison between subsistence values and logging royalties', unpublished M.Phil thesis, Massey University.

Cassells, R.M. (1993) 'Tropical rainforest: subsistence values compared with logging royalties' in A.C. Walsh (ed.) *Development That Works! Lessons from Asia-Pacific*. Amokura Publications, Palmerston North, pp.C3.1–C3.6.

Cassells, R.M. (1995) 'Social and land tenure assessment of Viru Harbour and North New Georgia Villages, Solomon Islands' unpublished consultancy report, R.M. Cassells, Palmerston North.

Cassells, R.M. (1996) 'Social forestry issues. Customary Land Reforestation Project, Solomon Islands' unpublished consultancy report, R.M. Cassells, Palmerston North.

Cater, E. (1993) 'Ecotourism in the Third World: problems for sustainable tourism development' *Tourism Management* 14,2 85–90.

Cater, E. and Lowman, G. (eds) (1994) *Ecotourism: A Sustainable Option?* Wiley, Chichester.

Ceballos-Lascurain, H. (1996) *Tourism, Ecotourism, and Protected Areas*. IUCN, Gland.

Central Planning Department (Tonga) (1993) 'Country Report on Population', unpublished paper, International Conference on Population and Development, Port Vila, Vanuatu.

Chambers, R. (1983) *Rural Development: Putting the Last First.* Longman, London.

Chambers, R. (1986) *Sustainable Livelihoods: An Opportunity for the World Commission for the Environment and Development.* Institute of Development Studies, University of Sussex, Brighton.

Chambers, R. (1994a) 'The origins and practice of participatory rural appraisal' *World Development* 22,7 953–69.

Chambers, R. (1994b) 'Participatory rural appraisal (PRA): analysis of experience' *World Development* 22,9 1253–68.

Chambers, R. (1997) *Whose Reality Counts? Putting the First Last.* Intermediate Technology Publications, London.

Chambers, R. and Conway, G.R. (1992) *Sustainable Rural Livelihoods: Practical Concepts for the 21st Century.* Discussion Paper No. 296, Institute of Development Studies, University of Sussex, Brighton.

Chand, G. (1991) 'France and South Pacific regionalism in the 1980s and 1990s' *Journal of Pacific Studies* 17 57–81.

Chandra, R. (1993) 'Breaking out of import-substitution industrialization: the case of Fiji' in D.G. Lockhart, D. Drakakis-Smith and J. Schembri (eds) *The Development Process in Small Island States.* Routledge, London, pp.205-227.

Chandra, R. (1994) 'Contemporary industrialisation in Fiji' in E. Waddell and P.D. Nunn (eds) *The Margin Fades: Geographical Itineraries in a World of Islands.* Institute of Pacific Studies, University of the South Pacific, Suva, pp.29–48.

Chandra, R. (1996) 'Manufacturing in Fiji: mixed results' *Pacific Economic Bulletin* 11,1 47–62.

Chapelle, T. (1978) 'Customary land tenure in Fiji: old truths and middle-aged myths', *Journal Polynesian Society* 87,2, 71–88.

Chapman, M. (1991) 'Pacific island movement and socioeconomic change: metaphors of misunderstanding' *Population and Development Review* 17,2 263–92.

Chung, J. (1988) 'Tropical cyclones and disaster relief' in J.D. Overton (ed.) *Rural Fiji.* Institute of Pacific Studies, University of the South Pacific, Suva, pp. 85–96.

Clarke, W.C. (1971) *Place and People: An Ecology of a New Guinean Community.* University of California Press, Berkeley.

Clarke, W.C. (1977) 'The structure of permanence: the relevance of self-subsistence communities for world ecosystem management' in T. P. Bayliss-Smith and R.G. Feacham (eds) *Subsistence and Survival.* Academic Press, London, pp. 363–84.

Clarke, W.C. (1978) 'Progressing with the past: environmentally sustainable modifications to traditional agricultural systems' in E.K. Fisk (ed.) *The Adaptation of Traditional Agriculture.* Development Studies Centre, Australian National University, Canberra, pp. 142–57.

Clarke, W.C. (1990) 'Learning from the past: traditional knowledge and sustainable development' *The Contemporary Pacific* 2,2 233–53.

Clarke, W.C. (1993) 'Learning from Ngirapo: indigenous knowledge and sustainable agricultural development' in E. Waddell and P.D. Nunn (eds) *The Margin Fades: Geographical Itineraries in a World of Islands.* Institute of

Pacific Studies, University of the South Pacific, Suva, pp.231–66.

Clarke, W.C. (1994) 'Traditional land use and agriculture in the Pacific Islands' in J Morrison, P. Gerathy and Linda Crowl (eds) *Science of Pacific Island Peoples: Land Use and Agriculture*. Institute of Pacific Studies, University of the South Pacific, Suva, pp.11–37.

Clarke, W.C. (1996) 'The sustainability of sustenance: land and agricultural production in the Third World' in I. Douglas, R. Huggett and M. Robinson (eds) *Companion Encyclopedia of Geography: The Environment and Humankind*. Routledge, London and New York, pp. 651–76.

Clarke, W.C. and Morrison, J. (1987) 'Land mismanagement and the development imperative in Fiji' in P. Blaikie and H.C. Brookfield *Land Degradation and Society*. Methuen, London, pp.176–85.

Clarke, W.C. and Thaman, R.R. (eds) (1993) *Agroforestry in the Pacific Islands: Systems for Sustainability*. United Nations University Press, Tokyo.

Cole, R.V. (1994) 'Land as security for private borrowing' in R. Crocombe and M. Meleisea (eds) *Land Issues in the Pacific*. MacMillan Brown Centre for Pacific Studies, Christchurch and Institute of Pacific Studies, University of the South Pacific, Suva, pp.43–51.

Cole, R.V. and Parry, T.G. (1986) 'Key issues in Pacific Island development' in R.V. Cole and T.G. Parry (eds) *Selected Issues in Pacific Island Development*. National Centre for Development Studies, Australian National University, Canberra, pp.1–20.

Collee, J. (1995) 'Stripping the Pacific Islands rainforests' *San Francisco Examiner* January 1, A14–A15.

Common, M. (1995) *Sustainability and Policy: Limits to Economics*. Cambridge University Press, Melbourne.

Connell, J. (1980) *Remittances and Rural Development: Migration, Dependency and Inequality in the South Pacific*. Development Studies Centre, Australian National University, Canberra.

Connell, J. (1982) 'Increasing urbanisation in the South Pacific: an inevitable development?' *New Zealand Population Review* 8,3 20–36.

Connell, J. (1983) *Migration, Employment and Development in the South Pacific - Cook Islands*. Country Report no.2. South Pacific Commission/ ILO, Noumea.

Connell, J. (1986) 'Small states, large aid: the benefits of benevolence in the South Pacific' in P. Elridge, D.K. Forbes and D. Porter (eds) *Australian Overseas Aid*. Croom Helm, Sydney and London, pp. 57–78.

Connell, J. (1987a) *Migration, Employment and Development in the South Pacific*. South Pacific Commission/ILO, Noumea.

Connell, J. (1987b) *New Caledonia or Kanaky? The Political History of a French Colony*. National Centre for Development Studies, Australian National University, Canberra.

Connell, J. (1988a) 'Contemporary issues in island micro-states' in M. Pacione (ed.) *The Geography of the Third World*. Routledge, London and New York, pp. 427–62.

Connell, J. (1988b) *Sovereignty and Survival: Island Microstates in the Third World*. Department Geography, University of Sydney, Sydney.

Connell, J. (1991a) 'Compensation and conflict: the Bougainville copper mine, Papua New Guinea' in J. Connell and R. Howitt (eds) *Mining and Indigenous*

Peoples in Australasia, Sydney University Press, Sydney, pp.55–76.

Connell, J. (1991b) 'Island microstates: the mirage of development' *The Contemporary Pacific*, 3,2 251–87.

Connell, J. and Howitt, R. (eds) (1991) *Mining and Indigenous Peoples in Australasia*. Sydney University Press, Sydney.

Connell J. and Lea J. (1993) *Planning the Future: Melanesian Cities in 2010*. National Centre for Development Studies, Australian National University, Canberra.

Connell, J. and Lea, J.P. (1995) *Pacific 2010: Urbanisation in Polynesia*. National Centre for Development Studies, Australian National University, Canberra.

Conroy, C. and Litvinoff, M. (eds) (1988) *The Greening of Aid: Sustainable Livelihoods in Practice*. Earthscan, London.

Convard, N. (1993) *Land-Based Pollutants Inventory for the South Pacific Region*. South Pacific Regional Environment Programme, Apia.

Cox, P.A. and Elmqvist, T. (1993) 'Ecocolonialism and indigenous knowledge systems: village controlled rainforest preserves in Samoa' *Pacific Conservation Biology* 1,1 6–13.

CPO (Central Planning Office) (1975) *Fiji's Seventh Development Plan 1976– 80*. CPO, Suva.

CPO (Central Planning Office) (1985) *Fiji's Ninth Development Plan 1986–90: Policies, Strategies and Programmes for National Development*. CPO, Suva.

Crocombe, R. (ed.) (1987a) *Land Tenure in the Pacific*. University of the South Pacific, Suva.

Crocombe, R. (1987b) 'The Cook Islands: fragmentation and emigration' in R. Crocombe (ed.) *Land Tenure in the Pacific*. University of the South Pacific, Suva pp. 59–73.

Crocombe, R. (1989) *The South Pacific: An Introduction*. Institute of Pacific Studies, University of the South Pacific, Suva.

Crocombe, R. (1992a) 'The future of democracy in the Pacific Islands' in R. Crocombe, U. Neemia, A. Ravuvu and W. Vom Busch (eds) *Culture and Democracy in the South Pacific*. Institute of Pacific Studies, University of the South Pacific, Suva, pp.9–28.

Crocombe, R. (1992b) *Pacific Neighbours: New Zealand's Relationship with Other Pacific Islands*. Institute of Pacific Studies, University of the South Pacific, Suva and MacMillan Brown Centre for Pacific Studies, University of Canterbury, Christchurch.

Crocombe, R. (1992c) *The South Pacific: An Introduction*. Institute of Pacific Studies, University of the South Pacific, Suva.

Crocombe, R. (1994) 'Trends and issues in Pacific Island land tenure' in R. Crocombe and M. Meleisea (eds) *Land Issues in the Pacific*. MacMillan Brown Centre for Pacific Studies, Christchurch and Institute of Pacific Studies, University of the South Pacific, Suva, pp.1–17.

Crocombe, R. (ed.) (1995) *Customary Land Tenure and Sustainable Development: Complementarity or Conflict?* South Pacific Commission, Noumea and Institute of Pacific Studies, Suva.

Crocombe, R. and Meleisea, M. (eds) (1994) *Land Issues in the Pacific*. MacMillan Brown Centre for Pacific Studies, University of Canterbury, Christchurch.

Curson, P.H. (1979) 'Migration, remittances and social networks among Cook Islanders' *Pacific Viewpoint* 20,2 185–98.

Danielsson, B. and Danielsson, M-T. (1992) 'In bondage to the bomb' in D. Robie (ed.) *Tu Galala: Social Change in the Pacific.* Bridget Williams Books, Wellington and Pluto Press, Annandale, pp.180–87.

Dasmann, R. (1988) 'National parks, nature conservation, and "future primitive"' in J.H. Bodley (ed.) *Tribal Peoples and Development Issues.* Mayfield, Mountain View, pp.301–10.

de Burlo, C. (1984) 'Indigenous response and participation in tourism in a Southwest Pacific Island nation Vanuatu' unpublished PhD thesis, Syracuse University.

Decloitre, P. (1995) 'A new approach to logging' *Pacific Islands Monthly* 65,7 28.

Delana, S., Raman, T., Segran, C., Sale, R., Tevaga, S. and Obadiah, S. (1988) 'Small-scale commercial fishing', in J.D. Overton (ed.) *Rural Fiji.* Institute of Pacific Studies, University of the South Pacific, Suva, pp.71–83.

Department of Agriculture and Forests (1975) *National Parks and Reserves Act 1974.* Government of Western Samoa, Apia.

Department of Statistics (1996) *Report on the Apia Urban Youth Survey.* Department of Statistics, Apia.

Development Cooperation Division (1996) 'A greenprint for the future' *Development Cooperation* (Ministry of Foreign Affairs and Trade, Wellington) 6, 8–9.

Dey, K. and Westerndorff, D. (1996) *Their Choice or Yours: Global Forces or Local Voices?* UNRISD Discussion Paper No.79. UNRISD, Paris.

Dodson, J. (ed.) (1992) *The Naive Lands: Prehistory and Environmental Change in Australia and the South-West Pacific.* Longman Cheshire, Melbourne .

Dommen, E. (1980) 'Some distinguishing characteristics of island states' *World Development* 8,12 931–43.

Dorrence, J.C. (1992) *The United States and the Pacific Islands.* Preager, Westport.

Douglas, N. and Douglas, N. (1994) *Pacific Island Yearbook.* Fiji Times, Suva.

Doulman, D.J (ed.) (1987) *Tuna Issues and Perspectives in the Pacific Islands Region.* East-West Center, Honolulu.

Doulman, D.J. (1989) 'Distant water fishing in the Central and Western Pacific Ocean: a status report' *Pacific Viewpoint* 30,1 4–21.

Duncan, R. (1994) 'A study of the economic benefits being foregone in the forestry sectors of Papua New Guinea, the Solomon Islands and Vanuatu', unpublished report prepared as part of the Melanesian Forestry Sector Study, National Centre for Development Studies, Australian National University, Canberra.

Dupon, J-F. (1993) 'Not always a pretty face: urban growth versus the environment in the Pacific Islands' *Environmental Case Studies* 6, South Pacific Regional Environment Programme, Apia.

Dwyer, L. (1989) 'Tourist hotel food and beverage imports in Fiji and Vanuatu' *Pacific Studies* 13,1 99–120.

Eaton, C. (1988) 'Vakavanua land tenure', in J.D. Overton (ed.) *Rural Fiji.* Institute of Pacific Studies, University of the South Pacific, Suva, pp.19–30.

Economist Intelligence Unit (1994) *Pacific Islands Country Profile 1994–5.* Economist Intelligence Unit Limited, London.

Edwards, M. (1993) 'How relevant is development studies?' in F. J. Schuurman (ed.) *Beyond the Impasse: New Directions in Development Theory.* Zed Books, London, pp.77–92.

Emberson-Bain, A. (1994) 'De-romancing the stones: gender, environment and mining in the Pacific', in A. Emberson-Bain (ed.) *Sustainable Development or Malignant Growth: Perspectives of Pacific Island Women*. Marama Publications, Suva, pp.91–110.

Escobar, A. (1995) 'Imagining a post-development era' in J. Crush (ed.) *Power of Development*. Routledge, London and New York, pp. 211–27.

Etherington, D.M. (1988) 'A policy perspective on coconut processing in the South Pacific islands' unpublished paper, Australian Agricultural Economics Conference, February 9–11.

Fairbairn, T.I.J. et al (1991) *The Pacific Islands: Politics, Economics and International Relations*. East-West Center, Honolulu .

Fana 'afi Le Tagoloa, A. (1992) 'The Samoan culture and government' in R. Crocombe, U. Neemia, A. Ravuvu and W. Vom Busch (eds) *Culture and Democracy in the South Pacific*. Institute of Pacific Studies, University of the South Pacific, Suva pp.117–38.

Feinberg, R. (1995) 'Introduction: politics of culture in the Pacific Islands' *Ethnology* , 34,2 91–98.

Fiji Times (1997) 'Bluefin tuna under threat' September 17.

Filer, C.S. (1994) 'The nature of the human threat to Papua New Guinea's biodiversity endowment' in N. Sekhran and S. Miller (eds) *Papua New Guinea Country Study on Biodiversity*. Conservation Resource Centre, Papua New Guinea Department of Environment and Conservation, Boroko, pp.187–99.

Filer, C.S. (1995) 'Participation, governance and social impact: planning of the Lihir gold mine' in D. Denoon, C. Ballard, G. Banks and P. Hancock (eds) *Conference Proceedings: Mining and Mineral Resource Policy Issues in Asia–Pacific*, Research School of Pacific and Asian Studies, Australian National University, Canberra, pp. 67–75.

Filer, C.S. and Jackson, R.T. (1989) *The Social and Economic Impact of a Gold Mine in Lihir. A Report to the Lihir Liaison Committee*. Lihir Liaison Committee, Port Moresby.

Fingelton, J. (1994) 'Forest resource management in the South Pacific: logging your way to development?', *Development Bulletin* 31: 19–22.

Finney, B. (1992) 'French Polynesia: a nuclear dependency' in A.B. Robillard (ed.) *Social Change in the Pacific Islands*. Kegan Paul, London, pp. 346–71.

Fisk, E.K. (1972) 'Motivation and modernization', *Pacific Perspective* 1,1: 21–33.

Fleming, E.M. (1986) 'Effects of price risk on agricultural exporters in the South Pacific: case study of Solomon Islands copra exports', *South Pacific Smallholder Project Occasional Paper No.5*, University of New England, Armidale.

Fleming, E.M. and Hardaker, J.B. (1995) *Pacific 2010: Strategies for Polynesian Agricultural Development*. National Centre for Development Studies, Australian National University, Canberra .

Food 2000 (1987) *Global Policies for Sustainable Agriculture*. Report of the Advisory Panel on Food Security to the World Commission on Environment and Development. Zed Books, London.

Forum Fisheries Agency (FFA) (1989) *Corporate Plan for the Forum Fisheries Agency 1990–1999*. FFA, Honiara.

Fosberg, F.R. (1965) 'The island ecosystem' in F.R. Fosberg (ed.) *Man's Place in the Island Ecosystem: A Symposium*. Bernice P. Bishop Museum Press, Honolulu, pp.1–6.

France, P. (1969) *The Charter of the Land. Custom and Colonisation in Fiji*. Oxford

University Press, London.

Fraser, H. (1996) 'Australia cuts aid to Solomons because of logging practices' *Pacific Report* 9, 1: 2.

Fraser, T. and Larsen, A. (1981) 'Consultants' final report: evaluation of reforestation project. North New Georgia', unpublished report, Fraser, Chandler and Larsen, Rotorua.

Frazer, I. (1997) 'The struggle for control of Solomon Island forests', *The Contemporary Pacific* 9, 1 39–72.

Friedmann, J. (1992) *Empowerment: The Politics of Alternative Development*. Blackwell, Cambridge.

Friedmann, J. and Rangan, H. (eds) (1993) *In Defense of Livelihood*. Kumarian Press, West Hartford.

Friesen, W. (1993) 'Melanesian economy on the periphery: migration and village economy in Choiseul', *Pacific Viewpoint* 34, 2: 193–214.

Fry, G. (1993) 'At the margin: the South Pacific and the changing regional order' in R.L. Leaver and J.L. Richardson (eds) *The Post-Cold War World: Diagnoses and Prognoses*. Allen and Unwin, Sydney, pp. 224–42.

Garrett, J. (1992) 'A change in relations, but for the best?', *Pacific Islands Monthly* 62, 2: 22–23.

Geddes, W.H. (1982) *Islands on the Line: Team Report*. Australian National University Press, Canberra.

Gerritsen, R. and MacIntyre, M. (1991) 'Dilemmas of distribution: the Misima gold mine, Papua New Guinea' in J. Connell and R. Howitt (eds) *Mining and Indigenous Peoples in Australasia*. Sydney University Press, Sydney, pp.35–54.

Ghai, D. and Vivian, J.M. (eds) (1992) *Grassroots Environmental Action: People's Participation in Sustainable Development*. Routledge, London .

Gillett, R. (1995) 'Aspects of the industry, trade and marketing of Pacific Island trochus', unpublished report prepared for ICECON and the World Bank.

Gillett R. (1997) 'Fisheries and employment in the Pacific Islands', unpublished paper, Suva.

Gillett, R. and Toloa, F. (1987) 'The importance of small-scale tuna fishing: a Tokelau case study' in D.J. Doulman (ed.) *Tuna Issues and Perspectives in the Pacific Islands Region*. East-West Center, Honolulu, pp. 177–90.

Gilpin, A. (1996) *Dictionary of Environment and Sustainable Development*. Wiley, Chichester.

Girardet, H. (1992) *The Gaia Atlas of Cities*. Gaia Books, London.

Government of Western Samoa (1982) *Western Samoa Socio-Economic Situation: Development Strategy and Assistance Needs*. Government of Western Samoa, Apia.

Government of Western Samoa (1991) *Seventh Development Plan 1992–94*. National Planning Office, Apia.

Government of Western Samoa (1993a) 'Country report on population', unpublished paper, International Conference on Population and Development, Port Vila, Vanuatu.

Government of Western Samoa (1993b) *Western Samoa Forestry Policy Review: Draft Forestry Policy Statement*. Forestry Division and Groome Poyry Forestry Review Team, Apia.

Griffen, C. and Monsell-Davis, M. (eds) (1986) *Fijians in Town*. Institute of Pacific Studies, University of the South Pacific, Suva.

Grynberg, R. (1993) 'Trade liberalisation in the post-Cold War era and its implications for the Fiji sugar industry', *Journal of Pacific Studies* 17: 132–60.

Grynberg, R. (1994) 'The Solomon Islands logging dilemma', *Pacific Islands Monthly* 64,3: 11–13.

Grynberg, R. (1995a) 'Guarding our last renewable resource', *Pacific Islands Monthly* 65,2 24–27.

Grynberg, R. (1995b) *The Impact of the Sugar Protocol of the Lomé Convention on the Fiji Economy*. Economics Division Working paper 95/8, Research School of Pacific Studies, Australian National University, Canberra.

Hadjor, K.B. (1993) *The Penguin Dictionary of Third World Terms*. Penguin Books, London.

Hall, C.M. (1994) 'Ecotourism in Australia, New Zealand and the South Pacific: appropriate tourism or a new form of ecological imperialism?' in E. Cater and G. Lowman (eds) *Ecotourism: A Sustainable Option?* Wiley, Chichester, pp.137–57.

Harcombe, D. (1993) *Solomon Islands: Travel Survival Kit*. Lonely Planet, Melbourne.

Hardaker, J.B. (1987) *Smallholder Agriculture in Tonga. Project Report, South Pacific Smallholder Project*, University of New England, Armidale.

Hardaker, J.B., Delforce, J.C., Fleming, E.M. and Sefanaia, S. (1986) 'Prospects for small holder development in the South Pacific', South *Pacific Smallholder Project Occasional Paper* No. 1, University of New England, Armidale.

Hardies-Boys, N. (1994) 'The rhetoric and reality of conservation aid in Western Samoa', unpublished M.A. thesis, University of Canterbury.

Hardoy, J. and Satterthwaite, D. (1989) *Squatter Citizen: Life in the Urban Third World*. Earthscan, London.

Hardoy, J., Mitlin, D. and Satterthwaite, D. (1992) *Environmental Problems in Third World Cities*. Earthscan, London.

Harrison, S. (1993) 'The commerce of cultures in Melanesia', *Man* 28, 1: 139–58.

Harvey, D. (1990) *The Condition of Postmodernity*. Blackwell, Cambridge.

Hata, K. (1996) 'Crediting seeds: sup sup gardens make the difference', internet: http://www.oneworld.org/news/bycountry/index.html .

Hau'ofa, E. (1993) 'Our sea of islands' in E. Waddell, V. Naidu and E. Hau'ofa (eds) *A New Oceania: Rediscovering Our Sea of Islands. School of Social and Economic Development*, University of the South Pacific, Suva, pp. 2–16.

Hau'ofa, E. (1994) 'Our sea of islands', *The Contemporary Pacific* 6, 1: 147–61.

Hayes, G. (1991) 'Migration, metascience and development policy in island Polynesia', *The Contemporary Pacific* 3, 1 1–58.

Haywood, K.M. and Walsh, L.J. (1996) 'Strategic tourism planning in Fiji' in L.C. Harrison and W. Husbands (eds) *Practicing Responsible Tourism: International Case Studies in Tourism Planning, Policy, and Development*. Wiley, New York, pp. 103–25.

Helu Thaman, K. (1994) 'Environment-friendly or the new sell? One woman's view of ecotourism in Pacific Island countries' in A. Emberson-Bain (ed.) *Sustainable Development or Malignant Growth? Perspectives of Pacific Island Women* Marama Publications, Suva, pp. 183–91.

Helu, I.F. (1992) 'Democracy bug bites Tonga' in R. Crocombe, U. Neemia, A. Ravuvu and W. Vom Busch (eds) *Culture and Democracy in the South Pacific*. Institute of Pacific Studies, University of the South Pacific, Suva, pp. 139–52.

Helu, I.F. (1997) 'Tradition and good governance', Discussion Paper 97/3, *State, Society and Governance in Melanesia,* Research School of Pacific and Asian Studies, Australian National University, Canberra.

Herr, R. (ed.) (1990) *The Forum Fisheries Agency: Achievements, Challenges and Prospects.* Institute of Pacific Studies, University of the South Pacific, Suva.

Hezel, F.X.S.J. (1992) 'The expensive taste for modernity: Caroline and Marshall Islands' in A.B. Robillard (ed.) *Social Change in the Pacific Islands.* Kegan Paul, London, pp. 203–19.

Hoadley, S. (1992) *The South Pacific Foreign Affairs Handbook.* Allen and Unwin, Sydney.

Hockings, J. (1989) *Traditional Architecture in the Gilbert Islands: A Cultural Perspective.* University of Queensland Press, St. Lucia.

Hooker, K.A. (1994) 'Return migration and the Cook Islands', unpublished MA thesis, University of Canterbury.

Houtz, R.E. (1962) 'The 1953 Suva earthquake and tsunami', *Bulletin of the Seismological Society of America* 52,1: 1–12.

Howard, M.C. (1988) *The Impact of the International Mining Industry on Native Peoples.* Transnational Corporations Research Project, University of Sydney, Sydney.

Howe, K. (1997) 'Nature, culture and history: the "knowing" of Oceania', unpublished Macmillan Brown Lecture, Department of History, Massey University, Palmerston North.

Hughes, P.J. and Sullivan, M.E. (1992) *The Environmental Effects of Mining and Petroleum Production in Papua New Guinea.* University of Papua New Guinea Press, Waigani, Port Moresby.

Hunter, C. (1995) 'Key concepts for tourism and the environment' in C. Hunter and H. Green (eds) *Tourism and the Environment: A Sustainable Relationship?* Routledge, London, pp. 52–92.

Hutching, G. (1996) 'Villagers make paper profit – without felling trees', internet, Gemini News Service:
http://www.oneworld.org/gemini/july/pacific.html.

Hvenegaard, G. (1994) 'Ecotourism: A status report and conceptual framework', *Journal of Tourism Studies* 5, 2: 24–35.

Hviding, E. (1989) 'Keeping the sea: aspects of marine tenure in Marovo Lagoon, Solomon Islands' in K. Ruddle and R.E. Johannes (eds) *Traditional Coastal Resource Management in the Pacific Basin: An Anthology.* UNESCO/ROSTEA, Jakarta, pp. 7–44.

Hviding, E. (1996) *Guardians of Marovo Lagoon: Practice, Place, and Politics in Maritime Melanesia.* University of Hawaii Press, Honolulu .

Hviding, E. (1997) 'Fisheries and coastal resources: knowledge and development in the Pacific Islands' in B. Burt and C. Clerk (eds) *Environment and Development in the Pacific Islands.* National Centre for Development Studies, Australian National University, Canberra and University of Papua New Guinea Press, Port Moresby, pp.123–42.

Hviding, E. and Baines, G.B.K. (1994) 'Community-based fisheries management, tradition and the challenges of development in Marovo', *Development and Change* 25,1 13–39.

Hyndman, D. (1991) 'Zipping down the Fly on the Ok Tedi Project' in J. Connell and R. Howitt (eds) *Mining and Indigenous Peoples in Australasia.* Sydney

University Press, Sydney, pp. 77–90.

Hyndman, D. (1994) *Ancestral Rain Forest and the Mountain of Gold: Indigenous Peoples and Mining in New Guinea*. Westview Press, Boulder.

Ingram, G.B. (1994) 'Institutional obstacles to conservation: Fegusson Island, Papua New Guinea', *Pacific Affairs* 67,1: 28–45.

Ingram, P. (1991) 'The status of women in the Cook Islands' unpublished country paper for the South Pacific Regional Seminar on the United Nations Convention on the Elimination of all Forms of Discrimination Against Women, Rarotonga.

IUCN (International Union for the Conservation of Nature and Natural Resources) (1997) *Beyond Fences: Seeking Social Sustainability in Conservation*. IUCN, Gland.

Jackson, R.T. (1991) 'Not without influence: villages, mining companies, and government in Papua New Guinea' in J. Connell and R. Howitt (eds) *Mining and Indigenous Peoples in Australasia*. Sydney University Press, Sydney, pp. 18–33.

Jalan, B. (ed:) (1982) *Problems and Policies in Small Economies*. Croom Helm, London and Canberra.

James, K. (1991) 'Migration and remittances: a Tongan village perspective' *Pacific Viewpoint* 32, 1 1–23.

James, K. (1993a) 'Cutting the ground from under them? Commercialisation, cultivation, and conservatism in Tonga', *The Contemporary Pacific* 5, 2: 215–42.

James, K. (1993b) 'The rhetoric and reality of change and development in small Pacific Island communities', *Pacific Viewpoint* 34,2: 135–52.

Johannes, R.E. (1977) 'Traditional law of the sea in Micronesia', *Micronesia* 13, 2: 121–7.

Johannes, R.E. (1981) *Words of the Lagoon: Fishing and Marine Lore in the Palau District of Micronesia*. University of California Press, Berkeley and Los Angeles.

Johannes, R.E. (1982) 'Traditional conservation methods and protected marine areas in Oceania', *Ambio* 11, 5: 258–61.

Joku, H. (1997) 'NGOs to demand inquiry', *The Independent*, 7 July.

Jones, P. (1995) 'Responding to urban change: observations on urbanisation, urban planning and urban management in the Pacific', Ministry of Home Affairs and Rural Development, Tarawa, Republic of Kiribati.

Jones, R. and Pinheiro, L. (1997) *Fiji: A Lonely Planet Travel Survival Kit*. Lonely Planet, Melbourne.

Kearns, F.J. (1965) 'The urban centre of Apia', *South Pacific Bulletin* 15, 4 47– 50.

Keesing, R. (1989) 'Creating the past: custom and identity in the contemporary Pacific', *Contemporary Pacific*, 1, 1&2 19–42.

Keesing, R. (1993) 'A tin with the meat taken out: a bleak anthropological view of unsustainable development in the Pacific' in T. Otto (ed.) *Pacific Island Trajectories: Five Personal Views*. Occasional Paper, Research School of Pacific Studies, Australian National University, Canberra, pp.29–55.

Keith-Reid, R. (1986) 'Was Bebe worst?', *Fiji Times*, 19 April.

Kelly, M. (1993) 'Tahitians', *Cultural Survival Quarterly*, Fall: 38.

King, B. (1992) 'Cultural tourism and its potential for Fiji', *Journal of Pacific Studies* 16: 74–89.

Kingdom of Tonga (1991) *Sixth Development Plan, 1991–1995.* Central Planning Department, Nuku'alofa.

Kingdom of Tonga Statistics Department (various years) *Annual Report,* Kingdom of Tonga Statistics Department, Nuku'alofa.

Kinnaird, V. and Hall, D. (eds) (1994) *Tourism: A Gender Analysis.* Wiley, Chichester.

Kirch, P.V. (1977) 'Valley agricultural systems in prehistoric Hawaii: an archaeological consideration', *Asian Perspectives* 20: 246–80.

Kirch, P.V. (1994) *The Wet and the Dry: Irrigation and Agricultural Intensification.* Cambridge University Press, Cambridge.

Kirch, P.V. (1997) 'Microcosmic histories: island perspectives on "global' change"' *American Anthropologist,* 99, 1: 30–42.

Kissling, C. (1987) 'Transport at the crossroads' in M.J. Taylor (ed.) *Fiji: Future Imperfect?* Allen and Unwin, Sydney, pp. 95–107.

Klinckhamers, P. (1992) *Western Samoa: Land-based Pollution Sources and their Effects on the Marine Environment.* South Pacific Regional Environment Programme, Apia.

Knapman, B. (1985) 'The rise and fall of the white sugar planter in Fiji, 1880–1925', *Pacific Studies* 9,1: 53–82.

Knapman, B. (1987) *Fiji's Economic History, 1874–1939.* National Centre for Development Studies, Australian National University, Canberra.

Knapman, B. (1994) 'Economic development and dependency' in K.R. Howe, R.C. Kiste and B.V. Lal (eds) *The Pacific Islands in the Twentieth Century.* Allen and Unwin, St Leonards, pp. 325–49.

Korten, D. (1995) *When Corporations Rule the World.* Kumarian, West Hartford.

Kuhlken, R. (1994) 'Tuatua ni Nakauvadra: a Fijian irrigated taro agrosystem' in J. Morrison, P. Gerathy and L. Crowl (eds) *Science of Pacific Island Peoples: Land Use and Agriculture.* Institute of Pacific Studies, University of the South Pacific, Suva, pp. 51–62.

Lagisa, L. (1997) 'The impacts of a major development project on women's lives: a case study of mining in Lihir, Papua New Guinea', unpublished MPhil thesis, Massey University.

Lal, P.N. (1984) 'Environmental implications of Coastal Development in Fiji', *Ambio* 13: 316–21.

Lamb, D. (1990) *Exploiting the Tropical Rainforest: An Account of Pulpwood Logging in Papua New Guinea.* UNESCO, Paris.

Lambert, B. (1963) 'Rank and ramage in the Northern Gilbert Islands', unpublished PhD thesis, University of California, Berkeley.

Larmour, P. (1984) 'Alienated land and independence in Melanesia', *Pacific Studies* 8, 1: 1–47.

Larmour, P. (1994) '"A foreign flower?" Democracy in the South Pacific', *Pacific Studies* 17, 1 45–77.

Larmour, P. and Qalo, R. (eds) (1985) *Decentralisation in the South Pacific.* University of the South Pacific, Suva.

Lawrence, J. (1997) 'Adult education and jobs, or sustainable livelihoods'. Paper presented to the UNESCO Panel on Changes in the World of Work, Hamburg, 12 July, internet:
http://www.undp.org/undp/seped/sl.htm.

Lawrence, R.J. (1983) *Atoll Economy: Social Change in Kiribati and Tuvalu no. 4:*

Tamana. Development Studies Centre, Australian National University, Canberra.

Lee, W. (1985) 'Women's groups in Papua New Guinea: shedding the legacy of drop scones and embroidered pillowcases' *Community Development Journal* 20,3: 222–36.

Le Heron, R. (1993) *Globalised Agriculture*. Pergamon Press, Oxford.

Lew, A. (1996) 'Adventure travel and ecotourism in Asia' *Annals of Tourism Research* 23, 3: 723–24.

Lihir Management Corporation (1995a) *Prospectus: Lihir Gold Limited*. Lihir Management Corporation, Port Moresby.

Lihir Management Corporation (1995b) *Lihir Gold Times, 1995 Annual Report*. Lihir Management Corporation, Lihir.

Linnekin, J. (1990) 'The politics of culture in the Pacific' in J. Linnekin and L. Poyer (eds) *Cultural Identity and Ethnicity in the Pacific*. University of Hawaii Press, Honolulu, pp. 149–74.

Liu, J. (1994) *Pacific Islands Ecotourism: A Public Policy and Planning Guide*. Pacific Business Center Program, University of Hawaii, Honolulu.

Loomis, T. (1990a) *Pacific Migrant Labour, Class and Racism in New Zealand*. Avebury, Aldershot.

Loomis, T. (1990b) 'Cook Island remittances' in J. Connell (ed.) *Migration and Development in the South Pacific*. National Centre for Development Studies, Australian National University, Canberra, pp. 61–81.

Lundsgaarde, H.P. (1974) 'The evolution of tenure principles on Tamana Island' in H.P. Lundsgaarde (ed.) *Land Tenure in Oceania*. University of Hawaii Press, Honolulu, pp. 179–214.

Lutero, P. (1994) 'Aid and development in relation to customary land tenure: some social and educational implications' in R. Crocombe and M. Meleisea (eds) *Land Issues in the Pacific*. MacMillan Brown Centre for Pacific Studies, Christchurch and Institute of Pacific Studies, University of the South Pacific, Suva, pp. 19–33.

Lynch, O.J. and Talbott, K. with Berdan, M.S. (1995) *Balancing Acts: Community Based Forest Management and National Law in Asia and the Pacific*. World Resources Institute, Washington DC.

Macpherson, C. (1992a) 'Some concluding thoughts on social change' in A.B. Robillard (ed.) *Social Change in the Pacific Islands*. Kegan Paul, London, pp. 428–51.

Macpherson, C. (1992b) 'Economic and political restructuring and the sustainability of migrant remittances: the case of Western Samoa', *The Contemporary Pacific*, 4, 1: 109–35.

Manner, H.I. (1994) 'The taro islets (Maa) of Puluwat Atoll' in J. Morrison, P. Gerathy and L. Crowl (eds) *Science of Pacific Island Peoples: Land Use and Agriculture*. Institute of Pacific Studies, University of the South Pacific, Suva, pp. 77–87.

Mansperger, M.C. (1995) 'Tourism and cultural change in small-scale societies' *Human Organization* 54, 1: 87–94.

Mantjoro, E. (1996) 'Traditional management of communal property resources: the practice of the Sasi system', *Ocean and Coastal Management* 32, 1: 17–37.

Marchand, M.H. and Parpart, J.L. (1995) *Feminism/Postmodernism/ Development*. Routledge, London.

Marcus, G.E. (1981) 'Power on the extreme periphery: the perspective of Tongan elites in the modern world system', *Pacific Viewpoint*, 22, 1: 48–64.

Marshall, G. (1990) 'The political economy of logging', *The Ecologist*, 20, 5: 174–81.

Maruia Society (1991) *A Protected Forest System for the Solomon Islands*. Maruia Society, Nelson.

Maude, H.E. (1963) *The Evolution of the Gilbertese Boti: An Ethnohistorical Interpretation*. The Polynesian Society, Wellington.

McCall, G. and Connell, J. (eds) (1993) *A World Perspective on Pacific Islander Migration: Australia, New Zealand and the USA*. Centre for Pacific Studies, University of New South Wales, Kensington.

McDiarmid, B. (1992) 'The environment: "Who gives a dam?"' in D. Robie (ed.) *Tu Galala: Social Change in the Pacific*. Bridget Williams Books/Pluto Press, Wellington and Annandale, pp. 80–91.

McGee, T.G. (1995) 'Metrofitting the emerging mega-urban regions of ASEAN: an overview' in T.G. McGee and M. Robinson (eds) *The Mega-Urban Regions of Southeast Asia*. University of British Columbia Press, Vancouver.

McGee, T.G. (1997) 'Globalisation, urbanisation and the emergence of sub-global regions: a case study of the Asia-Pacific region' in R.F. Watters and T.G. McGee (eds) *Asia-Pacific: New Geographies of the Pacific Rim*. Victoria University Press, Wellington, pp. 29–45.

McIlwaine, C. (1997) 'Third-World development: urbanizing for the future', *Progress in Human Geography*, 21, 3: 406–13.

McLisky, F.P. (1992) 'Tourism "off the beaten track": alternative tourism as an appropriate form of tourism in Fiji' unpublished MA thesis, University of Canterbury.

McMichael, P. (1996) *Development and Social Change: A Global Perspective*. Pine Forge Press, Thousand Oaks.

McNeeley, J.A. and Miller, K.R (eds) (1984) *National Parks, Conservation and Development: The Role of Protected Areas in Sustaining Society*. Smithsonian Institution, Washington DC.

McShane, O. (1995) 'The nuclear subsidies that make Tahiti a lesson in welfarism', *The Press* (Christchurch) 17 May, 11.

Meltzoff, S. and Li Puma, E. (1983) *A Japanese Fishing Joint Venture: Worker Experience and National Development in Solomon Islands*. ICLARM, Manila.

Merchant, C. (1992) *Radical Ecology: The Search for a Liveable World*. Routledge, New York.

Merchant, C. (1995) *Earthcare: Women and the Environment*. Routledge, New York.

Mies, M. and Shiva, V. (1993) *Ecofeminism*. Zed Books, London.

Milne, S. (1990) 'Tourism and economic development in Vanuatu', *Singapore Journal of Tropical Geography* 11, 1: 13–26.

MEHRD (Ministry of Education and Human Resource Development) (1991) Unpublished statistics on primary and secondary schooling in the Solomon Islands, Honiara.

Ministry of Foreign Affairs and Trade (1994) *Programme Profiles: New Zealand Official Development Assistance 1994–1995*. Ministry of Foreign Affairs and Trade, Wellington.

Ministry of Foreign Affairs and Trade (1995) *NZODA Programme Profiles*

1995–96. Ministry of Foreign Affairs and Trade, Wellington.

Moengangongo, S. (1992) *Land Tenure and Productivity: The Case of Tonga*. Institute of Rural Development, The University of the South Pacific, Suva.

Mogina, J. (1996) 'Wisdom for sustainable development: women's knowledge of forest resource use in Papua New Guinea', unpublished keynote speech at the 6th International Interdisciplinary Congress on Women, Adelaide, 21–26 April.

Molisa, G. (1983) *Black Stone*. Mana Publications, Suva.

Monsell-Davis, M. (1986) '"It's a man's game" – identity, social role, social change and delinquency in Suva' in C. Griffen and M. Monsell-Davis (eds) *Fijians in Town*. Institute of Pacific Studies, University of the South Pacific, Suva, pp.132–65.

Monsell-Davis, M. (1993) 'Urban exchange: safety-net or disincentive? Wantoks and relatives in the urban Pacific', *Canberra Anthropology*, 16, 2: 45–66.

Mossman, R. (1980) 'National parks and reserves in Western Samoa', unpublished paper prepared for UNESCO tourism workshop in Rarotonga, June 1980.

Mossman, R. and Berg, P. (1981) *Management Plan for O Le Pupu-Pu'e National Park*. Department of Agriculture and Forests, Apia.

Muller, L.T. (1996) 'Urbanisation: a paper on the effect of population growth and urbanisation on the demand and consumption of water and energy (namely electricity) for the period 1976–1986, Nuku'alofa, Kingdom of Tonga', unpublished MS, Central Planning Department, Nuku'alofa.

Munro, D. (1990) 'Transnational corporations of kin and the MIRAB system: the case of Tuvalu', *Pacific Viewpoint*, 31,1: 63–66.

Murray, W.E. (1998a) 'Globalisation and rural sustainable development in Chile – implications for the Pacific Islands', *Journal of Pacific Studies* (in press).

Murray, W.E. (1998b) 'Putting all your pumpkins in one basket – globalisation, political economy and neo-liberalism in Tonga' unpublished paper, Annual Conference of the Institute of British Geographers and the Royal Geographical Society, Kingston University, Guildford, 4–8 January.

Myers, N. (ed.) (1994) *The Gaia Atlas of Planet Management*. Gaia Books, London.

Naess, A. (1989) *Ecology, Community and Lifestyle*. Cambridge University Press, Cambridge.

Naidu, V. (1992) 'Social change and the survival of neo-tradition in Fiji' in A.B. Robillard (ed.) *Social Change in the Pacific Islands*. Kegan Paul, London, pp. 134–200.

National Reserve Bank of Tonga (1997) *Annual Report 1995–96*. National Reserve Bank of Tonga, Nuku'alofa.

Nelson, J.G. and Alder, E.A. (eds) (1992) *Toward a Greater Understanding and Use of the World Heritage Convention*. Occasional Paper No. 22, Heritage Resources Centre, University of Waterloo, Waterloo.

Newbury, C. (1972) 'Trade and plantations in Eastern Polynesia: the emergence of a dependent economy' in R.G. Ward (ed.) *Man in the Pacific Islands*. Oxford University Press, London, pp. 145–66.

Norgaard, R.B. (1994) *Development Betrayed: The End of Progress and a Coevolutionary Revisioning of the Future*. Routledge, London and New York.

Norton, R. (1993) 'Culture and identity in the South Pacific: a comparative analysis', *Man*, 28: 741–59.

Nunn, P.D. (1990) 'Recent environmental changes on Pacific Islands', *Geographical Journal* 156,2: 125–40.

Nunn, P.D. (1993) 'Beyond the naive lands: human history and environmental change in the Pacific Basin' in E. Waddell and P.D. Nunn (eds) *The Margin Fades: Geographical Itineraries in a World of Islands.* Institute of Pacific Studies, University of the South Pacific, Suva, pp. 5–27.

Nunn, P.D. (1994) *Oceanic Islands.* Blackwell, Oxford.

O'Riordan, T. (1981) *Environmentalism.* Pion, London.

O'Meara, J.T. (1995) 'From corporate to individual land tenure in Western Samoa' in R.G. Ward and E. Kingdon (eds) *Land, Custom and Practice in the South Pacific.* Cambridge University Press, Cambridge, pp.109–56.

Ogden, M.R. (1994) 'MIRAB and the Marshall Islands', *ISLA: A Journal of Micronesian Studies,* 2, 2: 237–72.

Olsson, G. (1992) 'Commitment, consensus or cash: an assessment, from the village point of view, of a rainforest preservation project' unpublished paper prepared for the Swedish Society for Nature Conservation, Stockholm.

Overton, J. (1987) 'Fijian land: pressing problems, possible tenure solutions', *Singapore Journal of Tropical Geography* 8, 2: 139–51.

Overton, J.D. (1988) 'The adoption of rice by village Fijians' in J.D. Overton (ed.) *Rural Fiji.* Institute of Pacific Studies, University of the South Pacific, Suva, pp. 147–64.

Overton, J.D. (1989) *Land and Differentiation in Rural Fiji.* National Centre for Development Studies, Australian National University, Canberra.

Overton, J.D. (1992a) 'The limits to accumulation: changing land tenure in Fiji', *Journal of Peasant Studies,* 19,2: 326–42.

Overton, J.D. (1992b) 'Farms, suburbs, or retirement homes: the transformation of village Fiji', *The Contemporary Pacific,* 5, 1: 45–74.

Overton, J. (1993a) 'Pacific futures? geography and change in the Pacific Islands', *New Zealand Geographer,* 49, 2: 48–55.

Overton, J.D. (1993b) 'Fiji: options for sustainable development', *Scottish Geographical Magazine,* 19, 3 164–170.

Overton, J.D. (1994) 'Land tenure and cash cropping in Fiji' in R. Crocombe and M. Meleisea (eds) *Land Issues in the Pacific.* MacMillan Brown Centre for Pacific Studies, University of Canterbury, Christchurch, pp. 117–31.

Overton, J.D. (1995) 'Land tenure in Fiji' unpublished report to the Fiji Constitution Review Commission, Suva.

Overton, J.D. (1996) 'Restructuring Oceania: regional reconfigurations of economic and political relations in the Pacific' in Y.M. Yeung (ed.) *Global Change and the Commonwealth.* Chinese University of Hong Kong, Hong Kong, pp.131–56.

Overton, J.D. (1998) 'Global markets and global citizens: an essay on vanishing borders in the Pacific Islands' in Lee Boon-Tong and Tengku Shamsul Bahrin (eds) *Vanishing Borders: The New International Order of the 21st Century.* Ashgate, Aldershot pp. 57–70.

Overton, J. and Chung, J. (1988) 'Ring-ditches in Tokatoka District, Fiji: a comment' *Domodomo* 1–4: 76–93.

Overton, J.D. and Purdie, N. (1997) 'Think local, act global? Reflections on sustainable development in the Pacific Islands', *Development Bulletin* 41: 37–9.

Pacific Islands Monthly (1994) 'US budget cuts lead to less aid for Pacific' *Pacific Islands Monthly* 64, 5: 5.

PacNews (1998) 'Sugar industry faces a massive loss', e-mail news service: pacnews@piba.org.vu.

Panos 1997 'Ecotourism: Paradise gained, or paradise lost?' internet: http://www.oneworld.org/panos/panos_eco2.html.

Park, G. (1992) 'National ecological survey of Western Samoa: report on stage III, presentation of the survey results to government and selected villages' unpublished report for the Department of Conservation, Wellington.

Parnaby, O.W. (1972) 'The labour trade' in R.G. Ward (ed.) *Man in the Pacific Islands*. Oxford University Press, London, pp. 124–44.

Parnwell, M. and Taylor, D. (1996) 'Environmental degradation, non-timber forest products and Iban communities in Sarawak' in M. Parnwell and R. Bryant (eds.) *Environmental Change in South-East Asia*. Routledge, London, pp. 269–300.

Parry, J.T. (1977) 'Ring ditch fortifications in the Rewa Delta, Fiji: air photo interpretation and analysis', *Bulletin of the Fiji Museum* 3, Suva.

Parry, J.T. (1981) 'Ring ditch fortifications in the Navua Delta, Fiji: air photo interpretation and analysis', *Bulletin of the Fiji Museum* 7, Suva.

Parry, J.T. (1987) 'The Sigatoka Valley – pathway to prehistory', *Bulletin of the Fiji Museum* 9, Suva.

Paul, J. (1993) 'Port Vila urban expansion plan', unpublished report prepared for the Government of the Republic of Vanuatu, Dunedin.

Pauli, M. (1987) 'Urban migrants in Taufusi, Apia' in L. Mason and P. Hereniko (eds) *In Search of a Home*. Institute of Pacific Studies, University of the South Pacific, Suva, pp. 236–40.

Pearce, D. (1993) *Blueprint 3: Measuring Sustainable Development*. Earthscan, London.

Pearce, D., Barbier, E. and Markandya, A. (1990) *Sustainable Development: Economics and Environment in the Third World*. Earthscan, London.

Pepper, D. (1993) *Ecosocialism: From Deep Ecology to Social Justice*. Routledge, London.

Pernetta, J.C. and Hughes, P.J. (eds) (1990) *Implications of Expected Climate Changes in the South Pacific Region: An Overview*. UNEP Regional Seas Reports and Studies No. 128, United Nations Environmental Programme, Nairobi.

Peteru, C. (1993) 'The need for institutional and legal change: a South Pacific non-governmental organisation perspective' in B. Boer (ed.) *Strengthening Environmental Legislation in the Pacific Region: Workshop Proceedings*. SPREP/UNEP, Apia, pp.96–103.

Pirie, P. (1994) *Demographic Transition in the Pacific Islands: The Situation in the Early 1990s*. Working Paper No.5 August 1994, East-West Centre, Honolulu.

Pitt, D.C. (1973/4) 'Identity, tradition and development' *Civilisations* 23/24, 112: 65–75.

Pond, W. (1997) 'The land as a tradeable commodity' *New Zealand Books: A Review*, 7, 5: 32–33.

Post Courier (1994) 'Vanuatu to ban export of logs', *Post Courier*, 10 November.

Puia Angiki, D. (1995a) '$7m scam surfaced', *Solomon Star*, 10 November.

Puia Angiki, D. (1995b) 'Harassment in logging camp', *Solomon Star*, 17 November.

Purdie, N.S. (1996) 'Reasserting the local in the global: local livelihoods and sustainable development in the proposed East-Rennell World Heritage Site, Solomon Islands' unpublished MPhil thesis, Massey University.

Quodling, P. (1991) *Bougainville: The Mine and the People*. Centre For Independent Studies, St Leonards.

Rahnema, M. (1992) 'Participation' in W. Sachs (ed.) *The Development Dictionary*. Zed Books, London, pp.116–31.

Rahnema, M. and Bawtree, V. (eds) (1997) *The Post-Development Reader*. Zed Books, London, pp. 94–101.

Raine P. (forthcoming) 'Who guards the guardians? Theoretical and practical criteria for environmental guardianship', unpublished PhD thesis, Massey University.

Rainforest Information Centre (Australia) (1995) *World Rainforest Report No. 32*. John Revington and the RIC/VDT EcoHome Project – PNG, Port Moresby.

Rakodi, C. and Devas, N. (1993) 'Conclusions: assessing the new approaches' in N. Devas and C. Rakodi (eds) *Managing Fast Growing Cities*. Longman, Burnt Mill, pp. 265–96.

Ranck, S.R. (1987) 'An attempt at autonomous development: The case of the Tufi guest houses, Papua New Guinea' in S. Britton and W.C. Clarke (eds) *Ambiguous Alternative: Tourism in Small Developing Countries*. University of the South Pacific, Suva, pp. 154–65.

Ransom, D. (1997) 'South Pacific: the last resort', *Pacific Islands Monthly*, 67, 6: 7–10.

Rashid, Y. (1995) 'Commercial sense or sheer madness' *Pacific Islands Monthly*, 65, 6: 15–16.

Ravenhill, J. (1985) *Collective Clientalism: The Lomé Convention and North-South Relations*. Columbia University Press, New York.

Ravuvu, A.D. (1983) *Vaka i Taukei: The Fijian Way of Life*. Institute of Pacific Studies, University of the South Pacific, Suva.

Ravuvu, A.D. (1987a) *The Fijian Ethos*. Institute of Pacific Studies, University of the South Pacific, Suva.

Ravuvu, A.D. (1987b) 'Fiji: contradictory ideologies and development' in A. Hooper, S. Britton, R. Crocombe, J. Huntsman and C. MacPherson (eds) *Class and Culture in the South Pacific*. Centre for Pacific Studies, University of Auckland, Auckland and Institute of Pacific Studies,University of the South Pacific, Suva, pp. 230–41.

Redclift, M. (1984) *Development and the Environmental Crisis: Red or Green Alternatives?* Methuen, London.

Redclift, M. (1991) *Sustainable Development: Exploring the Contradictions*. Routledge, London.

Rees, W.E. (1990) 'The ecology of sustainable development', *The Ecologist* , 20,1 18–23.

Rees, W.E. (1992) 'Ecological footprints and appropriated carrying capacity', *Environment and Urbanization*, 4,1 22–36.

Rees, W.E. (1996) 'Ecological footprints of the future', *People and the Planet* 5, 2: 6–8.

Richards, P. (1985) *Indigenous Agricultural Revolution: Ecology and Food Production in West Africa*. Hutchinson, London.

Robertson, T. and Tamanisau, A. (1992) 'Pacific overview: not so new world order' in D. Robie (ed.) *Tu Galala: Social Change in the Pacific*. Bridget Williams Books, Wellington, pp.23–38.

Robinson, K. (1991) 'Land rights, labour relations, and fertility in the Soroako Nickel project, Sulawesi' in J. Connell and R. Howitt (eds) *Mining and Indigenous Peoples in Australasia*. Sydney University Press, Sydney, pp.107–18.

Rosoman, G. (1995) 'Ecoforestry – towards a responsible plantation industry', *New Zealand Forestry*, 19, 4: 8–12.

Rowell, A. (1996) *Green Backlash: Global Subversion of the Environment Movement*. Routledge, London.

Roy, P. and Connell, J. (1989) 'The greenhouse effect: where have all the islands gone?', *Pacific Islands Monthly*, 59, 4: 16–21.

Royds Consulting Ltd (1997) 'Sanitation Master Plan for Port Vila' unpublished report prepared for the Asian Development Bank (TA:2597) and the Government of the Republic of Vanuatu, Manila.

Rudkin, B. and Hall, C.M. (1996) 'Unable to see the forest for the trees: ecotourism development in the Solomon Islands' in R. Butler and T. Hinch (eds) *Tourism and Indigenous Peoples*. International Thomson Business Press, London, pp.203–26.

Rutz, H.J. (1987) 'Capitalizing on culture: moral ironies in urban Fiji' *Comparative Studies of Society and History*, 29, 3, 533–57.

Sachs, W. (1991) 'Environment and development: the story of a dangerous liaison', *The Ecologist*, 21, 6: 252–57.

Satterthwaite, D. (1996) *Urban Poverty: Reconsidering its Scale and Nature*, Background Paper. Human Settlements Programme, International Institute for Environment and Development, London.

Saulei, S. and Aruga, J. (1994) 'The status and prospects of non-timber forest products development in Papua New Guinea', *Commonwealth Forestry Review*, 73, 2: 97–105.

Salleh, Ariel (1997) *Ecofeminism as Politics*. Zed Books, London.

Scheyvens, R.A. (1996) 'Engendering eco-timber production in the Solomon Islands', *Development Bulletin* , 39: 69–72.

Scheyvens, R.A. (1997) 'Sustaining women whilst sustaining the land? Engendering eco-timber production in the Solomon Islands' *Working Papers on Women and International Development*, Michigan State University, Lansing.

Scheyvens, R. and Overton, J. (1995) '"Doing well out of our doing good": A geography of New Zealand aid', *Pacific Viewpoint*, 36, 2: 192–207.

Schoeffel, P. (1985) 'Women in the fisheries of the South Pacific' in Cole, R.V. (ed.) *Women in Development in the South Pacific*. Development Studies Centre, Australian National University, Canberra, pp. 156–75.

Schoeffel, P. (1992) 'Concept for customary-based joint venture reforestation project' in E.D. Shield (ed.) *Plantation Opportunities in the Solomon Islands*. Project Working Paper 13, Australian International Development Assistance Bureau, Forestry Division, Ministry of Natural Resources, Honiara.

Schoeffel, P. (1994) 'Where are all the farmers?: Agriculture, land tenure and development in the Pacific Islands' in R. Crocombe and M. Meleisea (eds) *Land Issues in the Pacific*. MacMillan Brown Centre for Pacific Studies, Christchurch and Institute of Pacific Studies, University of the South Pacific, Suva, pp. 35–42.

Schoeffel, P. (1996a) *Sociocultural Issues and Economic Development in the Pacific*

Islands. Asian Development Bank, Manila.

Schoeffel, P. (1996b) 'A report of RETA 5548: analysis of sociocultural characteristics of economic systems of PDMCs' unpublished report, Asian Development Bank, Manila.

Schug, D.M. and Galea'i A.P (1987) 'American Samoa: the tuna industry and the economy' in D.J. Doulman (ed.) *Tuna Issues and Perspectives in the Pacific Islands Region*. East-West Center, Honolulu, pp. 191–202.

Schuurman, F.J. (ed.) (1993) *Beyond the Impasse: New Directions in Development Theory*. Zed Books, London.

Selwyn, P. (1980) 'Smallness and islandness', *World Development*, 8, 12: 945– 51.

Sevele, F. (1973) 'Regional inequalities in socio-economic development in Tonga: a preliminary study' unpublished Ph.D thesis, University of Canterbury, Christchurch.

Sewell, B. (1983) *Atoll Economy: Social Change in Kiribati and Tuvalu: Butaritari*. Development Studies Centre, Australian National University, Canberra.

Shepherd, A. (1998) *Rural Sustainable Development*, Macmillan, London.

Shield, E.D. (1992) 'Plantation opportunities in the Solomon Islands' *Project Working Paper* 13. Australian International Development Assistance Bureau, Forestry Division, Ministry of Natural Resources, Honiara.

Shiva, V. (1988) *Staying Alive: Women, Ecology and Survival in India*. Kali for Women, New Delhi.

Shiva, V. (1989) *Staying Alive: Women, Ecology and Development*. Zed Books, London.

Shiva, V. (1992) 'Recovering the real meaning of sustainability' in D.E. Cooper and J.A. Palmer (eds) *The Environment in Question*. Routledge, London, pp. 187–93.

Simon, D. (1989) 'Sustainable development: theoretical construct or attainable goal' *Environmental Conservation* 16, 1: 41–8.

Sindiga, I. (1995) 'Wildlife-based tourism in Kenya: land use conflicts and government compensation policies over protected areas', *Journal of Tourism Studies*, 6, 2: 45–55.

Sipolo, J. (1986), *Praying Parents*. Aruligo Book Centre, Honiara.

Sitarz, D. (ed.) (1994) *Agenda 21: The Earth Summit Strategy to Save Our Planet*. Earthpress, Boulder.

Slatter, C. (1987) 'Women factory workers in Fiji: The 'half a loaf' syndrome', *Journal of Pacific Studies* 13 47–59.

Slatter, C. (1994) 'For food or foreign exchange? Regional interests versus global imperatives in Pacific fisheries development' in A. Emberson-Bain (ed.) *Sustainable Development or Malignant Growth: Perspectives of Pacific Island Women*. Marama Publications, Suva, pp.131–48.

Snow, D. and Collee, J. (1996) 'The rape of an island paradise', *The Observer* 29 September, 4–5.

Sofer, M. (1985) 'Yaqona and peripheral economy', *Pacific Viewpoint* 26,2 415–36.

Sofield, T. (1991) 'Sustainable ethnic tourism in the South Pacific: some principles' *Journal of Tourism Studies* 2, 1: 56–72.

Sofield, T. (1993) 'Indigenous tourism development' *Annals of Tourism Research* 20: 729–50.

Sofield, T. (1994) 'Review essay: tourism in the South Pacific' *Annals of Tourism Research* 21: 207–19.

Solomon Islands Development Trust (1991) *Link* Vol. 23, Solomon Islands Development Trust, Honiara.

Solomon Islands Government (1986) *Census of Population, 1986*. Statistics Office, Ministry of Finance and Economic Planning, Honiara.

Solomon Star (1997) 'Returns from natural forest logging', *Solomon Star, 15* August.

South Pacific Commission (1995) *South Pacific Economies: Pocket Statistical Summary*. South Pacific Commission, Noumea.

South Pacific Commission (1996) *Pacific Islands Population Data Sheet*. South Pacific Commission, Noumea.

South Pacific Commission (1998) summary data on Pacific Islands, internet: http://www.spc.org.nc.

South Pacific Review (1993) 'Papua New Guinea: the mining and petroleum industry', *South Pacific Review*, November: 1.

South Sea Digest (1996) 'Logging threatens Solomons' forests', *South Sea Digest*, 19 April.

SPREP (South Pacific Regional Environment Programme) (1992) *The Pacific Way: Pacific Island Developing Countries Report to the United Nations Conference on Environment and Development*. SPREP, Apia.

SPREP (South Pacific Regional Environment Programme) (1993a) *Western Samoa: National Environment and Development Management Strategies*. SPREP, Apia.

SPREP (South Pacific Regional Environment Programme) (1993b) *Solomon Islands. National Environmental Management Strategy*. SPREP, Apia.

Spriggs, M. (1985) 'Prehistoric man-induced landscape enhancement in the Pacific: examples and implications' in I. Farrington (ed.) *Prehistoric Intensive Agriculture in the Tropics*. British Archaeological Reports, Oxford, pp. 409–34.

Spriggs, M. (1986) 'Landscape, land use and political transformation in Southern Melanesia' in P.V. Kirch (ed.) *Island Societies: Archaeological Approaches to Evolution and Transformation*. Cambridge University Press, Cambridge, pp. 6–19.

Statistics Department (1997) *Tonga Population Census 1996: Preliminary Results*. Kingdom of Tonga, Nuku'alofa.

Statistics Office (1993) *Report on the 1990 Census of Population, Volume I: Basic Information and Tables*. Kiribati Ministry of Finance, Bairiki, Tarawa.

Stayner, R. (ed.) (1992) *Local and Regional Impacts of Mining and Associated Developments in Australia*. Rural Development Centre, University of New England, Armidale.

Storey, D. (1998) 'Urban growth in a state of disarray: the (mis)management of Port Vila and the question of urban land', unpublished paper presented at the 12th Pacific History Association Conference, Honiara, Solomon Islands, 22–26 June.

Struhsaker, T.T. (1997) *Ecology of an African Rain Forest*. University Press of Florida, Gainesville.

Sturton, M. (1992) *Tonga – Development Through Agricultural Exports*. Economic Report No. 4, Pacific Islands Development Program, East-West Centre, Honolulu.

Swadling, P. (1977) 'Depletion of shellfish in the traditional gathering beds of Pari' in J.H. Winslow (ed.) *The Melanesian Environment*. Australian National

University Press, Canberra, pp. 182–7.

SWIFT Netherlands Foundation (1996) *Solomon Western Islands Fair Trade Newsletter* No.1.

Tacconi, L. and Bennett, J. (1995) 'Biodiversity conservation: the process of economic assessment and establishment of a protected area in Vanuatu', *Development and Change* 26: 89–110.

Taule'alo, I. (1993) *Western Samoa: State of the Environment Report*. SPREP, Apia.

Taylor, G. (1995) 'The community approach: does it really work?', *Tourism Management* 16, 7: 487–9.

Taylor, M. (1987) 'Issues in Fiji's development: economic rationality or aid with dignity?' in M. Taylor (ed.) *Fiji: Future Imperfect*. Allen and Unwin, Sydney, pp. 1–13.

Thakur, R. (1993) 'New Zealand and the South Pacific' *The Contemporary Pacific* 5, 1: 75–102.

Thaman, R.R. (1976) *The Tongan Agricultural System*. University of the South Pacific, Suva.

Thaman, R.R. (1978) 'Co-operative yam gardens: an adaptation of a traditional agricultural system to serve the needs of the developing Tongan market economy' in E.K. Fisk (ed.) *The Adaptation of Traditional Agriculture*. Development Studies Centre, Australian National University, Canberra, pp. 116–28.

Thaman, R.R. (1982) 'Hurricane Isaac and Tonga: a natural or cultural disaster?', *Review* 3, 8: 22–34.

Thaman, R.R. (1984a) 'Intensification of edible aroid cultivation in the Pacific Islands' in S. Chandra (ed.) *Edible Aroids*. Clarendon, Oxford, pp. 102–22.

Thaman, R.R. (1984b) 'Urban agriculture and home gardening in Fiji: a direct road to development and independence' *Transactions and Proceedings of the Fiji Society*, 14: 1–28.

Thaman, R.R. (1988) 'By the people and for the people: home gardening and national development in the Pacific Islands' in J. Hirst, J.D. Overton, B. Allen and Y. Byron (eds) *Small-Scale Agriculture*. Commonwealth Geographical Bureau and Department of Human Geography, Australian National University, Canberra, pp. 167–81.

Thaman, R.R. (1993) 'Pacific Island biodiversity: a basis for ecological, cultural and economic survival' in E. Waddell and P.D. Nunn (eds) *The Margin Fades: Geographical Itineraries in a World of Islands*. Institute of Pacific Studies, University of the South Pacific, Suva, pp. 49–65.

Thaman, R.R. and Murti, R. (1989) 'Oceanic drift gillnetting: a threat to Pacific Island fisheries', *SPACHEE Environmental News Alert* No. 1, South Pacific Action Committee for Human Ecology and the Environment, The University of the South Pacific, Suva.

Thaman, R.R. and Ravuvu, A.D. (1989) 'Ecopolitics and the destruction of the Pacific Island environment: a crisis of cultural survival', unpublished conference paper, 'Changing Directions – Ecopolitics IV', University of Adelaide, 21–24 September.

Thaman, R.R., Meleisea, M., and Makasiale, J. (1979) 'Agricultural diversity and traditional knowledge as insurance against natural disasters' Annex 10 in Natural Disaster Prevention Preparedness and Rehabilitation Meeting, 26–30 November 1979. Summary Record. South Pacific Bureau for Economic

Cooperation, Suva, pp .75–96.
The Cook Islands News (1998) 'Cook Islands population down to some 16,500' *The Cook Islands News*, 11 March.
The Ecologist (1993) *Whose Common Future?* Earthscan, London.
The Independent (1996) 'Timber certification means improved export market access: FSC', *The Independent* , 5 April, 16–17.
The Trading Post (1996) 'Vanuatu landowners win logging legal battle' 29 January.
Theopile, K. (1995) 'The forest as a business: is ecotourism the answer?', *Journal of Forestry* 93, 3: 25–7.
Thistlewaite, R., Sheppard, D. and Prescott, N. (1993) *The Kingdom of Tonga: Action Strategy for Managing the Environment*. SPREP, Apia.
Thomas, P. (1986) 'Western Samoa: a population profile for the eighties', *Islands/Australia Working Paper* No.86/14. National Centre for Development Studies, Australian National University, Canberra.
Thomas, P. (1987) 'Urban fringe development in Apia' in L. Mason and P. Hereniko (eds) *In Search of a Home*. Institute of Pacific Studies, University of the South Pacific, Suva, pp. 241–4.
Thomas, P. and Hill, H. (1987) 'Major issues in non-formal education in the South Pacific' in C.D. Throsby (ed.) *Human Resource Development in the Pacific*. National Centre for Development Studies, Australian National University, Canberra, pp. 105–30.
Thomlinson, E. and Getz, D. (1996) 'The question of scale in ecotourism: case study of two small ecotour operators in the Mundo Maya region of Central America', *Journal of Sustainable Tourism*, 4, 4: 183–200.
Times of Papua New Guinea (1994) 'Solomons suspends logging company', *Times of Papua New Guinea*, 4 August.
Tisdell, C. (1988) 'Sustainable development: differing perspectives of ecologists and economists, and relevance', *World Development* 16, 3: 373–84.
Tisdell, C. (1993) *Environmental Economics: Policies for Environmental Management and Sustainable Development*. Edward Elgar, London.
Tobia, B. (1997), 'Conservation Trust Fund plan gains general support', *Post Courier*, 19 May.
Tonga Development Bank (1993) *Annual Report*. Tonga Development Bank, Nuku'alofa.
ToVagira, M. (1990) 'Land and mineral rights for indigenous people in Papua New Guinea: a quest for justice, peace and integrity of creation', unpublished manuscript, Pontificia Universitas Lateranensis, Rome.
Trompf, G.W. (ed.) (1990) *Cargo Cults and Millenarian Movements*. Mouton de Gruyter, Berlin.
Tukai, M. (1988) 'Modernisation theory and a Fijian village' in J. D. Overton (ed.) *Rural Fiji*. Institute of Pacific Studies, University of the South Pacific, Suva, pp. 13–17.
Tuvuki, S.W. (1995) 'An analysis of the environmental planning framework for coastal developments in Fiji's Coral Coast tourist region', unpublished MPhil thesis, Massey University.
Ueteri-Taasi, I. (1996) 'EU concern over projects delay', *Solomon Star*, 2 April.
Underhill, Y. (1989) 'Population mobility as a household strategy: the case of Manihiki atoll, Cook Islands', unpublished MA thesis, University of Hawai'i.

UNDP (1994) *Pacific Human Development Report*. UNDP, Suva.

UNDP (1996) *The State of Human Settlements and Urbanisation in the Pacific Islands*. Regional Report for the United Nations Conference on Human Settlements (Habitat II), Istanbul 3–14 June 1996, UNDP, Suva.

UNDP (1997) *Sustaining Livelihoods; Promoting Informal Sector Growth in Pacific Island Countries*. UNDP, Suva.

United Nations (1995) *World Urbanization Prospects: The 1994 Revision*. Population Division, New York.

United Nations Pacific Operations Centre (1994) *Fiji: Trade Liberalisation Study*. United Nations Economic and Social Commission for Asia and the Pacific, Port Vila.

Valentine, C. (1963) 'Social status, political power and native responses to European influence in Oceania' *Anthropological Forum* 1: 3–55.

Valentine, P.S. (1993) 'Ecotourism and nature conservation: A definition with some recent developments in Micronesia', *Tourism Management*, 14, 2: 107–18.

van Diermen, P and Overton, J. (1998) 'Urban ecological footprints: a case study of Jakarta', *Working Paper 98/1*, Institute of Development Studies, Massey University, Palmerston North.

Varcoe, J.K. (1993) 'From the umu to the oven: emancipation for the women of the Cook islands?' unpublished MA thesis, University of Canterbury.

Veron, J.E.N. (1986) *Corals of Australia and the Indo-Pacific*. Angus and Robertson, North Ryde.

Vivian, J. (1992) 'Foundations for sustainable development: participation, empowerment and local resource management' in D. Ghai and J.M. Vivian (eds) *Grassroots Environmental Action: People's Participation in Sustainable Development*. Routledge, London, pp. 50–77.

Wackernagel, M. and Rees, W.E. (1996) *Our Ecological Footprint: Reducing Human Impact on the Earth*. New Society Publishers, Gabriola Island.

Waiko, J.D. (1993) *A Short History of Papua New Guinea*. Oxford University Press, Melbourne.

Wall, D. (1986) 'Coconut processing in the Pacific islands', *Islands/Australia, Working Paper 86/18*, National Centre for Development Studies, Australian National University, Canberra.

Wall, J.R.D. (1980) 'Proposals for land development after logging on North New Georgia. Solomon Islands', Overseas Development Administration Project Report 99. Land Resources Development Centre, Surrey.

Walsh, A.C. (1964) 'Urbanisation in Nuku'alofa, Tonga' *South Pacific Bulletin* 14, 2: 10–15.

Walsh, A.C. (1982) *Migration, Urbanisation and Development in South Pacific Countries*. Economic and Social Commission for Asia and the Pacific, United Nations, New York.

Walsh, A.C. (1984) 'The search for an appropriate housing policy in Fiji', *Third World Planning Review* 6, 2: 185–200.

Ward, R.G. (1967) 'The consequences of smallness in Polynesia' in B. Benedict (ed.) *Problems of Smaller Territories*. Athlone Press, London, pp. 81–96.

Ward, R.G. (1969) 'Land use and land alienation in Fiji to 1885', *Journal Pacific History* 4,1, 3–25.

Ward, R.G. (1980) 'The environmental context' in R.G. Ward and A. Proctor (eds) *South Pacific Agriculture Choices and Constraints: South Pacific Agricultural Survey 1979*. Australian National University, Canberra, pp. 3–25.

Ward, R.G. (1982) 'The effects of scale on social and economic organization' in R.J. May and H. Nelson (eds) *Melanesia: Beyond Diversity*. Research School of Pacific Studies, Australian National University, Canberra, pp. 181–91.

Ward, R.G. (1985) 'Land, land use and land availability' in H.C. Brookfield, F. Ellis and R.G. Ward, *Land Cane and Coconuts*. Department of Human Geography, Australian National University, Canberra, pp. 15–64.

Ward, R.G. (1989) 'Earth's empty quarter? the Pacific Islands in a Pacific century', *Geographical Journal*, 155,2, 235–46.

Ward, R.G. (1993) 'South Pacific Island futures: paradise, prosperity, or pauperism?', *The Contemporary Pacific*, 5, 1: 1–21.

Ward, R.G. (1995a) 'Deforestation in Western Samoa', *Pacific Viewpoint* 36, 1: 73–93.

Ward, R.G. (1995b) 'Land, law and custom: diverging realities in Fiji' in R.G. Ward and E. Kingdon (eds) *Land, Custom and Practice in the South Pacific*. Cambridge University Press, Cambridge, pp. 198–249. .

Ward R.G. (1997) 'Pacific Islands urbanisation: trends, issues and questions', unpublished keynote paper at the UNESCO/USP MOST workshop, Suva, 13–16 October.

Ward, R.G. and Kingdon, E. (eds) (1995a) *Land, Custom and Practice in the South Pacific*. Cambridge University Press, Cambridge.

Ward, R.G. and Kingdon, E. (1995b) 'Land tenure in the Pacific Islands' in R.G. Ward and E. Kingdon (eds) *Land, Custom and Practice in the South Pacific*. Cambridge University Press, Cambridge, pp.36–64.

Ward, R.G. and Proctor, A. (eds) (1980) *South Pacific Agriculture: Choices and Constraints*. Asian Development Bank, Manila and Australian National University Press, Canberra.

Wartho, R. (1995) 'Conceptualising Oceania in the new world disorders', *Pacific Viewpoint* 36, 2: 211–26.

Weaver, S. (1991) 'Taking tourism to the bush', *Pacific Islands Monthly*, 61, 12: 54–5.

Weaver, S. (1992) 'Nature tourism as a means of protecting indigenous forest resources in Fiji', *Journal of Pacific Studies*, 16: 63–73.

Weaver, S. (1994) 'The reenchantment of Fiji's forests: a postmodern approach to ecological sustainability' unpublished PhD thesis, University of Canterbury.

Wells, B. and Brandon, K. (1992) *People and Parks: Linking Protected Area Management with Local Communities*. World Bank, World Wildlife Fund and USAID, Washington.

West, P.C. and Brechin, S.R. (eds) (1991) *Resident Peoples and National Parks: Social Dilemmas and Strategies in International Conservation*. University of Arizona, Tucson.

Whatmore, S. (1995) 'From farming to agribusiness: the global agro-food system', in R.J. Johnston, P.J. Taylor and M.J. Watts (eds) *Geographies of Global Change*, Blackwell, London, pp. 36–49.

White, G. and Lindstrom, L. (1993) 'Oceania: islands, land, people', *Cultural Survival Quarterly* Fall: 32–4.

Wiens, H.J. (1962) *Atoll Environment and Ecology*. Yale University Press, New Haven.

Wijewardana, D. (1995) 'Sustainable management of forests: current international debate', *New Zealand Forestry* 39, 4: 45.

Wilkinson, P. and Pratiwi, W. (1995) 'Gender and tourism in an Indonesian Village', *Annals of Tourism Research*, 22, 2: 283–99.

Winslow, D. (1991) 'Sustainable development in New Caledonia', *Pacific Affairs*, 64, 4: 489–505.

Women of Vanuatu (1983) 'Integration of women in the development process', *Pacific Perspective* 11, 2: 1–4.

Wooff, W. (1997) *Achieving Successful Forestry Plantations*. International Plantation Conference Proceedings, Kuala Lumpur.

World Bank (1992) *World Development Report 1992*. Oxford University Press, New York.

World Bank (1993) *Pacific Island Economies: Toward Efficient and Sustainable Growth*. EAP, Washington DC.

World Bank (1994) *World Development Report 1994*. Oxford University Press, New York.

World Bank (1995) *Managing Urban Environmental Sanitation Services in Selected Pacific Island Countries*. EAP, Washington DC.

World Commission on Environment and Development (WCED) (1987) *Our Common Future*. Oxford University Press, Oxford.

World Resources Institute (1996) *World Resources 1996–97*. Oxford University Press, New York.

Worsley, P. (1968) *The Trumpet Shall Sound: A Study of 'Cargo Cults' in Melanesia*. Schocken Books, New York.

Wright, A. and Hill, L. (eds) (1993) *Nearshore Marine Resources of the South Pacific: Information for Fisheries Development and Management*. Institute of Pacific Studies, University of the South Pacific, Suva and Forum Fisheries Agency, Honiara.

Wright, A.C.S. (1962) 'Some terrace systems of the Western Hemisphere and Pacific Islands', *Pacific Viewpoint* 3, 1: 97–101.

Wyrtki, K. (1990) 'Sea level rise: the facts and the future', *Pacific Science* 44, 1: 1–16.

Yadi, A. (1997) 'Timber companies call for more, better incentives' *The Independent* July 3: 23.

Yen, D.E. (1974) *The Sweet Potato and Oceania: An Essay in Ethnobotany*. Bulletin 236, Bernice P. Bishop Museum, Honolulu.

Young, E. (1997) 'Striving for development and sustainability' Briefing Paper No. 47, Australian Development Studies Network, Australian National University, Canberra.

Ziffer, K. (1989) *Ecotourism: The Uneasy Alliance*. Conservation International, Washington DC.

INDEX